PERILOUS FIGHT

PERILOUS FIGHT

*America's Intrepid War with
Britain on the High Seas,
1812–1815*

Stephen Budiansky

ALFRED A. KNOPF  NEW YORK 2010

THIS IS A BORZOI BOOK
PUBLISHED BY ALFRED A. KNOPF

Copyright © 2010 by Stephen Budiansky

All rights reserved. Published in the United States by Alfred A.
Knopf, a division of Random House, Inc., New York, and in
Canada by Random House of Canada Limited, Toronto.

www.aaknopf.com

Knopf, Borzoi Books, and the colophon are registered
trademarks of Random House, Inc.

Maps and diagrams by Dave Merrill

Library of Congress Cataloging-in-Publication Data
Budiansky, Stephen.
Perilous fight : America's intrepid war with Britain on the high seas,
1812–1815 / Stephen Budiansky.—1st ed.
p. cm.
Includes bibliographical references and index.
ISBN 978-0-307-27069-6
1. United States—History—War of 1812—Naval operations.
2. United States—History, Naval—To 1900.   I. Title.
E360.B87   2010
973.5'2—dc22   2010037005

Jacket painting: *Action Between USS* Constitution *and HMS* Guerriere,
19 August 1812 by Anton Otto Fischer. Courtesy Miss Katrina S.
Fischer. U.S. Naval Historical Center Photograph.
Jacket design by Joe Montgomery

Manufactured in the United States of America

First Edition

Contents

Maps and Diagrams

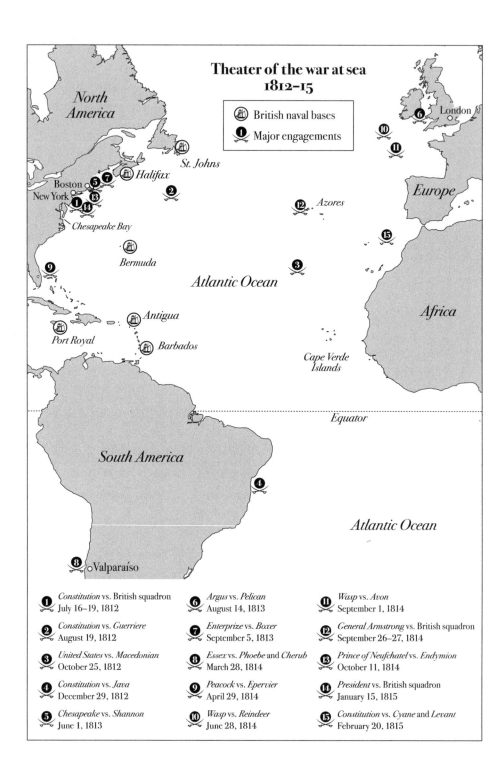

Theater of the war at sea
1812–15

- 🏛 British naval bases
- ⚔ Major engagements

North America

St. Johns

Boston
New York
Halifax

Chesapeake Bay

Bermuda

Atlantic Ocean

Antigua

Port Royal

Barbados

Cape Verde Islands

Europe

London

Azores

Africa

Equator

South America

Valparaíso

Atlantic Ocean

❶ *Constitution* vs. British squadron
July 16–19, 1812

❷ *Constitution* vs. *Guerriere*
August 19, 1812

❸ *United States* vs. *Macedonian*
October 25, 1812

❹ *Constitution* vs. *Java*
December 29, 1812

❺ *Chesapeake* vs. *Shannon*
June 1, 1813

❻ *Argus* vs. *Pelican*
August 14, 1813

❼ *Enterprize* vs. *Boxer*
September 5, 1813

❽ *Essex* vs. *Phoebe* and *Cherub*
March 28, 1814

❾ *Peacock* vs. *Epervier*
April 29, 1814

❿ *Wasp* vs. *Reindeer*
June 28, 1814

⓫ *Wasp* vs. *Avon*
September 1, 1814

⓬ *General Armstrong* vs. British squadron
September 26–27, 1814

⓭ *Prince of Neufchatel* vs. *Endymion*
October 11, 1814

⓮ *President* vs. British squadron
January 15, 1815

⓯ *Constitution* vs. *Cyane* and *Levant*
February 20, 1815

Prologue

MANY WARS have been called "the forgotten war": those words have
become a catchphrase much beloved of military historians seeking to
excuse their obsession with obscurity. But rarely was a war—or at least
large parts of a war—forgotten with such swiftness, and such mutual
determination, as the War of 1812. America and Britain both had
things they wanted to forget, and forget quickly, about this often brutal
three-year fight that raged across half a globe, from the wilderness of
the northwestern forests to the capital cities of Canada and the United
States, from the seas off Chile to the mouth of the English Channel.
The forgetting began almost as soon as the last shot was fired, and it has
been going on ever since.

It would be decades before the war even had a name; until the 1850s
this war that left thirty thousand dead, that pushed the fledgling American republic to the brink of bankruptcy and secession, that brought
down some of the loftiest military reputations of the Revolutionary
generation to ruin and disgrace, that saw hundreds of American citizens executed by firing squad for desertion, was most often just called
"the late war" or "the late war with Great Britain." "The War of 1812"
came into widespread use only after the Mexican War of 1846–48
usurped the place of the "late war" in American memory. It proved a
memorable phrase, yet like "the late war," it sidestepped any memory
of why the war had been fought, or even whom it had been fought
against.[1]

Americans above all wanted to forget the disastrously mismanaged land campaign, which had been marked from the start by miscalculation, blunders, incompetence, and monumental overconfidence. No one had escaped humiliation; the wisest men had predicted easy success and quick victory, and had wound up with egg on their faces. A month into the war Thomas Jefferson, from his quiet retirement at Monticello, had smugly assured a fellow Republican politician that "the acquisition of Canada this year, as far as the neighborhood of Quebec, will be a mere matter of marching." One more year, Jefferson added, would bring the "final expulsion of England from the American continent."[2]

Two weeks after Jefferson's pronouncement, in the very opening of the offensive against British forces to the north, the American brigadier general William Hull surrendered his entire army at Detroit without firing a shot. He was subsequently court-martialed, convicted of cowardice, and sentenced to be shot by a firing squad until President Madison granted him a reprieve based on his meritorious service in the Revolution. DISASTER ON DISASTER ON LAND read the headlines in the anti-administration newspapers that winter as the debacles of the war's opening months were repeated again and again.[3]

Along with the military blunders were a string of political embarrassments that both American political parties were eager to disown in the war's aftermath. Not until the Vietnam War a century and a half later would a decision to go to war so divide the nation, and impassioned feelings had led to many injudicious words and ill-considered stances. The Federalists, the party of Alexander Hamilton and John Adams, whose stronghold was mercantile New England, had voted in Congress to a man to oppose the declaration of war, and were unsparing in their bitter denunciations. Sermons preached week after week from northern Congregational pulpits added religious censure to the torrent of inflammatory words, warning that any "accomplice in the wickedness" of Mr. Madison in such an iniquitous and unjust war would become a very murderer in the sight of God, "the blackest of crimes" on his conscience, "the guilt of blood upon his soul." By the end of 1814 disunion was being bruited in the northeastern states. But with the return of peace all such talk simply sounded wild, if not outright treasonous, and the Federalists desperately wanted to bury the recent political past.[4]

The Republicans had their own partisan excesses to live down, and they too quickly contracted a convenient case of amnesia, forgetting how for years they had denounced the very existence of an American navy as an evil of evils, a road to ruinous tyranny, an overweening Federalist ambition incompatible with the common-man values of a free republic. On the very brink of the war that they were clamoring for, the Republican Congress had voted down a modest naval expansion that the Federalists had strongly backed.

And so the Federalists had opposed the war, the Republicans had opposed the navy, and so the one thing they could agree on after it was all over was how gloriously the tiny American navy had triumphed. For decades afterward the whole complex history of the war was reduced to a simple romantic tale of patriotic pride and derring-do. The stories of a few glorious single-ship actions fought by heroic American captains would be the story of the war to generations of Americans. The glory was real and merited, yet it was a only a fraction of the story of the whole war, a fraction even of the story of the whole *naval* war. But it was the part that would command almost all the attention whenever the War of 1812 was periodically revisited by popular writers, notably in 1882 by a young Theodore Roosevelt (who nearly two decades later would become assistant secretary of the navy) and in 1956 by the novelist C. S. Forester (who two decades earlier had begun to write his Horatio Hornblower stories).

The one thing Americans could agree upon was precisely the one thing Great Britain wanted to forget: the humiliations her all-powerful Royal Navy had sustained on the high seas, the astonishing wounds to her prestige and pride she had suffered at the hands of the same upstart rival for the second time in thirty years. And so this second war with America became little more than a footnote to the contemporaneous, and much more important, Napoleonic Wars. In Britain too it became ever after a war without a real name, to this day something to be found in scholarly indexes under the musty title "Anglo-American War, 1812–15." In his monumental fifteen-hour-long television documentary of the history of Britain, the British historian Simon Schama devoted less than one sentence to the war. Ask even a well-educated Briton today about the War of 1812 and you are likely to get a blank stare followed by a question about whether it has something to do with the piece by Tchaikovsky.

Where amnesia induced by political expedience and national shame left off, the haze of quaintness took over. Some of the nostalgia about the war was honestly come by: the world of sailing ships and sea battles would just a few generations later seem as remote and about as real as the Knights of the Round Table. The historian Henry Adams, the grandson and great-grandson of presidents, mused in his 1907 auto-biography whether the "American boy of 1854 stood nearer the year 1 than to the year 1900" in the world he was born into, in the education he received, and in the habits of mind he was inculcated with.[5] Like the year 1854, the year 1812 was barely beyond the medieval in its technolo-gies and its rhythms of life, in its lingering feudal codes of personal and family honor. Nine-tenths of the seven million Americans alive in 1812 lived on farms, rising with the sun and going to bed with dusk, using tools unchanged for a thousand years; the rest lived in a few small cities of ten or twenty or thirty thousand hugging the Atlantic coast.

By the turn of the twentieth century literally everything had changed. One can read the memoirs and letters of soldiers and seamen from World War II or even World War I and instantly know these men: they were our fathers and grandfathers; they looked on the world much as we do; their jokes may be corny but are never incomprehensible; the mechanized, ordered warfare they fought is awful but familiar. The men of the War of 1812 can seem at times to be from another world entirely. The archaic tools with which they waged war are almost the least of it; their assumptions, their motives, their ways of thinking take work to get our minds around. The officers who commanded America's fledgling navy of 1812 really did fight duels over tiny aspersions to honor, things we would literally laugh at today; they really did in the midst of war engage in the most astonishing acts of chivalry toward their foes; they really did endure suffering of an unspeakable blackness with a stoicism that can seem superhuman to a modern sensibility.

They also squabbled over money and promotions, lied and schemed, fornicated and drank, stabbed each other in the back when it suited them, and wrote very bad poetry. One of the enduring reasons to study war is that it shines a light on humanity hidden in ordinary times; it lays bare what is so often successfully hidden.

And how they did reveal themselves, if we care to look: not just the officers but the common men, too. The American Civil War was the first war in which the voice of the common soldier came to the fore, but a surprising number of ordinary American seamen from the War of 1812 were literate: 70 percent could sign their names, 30 percent with a practiced penmanship that clearly reflected formal schooling.[6] A good many of them wrote letters home, or kept journals that ranged from the pedestrian and the mechanical to the eloquent and the wry, and along with some shipboard officers—these were mostly surgeons or chaplains—and a few of the more earnest midshipmen, some even possessed enough literary ambition to publish memoirs that, while they have to be taken with a grain of salt in places, are nonetheless full of life and surprises.

And then no one wrote as much as those occasional amazing Royal Navy captains of the era, soliloquizing in long, long serial letters nominally to lonely wives back home that were really inner dialogues with their own lonely selves. In an art that long blockade duty seems to have honed, they bared their souls as few of their contemporaries ever dared.

Newspapers of the day are not always a reliable source, but they too are full of life and surprises. News traveled much faster than we might imagine in the pre-telegraph era, and the press of the early American republic has a vitality and wide-awakeness, an excitement at repeating news, gossip, rumors, plagiarized snatches from newspapers just arrived from the next city or state or foreign port, an animation and immediacy that loses nothing from being viewed across the intervening span of two centuries. In 1812 there were some four hundred newspapers published in America, two dozen of them dailies; Boston alone boasted a dozen newspapers for a population of thirty thousand.[7] They were serious and sarcastic, authoritative and vituperative; capable, as in Baltimore in the months after the declaration of war, of igniting lethal riots with their invective; but in their densely covered four broadsheet pages they also printed long verbatim extracts of official documents and foreign reports, songs and poems, accounts of dinners and funerals, prayers and Fourth of July orations, and ephemeral quips and retorts of the day that would otherwise have been lost to history.

Another unfailingly rich source of eyewitness views and contemporary attitudes is the British *Naval Chronicle*, a publication founded in 1799 that continued its monthly installments until 1818. Aimed at both a core professional audience of Royal Navy officers and a broader British public that had begun to follow the exploits of the navy through its heyday in the French Revolutionary and Napoleonic wars, the *Chronicle* included in every issue lists of promotions, biographies of notable officers, articles on navigation and scientific developments, official and unofficial reports recounting actions and battles, still more bad poems, and a surprisingly open and self-critical forum in which active and retired officers exchanged frank views—though often under pseudonyms—about the management and mismanagement of the service.

All of these help to reconstruct the woof and warp of the life and times of the men of 1812. A true account of the naval war of 1812 is first and foremost, like all true military histories, an account of humanity revealed under extraordinary circumstances. Like all wars, the War of 1812 is worth a close reading on this score alone.

This war is also one worth examining, and remembering, for the strikingly modern lessons it holds for the art of waging battle against a vastly superior opponent. Much of this story is embodied in the strikingly modern person of William Jones, America's secretary of the navy for the most critical two years of the conflict, a man well ahead of his time who grasped that war is as much about strategy, politics, public relations, finances, manpower, and logistics as it is about fighting. Jones, ever unflappable and ever with a clear eye and a cool head, knew that the war was never to be won by the single-ship engagements that so electrified the American public, not when facing an opponent who held a hundred-to-one numerical advantage in ships and men. Jones made this clear in May 1814 when he wrote President Madison with the news that the American sloop of war *Peacock* had taken HMS *Epervier* off Cape Canaveral, Florida. "I like these little events," Jones stated. "They keep alive the national feeling and produce an effect infinitely beyond their intrinsic importance."[8]

His refusal to be misled about the "intrinsic importance" of "these little events," even while acknowledging their value in bolstering public feeling, was the heart of the matter. Jones never lost sight that his own quietly resolute strategy of hitting Britain where it really hurt, in her vulnerable commerce and not her powerful navy, was what counted, and he tirelessly reiterated the point to his glory-seeking captains. Keeping the Royal Navy tied up and distracted by hit-and-run raids against Britain's overextended merchant fleets would be a way to turn Britain's vast presence on the oceans against itself. A later age would call this "asymmetric warfare," and it would become the subject of intensive military study in the twentieth and twenty-first centuries as guerilla and insurgency warfare found the United States more and more often playing the muscle-bound Goliath. How America once skillfully played the nimble David is an enduring lesson well worth revisiting.

If popular accounts of the War of 1812 romanticized the clashes on the high seas, the work of modern academic historians went to the other extreme ever since Henry Adams's incisive study of Jefferson's and Madison's presidencies revealed the enormous political and diplomatic complexities that lay behind the conflict. Untangling all the skeins of frontier and party politics, diplomatic maneuvering, and European statecraft that became raveled together in the war's prosecution and inconclusive resolution has tended to occupy so much of modern historians' attention that the actual fighting often seems to vanish altogether from their accounts by the time one reaches the end.

But there is a much stronger connection between the strategy and prosecution of America's naval campaign and the lasting political and diplomatic consequences of the war than has generally been appreciated. Writing a century after the war's end, with a bit of hyperbole but an essence of truth, Charles F. Adams Jr., another scion of the presidential dynasty, dated the exact moment of America's birth as a world power to Wednesday, August 19, 1812, 6:30 p.m.—the instant the British frigate *Guerriere* struck her flag to America's *Constitution*.[9]

However inconclusive the formal treaty ending the war may have been, the European nations never again attempted to interfere with American sailors or America's oceangoing trade, the two great issues that had driven America to war. The war on land was a dismal stalemate, but the new de facto realities that the American navy established with its success after success at sea ensured that the war would have a lasting consequence that went well beyond the de jure terms negotiated by diplomats. The British diplomat Augustus J. Foster, who served as his country's minister to America in 1811 and 1812, did not hesitate to acknowledge the war's real, and enduring, significance.

"The Americans," he said simply, ". . . have brought us to speak of them with respect."[10]

ANYONE WHO writes about the navy of America's early years walks in the footsteps of a remarkable group of scholars at the U.S. Navy's Naval Historical Center (now the Naval History & Heritage Command), who for decades have tirelessly edited and made accessible in published form compendious collections of original documents, most recently three monumental volumes relating to the War of 1812. These works are models of scholarship, clarity, and judicious selection, as well as being beautifully produced books that are a true national treasure. I would add my personal thanks to Charles E. Brodine Jr. and Margherita M. Desy of the historical center for sharing their knowledge, expertise, and time in many ways. Mr. Brodine went well above and beyond the call of duty in generously sharing with me several hard-to-find images that appear in this book, as well as helping me locate other key materials; Ms. Desy spent most of a day giving me a fascinating and deeply informed tour of the magnificently restored frigate *Constitution* in Boston and subsequently answering my many questions about shipbuilding, seamanship in the age of sail, and much else. I am also very much indebted to Margherita Desy, Frederick Leiner, and William Cook for reading my manuscript and providing many corrections and suggestions and much sage advice.

I would like to thank the staffs of the Historical Society of Pennsylvania; the National Maritime Museum in Greenwich, England; The National Archives in London; the Library of Congress Manuscript Division; the Library Company of Philadelphia; the Earl Gregg Swem Library Special Collections Research Center at the College of William and Mary; the South Caroliniana Library; and the Duke University Special Collections Library for their untiring professionalism and eagerness to assist. And I again would like to give my personal thanks to my dear friends Peter and Celia David, who have both put me up and put up with me on my research trips to London.

PERILOUS
FIGHT

Waring under bare Poles ——— Scudding.

Fig.183

Fig.484

Fig.485

Fig.486

Fig.487

Method of sailing a ship in distressed condition (Lever, *Young Officer's Sheet Anchor*)

CHAPTER I

In Barbary

THAT AMERICA would have a navy at all in 1812 on the eve of her mad war against Britain was the direct result of events of a decade before that had spoken more to the young nation's heart than to her mind. The American mind was dead set against the temptations that the republic's founders believed always led governments to war and tyranny. A solid majority of America's political leaders opposed on principle the very notion of a standing navy, a solid majority of Americans opposed the taxes that would be required to pay for one, and no sane American of any political inclination thought that any navy their country could ever possess would be able to contend with those of the great European powers.

Yet from the Anglophile merchants of New England to the backwoods farmers on the frontier, Americans had been stirred by the glory that had been won by the captains and men of the tiny United States navy in worlds far away ever since its founding in 1794, and it was that glory that had kept the service alive against all rational calculation to the contrary.

Edward Preble had no illusions about the price to be paid for that glory. "People who handle dangerous weapons," he once wrote, "must expect wounds and Death."[1] Preble was a man of action to the core, possessed of a legendary decisiveness and a volcanic temper. Just a year before joining his country's young navy in 1798 as a not-so-young thirty-seven-year-old lieutenant, Preble had taken exception to something a fellow merchant sailor had said to him in Boston, and cracked him over the head with a musket. Preble ended up paying his victim's room and board and medical bills while he recovered, then gave him $200 for his troubles; he never apologized, though.[2]

The first week of February 1804 found Commodore Edward Preble, forty-two years old, captain of the frigate *Constitution* and commander of America's six-ship Mediterranean squadron, going prematurely bald and gray. His dark blue eyes were as fierce as ever, but he was increasingly given to bouts of racking physical debilitation from a griping stomach complaint that laid him low for days at a time. On the outside he usually managed to keep up a front of self-control and even optimism; inside he was blackened by darts of despair at the task before him, at his mission in life, at the distressing run of bad luck that kept coming his way.

Just a year before taking command of the *Constitution* the previous May, he had tried to resign his commission from the navy altogether, pleading his shattered state of health, which had kept him bedridden more often than not for weeks on end. Writing the secretary of the navy, Robert Smith, with his decision, Preble had enclosed a statement from his physician confirming that he was "reduced to a distressing state of debility and emaciation," adding, "he is extremely susceptible of injury from the cares and fatigues of business." His ship's surgeon agreed that the burdens of the job had proved too much for a man of Preble's hard-driving and easily provoked temperament.[3]

But Secretary Smith had spurned the resignation, ordering Preble on furlough to get some rest, and slowly his health had improved enough for him to return to the endless vexations of commanding one of the three plum ships of the tiny American fleet. For more than two years the American squadron in the Mediterranean had been waging an anemic battle against the Barbary corsairs that were raiding American ships traversing the region. For centuries the semi-independent Muslim states of Tunis, Algiers, and Tripoli had flourished on piracy and tribute extorted from European shippers that sailed the Mediterranean. On May 14, 1801, the pasha of Tripoli had made known his dissatisfaction with the amount of tribute he had been receiving from the United States in return for allowing American ships to pass unmolested: in a symbolic declaration of war, the pasha had sent his men to chop down the flagstaff in front of the American consul's residence.

Little had happened since. The American naval force found it could not effectively blockade Tripoli's harbor and had been reduced to defensive measures, convoying American ships rather than directly confronting the Tripolitan corsairs. American consuls in the region warned that the United States' prestige was plummeting—as was her navy's, both at home and abroad. Jefferson's cabinet, true to the antinavalist credo of the Republican party, was strongly inclined to simply pay off the pasha and be done with it; Treasury Secretary Albert Gallatin wrote the president that he considered the decision "a mere matter of calculation whether the purchase of peace is not cheaper than the expense of a war."[4]

Preble's and the *Constitution*'s mission was to prove them wrong; or at least to prove that the navy had some value at all. Painfully aware how much was riding on their mission, the secretary of the navy confidently let be it known in Washington that Preble would be on station ten weeks from the date of receiving his orders. Instead, the months had slipped by as Preble struggled to get his ship seaworthy. The *Constitution* was only five years old but was literally rotting away at her moorings. She had served with distinction during America's undeclared naval war with France from 1798 to 1800—the Quasi War, as it came to be called, triggered by French captures of American merchant ships trading with Britain and then by a wave of popular anger over the XYZ Affair, when an American delegation sent to Paris to resolve the rising tensions was approached by three agents of the French government who demanded a large bribe. In May 1800, a detachment of sailors and marines from the *Constitution* staged a daring cutting-out raid on a harbor in Haiti, seizing a French privateer and recapturing an American merchant brig; two days later the *Constitution*'s men exhibited equal derring-do in snatching another French privateer from under the guns of a nearby port in Hispaniola. But with the signing of a peace treaty between America and France in September 1800, the ship had returned to Boston after one final cruise in the West Indies, and since June 1802 she had lain utterly neglected, accumulating weeds and decay, in the Charles River near Boston's Charlestown Navy Yard.

On May 20, 1803, Preble had come aboard, inspected her skeleton crew of one midshipman, one boatswain, and twelve men, and ordered a caulking stage brought alongside so he could examine the ship's bottom. The next day he climbed out onto the stage armed with a rake and began pulling up swaths of sea grass that had grown through gaping holes in the copper sheathing below the waterline.

Through the spring and summer of 1803 Preble worked day after day, morning to night, making "every exertion in my power," he wrote an old acquaintance, denying himself even "the pleasure of dining with a friend" as he urged the work on.[5] Every seam of the frigate's planking had to be recaulked, a job that required all of the officers' rooms alongside the wardroom to be knocked out. There were cables to be made and tarred, ballast to be brought in, fifty-four thousand gallons of water in casks to be loaded, all new yards to be fitted, all of the ship's rigging to be removed and rerigged. For the damaged copper sheathing to be replaced, the ship first had to be brought over to a wharf at Boston's North End, just across the mouth of the Charles River, and all her guns and nearly all her ballast laboriously removed. Then the gunports had to be hammered shut and temporarily caulked tight to make them waterproof, everything that might slide around had to be unloaded and the rudder unshipped, and then each day she was tipped over and held at a frightening angle by huge ten-inch-thick ropes running from her lower masts to a capstan on the wharf alongside. Massive poles braced the masts against the edge of the deck to take the strain as the ship was heaved over, exposing her side all the way down to the keel, while relieving tackles running from the opposite side made sure she did not capsize altogether. Carpenters set to work from a stage, ripping off the old copper sheets and filling the exposed seams beneath with oakum. Then came a coating of tallow, tar, and turpentine; then sheets of tarred paper roofing felt; then finally the new sheets of copper hammered on. Sailing Master Nathaniel Haraden—his nickname was "Jumping Billy"—oversaw the backbreaking schedule; work started at 5:15 each morning, and the laborers kept at it until seven at night, with an hour off for breakfast and dinner and fifteen minutes for grog at eleven and four. Some captains had found Haraden hard to take for having "assumed too much" in telling them how to run their ship, but the fact was no one knew the *Constitution* better, and the log Haraden kept of the repair operation spoke of a man justifiably proud of his mastery of the myriad technical complexities the job entailed. Preble told Secretary of the Navy Smith he thought Haraden knew his job and that he could keep him in line when he had to.[6]

By August 9 the *Constitution* at last was ready to sail, awaiting only a favorable wind to carry her out of Boston harbor. Preble wrote a farewell letter to an old friend from Maine, Henry Dearborn, now Thomas Jefferson's secretary of war. "I assure you I am not in pursuit of pleasure—excepting such as the destruction of the piratical vessels in the Mediterranean can afford me," Preble wrote. "If Tripoli does not make peace, I shall hazard to destroy their vessels in port if I cannot meet them at sea."

And he added: "None but a real friend would have given me the kind advice which you have respecting the government of temper. Be assured it shall be attended to."[7]

. . .

NOTHING ABOUT his command was calculated to improve the new commodore's temper. One early and spirited display of his legendary short fuse, however, did him some good with the officers and men under his command who were already growing weary of what one midshipman, Charles Morris, termed their captain's "ebullitions of temper." Nearing the Straits of Gibraltar on the evening of September 10, the *Constitution*'s lookout had spotted through the lowering haze just at sunset a distant sail, tracking the same course but far ahead. A few hours later, dark night settled in and they were suddenly on her: the same ship, apparently, and almost certainly a ship of war. The *Constitution*'s crew was brought swiftly and silently to their action quarters—no beating of the drums, but every gun crew at its station, gunports open and guns run out, the men peering down their barrels at the stranger, slow matches smoldering at the ready to set off their charges the instant the order to fire came. Only then did Preble give the customary hail.

"What ship is that?"

Across the water a defiant echo came back: "What ship is that?"

"This is the United States ship *Constitution*. What ship is *that*?"

Again the question was repeated, again with the same result. At which Preble grabbed the speaking trumpet and, his voice strained with rage, shouted, "I am now going to hail you one last time. If a proper answer is not returned, I will fire a shot into you."

"If you fire a shot, I will fire a broadside."

"*What ship is that?*" Preble thundered one last time.

"This is His Britannic Majesty's ship *Donnegal*, eighty-four guns, Sir Richard Strahan, an English commodore. Send your boat on board."

Now the volcano erupted. Leaping to the netting, Preble bellowed, "This is the United States ship *Constitution*, forty-four guns, Edward Preble, an *American* commodore, who will be *damned* before he sends his boat aboard *any* vessel." And then, turning to his crew, he bellowed an equally loud, and theatrical, aside. "Blow on your matches, boys!"

An ominous silence ensued, broken by the sound of a boat splashing down and rowing across. A shamefaced British lieutenant came on deck and apologetically explained that his ship was in fact the frigate *Maidstone*, no eighty-four-gun ship of the line at all. Her lookouts had been caught napping, and they had not seen the *Constitution* until they heard her hail; they had no expectation of encountering an American ship of war in these waters, and uncertain of her true identity and desperate to buy time to get their own men to quarters, they had stalled and dissembled.

The apologies were accepted; more important, as Morris later recalled, "this was the first occasion that had offered to show us what we might expect from our commander, and the spirit and decision which he displayed were hailed with pleasure by all, and at once mitigated the unfriendly feelings" that their commander's irascibility had produced.[8]

Throughout the fall of 1803 the commodore was vexed by the subtleties of Levantine politics, the difficulties of securing reliable translations of Arabic and Turkish documents, and a furious altercation with Commodore John Rodgers, who insisted that as senior captain, owing to the earlier date of his commission, only *he* was entitled to fly a commodore's broad pennant on the Mediterranean station. Then disaster: on November 24, on the passage from Gibraltar to Malta, the *Constitution* spoke a passing British frigate that gave them the appalling news that the Tripolitans had captured the American frigate *Philadelphia* and all her crew on the last day of October. The available facts were few but devastating. Chasing a corsair running into Tripoli harbor, the American frigate had struck a shoal and helplessly surrendered to Tripolitan gunboats that had poured out from the town; the enemy had since refloated her, and she now stood in Tripoli harbor, snug under the guns of the forts that ringed the shoreline. "This affair distresses me beyond description," Preble confessed to the secretary of the navy in a dispatch two weeks later, "and very much deranges my plans of operation for the present."

Although Preble never publicly let slip a word of criticism of the *Philadelphia*'s officers, he poured out his despair and dismay in his private letters. To the secretary he continued:

> I fear our national character will sustain an injury with the
> Barbarians—would to God, that the Officers and crew of the
> Philadelphia, had one and all, determined to prefer death to
> slavery; it is possible that such a determination might save them
> from either. . . . If it had not been for the Capture of the
> Philadelphia, I have no doubt, but we should have had peace
> with Tripoly in the Spring; but I now have no hopes of such an
> event— . . . I do not believe the Philadelphia will ever be of
> service to Tripoly; I shall hazard much to destroy her—it will
> undoubtedly cost us many lives, but it must be done. I am

surprised she was not rendered useless, before her Colours were
struck.[9]

And in a letter to his wife, he laid bare how much the circumstances of
the *Philadelphia*'s loss had racked him, heart and soul, beyond the blow
to his operational plans: "Captain Bainbridge, together with all his officers and crew, amounting to 307 men, are slaves and are treated in the
most cruel manner, without a prospect of ever again beholding their
friends. I hope to God such will never be my fate! The thought of never
again seeing you would drive me to distraction . . . May Heaven preserve us both. . . . I most sincerely pity the cruel fate of poor Bainbridge. I know not what will become of them. I suspect very few will
ever see home again."[10] There were reports that the pasha of Tripoli
was going to demand $3 million as ransom for his prisoners. "A pretty
good asking price," Preble sarcastically observed.[11]

Adding to Preble's troubles were a raft of vexations large and small.
The *Constitution* was in need of repairs again. Chafing under Preble's
stern discipline, a half-dozen crew members had deserted and taken
refuge on British warships; he was constantly doling out punishments
for drunkenness and neglect of duty, two or three dozen lashes apiece,
throwing a man in irons for "impertinence."

Syracuse, the port town in southern Sicily where Preble had decided
to base his squadron and where the *Constitution* began to undergo three
weeks of repairs in late November, proved a constant headache, and a
discipline problem too. Things had started well. The local officials and
leading citizens hastened to make the Americans welcome, and the
town's somnambulant economy had undergone an instant revival with
the sudden influx of dollars. Two new hotels in the "English style" had
opened to cater to the Americans; the leading opera singers of Sicily
had hastened to Syracuse when word went out across the island that
American officers showed their appreciation for their favorite perform-
ers by throwing gold coins on the stage. "The Inhabitants are extremely
friendly and civil, and our Sailors cannot desert," Preble optimistically
reported to Secretary Smith on December 10, 1803.[12]

On the other hand, that very dependency on the American trade
had quickly translated into a swaggering contempt on the part of Preble's young officers for local law and authority. It was an attitude unin-
tentionally encouraged by Preble himself, who had set the tone with his
own high-handed impatience with the mostly innocent pettifogging of

the local governor, an indecisive man who brought out the worst of the commodore's temper. Preble so cowed the poor man that the Americans were soon a law unto themselves. All an American officer had to do was utter the magic words "I shall inform the commodore." Disciplining the cocky Americans ultimately fell to the commodore himself, who was distracted by a thousand other details. In the end he admitted somewhat helplessly that "great irregularities have been committed by some of our officers" and passed the problem on to his successor, saying he hoped the new commander might "make an example" of some of the worst offenders.

But the town was also frankly dangerous, as well as dreary, filthy, wretchedly poor, and depressingly decayed from its ancient grandeur of classical times. Mobs of beggars followed the Americans in the streets; at night gangs of cutthroats marauded more or less at will. Lieutenant Stephen Decatur and Midshipman Thomas Macdonough were returning to their ship, the brig *Enterprize,* one night not long after the Americans' arrival when they were accosted by three armed men in a narrow street. The officers drew their swords and, keeping their backs to a wall, fought off their attackers, wounding two. All three of the assailants then fled, and Macdonough chased one of the men into a nearby house and up to the roof, where the man tried to escape capture by leaping to the ground—killing himself in the fall.

The Sicilian nobility did not wear well either. They kept up a show of ostentation, but soon there was a story making the rounds about the dinner party given by Lieutenant Decatur aboard the *Enterprize* during which one of the guests, a Baron Cannarella, was intercepted by Decatur's servant as he was about to slip two silver spoons into his pocket. (The servant held out his tray and deadpanned, "When you have done looking at them, sir?")[13]

It would be months before Preble's urgent request for reinforcements, especially a frigate to replace the *Philadelphia,* could reach Washington and be acted on, and so his reduced squadron, now consisting of one frigate, two eighteen-gun brigs, and three schooners, settled in for the winter, biding their time in their less than completely easy new home.

But something was afoot; a careful observer could see the commodore was in a state of expectant tension as the new year began. On February 3, 1804, Preble wrote to several of the American consuls in the Mediterranean and to Secretary of the Navy Smith, informing them that he had somewhat surprisingly decided to condemn, and take into his service as a lawful prize, a vessel he had stopped and boarded off Tripoli in late December. She was a ketch, a tall two-masted vessel, fore and aft rigged like a schooner. Though sailing under Ottoman colors when Preble had halted her, her crew had acted more than a little suspiciously—showing outright panic when the *Constitution* revealed herself to be American, hauling down the false British colors she had been flying and raising the Stars and Stripes in their place. On searching the ketch, the *Constitution*'s boarding party had found sidearms and clothes apparently belonging to officers of the *Philadelphia.*

Since then, a Maltese merchant captain who had been in Tripoli harbor the day the *Philadelphia* was taken had come forward; Salvador Catalano told Preble that he had seen the very same ketch haul down her Turkish colors, raise the Tripolitan flag, and take aboard a hundred soldiers, then make her way out to the stranded *Philadelphia,* where she led the way, plundering and taking the American crew prisoner.

American navy department regulations required prizes to be sent back to the United States for adjudication and condemnation by a prize court, but Preble brushed that aside, pointing out in his dispatches that "there cannot be the smallest doubt of her being a lawful prize" and that in any case—and this had lame excuse written all over it—"she is not a proper Vessel to cross the Atlantic at this season of the year."[14]

The crew, and forty-two slaves who were being shipped in her hold, were removed from the ketch, and soon the vessel was a beehive of activity. Lieutenant Decatur was seen leading daily work parties of his officers and men: towing her to the mole; ferrying boatloads of weapons, muskets, cutlasses, boarding pikes, and tomahawks from the *Constitution;* bringing up two guns from the hold. The commodore was now calling the ketch the *Intrepid.* On January 31, Preble ordered Lieutenant Charles Stewart to prepare his eighteen-gun brig *Syren* for a cruise and be ready to sail "as soon as the Signal is made."[15]

On the same day that Preble had written the American consuls of his decision to condemn the ketch as a lawful prize, the *Constitution*'s sailing master, Nathaniel Haraden, noted in his logbook: "Towards evening sailed the Syren and the Prize. The prize was commanded by Capt Decatur and had on board 70 of the Enterprizes men and Officers. Six Officers from the Constitution were also on board her. They stood out to the South^d and are bound on some Secret Expedition."[16]

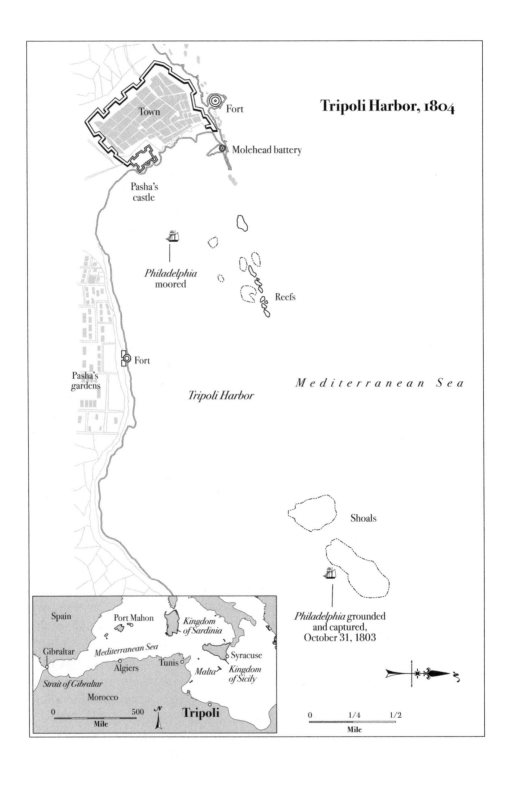

Tripoli Harbor, 1804

Town

Fort

Molehead battery

Pasha's castle

Philadelphia moored

Reefs

M e d i t e r r a n e a n   S e a

Fort

Pasha's gardens

Tripoli Harbor

Shoals

Philadelphia grounded and captured, October 31, 1803

Spain

Port Mahon

Kingdom of Sardinia

Gibraltar

Mediterranean Sea

Algiers

Tunis

Syracuse

Malta

Kingdom of Sicily

Strait of Gibraltar

Morocco

0   500

Mile

Tripoli

N

0   1/4   1/2

Mile

STEPHEN DECATUR Jr. was young, twenty-five years old, but he had already made a mark for himself in the American navy as a natural leader, one who inspired men rather than bludgeoned them into doing their duty. Brought up in Philadelphia, the political and maritime capital of the young nation, son of a captain of the American navy who commanded the *Philadelphia* during the Quasi War with France, Decatur perfectly looked the part of the dashing naval officer. Tall, trim, broad-shouldered, an excellent shot, a strong swimmer, a good horseback rider, with a mop of curly dark hair, slightly rakish sideburns, and puppy-dog brown eyes, he was the stuff nineteenth-century heroes were made of. He was also known for an aversion to corporal punishment as a means of discipline in an age when that was the norm, and was "proverbial among sailors, for the good treatment of his men," said one marine private who hadn't a good word to say about anyone else.[17] Preble had singled out Decatur for this job, taking a chance on a man who had not yet distinguished himself with any great feat but who seemed to have the drive and dash that it would take.

Ten days went by with no word or sign.

On February 12, unable any longer to hide his apprehensions of disaster, Preble ordered a lookout posted on the masthead of the *Constitution* to keep watch for Decatur's or Stewart's return.

Another week passed; then, at ten in the morning on the nineteenth, a Sunday, there they were, both American ships, running into the harbor. Atop the *Constitution* three numeric signal flags, no doubt long at the ready, flashed out at once: 2-2-7.

A tense minute passed as the *Syren*'s signal officer flipped through the signal book to locate the meaning—"Business or enterprise, have you completed, that you was sent on?"—and assembled an answering hoist. And then the flags Preble had been waiting for broke forth gloriously on the *Syren*'s peak: 2-3-2, "Business, I have completed, that I was sent on."[18]

The commodore spent much of the rest of the day pouring out his relief in a flood of correspondence, beginning with a letter to the secretary of the navy, to whom he could convey the first good news he had had for nearly a year.

At 10 AM the *Syren* and Ketch *Intrepid* arrived from the coast of Tripoly after having executed my orders highly to my satisfaction,

by effecting the complete destruction of the Frigate late the
Philadelphia in the Harbour of Tripoly on the night of the 16th Inst
by burning her with all her Materials. The Frigate was moored in
a situation from whence she could not be brought out. Of course
it became an object of the first importance to destroy her. It has
been effected by Lieut Decatur and the Officers and Crew under
his command in the most gallant manner. His conduct and that
of his brave Officers and Crew is above all praise.

Later that day the commodore dashed off a second letter to Secretary
Smith.

> Sir,
> Lieutenant Decatur is an Officer of too much Value to be
> neglected. The important service he has rendered in destroying
> an Enemy's frigate of 40 Guns, and the gallant manner in which
> he performed it, in a small vessel of only 60 Tons and 4 Guns,
> under the Enemy's Batteries, surrounded by their corsairs and
> armed Boats, the crews of which, stood appalled at his intrepidity
> and daring, would in any Navy in Europe insure him
> instantaneous promotion to the rank of post Captain. I wish as a
> stimulus, it could be done in this instance; it would eventually be
> of real service to our Navy. I beg most earnestly to recommend
> him to the President, that he may be rewarded according to his
> merit.[19]

Preble's elation—an ebullition of joy rather than temper, for once—
only increased as the full details of Decatur's feat became known. It was
a coup of the first order, a model naval operation, a redemption after
months of shame.

The two ships had left Syracuse in company in a moderate breeze
and pleasant weather at five p.m. on the third, the small and none too
strongly built *Intrepid* at one point taken under tow by the *Syren* as they
cleared the southernmost reach of the harbor.

On board the *Intrepid* was a crew of sixty-four volunteers from the
Enterprize, along with all of the *Enterprize*'s officers, among them Mid-
shipman Macdonough; Decatur's second in command, Lieutenant
James Lawrence; and Lieutenant Joseph Bainbridge, brother of the
Philadelphia's now imprisoned captain. From the *Constitution* Preble had

sent five midshipmen, including nineteen-year-old Charles Morris, to complete the company. Salvador Catalano, the Maltese merchant captain who had confirmed the ketch's identity and who knew Tripoli harbor well, had volunteered to serve as pilot. Surgeon's mate Lewis Heermann, who had been confidentially informed of the mission in advance and asked by Decatur for an official report on any men or officers who ought to be excluded for physical causes, begged to be allowed to go along too. Decatur had proposed having Heermann sail on the *Syren,* which was to stand outside Tripoli harbor during the actual attack, but Heermann argued he'd be of more use accompanying the men directly into action, where his "professional services might be the most useful." Decatur at last relented, so long as the doctor promised to "get into a place of safety" on the ketch "in the moment of danger." Heermann replied that he considered "the permission you have given me to go in as an order."[20]

Only after they were under way did the crews finally learn their true destination: the cover story Preble had put out was that they were bound for Malta so the *Intrepid* could be rerigged. On board the *Syren* all hands were mustered at nine the following morning and the commodore's orders read aloud. They would "proceed with all possible dispatch for the Coast of Tripoly." Before nearing the coast they were to disguise the brig "to give the appearance of a Merchant Vessel": striking down the topgallant masts that unmistakably marked a man-of-war, repainting her sides with a new color, housing the guns and shutting the gunports, concealing her deck with quarter cloths. The *Intrepid,* less likely to raise suspicion, would make its way into the harbor first under cover of night, supported by the *Syren*'s boats; on reaching the *Philadelphia,* they would board and burn her, having equipped themselves with "combustibles" for the purpose. Since "on boarding the Frigate it is probable you will meet with Resistance," the commodore cautioned, "it will be well in order to prevent alarm to carry all by Sword."

He concluded: "The destruction of the Frigate is of National importance, and I rely with confidence on your Valor Judgment & Enterprize in contributing all the means in your power to effect it. Whatever may be your success you will return if possible directly to this place.

"May the Almighty take you under his protection and prosper you in this Enterprize."

The crew let out three hearty cheers. When Stewart asked for volunteers from the *Syren*'s crew to take part in the actual attack, the entire crew stepped forward.[21]

THE PASSAGE to Tripoli was miserable. The *Intrepid* was barely seaworthy. Conditions aboard would have been bad under the best of circumstances, but crowded with a vastly larger crew than she was ever intended to carry, the ketch bordered on the uninhabitable. Decatur, the three lieutenants, and the surgeon were packed into the tiny cabin; the six midshipmen and the pilot slept on a platform laid atop the water casks on one side of the hold, with barely enough room to squeeze in under the deck; the eight marines occupied a corresponding arrangement on the other side; and the men were left to their own devices to find a place among or on the casks. The officers had embarked with less than an hour's notice and been told to bring only a single change of clothing. "To these inconveniences were added . . . the attacks of innumerable vermin, which our predecessors the slaves had left behind them," recalled Midshipman Morris. The ship's provisions, also hastily loaded, turned out to be putrid when the casks were opened.

Still, spirits were high, the weather was unusually fair and mild, and the afternoon of February 7, 1804, found the two ships approaching their destination. But there were already indications of a coming gale; the wind was out of the west and freshening. When Morris and Catalano went ahead in a boat to scout the approach to the harbor, they found the surf breaking right across the narrow harbor entrance, hemmed in by a series of menacing shoals and reefs, and Catalano declared that "if we attempted to go in we would never come out again." Decatur ordered the attack called off, and with the wind shifting to the north and mounting quickly to gale force, the ships had to laboriously tack their way windward through the night to be out of sight of the town when dawn broke. The *Syren*'s anchor was wedged so tight in the rocky bottom it took half the night to try to haul it in; three times the men at the capstan were knocked down by the bars, and several were seriously injured when the cable parted under the strain. In the end, the brig rolling up to its gunwales and daylight approaching, Stewart ordered the cable cut and the anchor left behind. And then the wind began to blow in earnest.[22]

For four days they were blown eastward, scudding on nearly bare poles, the crew so sick most of the time that they didn't have to worry about contending with their rotten food. The gale finally blew itself out on the tenth, and then began an arduous five days of working back westward. The storm, the hardships on board, the disappointment of the abandoned first attempt were beginning to take their toll. Morale was dropping dangerously; they had surely been seen from shore by now, the men were saying; the town would be thoroughly alarmed and the *Philadelphia* so heavily guarded that they didn't stand a chance.

On the fifteenth they were again nearing Tripoli. Again the attempt had to be abandoned as night fell before they had come close enough to catch sight of the town and take a bearing; it was now impossible to find the harbor entrance in the dark.

The morning of the sixteenth of February began with light winds, pleasant weather, and a smooth sea: an auspicious start. The two vessels kept far apart during the day. Now the timing was critical; Decatur aimed to reach the harbor entrance just after dark while not arousing suspicions by obviously loitering outside the harbor. "The lightness of the wind allowed us to keep up all appearance of an anxious desire to reach the harbor before night," recalled Morris; all sail set, to aid the deception a drag of spars, lumber, and ladder was dropped astern to further check their speed. The *Intrepid* aimed to pass as a Maltese trader, flying English colors; the crew was now completely concealed below save a half dozen on deck dressed in Maltese garb. As the sun set behind the white walls of the city and castle, the *Intrepid* was two miles from the eastern entrance of the harbor, the *Syren* about three miles behind. In the last glow of light they saw the English consul's house along the shore raise the English colors in recognition of theirs.

The plan was to drop anchor under cover of dark and wait for the boats of the *Syren* to come up before entering the harbor. But the wind was now dropping rapidly, and Decatur began to fear that unless he went ahead at once there would not be enough wind to carry the *Intrepid* in at all. Observing that "the fewer the number the greater the honor," he gave orders to proceed without the planned reinforcements.

The wind wafted them slowly into the harbor, a crescent moon barely lighting the looming batteries of the forts that ringed the shoreline, the water smooth. Then the *Philadelphia* came into view, anchored just four hundred yards from the castle, seven hundred yards from the battery on the molehead, with a few smaller ships nearby. The *Intrepid* made straight for the frigate, her crew now stretched out on the deck, swords, axes, pikes at the ready. "At last the anxious silence was broken by a hail . . . demanding our character and object," Morris recalled. Catalano, speaking in Arabic, answered that they had come from Malta to load cattle for the British garrison there, and they had lost their anchor in the gale. Could they tie up to the frigate for the night? Permission was granted.

Catalano kept up a running conversation as the gap between the two ships narrowed. The guard on the frigate asked what the other large ship was that they had seen in the offing. Catalano replied it was the *Transfer,* a brig that the pasha had purchased from the British in Malta, and which the Tripolitans were expecting.

Just as the *Intrepid* was about to make contact alongside the *Philadelphia,* the wind shifted, blowing directly from the frigate, sending the ketch about twenty yards off. "This was a moment of great anxiety," Morris remembered. "We were directly under her guns, motionless and powerless, except by exertions which might betray our character." But the *Intrepid* was towing one of the *Syren*'s boats, which had been sent over a few days earlier, and with a coolness that bordered on the preternatural, the boat was "leisurely manned" and rowed toward the frigate carrying a line. They were met by a boat from the frigate with another rope, and the two lines were made fast; the *Intrepid*'s boat returned, and the rope was passed onto the deck where the crew, still hidden, began hauling in the line as they lay facedown, slowly closing the distance between the vessels once again.

There were still a few yards to go when the Tripolitans realized at last that something was wrong. A cry went up from the guard on the frigate's deck. *"Americanos! Americanos!"* The captain of the guard hailed Catalano and asked if there were any Americans on board; Catalano replied they were only Italians and Englishmen. Again the guard shouted a warning, and the Tripolitan captain, now convinced, shouted out an order to cut the line. The strain of keeping up the pretense suddenly became too much for the Maltese pilot: Catalano cried out to Decatur, "Board, Captain, board!"

Decatur's booming voice responded at once with a peremptory command that froze every man in his spot: *"No order to be obeyed but that of the commanding officer!"*

A few more agonizing seconds passed as the last gap closed. Then, leaping onto the frigate's main chains, Decatur shouted, *"Board!"*[23]

"Not a man had been seen or heard to breathe a moment before," recalled Heermann, the surgeon's mate who had begged to be included on the mission; "at the next, the boarders hung on the ship's side like cluster bees; and, in another instant, every man was on board the frigate."

Morris had leapt at the same moment as Decatur, an instant before the actual order to board was given, and happened to reach the deck first, all apparently unbeknownst to Decatur. Morris turned just in time to see Decatur coming over the rail with his sword arm lifted, ready to strike him; Morris shouted the watchword—"Philadelphia"—just in time to avoid becoming the first, self-inflicted casualty of the operation.

Several of the guards promptly leapt over the opposite rail and swam the short distance to shore; others got aboard a boat and fled. But a few turned to fight, and the minutes that followed were pure butchery. To avoid spreading the alarm, no firearms were used; it was all stabbing and slashing at close quarters, the dead heaved over the side when it was done.

But the whooping and screaming of the Tripolitans had spread the alarm nonetheless, and a hail of musket fire began from two xebecs lying near. Decatur sent a rocket arcing into the sky to signal the *Syren* that the *Philadelphia* had been taken; it was answered by a cannonade from the castle and the other batteries around the harbor.

The boarding party had been divided into teams, each under a lieutenant and each assigned a part of the ship to set afire; watching from the *Intrepid,* where he had dutifully remained, Heermann saw the frigate's gun deck "all of a sudden beautifully illuminated" by the lanterns the men carried as they moved to their stations. Then Decatur was on the deck, making his way forward to aft, shouting the command "Fire!" down each hatchway, and in a minute billows of smoke and flame were pouring from every corner of the ship. Decatur was the last to get off, "literally followed by the flames," Heermann said.[24]

As the fire ran up the rigging and set the tops ablaze, the *Intrepid's* men, now giddy with their triumph, stood transfixed at the spectacular "bonfire"—and more than a bit oblivious to the extreme danger they were still in. In approaching the *Philadelphia,* they had deliberately placed themselves on the lee side to ease their getaway; now the bow was shoved off and the jib set, but the huge draft created by the fire repeatedly drew the ketch back in, and her main boom became entangled with the large ship's quarter gallery. The men were still noisily laughing and clowning when a furious Decatur leapt atop the companionway, drew his sword, and announced he would cut down the first man who made another sound. That promptly restored order. The boats were got out to tow the bow around, the sweeps were manned, and slowly and laboriously the ketch was brought off and the land breeze began to carry her out to sea. A single cannonball passed through the ketch's topgallant sail, but the fire from the shore was otherwise mercifully inaccurate. There had been no loss of life and but a single casualty among the *Intrepid*'s crew.

At eleven o'clock the men aboard the *Syren* saw the blazing tops of the frigate's masts fall over, and at midnight the fire burned through her cables and she drifted slowly ashore in the direction of the pasha's castle. Then, as the flames and heat reached her guns, they went off one after another, a derisory ghostly cannonade taking the Americans' final revenge, a few of the shots actually striking the castle walls.

By six the next morning the *Syren* and the *Intrepid* were forty miles to sea. They could still see the glow of the burning ship on the horizon.[25]

THE DESTRUCTION of the *Philadelphia* brought a rare moment of relief to the agonizing apprehensions that had weighed on Captain William Bainbridge since surrendering his ship in October. In the house in Tripoli where the officers of the *Philadelphia* were being held, they were awakened the night of Decatur's raid by "a most hideous yelling and screaming from one end of the town to the other," mingled with a "thundering of cannon from the castle." Opening a window, they were able to look out to the harbor and see the frigate ablaze. "A most sublime sight," Bainbridge wrote, "and very gratifying to us."

The next morning a strong guard appeared at the door. The pasha, who had watched the entire spectacle from a front-row seat in his own quarters overlooking the harbor, was said to be in a rage. The *Philadelphia*'s surgeon's mate, Jonathan Cowdery, was curtly informed he would no longer be permitted to tend to the sick members of the crew or any of the other patients in the city that he had been treating, including the pasha's own daughter. There were rumors the officers would be moved to the castle; or, as Bainbridge put it, "what they call a Castle, which in fact was a most loathsome prison."[26]

But most of these shows of displeasure abated almost as soon as they had arisen. Despite Preble's pangs back in December as he contemplated Bainbridge's captivity—a "slave, treated in the most cruel manner"—the *Philadelphia*'s officers had, in fact, enjoyed considerable freedom and privileges since they had landed in the pasha's hands, and that was not about to change for the very simple reason that, as the pasha very well knew, they were literally worth their weight in gold. The officers had been allowed to take up residence in the spacious house previously occupied by the last American consul in Tripoli before the war began. The Danish consul was allowed to visit them every day and supplied them with bedding and arranged for credit with local money-lenders. After signing a pledge that they would not attempt to escape, the prisoners were eventually allowed to stroll around the town and even the countryside; Cowdery was regularly invited to visit the pasha's gardens and often left loaded down with baskets of oranges, figs, dates, pomegranates, and olives, gifts from the pasha and his ministers.

The initial indignities of the first hours after their capture—they were stripped of their money, uniforms, and swords; their pockets were searched; even their boots were pulled off to see if anything of value had been concealed there—still rankled, all the more when they saw the local citizens parading around in their clothes, and even more when the local clothes dealers showed up to offer them back at an exorbitant price. But all in all it was not a terribly arduous captivity for the officers.[27]

What really made life a burden to Captain Bainbridge was the dread of what would become of his honor and reputation. "My situation in prison is entirely supportable," he wrote his wife the day after the disaster, ". . . but if my professional character be blotched—if an attempt be made to taint my honour—if I am censured, if it does not kill me, it would at least deprive me of the power of looking any of my race in the face." So maddened was he at moments by contemplating the loss of "the beautiful frigate which was placed under my command," he said, "that I cannot refrain from exclaiming that it would have been a merciful dispensation of Providence if my head had been shot off by the enemy, while our vessel lay rolling on the rocks."[28]

Bainbridge once referred to himself as "the Child of Adversity," and this was not the first humiliation he had suffered in his naval career.[29] In 1798, during the Quasi War, he had surrendered without a shot his very first command, the eighteen-gun schooner *Retaliation*, to two French frigates that he had embarrassingly mistaken for British vessels he had spoken the day before and carelessly approached. Two years later he had suffered the torment of having to carry tribute to the dey of Algiers under the terms of the treaty the United States had accepted as cheaper than building a navy that could resist the Barbary corsairs' depredations on American merchantmen. After unloading a shipment of guns, lumber, nails, and other supplies in Algiers, Bainbridge was summoned by the dey and told he must now run an additional errand with his warship. The dey needed to send his ambassador to Constantinople, along with a retinue of a hundred followers, a hundred black slaves, four horses, a hundred and fifty sheep, twenty-five horned cattle, four lions, four tigers, four antelopes, and twelve parrots, a lavish tribute that the dey hoped would restore his good graces with the sultan, with whom he was just at the moment out of favor. The humiliation was completed by the dey's insistence that Bainbridge's ship, the *George Washington,* a thirty-two-gun converted merchantman, fly the Algerian flag on this mission. When Bainbridge balked, the dey hinted that the only alternative was war. "You can, my friends, see how unpleasantly I am situated," Bainbridge wrote William Jones and Samuel Clarke, old friends from Philadelphia, owners of a merchant shipping partnership he had sailed for in his days as a very young merchant captain. "If I go it will take a period of six months and for that space of time I shall be in the worst of purgatories, having two hundred infidels on board, being in a country where the United States is not known, no person to call on in case of emergency and not able to speak the language in a land where the plague ravishes and at the mercy of Devils." The day of his departure, the *George Washington*'s log recorded, "The pendant of the United States was struck and the Algerian Flag hoisted on the Main top Gallant royal head mast . . . some tears fell at this Instance of national Humility."[30]

But Bainbridge had a streak of bullying self-pity that had served him well in the past, and it did not take long for him to put it to use again in this latest humiliation. He had all of Decatur's pride and vanity and touchy sense of honor with none of his dash; he was not a handsome man, with a rectangular head, heavy jowls, a florid complexion, thick lips, a deeply cleft chin, and a pugnacious air. Even Bainbridge's admirers noted his "vehemence" and how when one of his "fierce" storms came over him he could barely speak, caught in a stammer that sounded like he was saying "unto unto unto" before he could get his words out.[31]

In only one of his letters following the loss of the *Philadelphia* did Bainbridge even come close to admitting responsibility for the disaster. He acknowledged to Preble that if he had not sent the schooner *Vixen* away a week before (on what he surely should have known was an ill-advised wild goose chase: two Tripolitan men-of-war were rumored to be *somewhere* on a cruise, but the report Bainbridge received from a passing merchant brig did not even say where they might be), it might have been possible to prevent the calamity.[32] The *Vixen* could easily have come to his aid and helped tow the frigate off the rocks.

After that he became ever more stridently self-justifying, demanding to friends that they write back and reassure him he was not to blame. "Striking on the Rocks was an accident not possible for me to guard against," he wrote Preble. The shoal was not marked on any charts. He had done "every thing" in his power to get the ship off: backing the sails, lightening the bows by throwing most of the guns overboard, finally cutting the foremast clear away; it was, however, "impossible." Attempting to fight off the Tripolitan gunboats "would be only a sacrificing [of] lives without effecting our enemy or rendering the least service to Our Country . . . a want of courage can never be imputed when there is no chance of resistance." The embarrassing fact that the Tripolitans had floated the frigate off the shoal forty hours later "adds to our calamity, but . . . we feel some consolation in knowing that it is not the first instance where ships have been from necessity (of running aground) obligded to surrender, and afterwards got off by the enemy . . . witness the *Hannibal* at Algesiras, the *Jason* off St. Maloes, and several others."[33]

No doubt at Bainbridge's behest, the officers of the *Philadelphia* quickly closed ranks too, drawing up and sending to their captain a memorial on the first day of their captivity assuring him of their "highest and most sincere respect," their "full approbation of your conduct," and vouching that "every exertion was made . . . which either courage or abilities could have dictated." But some of their consciences were far from clear over their own responsibility for the loss of the ship, which likely explained the eagerness to embrace Bainbridge's assurances that it had been an unavoidable "accident." Lieutenant David Porter had apparently urged Bainbridge repeatedly to continue the chase and insisted they were in no danger, even though they had no pilot aboard who knew the local waters; the moment the ship struck the reef, reported one of the ship's men, Porter had turned as white as a sheet.[34]

Bainbridge importuned friends to send copies of American newspapers, and soon after the first reports of the *Philadelphia*'s loss reached the United States in March 1804, the American press had indeed rallied to Bainbridge's support. The Republican newspapers hastened to absolve blame anywhere by labeling it "one of those inevitable misfortunes which no human foresight could have seen," the Federalist prints equally acquitting the ship's officers as they rushed to use the event to pillory the Jefferson administration for its "miserable, starveling, niggardly species of economy which by saving a dollar ruins a nation."[35]

As ALWAYS, the common sailors had a different story to tell; from the start they had loathed their captain and were far from convinced that he had done all he might have to resist capture.

They had also suffered a brutality in captivity that the officers escaped. The 283 crewmen were confined in a stone warehouse outside the castle that measured eighty by twenty-five feet—seven square feet to a man—with a rough dirt floor and a small grated skylight the only source of light or air. Accounts published afterward by one of the captives, William Ray, a marine private, recounted vicious beatings by the guards. A favorite was the bastinado on the bare soles of the feet: the prisoner would be thrown on his back, his ankles bound together and raised so the soles were nearly horizontal, and then two men, each armed with a three-foot bamboo staff as thick as a walking stick, would roll up their sleeves and swing down on the bottoms of the victim's feet with all their might.

The officers whiled away their days at the consul's house with books and other diversions. A few days after their arrival Bainbridge ordered Porter to organize what he called "the College of Students," instructing the midshipmen each day after breakfast in navigation and naval tactics. The Danish consul supplied the American officers with a volume of collected plays, which they proceeded to stage complete with scenery and costumes they set to work building and sewing. The crew meanwhile was set to hard labor, hauling three-ton stones in hand-pulled carts, boring cannons, unloading casks of gunpowder and supplies from the frigate, shoveling out an old wreck buried in the sand of the beach as they worked up to their armpits in the cold surf. Their diet was little more than bread, olive oil, and couscous.[36]

Like the officers, the men had openly rejoiced in the success of Decatur's raid; unlike the officers, they suffered the full force of the pasha's humiliated rage. Ray recounted what happened next:

Early in the morning, and much earlier than usual, our prison doors were unbolted, and the keepers . . . rushed in amongst us and began to beat every one they could see, spitting in our faces and hissing like the serpents of hell. We could not suppress our emotions, nor disguise our joy . . . which exasperated them more and more, so that every boy we met in the streets would spit on us and pelt us with stones; our tasks were doubled, our bread withheld, and every driver exercised cruelties tenfold more rigid and intolerable than before.[37]

But Ray's bitterest recollections were of the indifference Bainbridge and the other officers showed for the men's plight. "At numerous times, when we were on the very brink of starvation, and petitioned Captain Bainbridge for some part of our pay or rations, he invariably gave us to understand that it was entirely out of his power to do anything for us," Ray wrote. The men resorted to petitioning Preble, and even the pasha, directly, and with more success (the pasha agreed to provide barrels of pork unloaded from the frigate to supplement the men's meager rations).[38]

Soon after their arrival the men had been questioned closely by the pasha's admiral about the circumstances of the ship's surrender. Murad Reis was a character who would have been scarcely credible on the pages of a novel. Born in Scotland, he was originally known as Peter Lisle. In his younger years he had traveled to New England, where he developed a strong aversion to America and Americans; then in 1796 he took passage on a schooner out of Boston that was captured by Tripolitan marauders when it reached the Mediterranean. Seizing opportunity with remarkable panache, Lisle proceeded in quick succession to convert to Islam, marry the pasha's sister, talk the pasha into declaring war against America, and assume personal command of the captured schooner, now fitted out as a twenty-six-gun man-of-war in the Tripolitan navy.

The "renegade Scotchman," as the Americans called him, asked the men bluntly whether their captain was "a coward, or a traitor": Reis said he had to be one or the other. Reis went on to express incredulity that the Americans had given up so easily. They might have known the frigate would float off the rocks as soon as the wind shifted, Reis pointed out; they might have realized that he had no intention of trying to board a frigate manned by three hundred well-armed men, or risk destroying such a valuable potential prize by firing his guns at the hull.

It was a telling point. While Bainbridge did order the ship scuttled and the magazine drowned, the flag was struck before the work was finished, and the Tripolitans, when they rushed aboard, were quickly able to plug the leaks. At a very minimum he could have played for time. And Ray noted that the crew was more than willing to fight; the only damage the Tripolitan gunboats had done up to the moment of the frigate's surrender was to the rigging and sails: they were deliberately aiming high. "The man who was at the ensign halyards positively refused to obey the captain's orders, when he was ordered to lower the flag," Ray recalled. "He was threatened to be run through and a midshipman seized the halyards, and executed the command, to the general murmuring of the crew." Ray also noted that Bainbridge had impatiently spurned the suggestion of the ship's boatswain to try kedging the ship off by hauling in a line from an anchor cast astern, which might well have worked. But, as Ray bitterly observed, Bainbridge had once told a seaman, "You have no right to think"; that attitude seemed to be his guiding rule in this case as well.[39]

When Ray's memoir was published in 1808, Bainbridge retorted that its author was "an ungrateful wretch who has no character to lose." But there was little doubt that the feelings of contempt between Captain Bainbridge and the crews who served under him were widely shared and mutual. Bainbridge had a well-earned reputation as a hard horse, a flogging captain; Preble might have been a stern disciplinarian but Bainbridge was a brute, regularly meting out punishments of thirty-six lashes, putting a man in irons for six weeks for drunkenness, habitually addressing his crews as "you damned rascals." As a merchant captain he had personally quelled two attempted mutinies with his own fists; as captain of the *George Washington* he had fractured a man's skull hitting him over the head with the flat of a sword. While captive in Tripoli, Bainbridge expressed quite plainly what he thought of his crewmen in a letter to Preble: "I believe there never was so depraved a set of mortals as Sailors are; under discipline they are peaceable & serviceable;—divest them of that, and they constitute a perfect rable." The feeling was returned in full. Thirteen men of the *Philadelphia* deserted at the very start of the cruise to avoid serving under Bainbridge. Ray in his memoir claimed that the *Philadelphia*'s crew was near mutiny at the time the ship struck the shoal in Tripoli harbor.[40]

Part of what so rankled the men of the American navy was how such treatment, and such attitudes, smacked of the despotism their nation had just finished fighting a revolution to be rid of. American seamen who left a record of their views frequently commented on their rights as free Americans and their resentments at the "petty tyranny" exercised by their officers.

A man on the *Constitution* who was about be flogged burst forth in what a shipmate described as a "patriotic speech": "I thought it was a free country; but I was mistaken. My father was American born, and my mother too. I expected to be treated as an American myself; but I find I'm not." ("Down with him and put him in irons," responded an unimpressed lieutenant.) "Such outrages on human nature ought not to be permitted by a government that boasts of liberty," agreed James Durand, who as a seaman aboard the frigate *John Adams* in 1804 saw men given eighteen lashes for such "crimes" as spitting on the deck. But, as Durand observed, "no monarch in the world is more absolute than the Captain of a Man-of-war." John Rea, who served as an ordinary seaman on the *George Washington* under Bainbridge, bitterly ridiculed all the ceremony that emphasized the captain's kingly authority: the ritual reading of the articles of war every Sunday to the assembled men, the mustering of the crew to witness punishment, the strictures against speaking back to an officer or expressing so much as an opinion; "all that ridiculous and absurd parade, common on board of *English Men-of-War.*"

Especially galling was the lordly attitude of the midshipmen. Following the Royal Navy model, these officers-in-training were referred to as "young gentlemen" (all officers were by definition "gentlemen"), but Rea dismissed them as "brats of boys, twelve or fifteen years old, who six months before had not even seen salt water, strutting in livery about a Ship's decks, damning and flashing old experienced sailors."[41]

The floggings and discipline, the hieratical rituals, the rigid distinctions between officers (who were "gentlemen") and men (who were not) had indeed all been copied almost slavishly from the British example. When Preble, in command of the frigate *Essex,* had put in at Cape Town in March 1800 and had dined night after night with the officers of the British squadron there, he used the opportunity to acquire copies of British naval manuals and squadron orders, diligently studying and marking them up. The American navy's regulations, first issued in 1798 and revised in 1802, drew directly, often word for word, from the British *Regulations and Instructions Relating to His Majesty's Service at Sea.* It was a natural recourse: the British navy was the most admired and powerful in the world; the two nations shared a common language and heritage.

But the British example was already proving an uneasy fit with this new man, the American.[42]

THE TRIPOLITAN war dragged on for another year and a half. The *Constitution* came in several times to bombard the town; a harebrained scheme was hatched by William Eaton, the former American consul in Tunis (a sergeant in George Washington's army, he was now calling himself "General" Eaton) to gather a band of Arab mercenaries in Cairo, march hundreds of miles across the desert, and replace the pasha of Tripoli with his presumably more compliant brother. But the bombardments were indecisive, and Eaton's expedition was beset by repeated mutinies and delays. Eight United States marines who took part in the march did play a conspicuous part in bravely taking the fort at Darnah, five hundred miles east of Tripoli, which was as far as the expedition ever got; if it was not exactly "the shores of Tripoli" subsequently referred to in the famous first line of the "Marines' Hymn," their action may have helped put pressure on the pasha to come to terms.

In September 1804 the *Intrepid* had been sent into Tripoli harbor packed with five tons of powder and 150 shells. It was to blow up the Tripolitan gunboats and galleys while they lay at their anchorage at night, the crew escaping in two boats after the fuse was lit, but something went wrong and the ketch exploded prematurely, killing all thirteen men aboard. Preble thought the ship might have been boarded, and Lieutenant Richard Somers had bravely decided to blow up his command rather than surrender. His praise for Somers brought a hurt complaint from Bainbridge, who was convinced it was a slap at him for failing to do the same with the *Philadelphia*. Preble ended up apologizing to Bainbridge. Dr. Cowdery drew the job of supervising the burial of some of the corpses that had washed up on the shore afterward. They had been mangled by stray dogs when the pasha for days refused to allow them to be collected, after which the remains were placed on public display and the local populace was invited to hurl insults at them before they were finally buried.[43]

In the end a treaty was signed in June 1805, the ceremony taking place in the great cabin of the *Constitution;* the United States would pay no tribute but agreed to a $60,000 ransom for the captives in Tripoli. A twenty-one-gun salute echoed from the castle and was returned by the

Constitution. The prisoners got so drunk (despite the strictures of Islam, some of the town's Jewish and Christian shopkeepers sold alcohol) that Bainbridge delayed bringing them aboard the *Constitution* for a day until they were clean and presentable. Six men had died during their captivity; five others had "turned Turk," converting to Islam, and either chose—or were not given any other choice by the pasha—to remain behind.

Dr. Cowdery was so worried that he would not be permitted to leave either—the pasha had at one point assured him he would not take $20,000 for his release, so valuable a physician had he proved to be—that the doctor deliberately botched an operation on a Tripolitan soldier whose hand had been shattered by a bursting blunderbuss: "I amputated all his fingers but one, with a dull knife, and dressed them in a bungling manner, in the hopes of losing my credibility as a surgeon in this part of the country."[44]

On his return to America, Bainbridge was feted at huge banquets at Richmond, Fredericksburg, Alexandria, and Washington. He basked in it all. Preble, who had been replaced in his command in September 1804, had been welcomed as a conquering hero too; President Jefferson invited him to dine at the White House and Rembrandt Peale painted his portrait. But he was not so sure about it all. "The people are disposed to think that I have rendered some service to my country," he cautiously told his wife. Three years later he was dead, at age forty-six. Though studiously avoiding public controversy, he had privately told friends the treaty with Tripoli was "ignominious" and a "sacrifice of national honor." Bainbridge may or may not have remembered the words he himself had written the navy department on first arriving in the Mediterranean, back in September of 1800. "Had we 10 or 12 frigates and sloops in these seas," Bainbridge insisted, "we should not experience these mortifying degradations."[45]

CHAPTER 2

Honor's Shoals

From the *Boston Patriot*,
February 29, 1812.

No visit to America was complete for the British traveler of the early 1800s without a letter home laden with disdain for the vulgarity of the inhabitants. Americans were crude, loud, boastful, grasping—and they were ingrates to boot. Augustus J. Foster, secretary to the British legation in 1804, asserted that "from the Province of Maine to the borders of Florida, you would not find 30 men of Truth, Honour, or Integrity. Corruption, Immorality, Irreligion, and above all, self-interest, have corroded the very pillars on which their Liberty rests." No more than five members of Congress could be considered gentlemen; the rest habitually appeared in "the filthiest dresses." American women were "a spying, inquisitive, vulgar, and most ignorant race." President Jefferson himself "is dressed and looks extremely like a plain farmer, and wears his slippers down at the heels."[1]

Those slippers had nearly caused a diplomatic incident themselves.

When Foster's principal, the new British minister Anthony Merry, came to present his credentials to the president, he arrived in full court dress, sash, ceremonial sword, and all. President Jefferson appeared in an old brown coat, faded corduroys, much-soiled linen, and those worn-down slippers. Merry was sure it was a calculated insult to him personally, and to his country officially. The British minister spent the next several months accumulating imagined insults from other displays of American informality, above all the careless egalitarianism of Jefferson's hospitality at the White House. Jefferson made a point of dispensing with all the elaborate European rules of precedence of place in seating guests at his dinner table; his rule was what he termed *"pêle-mêle"*: guests found their own seats. This was all news to Merry, who was mortified when Mrs. Merry was not seated next to the president and he found himself elbowed aside by a member of the House of Representatives as he was about to sit down next to the wife of the Spanish minister. Even an official note from Secretary of State James Madison explaining the customs of his host country failed to convince Merry that it was anything but a premeditated plan to give offense.[2]

The deeper problem was that most Britons did not really think of the America of 1800 as a real country. The Revolution had given America independence in name, but her claims to a place among the civilized nations of the world struck even sympathetic British observers as pretentious or simply laughable. America's similarities to Britain only showed her enduring dependence on the mother country; her differences only reflected degeneracy or immaturity, proving how helpless the former colony was on her own. British critics found literally nothing praiseworthy about life in America. In science, art, and literature America was a nullity; "the destruction of her whole literature would not occasion so much regret as we feel for the loss of a few leaves from an antient classic," pronounced the *Edinburgh Review*. American conversation consisted of nosy cross-examination of strangers. America's colleges were little better than grammar schools. The food was ill-cooked, the drinking excessive, the inns crowded, the street brawls savage.[3]

Above all, America's government was a rickety experiment, indecisive and incapable of ever rising to the level of the world's great powers. The Irish poet Thomas Moore, who visited America in 1804, saw in the vulgarity and roughness of American society a reflection of a government system fatally weakened by airy ideals of republicanism and lacking the steadying influence of a gentry and hereditary aristocracy. "The mail takes twelve passengers, which generally consist of squalling children, stinking negroes, and republicans smoking cigars," Moore complained. "How often it has occurred to me that nothing can be more emblematic of the *government* of this country than its *stages,* filled with a motley mixture, all 'hail fellows well met,' driving through mud and filth, which *bespatters* them as they *raise* it, and risking an *upset* at every step."[4]

America's grasping commercialism and braying talk of liberty, most Britons felt, were all of a piece with its upstart vulgarity. An honest recognition of America's ongoing dependency on Britain for its very survival, economically and politically, ought to make Americans more grateful and less strident: more willing to accept the place Britain wished to assign her as a very junior partner; happy to behave, in other words, more as the colony they really, in fact, still were, not the excessively proud nation their upset victory at Yorktown had led them to declare themselves to be. "The Alps and Apennines of America are the British Navy," asserted the *Times* of London. "If ever that should be removed, a short time will suffice to establish the head-quarters of a Duke-Marshal at Washington, and to divide the territory of the Union into military prefectures." The even more jingoistic British newspaper the *Courier* chimed in with the observation that while America was arguably *advantageous* to Great Britain, Great Britain was *necessary* to America: "It is British capital, which directly or indirectly, sets half the industry of America in motion: it is the British fleets that give it protection and security."[5]

LIKE ALL caricatures, the picture of America painted by British travelers and opinion writers captured some truths. On a visit to Monticello during the summer of 1805, Augustus Foster observed with more perception and nuance, and less of the automatic disdain that had animated his earlier impressions of America, the contradictions of American democracy, and of the leader who was supposed to embody its values. The president who made a show of democratic simplicity, riding his horse unaccompanied about Washington in his worn coat, spent freely on his own comforts at home atop his mountain retreat in Virginia. There were all the gadgets Jefferson's guests were expected to admire: the cart equipped with an odometer, the spiral rotating clothes rack. And then Foster, the English aristocrat, found that his own views on human equality and liberty were far more broad-minded than Jefferson's, at least when it came to extending the American notion of liberty to the black race. Foster thought it self-evident that blacks were "as capable to the full of profiting by the advantages of Education as any other of any Shade whatever," but the Republican president told him that "the Mental Qualities of the Negro Race" fitted them only "to carry Burthens" and that freedom would only render them more miserable; the American champion of democratic equality dismissed emancipation of the slaves as "an English Hobby," much as the tea tax had been. And Jefferson the extoller of agrarian virtue was "considered a very bad Farmer," Foster found in conversation with others nearby; a whole hillside of Monticello had been so negligently cultivated as to have eroded away into gullies so deep that "Houses afterwards might be buried" in them. "They have been obliged to scatter Scotch Broom Seed over it, which at least succeeded in at least hiding the Cavities." Like the country itself, America's third president was much given to "speculative doctrines on imaginary perfection" that did not always comport with reality.[6]

The reality was that America in the first decade of the new century was poor, weak, and backward. By many measures there had been little progress from colonial days. Compared with London, with its one million people, America's great cities were little more than overgrown medieval villages. Boston had actually lost population for several years following the Revolution; by 1800 its population stood at 25,000, little more than what it had been thirty years earlier. New York had 60,000, Baltimore 13,000, Charleston 18,000. With the possible sole exception of Philadelphia—whose 70,000 residents enjoyed neatly laid-out blocks, streetlights, drains, and wooden pipes that brought in fresh water—they also had no sanitation to speak of, bad paving, an abundance of dramshops, and periodic outbreaks of yellow fever and other deadly epidemics that sent the residents fleeing for the hills. The still-unpaid cost of the war against Britain, a debt of $82 million, pressed like a dead weight on the national economy; the entire capitalization of all the banks in the country amounted to but a third as much.

Travel was arduous, erratic, and unbelievably expensive; even in settled New England, stagecoaches crept along barely travelable roads at an average pace of four miles an hour, taking three days from Boston to New York, two days from New York to Philadelphia. From Baltimore to Washington—where the new federal city, all hope and little reality, was rising on a malarial backwater with nothing to show yet but a single row of brick houses, a few log cabins, the half-finished White House, and, a mile and a half away across a bramble-tangled swamp, the two wings of the Capitol still unconnected by a center—there was a stagecoach but no road at all; the driver chose among meandering tracks in the woods and hoped for the best. To go from Baltimore to New York cost $21, a month's average wages.[7]

South of Washington there were no public conveyances to be had at all, no roads that wagons could traverse, no bank between Alexandria, Virginia, and Charleston, South Carolina, and no call for one. Three-quarters of the nation's workforce of 1.9 million worked on farms, almost all practicing methods unchanged for a thousand years before, steadily exhausting the soil, making whatever clothes they wore themselves, threshing grain with two sticks bound by a leather hinge or trodding it with horses or oxen. Two thousand men in the entire nation, about evenly divided between textiles and primary iron and steel production, earned their wages in basic manufacturing. Houses, even of the wealthiest planters, were run-down; a French visitor to Virginia at this time found genteel poverty the norm: "one finds a well-served table, covered with silver, where for ten years half the window panes have been missing, and where they will be missed for ten years more."[8]

Most Americans still reckoned money in shillings and never saw an American coin larger than a cent. The loose ties that linked the states together had changed little from colonial times. The new capital was meant to be an affirming symbol of nationhood, but as the historian Henry Adams would later wryly observe, "the contrast between the immensity of the task and the paucity of the means" seemed only to suggest that the nation itself was no more than a "magnificent scheme." The unraised columns of the Capitol were a symbol not of national affirmation but of a people given to grandiose and loudly proclaimed plans incapable of fulfillment. Pierre L'Enfant's grand design of broad avenues and long vistas existed only in the imagination across an ugly expanse of tree stumps. Expectations that Washington would grow like any other city and become a place of commerce and culture had been roundly disappointed; the legislators lodged together in boarding-houses, two to a room, living "like bears," complained one senator, "brutalized and stupefied" by having nothing to do but talk politics morning and night, having to send to Baltimore for all but the most ordinary necessities. "Is national independence a dream?" asked the citizens of Mobile, part of Jefferson's grand Louisiana Purchase of 1803, struggling as they were to eke out a miserable living on a frontier a thousand miles away.[9]

The one bright spot in all this was America's maritime trade: it was absolutely booming. By 1805 the American merchant fleet engaged in foreign trade was growing by seventy thousand tons of shipping a year, well on its way to reaching a million tons by the end of the decade, double what it was in 1800 when America already boasted the world's largest merchant fleet of any neutral nation. From Salem, Boston, New York, Philadelphia, Baltimore, Charleston, American-built ships laden with American-grown cotton, wheat, and tobacco set sail across the Atlantic, the Caribbean, and even more distant seas. American exports passed $100 million a year, quadruple the figure of just a decade earlier. And it was not just American products they were carrying; Yankee ships were showing up wherever there were goods to be carried and money to be made. William Jones, merchant captain of Philadelphia, was already following a well-worn path for American traders when he sailed to India in 1803 and Canton in 1805, taking a share of the lucrative Chinese opium trade.

Customs duties were the national government's only reliable source of revenue, and the expansion of foreign trade brought millions flooding into the United States Treasury. Jefferson's administration ran a surplus every year, making it possible to pay down the debt that the president had called a "moral canker" on the body politic of the young nation. Federal revenues grew from $10 million at the start of Jefferson's presidency in 1801 to $16 million by the end of his second term, allowing his treasury secretary, Albert Gallatin, to announce in 1808 that $25 million of the $82 million national debt had been erased.[10]

America's growing merchant fleet created a huge demand for labor to man all the new ships: four thousand new sailors were needed each year just to keep pace with the expansion. By 1807 some fifty thousand seafarers would be employed on American merchant ships. It was a young man's occupation, and a distinctly urban one. Nearly all American seafarers came from towns or cities along the coast; half were from the twelve largest coastal cities. Most went to sea between the ages of sixteen and twenty and stayed at it only a few years; half were between the ages of twenty and twenty-four, and only 10 percent remained at sea for more than fifteen years. For a young American of 1800 it was not a way of life but an adventure and a way to make some quick money, since the wages paid merchant seamen had risen swiftly with demand, and American seamen were soon earning $18 a month at a time when their counterparts in the British merchant marine and the Royal Navy were paid less than half that. Some American shipowners were offering as much as $30 or $35 a month when that was what it took to man their vessels.

It was also an exceedingly dangerous occupation. The physical descriptions entered in seamen's certificates issued by the United States in the first two decades of the nineteenth century in almost every case include a mention of scars and deformities: most sailors had smashed, split, bent, or broken fingers, missing nails, or missing fingertips; one in ten were partially disabled with missing eyes, lame legs, or ruptures.[11]

Significantly, more than 15 percent of American seafarers at this time were free African Americans; that was two or three or even four times the percentage of the black population in the places they came from. Half of black seafarers worked as stewards or cooks, but the other half were regular seamen. It was an opportunity for equal pay and equal respect that simply did not exist anywhere else in American society at the time. "To drive carriage, carry a market basket after the boss, and brush his boots, or saw wood and run errands, was as high as a colored man could rise" on land, recalled William Brown, whose father, Noah, had been a sailor on merchant ships in Rhode Island in the first years of the 1800s. But at sea, noted one traveler of a slightly later period, "the Negro feels as a man." Black seafarers responded to the opportunity by sticking with the life at sea much longer than their white counterparts: they were on average older, more likely to be married, more likely to be tied to one home port. That meant they were also more experienced. On many Yankee ships African American sailors ranked higher, and earned more, than white hands.

African Americans were almost never officers—there were limits—but many observers commented on the equality and lack of racial animosity that existed among American sailors in the first decades of the nineteenth century. They messed together and worked together. Racial boundaries retreated in the face of the far more salient boundaries that the rules and regimentation of shipboard ritual imposed; ironically, the very depersonalization and dehumanization that all sailors suffered made race recede in significance along with every other claim to individual, human consideration that a ship's captain made perfectly clear he didn't give a damn about. A visitor to New Orleans around 1800 noted with wonder that black seamen might "give twenty lashes with the end of a rope to white sailors, but ashore they dare not even look them in the face."

It would not last: by 1840 segregation was already becoming the norm on American ships, and more and more the only jobs open to African Americans at sea were the familiar and degradingly menial ones of servant, messman, and cook. But in the formative years of the young republic, African Americans would carry a hugely disproportionate burden in the emergence of the nation as a force to be reckoned with on the high seas.[12]

BRITISH OPINION divided on whether the swelling tide of American merchant vessels was a good thing or a bad thing. A few radical members of Parliament regularly rose from the Whig party's opposition benches to praise all things American. Samuel Whitbread, whose successful brewing business had made him a fortune—and an emblem of the self-made man who was beginning to challenge the landed aristocracy's traditional hold on power—declared that he viewed America's successful Revolution with "reverence and admiration," and made clear he welcomed American progress on any and all fronts as a boon to humankind.[13]

Others saw perfectly practical reasons to welcome America's growing commercial prosperity. America was the market for half of Britain's textile exports in 1806, a third of all her exported goods—worth some $50 million a year. America, for her part, supplied Britain with the wheat she needed to feed herself, shipping twice as much as the rest of the world combined, along with some fifty million tons of cotton a year to keep her mills running. Anticipating free-trade arguments that would take nearly two centuries to become commonplace, the Scottish Whig politician Henry Brougham argued that trying to protect traditional British monopolies on the oceangoing trade only hurt Britain's prosperity in the long run; the American shipping trade provided an outlet for British manufactures and put money in the pockets of Britain's best customers. "Can any but the veriest driveller in political science, doubt for a moment that her gains are our gains," Brougham wrote of America in 1808, ". . . that the less she traded with other nations, the less she will trade with ourselves; and that to confine her foreign commerce to her trade with England, would be to diminish, if not to destroy this trade also."

That was a compelling argument for many of Britain's emerging

industrial class. But it was the "drivellers" who spoke far louder, clinging to a traditional view that equated the strength of Great Britain with
her hegemony of the seas, pure and simple: British merchantmen no
less than the Royal Navy were why Britannia ruled the waves. Shipbuilders, shipowners, and the trades that supplied them formed a powerful bloc that violently opposed any concessions to rival trading
nations, and in particular any weakening of the Navigation Acts, which
barred non-English ships from carrying goods to or from English
colonies. They noted with alarm that America had already elbowed
aside Britain in the trade between the two countries; British tonnage
engaged in that transatlantic commerce had plummeted from 72,000
to 14,000, and there was no end to America's appetite for more. "Our
liberality was but that of the prodigal who gives without return,"
declared Lord Sheffield, a venerable proponent of the Navigation Acts.
America's gains, insisted the traditionalists, inescapably were Britain's
losses.[14]

Calls to crack down on the encroaching American trade sharply
intensified with the resumption of Britain's war with France in May
1803. As the Royal Navy swept French and Spanish merchantmen from
the sea, neutral American shippers swept in. "Their own fair Trade has
increased immensely & yet they would have the carrying all the French
& Spanish," fumed Augustus Foster. "There is not, thanks to our Tars,
a single French or Spanish merchantman that now navigates these
Seas—& these Jews want to navigate for them."[15] It was sometimes
hard to tell which the British resented more, the money the Americans
were making or the aid they were giving their enemy, but there were
clear signs that a harsh reaction was coming.

In summer 1804 the British frigate *Leander* appeared off Sandy Hook
at the entrance to New York harbor. Along with two other British warships, the frigate *Cambrian* and the sloop of war *Driver*, the *Leander* had
been in and out of New York since the spring, ostensibly to keep watch
on two French frigates that had taken refuge in the harbor. On one
occasion *Cambrian* and *Driver* had sailed into port and anchored directly
abreast of the French ships in an attempt to rattle their foes.[16]

On her return in August 1804, the *Leander* began to make clear that
the British navy now had an additional mission on the American coast,
and that was the systematic harassment of American shipping. "With
the outward-bound vessels we had little or nothing to do," recalled Basil
Hall, then a young midshipman aboard the *Leander*. But every Ameri-

can ship returning from Europe was halted and boarded, just outside of the United States' three-mile territorial limit:

> Every morning, at daybreak, during our stay off New York, we set about arresting the progress of all the vessels we saw, firing off guns to the right and left, to make every ship that was running in, heave to, or wait, until we had leisure to send a boat aboard, "to see," in our lingo, "what she was made of." I have frequently known a dozen, and sometimes a couple of dozen ships, lying a league or two off the port, losing their fair wind, their tide, and worse than all, their market, for many hours, sometimes the whole day, before our search was completed. . . . When any circumstance in the ship's papers looked suspicious, the boarding officer brought the master and his documents to the Leander, where they were further examined by the captain; and if anything more important was then elicited, by an examination of the parties or their papers, to justify the idea that the cargo was French, and not American . . . the ship was forthwith detained. She was then manned with an English crew from the ships of war, and ordered off to Halifax.[17]

Neutral trade was governed by what was, in effect, a body of international common law, a set of precedents and rulings that had been accumulating for centuries, enforced by the admiralty courts of each nation. The basic principles were widely recognized and accepted as part of the "law of nations" that governed the rules of civilized warfare. A belligerent could legally make a prize of any of his enemy's merchant vessels encountered on the high seas. He could not, however, interfere with neutral vessels trading with the enemy so long as they did not carry contraband—material such as weapons or ammunition that directly aided the enemy's military forces. The more traditional rules that British courts enforced held that noncontraband goods *owned* by a belligerent could also be seized on the high seas, even when transported by a neutral vessel. American policy favored a more encompassing definition of neutrality: "free vessels make free goods." This difference would often be cited as one of the key points of dispute in the war to come between Britain and America, but the truth was it was largely moot by 1804; American shippers by then had access to enough credit that the goods they transported were almost always purchased on their own account, so American ships carried American goods. By either the British or the American definition, the ships and their cargo were neutral and not subject to seizure.

The British rule may have provided slightly more convenient legal window dressing for the pretexts British captains began to use as they stepped up the campaign against American shipping, but it was manifest they were going to find pretexts no matter what. Hundreds of American ships were halted and seized on the flimsiest evidence—a ship's paper not drawn up in correct form, a bill of lading that the British captain declared *might* have been forged, a piece of private correspondence referring to business transactions in France—and sent in to Halifax or Bermuda or the West Indies for adjudication by the British vice admiralty courts that operated at these colonial outposts. The ships' owners faced months of lost time while their ships were held and their cargoes frozen, and contesting the legality of the seizure incurred thousands of dollars in legal fees and court charges for the ship's owner, win or lose. And then the captor could threaten to carry the case to the Lords Commissioners of Appeal in London, which guaranteed to tie up the matter for a minimum of another year, virtually forcing the owner to compromise in order to have the appeal dropped. And after all that, upon the release of his ship, he faced the good chance that his vessel would be seized yet again by another British ship on his way home, starting the process all over again. There were never any official repercussions for a British navy captain who was overly zealous in stopping and seizing American ships; none was ever disciplined. Although in egregious cases the vice admiralty courts could find the capturing ship's captain liable and award the owner costs and damages, the sanction was never applied with the frequency or certainty required to offset the much greater rewards that captors regularly reaped even in dubious seizures.

Knowing this allowed the even less scrupulous British privateers, who eagerly began to join in the game, to extort ransoms of $500 or $1,000 apiece from the owners of merchant ships they stopped on scarcely any pretext at all. It was a small price to pay for staying out of the clutches of the British legal system.[18]

IN 1805 the tensions that would finally erupt seven years later into full-blown war took a sharp jump as a result of a British legal ruling that vastly widened the scope of the for-now-undeclared British war on American neutral commerce. In May 1805 the British vice admiralty court in Nassau, Bahamas, ruled that any American ship carrying goods between France and her colonies could legally be seized, regardless of who owned the goods or where the voyage began. As a direct consequence, British cruisers everywhere began snapping up every American merchant ship they encountered crossing the Atlantic.

The legal reasoning in the case, which involved the merchant brig *Essex,* revolved around a British precedent known as the Rule of 1756, established during the Seven Years' War of 1756–63 between Britain and France. The rule held that a neutral could not carry on in wartime a trade that was closed to him in peacetime. France, like most European powers, restricted trade to her colonies to French vessels. For a neutral to come in and take up that trade in wartime was, from the British viewpoint, not a neutral act at all, but rather was using the cover of neutrality to reconstitute the commerce of an enemy that had been legitimately destroyed by the not inconsiderable exertions of the Royal Navy.

The 1803 revival of hostilities between Britain and France had produced a bonanza for American merchants carrying sugar and coffee from the French West Indies to France, precisely the sort of trade barred by the Rule of 1756. To skirt the rule, American ships would break their voyage by touching at an American port, sometimes even unloading their cargo onto the wharves and paying import duties before reloading the goods and "re-exporting" them. An earlier British admiralty court decision had seemed to sanction this practice, and American shippers immediately started to run away with this trade; American re-exports doubled in just two years, reaching $60 million in 1805. The *Essex* decision slammed the door on this legal charade. "I cannot hesitate in denying to a fraudulently circuitous voyage, those immunities which are withheld from a direct one," the judge of the British vice admiralty court ruled in affirming the validity of the *Essex's* seizure.[19]

The decision caused an uproar in the United States when news of it finally arrived in late 1805, not least because it had come without warning and scores of American ships were taken before American shippers could learn of the change in policy. Hard on its heels there arrived from England a furious attack on American motives that literally added insult to the injury. *War in Disguise: or, The Frauds of the Neutral Flags* was published anonymously but was almost immediately known to be the work of James Stephen, a British lawyer with close ties to the government. James Monroe, the American minister in London, sent a copy back to Washington along with the report that everyone in London knew it was "a ministerial work, or rather under its auspices." Those suspicions were amply confirmed when Stephen was shortly afterward rewarded with a safe seat in Parliament.

War in Disguise was hugely influential in Britain, throwing America's supporters on the defensive by skillfully casting America not as an innocent wronged but as an actual aggressor, and a deceitful and treacherous one at that. Affirming the correctness of the *Essex* decision—"that a neutral has no right to deliver a belligerent from the pressure of his enemy's hostilities, by trading with his colonies in time of war in a way that was prohibited in time of peace"—Stephen went on to accuse America of engaging in conduct that was tantamount to war. Far from America having had *her* neutral rights violated, America had trespassed Britain's belligerent rights. Cutting off France from the wealth of her colonies was Britain's most effective weapon against Napoleon, and the "abuse of the neutral flag" by America to restore that commerce was little more than a French ruse de guerre: American ships had been "made French by adoption." Moreover, Americans knew it and were lying through their teeth when they tried to say otherwise. American merchants had perpetrated "fraud and perjury," had violated "the obligations of truth and justice in order to profit unduly by the war," had corrupted the very morals of American society in the process. American protests were not only baseless, but immoral.

Stephen concluded by suggesting that Americans were much too wise to fail to see where their true interests lay; Britain was the true defender of liberty. Nor did Britain seek war with a neutral nation. But such a war, he threatened, was infinitely better than "the sacrifice of our maritime rights."[20]

From New York, where the seizure of American merchantmen continued apace, the city's merchants presented a memorial protesting the "the humiliating and oppressive conduct of ships of war in the vicinity of our coasts and harbors." From the Caribbean to the Atlantic seaboard to the approaches of the ports of Europe, an American ship was being seized every day or two; at any given time there was $10 million worth of American property awaiting adjudication and possible condemnation in British prize courts. Insurance premiums on cargoes carried by American ships quadrupled.

A few months later the humiliations boiled over into a riot, and a rage burning and lasting enough that it might have kindled instant war had the country's leaders fanned it. On the evening of April 25, 1806, the *Leander, Cambrian,* and *Driver* were carrying on their usual routine of lobbing cannonballs across the bows of merchantmen passing into New York when a shot from the *Leander* struck a small coasting sloop inside the harbor. The British captain claimed the sloop had by unlucky chance been in line with the shot, far behind the vessel he was halting. Whatever the facts, the ball struck the helmsman of the sloop, John Pierce, immediately killing him in a particularly gruesome manner: he was completely decapitated.

The sloop's captain was Pierce's brother, and he made his way back to the city, quickly gathered a furious mob, and paraded the mangled body and severed head of the dead man through the streets. The next day a party from the *Leander* returning to their ship with a load of provisions was intercepted by a mob; the supplies were grabbed and placed on twenty carts that were triumphantly wheeled around the city, drums beating, British colors flying under the American flag from a pole on the lead cart. On reaching the Alms House, the crowd presented their prize for the use of the poor and burned the British flag.

Four of *Leander's* officers caught ashore were thrown in jail for their own protection; protest meetings were called; Pierce was given a huge public funeral; and with a local election scheduled to begin the next day, both political parties made hay of the issue, especially the Federalists, who indignantly blamed the Republicans for refusing to support the construction of a navy that could prevent such affronts. For days Thomas Barclay, the British consul general in New York, hid in his house, fearing he would be killed if he showed his face in public. He wrote reams of letters expressing his regret for the mistake and desperately trying to get the *Leander's* officers freed; eventually the city authorities secretly released them and hustled them back aboard their ship.[21]

Talk of war began to sound more than just theatrical. "How long must we bear these violations of our National honor, property, and loss of our fellow Citizens," William Bainbridge wrote Edward Preble when he heard the news. "—O Lord! Grant us a more honorable Peace or a sanguinary war!"[22]

Publicly, Jefferson ordered American ports forever closed to the three British ships and the *Leander's* captain arrested if he ever were found within American jurisdiction. Privately, the president admitted his first doubts about his party's rigid opposition to a standing navy as a threat to liberty and a burdensome expenditure that would lead to oppressive taxation and growing government power. To Jacob Crown-inshield, a wealthy Salem merchant and Jeffersonian member of Congress, he wrote a few weeks after the event, "Although the scenes which were acted on shore were overdone with electioneering views, yet the act of the British officer was an atrocious violation of our territorial rights." He lamented that America did not have three frigates to send at once to New York or, even better, some ships of the line building. "That we should have a squadron properly composed to prevent the blockading of our ports," Jefferson added, "is indispensable."[23]

A couple of months earlier he had conceded a more fundamental doubt about the country's overall direction. "The love of peace which we sincerely feel & profess," he wrote one of his correspondents in February, "has begun to produce an opinion in Europe that our government is entirely in Quaker principles."[24]

WHEN THE news of the *Essex* decision reached Washington, Secretary of State Madison sat down, took up his pen, and produced his own painstaking, lawyerly rebuttal. Exhaustively analyzing the legal precedents, history, justice, and logic of the rules governing neutral trade, Madison concluded that the Rule of 1756 had no basis in the law of nations. The secretary of state had his argument printed as a 204-page booklet and presented every member of Congress with a personal copy. *An Examination of the British Doctrine, Which Subjects to Capture a Neutral Trade, Not Open in Time of Peace* was thorough, closely argued, solidly reasoned, and absolutely, mind-numbingly dull. Massachusetts senator John Quincy Adams, son of the former president and an eminent scholar, pronounced himself "much pleased" with Madison's effort—and admitted privately that it took him eight days to get through it. Senator William Plumer of New Hampshire more forthrightly confessed, "I never read a book that fatigued me more than this pamphlet."

But it was John Randolph, the flamboyant maverick congressman from Virginia, "old Republican," constant thorn in the side of the Jefferson administration, owner of a plantation fittingly named Bizarre, who put his finger on the heart of the matter. Flinging Madison's booklet contemptuously to the floor of the House, he pronounced it "a shilling pamphlet hurled against eight hundred ships of war."[25]

The fact was that the British could do whatever they wanted. The

fact was that for all of James Stephen's outrage over American treachery in engaging in trade with France, Britain was perfectly happy to
engage in the same trade herself. British merchant ships regularly carried goods to Napoleon's empire; when Americans pointed out the
utter hypocrisy of their stance, British defenders of maritime interests
glibly replied with an argument that went little beyond the principle of
might makes right. As the jingoistic London newspaper the *Courier*
would put it, "The sea is ours, and we must maintain the doctrine that
no nation, no fleet, no cock-boat shall sail upon it without our permission." Even Lord Grenville, a leader of the opposition, seemed per-
plexed by American accusations of inconsistency. A certain amount of
trade with the Continent and the French colonies *had* to proceed, even
with the British blockade, he observed; and since Britain could not
carry on her war against France without a strong economy, it was manifest that Britain should be the one to benefit from this inevitable trade.
Grenville professed himself irritated by "the stress w^h. Jefferson lays on
the supposed unreasonableness of our claim to deprive other nations of
a trade w^h. we carry on ourselves. . . . we *have* a right to prevent that w^h.
is injurious to us, & may if we think right relax that right in cases where
we think the advantage to ourselves compensates or overbalances the
injury."

In Washington, Merry, the British minister, confidently informed
London after the *Leander* affair that America was too weak to take any
meaningful action; a firm stand resisting any American claims would
"only be attended by the salutary effect of commanding from the
[American] Government the respect which they have recently lost
toward Great Britain."[26]

Jefferson may have come to believe that a reinvigorated navy had
become "indispensable," but his long-standing ideological opposition
to having a navy at all left him in a weak position to exercise much leadership on the subject. Jefferson had come into office in 1801 vowing to
reduce debt, taxes, and expenditures, and Secretary of the Treasury
Albert Gallatin, puzzling over where to find $2.7 million to cut from the
government's $5 million annual spending—that was the amount he cal-
culated would be needed to cover his planned reductions in the national
debt—saw the navy's $2.1 million as an irresistible target. Gallatin
thought $1 million was a perfectly adequate figure for a navy to live
with, insisting that America would gain more strength by reducing its
debt than from anything a navy could do. The example of Britain

showed the dangers of endless expenditure once a country started
down the road of naval expansion: Britain had incurred a staggering
debt of £300 million (about $1.3 billion) in building up its navy. Gallatin
produced calculations for Congress proving that a navy *always* cost
more than the value of the commerce it saved. Moreover, as a matter of
basic principle, commercial interests had no claim to the government's
protection once they ventured beyond the territory of the United
States. By the same token, a navy would be useless in defending American territory in the unlikely event of a seaborne invasion from abroad,
since any nation that could carry out such an attack would have to possess a fleet of such overwhelming might that no American navy could
possibly contend with it.[27]

In his first year in office Jefferson hatched one of his usual fantastic
schemes, an eight-hundred-foot-long dry dock that would hold the
entire American navy in storage until it was needed again. Excavated
out of the banks of the Eastern Branch of the Potomac (now the Ana-
costia River) east of the Washington Navy Yard, the dock would fill the
entire area between Ninth and Tenth streets from the river to the inter-
section of Georgia and Virginia avenues. Covered with a sheet-iron
roof—like the Paris corn market, Jefferson suggested—as many as
twelve frigates could thus be preserved indefinitely in a state of suspended animation, "under the eye of the executive administration" and
safely beyond the temptations of military adventurism. Congress predictably balked at the half-million-dollar cost of the project, but the
Republican majority gladly went along with the slashing cutbacks in the
navy Jefferson and Gallatin proposed along with it.

In that political climate it was next to impossible to find anyone willing to serve as head of the Navy Department. At one point Jefferson
joked, "I believe I shall have to advertise for a Secretary of the Navy."
Robert Smith, a Baltimore lawyer who finally agreed to take the position after four other men had turned it down, found that his first task
was to write to two-thirds of the navy's officers, dismissing them from
the service in obedience to the terms of the naval Peace Establishment
Act, passed by Congress in March 1801.[28]

The Tripolitan war had brought a modest reversal in course, but
with its end in June 1805, all but one of six original frigates authorized
back in 1794—in the bill that had first created the United States navy—
were being laid up or dismantled; only the *Constitution* remained on
active service, in the Mediterranean. During the Quasi War with

France the materials needed to build six seventy-four-gun ships of the line had been purchased, but the war ended before construction could begin, and for nearly a decade the timbers had been sitting in storage at the navy's shipyards in Portsmouth, Boston, New York, Philadelphia, Washington, and Norfolk. The most Jefferson was willing to do now was diffidently observe to Congress that it was up to "the will of the Legislature" whether to build those ships.

Edward Preble and several other navy officers went to Washington to lobby for the cause shortly after Congress began its session in December 1805, but Preble quickly saw it for the hopeless task it was. "What we are to do for a Navy," he wrote his fellow captain James Barron, "God only knows." Another naval officer surveyed the views of Congress in early 1806 and reported that "some of the gentlemen think the most economical plan is to let [the six frigates] rot; others to sell half for the repairs of three; and almost all are of the opinion that six seventy-fours would ruin the country." When a bill authorizing construction of the ships of the line came up for a vote in late March 1806, it was defeated by a two-to-one margin. The amendments to the Peace Establishment Act that finally passed at the end of April limited the number of seamen on active duty to 925, cut the number of captains from 15 to 13, and authorized new expenditures of $400,000 for harbor defenses only. Most naval officers were already Federalists by inclination, and Republican opposition to the navy cemented their political allegiance. James Barron received a handwritten note from the president the next spring offering his "friendly salutations" and asking if Captain Barron might carry a letter for him to Malta and arrange for a pipe of Malta Madeira to be sent back to him. Barron scrawled a surly comment on the back: "From that infamous Hypocrite T. Jefferson."

Captain William Bainbridge requested and received a leave of absence from the navy in June 1806 to sail as a merchant captain, and a number of other experienced officers took the same course. Master Commandant Isaac Chauncey wrote Preble that he had obtained a furlough and was heading for China: "I see no prospect of Congress doing any thing for the Navy or officers therefore the sooner we can get good employ in private Ships the better at least for those who has no fortunes to depend on."[29]

Two hundred fifty thousand dollars of the congressional appropriation for harbor defenses was set aside for the construction of up to fifty small gunboats. These were another one of Jefferson's hobbyhorses:

small, one- or two-masted sloop-rigged vessels, typically no more than fifty feet long and eighteen or even ten feet wide, armed with one or two guns mounted on swivels; all in all, more like a Chesapeake oyster boat than a ship of war. The idea was that two hundred or so could be built cheaply and distributed up and down the coast to defend American harbors—fifty for Boston and other harbors north of Cape Cod, fifty for New York and Long Island Sound, twenty for the Chesapeake, twenty-five for Charleston and Savannah (Jefferson worked all the numbers out himself). In a calm they could be rowed with oars, and most of the time they could be manned by skeleton crews or even "hauled up under sheds" when not in use, Jefferson suggested.

Jefferson thought them the perfect embodiment of republican ideals, the perfect answer to the deep-seated fear among his party's faithful that a standing navy would be as dangerous an invitation to despotism as a standing army. American naval power, the Republicans insisted, would only entangle the nation in wars and foreign intrigues and do the bidding of the detested commercial classes and money men at the expense of the honest republican agrarians who were the backbone of American liberty and virtue. Contesting with the British navy on the high seas was impossible, and even were it not, it would only corrupt American values. "I deem it no sacrifice of dignity to say to the Leviathan of the deep: We are unable to contend with you in your own element," Congressman Randolph proclaimed in one of the hourslong harangues he regularly delivered on the House floor.

The American carrying trade was itself an evil by this way of thinking, not even worth trying to defend. Randolph derided it as "a mere fungus—a mushroom production of war in Europe" that would vanish as soon as peace between Britain and France returned and European shippers reclaimed their customary trade routes. Congressman George Washington Campbell of Tennessee went even further, ruing the day America ever first succumbed to the seductive vice of commerce: "It would have been well for us if the American flag had never floated on the ocean . . . to waft to this country the luxuries and vices of European nations, that effeminate and corrupt our people, to excite the jealousies and cupidity of those Powers whose existence, in a great degree, depends on commerce, and to court their aggressions and embroil us in their unjust and bloody contests."[30]

The gunboats, as Jefferson conceived of them, would answer most of these objections, or at least offer a palatable compromise that he thought most Republicans could swallow. Gunboats were obviously defensive, restricted to protecting American territory; since they could barely navigate open waters, they could never "become an excitement to engage in offensive maritime war." They were thrifty: at $5,000 apiece, a mere one-fortieth the cost of a frigate or one-seventieth the cost of a ship of the line. They even could be manned in time of need by a kind of maritime citizen militia, Jefferson suggested.[31]

The trouble was they were also ridiculous. In anything but a flat calm their guns proved impossible to aim with any reliability: even a light chop made the boats pitch and roll violently. In even moderate seas the guns had to be stowed below to keep the boats from capsizing from their top-heaviness; then it turned out that the recoil when the guns were fired in any direction other than nearly straight fore or aft also caused the boats to capsize. Their low gunwales afforded no protection to the crew from musket fire, while a single cannonball could reduce them to splinters.

Even their economy swiftly proved illusory as construction costs doubled. While that still meant that twenty gunboats could be built for the price of one frigate, their manpower needs were no bargain at all; twenty gunboats required twice as many men, and five times as many officers, as a single frigate. It cost something like $120,000 a year to man and maintain one large frigate of fifty-six guns, three times that much for gunboats that carried an equivalent number of guns.[32]

Naval officers loathed the gunboats and complained that they undermined the only real system the navy had for bringing up young officers and teaching them the arts of seamanship and command: namely by having midshipmen enter the navy as adolescents and learn from the example of the senior captains they served under. But the gunboats, often captained by an officer no more senior than an older midshipman, provided no such opportunities and quickly acquired a reputation for lax discipline, or worse. Complaints of drunkenness and insubordination were rife. One distraught mother of a midshipman wrote to the secretary of the navy that aboard a gunboat her son had had "no opportunity to acquire a practical knowledge of his profession; he is exposed to the contagion of vicious example; gains not the advantage of discipline; forms not the valuable manners of an officer; and thus has every prospect for future service to his country blasted and destroyed."

When one gunboat capsized and sank in six fathoms of water,

Stephen Decatur sarcastically asked, "What would be the real national loss if *all* gunboats were sunk in a hundred fathoms of water?"

In the end, 177 would be built for $1.5 million. That would have bought the American navy eight new forty-four-gun frigates or five mighty seventy-four-gun ships of the line.[33]

THE GROWING British harassment of American trade from 1804 on stirred American resentment, but what turned resentment into fury was a sudden increase in the longstanding and long-detested Royal Navy practice of seizing sailors from merchant ships and forcibly impressing them into British naval service. As the war with France created a surging demand for sailors to man the fleet, it became a daily occurrence for British warships to stop and board any passing American merchant vessels and pull off a few experienced seamen. That the British claimed the men it took were all British subjects did little to assuage American anger, especially since Britain arrogantly insisted that anyone born in Britain remained a British subject, forever owing allegiance to the British crown even if he had since become a naturalized American.

Yet even during the colonial years Americans had loathed and at times violently resisted impressment. In November 1747 a press gang from a British man-of-war had come ashore in Boston and rounded up sailors, shipbuilders' apprentices, and laboring land men, triggering three days of rioting. An angry mob of "seamen and other lewd and profligate persons . . . arm'd with cutlasses and other weapons," as Massachusetts's colonial governor indignantly put it, chased British naval officers through the streets and forced its way into the first floor of the town hall when the officers holed up there to try to escape. The rioters broke into the council chambers and hurled brickbats at the governor and his council, dragged off an undersheriff guarding the governor's house and beat him and threw him in the town's stocks, and hauled up a navy barge and threatened to set it on fire in the governor's courtyard. The governor tried to call out the militia to quell the disturbance, but the militiamen refused to obey the order to muster.

Declaring that he "did not think it consistent with the Honour of His Majesty's Government to remain longer in the Midst of it," the governor then ran for his life, taking shelter in Castle William, a stone fort manned by British army troops on one of the islands in the harbor. Eventually some of the impressed men were released in exchange for naval officers held hostage by the mob. Two decades later, in 1769, John Adams successfully defended an American sailor who killed the lieutenant of a British frigate when he tried to press him and other crewmen as their merchant ship was returning to Massachusetts after a voyage to Europe; the judge ruled it justifiable homicide.[34]

The practice of impressing American seamen continued nonetheless. Even after the Revolution, British warships regularly took sailors out of passing American merchant vessels. Many crewmen on American ships were indeed British subjects, but the Royal Navy's officers were never very particular when they needed a few prime hands to fill out their ship's company. American consuls and notaries had begun to provide American seamen with certificates authenticating their citizenship specifically to protect them against the press, but British naval captains routinely brushed these proofs aside. "I could get one, if I was in America, for half a crown, as good as that," sneered one Royal Navy captain when an American sailor showed him his certificate. Declaring an impressed American to be a Scotsman or Irishman was another favorite pretext; any sailor with a *Mc* or *Mac* or *M'* in his name who protested against being pressed was almost certain to hear some variation on what was obviously a well-worn line making the rounds among Royal Navy officers, given how many times it was recounted by their victims: "Do you call yourself a Yankee, you damned Scotch rascal?" Another British captain said, "I have plenty like you on board and I do not believe you was ever in any part of the United States. You are either Scotch or Irish."[35]

The start of Britain's war against Napoleon in 1803 turned an occasional annoyance into a major assault on American sovereignty. The Royal Navy's manpower demands were proving insatiable: from 1803 on, the number of sailors and marines needed to man the fleet grew almost steadily at a rate of 12,000 year as the force more than doubled from 60,000 in 1803 to 145,000 by 1812.[36] But even that did not tell the whole story because of the waves of desertions constantly taking place. To try to stem the loss of men, the navy instituted horrific punishments; deserters faced hanging or worse. James Durand, an American seaman who was trapped in the British service for six years after being pressed from a merchant ship in August 1809, witnessed one of these punishments carried out on a fellow American who had repeatedly tried to escape. He was sentenced to be whipped through the fleet, a total of three hundred lashes. The prisoner was stripped from the waist up, seized to a gallows erected in a large boat, and as the band played the rogue's march was rowed from one warship to the next in the harbor. At each stop the boatswain's mate of the ship came on board and delivered twenty-five lashes to the man's bare back with the cat-o'-nine-tails. It was little but a long-drawn-out death sentence. "Alongside the last ship he expired under the brutality of the punishment," Durand wrote. "So they gave his body ten lashes after he had died."[37]

But even that threat could not keep more than six thousand men from deserting each year, willing to risk the chance of draconian punishment rather than the certainty of the continued brutality of life aboard a man-of-war. Between the deserters, and the new ships to be manned, and the fifteen hundred men a year invalided out of the service from injury or sickness, the Royal Navy needed to find close to twenty thousand new men a year.[38] A semibenevolent patriotic organization called the Marine Society offered to outfit destitute boys and men with a new suit of clothes and a few days of good food and tutoring if they would volunteer; that provided a thousand a year driven mostly by desperation. A few dreamy, naive young men from working families were drawn by visions of adventure—"I had read Robinson Crusoe many times over and longed for the sea," said the son of an Edinburgh cooper who enlisted. But most of the "volunteers" were the so-called quota men that the magistrates of each county had to produce in two large drafts in 1795, supplemented in the following years by a steady stream of various small-time thieves, beggars, pickpockets, and other local nuisances from the local jails, including the occasional dissipated scion of a gentlemanly family who had fallen into drink, debt, or other dissolution that made getting out of the country as quickly as possible an attractive option.[39]

Volunteers, willing and otherwise, could satisfy only a small fraction of what the navy needed during its rapid buildups. By 1800 the Impress Service was a permanent institution, commanding the full-time services of one admiral, forty-seven captains, and eighty lieutenants whose job it was to make up the difference. "Gentlemen," officers of merchant ships at sea, and sometimes fishermen were exempt from the press, but otherwise the law permitted the navy to forcibly take any "persons using the sea." That generally meant merchant seamen, but in practice it was interpreted imaginatively. Impress officers routinely declared that a man who had just been dragged in off the streets of a seaport town "looked like" a sailor, and that was good enough.[40] Merchant ships at sea were in many ways the favorite target of the press, however, since they were sure to contain experienced sailors. A Royal Navy captain almost never passed up the chance to press a few "prime seamen" from a passing ship.

In London, James Monroe's consulate was soon inundated with pleas from friends and families of American seamen who had been forcibly taken into British service. The American agent for seamen in London tallied 6,057 American sailors who had applied for release from the Royal Navy from 1803 to 1810, and the American secretary of state reported 200 more cases that had been filed directly with his office.[41] Although the British government professed itself willing to discharge American citizens who had been wrongfully impressed, a sailor trying to get his release from the Royal Navy faced a Kafkaesque series of obstacles. To start with, any impressed man who accepted pay was deemed to have "volunteered" and thus was ineligible for release. James Durand had been grabbed in his sleep belowdecks on a merchant brig in Plymouth harbor by a press gang that had come alongside in a boat from the frigate *Narcissus* and forced to leave behind all his clothes, money, and papers. A few days later the captain summoned him to the quarterdeck and offered him five pounds if he would enter the ship's company. When Durand protested that he was an American, the captain replied, "If you will not work I'll flog you until you're glad to set about it. Go below, for I won't hear another word out of you." Below he found twelve other Americans who had been impressed earlier; one said he had been given four dozen lashes, and advised Durand to do as the captain bid him.

All manner of dodges were used to keep improperly impressed Americans from having their cases heard. Samuel Dalton of Salem, who was taken by the British in 1803, wrote letter after letter to his family and American consuls, desperately trying to have proofs of his citizenship forwarded to the Admiralty, and was thwarted at every turn. His mail was intercepted; when the American consul in London tried to file for a writ of habeas corpus, the magistrate kept rejecting it on technical grounds. First the magistrate said there was no evidence that Dalton actually was serving in His Majesty's navy. The consul filed a deposition from a fellow seaman attesting that he had seen Dalton aboard the British ship of the line *Namur*. The magistrate rejected that petition because the seaman had not attested that Dalton had asked him to help secure his release. The consul obtained another deposition from the witness, only to have it rejected this time on the grounds that the man had not sworn that he believed Dalton was an American. "I am like a man that is out of his mind," Dalton wrote his mother six years into what would be an eleven-year ordeal to obtain his freedom.

Britain's naval supporters noisily defended impressment as a self-evident necessity, a right founded on "immemorial usage," and dismissed American protests as "almost ridiculous" given the "right which we undoubtedly possess of reclaiming runaway seamen." Ceding the right to stop and search American ships and remove British sailors would create a safe haven for deserters, they insisted. Many British writers also insisted that any supposed American sailors taken in the press were in fact native-born Britons, and that the entire dispute between the two countries over impressment turned largely on their differing definitions of nationality and the right of naturalization. In fact, however, just the opposite was the case; nearly all of the American citizens seized in the press had been born in the United States.[42]

The figure 6,257 began to appear in large outline type in Republican newspapers as American public outrage smoldered. Many of the British ships that invested American ports, seizing returning American merchantmen as prizes, also started pressing men out of them while they were at it. Each day's shipping news contained reports of men taken: the ship *Hannah and Elizah* of New Bedford bound for New Holland on a whaling voyage, forced to put back after the *Leander* took ten of her crew; the brig *William*, three seamen and three passengers pressed by *Leander;* the ship *Actress,* sailed from New York and forced to return, having had two of her best seamen taken off by *Leander;* the schooner *Swallow* sailing in company with *Nancy* from Baltimore, boarded by the British frigate *La Desiree,* which impressed three men from *Swallow* and thirteen from *Nancy;* twelve fishermen from Salem and Marblehead impressed on the banks by the English frigate *Ville de Milan.* Once in a while a ship ordered to Halifax was retaken en route when the American crew overpowered their captors and put back into an American port, but there was no resisting the British boarding parties that pulled men off as a frigate stood by, its entire broadside of guns run out, smoldering matches at the ready.[43]

There was obviously a spurious precision to the 6,257 figure, and both at the time and later there would be much controversy over the true number of impressed American sailors, but the best analysis suggests that it was not far off that widely popularized number. By 1812 the

British had ordered the release of nearly 2,000 Americans who success-fully protested their impressment; nearly 2,000 more Americans forcibly serving on British warships were discharged from service and held as enemy prisoners at the start of the war in 1812. So even by Britain's own definitions and admission, 4,000 was a bare minimum for the number of American citizens forced since 1803 to serve against their will in the Royal Navy. The true figure may easily have been as high as 8,000 or 10,000.[44]

A bill introduced in Congress in the 1806 session sought to define impressment as piracy, punishable by death. Representative Randolph, nothing if not consistent, opposed any such American efforts as empty gestures and argued that British impressment only offered a further demonstration of the inherent evils of a standing navy: an American navy would soon be forced to adopt the same detestable practice to fill its ranks.[45]

Others with a keener grasp of public opinion and the dynamics of the relations between nations recognized the British behavior for the political dynamite it was, the galling humiliation to national sovereignty it represented. "That an officer from a foreign ship should pronounce any person he pleased, on board an American ship on the high seas, not to be an American Citizen, but a British subject, & carry his interested decision on the most important of all questions to a freeman into exe-cution on the spot is so anomalous in principle, so grievous in practice, and so abominable in abuse, that the pretension must finally yield," wrote Madison, summing up the case.

More to the point was John Quincy Adams. "The practice of impressment," he said, "is the only ineradicable wound, which, if per-sisted in, can terminate no otherwise than by war."[46]

THE UNITED States frigate *Chesapeake* had been laid up "in ordinary"—out of service but still officially in commission—for four years in the navy yard in Washington when William Henry Allen received orders at the end of January 1807 to join her as third lieu-tenant. The ship was being brought back into service to finally relieve the *Constitution*, which had remained on station in the Mediterranean ever since the end of the Tripolitan war. On her way she was to deliver to Minorca the new American consul, a naval surgeon named Dr. John Bullus, who was a close friend of Thomas Jefferson's.

The first order of business for the officers was to ship a crew. Henry Allen traveled to Philadelphia to try to find up to 170 seamen and boys; other recruiters went to New York and Norfolk. By the end of March, Allen had managed to get 47 men aboard a packet boat safely on their way to join the ship, but it had not been easy. "My guardian genius of good fortune certainly slumbered a little when she suffered me to be sent here," Allen wrote his father. "What do you think of 60 or 80 Sailors, no doubt some of them wild Irishmen, let loose in this city after you have advanced them from 18 to 70 dollars each . . . I never had so much trouble with a pack of rascals in my life." Of the 57 men he finally recruited, he had to release one after the man's wife appeared, begging for his release and "*overpersuaded* me"; three others proved to be unfit for one reason or another, and six disappeared with the advance pay Allen had given them.[47]

By May 9, when the *Chesapeake* at last set out from the navy yard, she was still 60 men short. During the transit from Washington to Norfolk, where the ship was to complete her final fitting out for sea, 60 to 85 men were sick the entire time from a virulent infection that had torn through the crew. At nine in the morning of the first day, less than a mile into the two-hundred-mile first leg of her voyage, the frigate struck and grounded on the sandbar where the Eastern Branch joins the Potomac. A day of heaving off with the anchors was followed by a day of unloading supplies and shot onto a tender. On the seventeenth the green crew was trying to strike down the fore topgallant yard to fix a line that had been improperly rigged when the spar came loose and crashed to the deck, killing two crewmen and seriously injuring a third. A few days later another seaman fell overboard and drowned. Three of the sick men died over the next two weeks; a dozen of the crew made off with the ship's boats and deserted; then the ship struck on Mattawoman shoals farther down the Potomac, and the cable broke when the crew tried to heave the ship off using a stern anchor. On June 4 she finally arrived at Hampton Roads. But there were other, deeper problems with this ship, which the crew was already feeling was cursed with ill luck: tensions between the officers and their captain, incomprehensible lapses in routine preparations of the ship's armaments, chaotic arrangements for accommodating passengers who kept being added to the ship's charge.

The ship's senior officer was James Barron. At age thirty-nine he was one of the navy's senior captains, having been advanced to the rank in 1799 at the same time as Edward Preble and John Rodgers. He was an expert seaman from a maritime family; his father had been the commander in chief of Virginia's state navy during the Revolution, his older brother Samuel was a commodore in the Mediterranean during the Tripolitan war, where Barron had served too, as captain of the frigate *President*. He was, however, said to be more of a seaman than a fighting man. He had seen no fighting in either the Quasi War or the Mediterranean, his duties never seeming to go beyond routine patrolling. That was not necessarily his fault, but whether as cause or effect, he seemed to lack the rage for glory that drove so many of his fellow officers.

He was tall, over six feet, and strongly built but also overweight and nearsighted, giving him a perpetual squint. He was amiable and made friends easily. He had also acquired his share of enemies. An apparently offhand but too familiar remark to Stephen Decatur had resulted in a noticeable frostiness between them of late. Strolling through Norfolk one day in February 1806 with Decatur and some other navy officers, Barron had tried to defend Decatur from the ribbing one of the others started to give him about "the particular attraction" that brought him to town. Barron spoke up and said that no, he knew that Decatur's affections were elsewhere engaged. That, anyway, was how things stood as far as Barron knew; Decatur had told him earlier of his engagement to a woman in Philadelphia. What Barron didn't know, but which the other officers apparently did, was that Decatur had since met Susan Wheeler, the daughter of Norfolk's mayor, had fallen head over heels for her, and was planning to marry her just a few weeks later—having abruptly broken off his other engagement, a fact he didn't particularly care to have made public. Mortified at having his less than completely honorable conduct brought to light, Decatur had turned on his heels and walked off. Barron was notably absent from the list of guests at the wedding.[48]

Barron had also made a bitter enemy of John Rodgers. That in itself was not terribly surprising; Rodgers picked fights with everyone. Rodgers had once addressed a furious letter to Edward Preble stating that while their present duties constrained him "from requiring you to explain your observation on the comparative good order" of their respective ships "and other incoherent remarks" Preble had made, "when we meet in the United States you shall then be explicitly informed of my opinion of your conduct."[49] Although nothing further happened in that instance, Rodgers's feud with Barron came within a whisker of an actual duel in February 1807. Rodgers thought Barron had tried to thwart his chances to assume command of the Mediterranean squadron when Samuel Barron had fallen ill; when Rodgers did get the appointment and Barron wrote to congratulate him, Rodgers dismissed him in a message sent through Bainbridge as "two faced" and a "Judas," and dared Barron to send him a challenge when they returned to America. "I shall impute it to a want of what no gentleman—one who wears a uniform—should be deficient in" should Barron fail to do so, he added for good measure.[50]

Both men named seconds, and the dictates of honor at that point took charge; any hint of wanting to avoid a "meeting" would now be taken as a sign of cowardice, which was worse than swallowing whatever the original affront had been. Barron was particularly touchy since delays caused first by an illness and then by an order from the secretary of the navy forbidding him to leave Norfolk—in an attempt to avert the impending duel—had started rumors that he was trying to back out. That forced Barron to declare that if Rodgers "will come to Norfolk and accede to my terms of *short distance*"—meaning an almost certainly fatal outcome for one or both of the men—he was ready; failing that, he later proposed, he would have no alternative but "breaking my orders and seeking you where you are to be found." As the men were on the verge of meeting in Havre de Grace, Maryland, the seconds negotiated an agreement. A letter from them to Rodgers was published, declaring that Barron "does not now perceive the necessity of calling on you," though he remained "injured by the style of your reply," and at the same time expressing their certainty that Rodgers could not "entertain a suspicion dishonorable to captain Barron" and had spoken out of "instantaneous irritation" only.[51]

Whatever the truth about Barron's courage or lack thereof, most of the *Chesapeake* lieutenants were Rodgers's protégés, and most were willing to put a doubtful interpretation on Barron's conduct in this affair of honor. Meanwhile, though, they had seen little of their commanding officer. Barron left the job of bringing the ship down to Master Commandant Charles Gordon, his second in command. Barron traveled to his home in Hampton to wait for their arrival. Before leaving the navy yard, Barron had complained that the gunpowder supplied by the navy yard was "not fit for service." The navy department replied that he could have it "remanufactured" when he reached Malta.[52] As Gordon brought the ship past Mount Vernon on the way down the Potomac, he ordered the customary sixteen-gun salute to the grave of George Washington. Henry Allen, who was in charge of carrying out the salute, found to his consternation that half of the cartridges were the wrong size for the guns. Gordon, furious, ordered the gunner placed under arrest. Just below Mount Vernon, Dr. Bullus and his wife, three children, and two servants came aboard. Their small mountain of baggage, crated furniture, and household paraphernalia was stowed as best it could be about the frigate's gun deck.

At Norfolk still more passengers and baggage joined the ship. Gaetano Carusi, with his wife and family, and several other Italian musicians were returning home after two utterly miserable years in the service of the United States. Recruited to lead the newly created Marine Band, practically browbeaten by American officers in Sicily into coming to Washington at the meager pay of $12 a month, Carusi had experienced nothing but one disappointment after another. (At one point, the commandant of the Marine Corps, who wanted nothing to do with the musicians, put them to work digging latrines in the hope of getting them to quit.) Paying $40 out of his own pocket to get to Norfolk, Carusi was relieved to be seeing the last of a country that, he said, had only "deceived, betrayed, and insulted" him.[53]

Twelve miles east of Norfolk, at the mouth of the Chesapeake, lay Lynnhaven Bay, the habitual anchoring point of a strong British squadron that had been operating in the area since the summer of 1806. Relations between the British and the locals had generally been much better than they were in New York. The British ships had arrived there after chasing three French warships into Annapolis, and had remained ever since to keep the French bottled up. British officers frequently went into Norfolk and were generally welcomed as an addition to the social life of the town; they were even more enthusiastically welcomed by the farmers of Princess Anne County, who suddenly had a new and very high-paying customer for their cattle and produce right at their doorstep.

The proximity to American soil was also welcomed by more than a few British sailors, who began deserting at a steady clip. In February 1807, while the officers of the frigate *Melampus* were giving a party on board for some of the ladies and gentlemen from Norfolk they had become acquainted with, five of the crew jumped into the captain's gig and rowed like madmen for shore. A sentry on deck challenged them with a hail; that was followed by a volley of musket fire from the ship's marines, but the men reached Sewell's Point safely, gave three cheers, and vanished into the countryside. A few weeks later a boat crew sent from the sloop of war *Halifax* to retrieve a kedge anchor took advantage of a rain squall that hid them from view of the ship to beat it to shore, threatening the midshipman who was in command of the party that they would beat his brains out if he tried to stop them. Musket fire and then a cannon shot echoed from the *Halifax*, but the boat was soon completely shrouded in the mist and lowering dusk, and it too reached Sewell's Point.

Within days four of the deserters were aboard the *Chesapeake*, having signed on to her crew. Three were Americans, all from the *Melampus*: Daniel Martin, an African American man from Westport, Massachusetts; William Ware, an "Indian looking" black man from Maryland; and John Strachan, a white man from Maryland's Eastern Shore. The fourth, Jenkin Ratford from the *Halifax*, was English, which the American recruiter in Norfolk apparently knew perfectly well, since he asked him if he didn't have "a second name" to use; Ratford was entered on the ship's books as John Wilson.

The *Halifax*'s captain stormed into Norfolk to demand his men back and was treated to something of a practical-joke runaround, made worse when he encountered Ratford himself on the street. In his joy of liberation in what he loudly declared to be "the Land of Liberty," Ratford unleashed a string of verbal abuse at his former captain that he had no doubt been saving up for years. The captain confronted the American lieutenant in charge of the recruiting rendezvous, who referred him to the local civil authorities; he then went to the mayor, who referred him to Decatur, as commander of the Norfolk Navy Yard; Decatur referred him back to the recruiter. Allen heard rumors in town that the British were prepared to take the men back by force.[54]

On the morning of June 21, the fifty-gun ship of the line *Leopard* ran up Lynnhaven Bay and dropped her anchor by the *Melampus* and the seventy-four-gun ship of the line *Bellona*. On her way from Halifax, the *Leopard* had stopped and searched a dozen American merchant ships and pressed several men from them; just two days earlier she had seized an American schooner off the Delaware capes carrying sugar and coffee to Philadelphia from Havana, taken the crew aboard, and torn up their American protection certificates.[55]

A few hours after the *Leopard*'s arrival, Commodore Barron went aboard the *Chesapeake,* and the American frigate at last weighed anchor and dropped down the roads, preparing to stand to sea the next morning.

HENRY ALLEN was on deck as officer of the watch as the *Chesapeake* passed the British ships in Lynnhaven Bay at about nine on the morning of June 22, 1807. A signal broke out on the *Bellona,* and soon Allen noticed the *Leopard* standing out under easy sail ahead of them, apparently in no hurry to take advantage of the favorable southwesterly wind to get to sea.

At noon, as the *Chesapeake* approached the mouth of the Chesapeake Bay, the wind shifted to the southeast, forcing her to tack several times to clear the land. By now the *Leopard* was several miles to the south and unmistakably began dogging the American's course, tacking when she tacked, always staying to windward, steadily closing their gap to a mile. Allen's unease grew as he saw that the *Leopard*'s lower gunports were open. "This fellow is coming on board of us to demand deserters and if they are not delivered up we shall have hell to hold," muttered the ship's sailing master.[56] From time to time Barron and Gordon cast a glance at the British ship but said nothing. At 2:30 dinner was served in the captain's cabin, and the ship's commanding officers went below.

It was the normal courtesy for a ship wishing to speak another to come up on her leeward side. But around three, as the *Chesapeake* slowed to put off the Norfolk pilot, the *Leopard* suddenly shot up on her windward quarter, fifty or sixty yards away. All her guns were run out, their tompions removed. The *Leopard*'s captain, Salusbury Pryce Humphreys, hailed that he had dispatches for the commander of the *Chesapeake;* Barron shouted back for him to send a boat aboard and he would heave to.

Standard orders for every warship of every navy of the world called for beating to quarters when approaching another ship of war, sending her crew running to battle stations on the signal traditionally given by the beating of the marines' snare drum. Barron would later insist that he had neglected to do so because he had no clue of any unfriendly intentions on the part of the British ship, even when he saw the *Leopard*'s guns run out. If so, he was certainly disabused of the notion a minute later, when he read the astonishing order handed to him in his cabin by the *Leopard*'s lieutenant. Even the British recognized that a foreign "national ship" was sovereign territory. The order from Vice

Admiral George Cranfield Berkeley, commander in chief of the North American station, was addressed to all the British ships under his command, and as much as it tried to disguise the fact, it was an act of territorial infringement tantamount to war:

> Whereas many Seamen, subjects of His Brittanic Majesty, and serving in His Ships and Vessels as per margin, while at Anchor in the Chesapeak deserted and entered On Board the United States frigate called the *Chesapeak,* and openly paraded the Streets of Norfolk in sight of their Officers under the American flag, protected by the Magistrates of the Town, and the Recruiting Officer belonging to the above mentioned American Frigate . . . the Captains & Commander of His Majestys Ships and Vessels under my Command are therefore hereby required and directed in case of meeting with the American frigate the *Chesapeak* at Sea, and without the limits of the United States to shew to the Captain of her this Order; and to require to search his Ship for the deserters from the before mentioned Ships. . . . and if a similar demand should be made by the American, he is to be permitted to search for any Deserters from their Service, according to the Customs and usage of Civilized Nations in terms of peace and Amity with each other.[57]

Attached was a note from Humphreys, which he would later explain was his attempt "as a gentleman, to soften and ameliorate the apparent severity and harshness" of Berkeley's order that it was his duty to obey:

> The Captain of the *Leopard* will not presume to say anything in addition to what the Commander in Chief has stated, more than to express a hope, that every circumstance respecting them may be adjusted, in a manner that the harmony subsisting between the two countries, may remain undisturbed.[58]

Barron asked the lieutenant to sit down while he wrote a reply. A half hour passed and the lieutenant began getting very uncomfortable. A signal broke out on the *Leopard*. Finally, after another ten minutes, Barron handed over his answer. In it he stated that he knew of no deserters on his ship, but added that he was "instructed never to permit the crew of any ship that I command to be mustered by any other but her own officers."

Only as the lieutenant was being rowed back did Barron finally order Gordon to get the men to quarters, but even then he phrased it in a hesitant way, saying only, "You had better get your gun deck clear"; Gordon thought that might mean only to be *ready* to beat to quarters. After several more minutes' hesitation, Barron told Gordon to bring the men to quarters, but without a drumroll or letting the men show themselves through the gunports so the British could not "charge us with making the first hostile show."

The result was utter confusion. The marine drummer, not understanding this unusual order, started beating his drum only to be hit by Gordon with the hilt of his sword to stop him. Many of the crew didn't know what to make of that and thought the order had been countermanded. The gun deck was jammed with equipment and supplies and Dr. Bullus's luggage and furniture. Henry Allen rushed to his station as captain of the second division of guns and tried to get his men to start clearing away 720 feet of six-inch anchor cable that lay directly behind the guns, throwing barrels and casks down the main hatch, carrying down to the cockpit two decks below nine of the sick men who'd had their hammocks strung directly over the guns. Just then came a single shot from the *Leopard,* then another, then a crashing broadside that cut through the *Chesapeake*'s masts and sails.

The *Chesapeake*'s befuddled gunner was struggling in the magazine to load powder horns to prime the guns: he had neglected to fill more than three of them beforehand. The flintlocks for the guns were not properly fitted, and the slow matches that were always supposed to be ready as a backup had not been prepared either. Allen sent a midshipman running to get an iron, known as a loggerhead, heating in the galley stove to set off the primer.

Two more broadsides hit directly into the hull. One set loose a shower of splinters on the deck above that tore into Barron's leg, carrying off a good chunk of his right calf. But the gun deck took the brunt. A twenty-four-pound ball hit one of Allen's men directly in the chest, killing him instantly and spattering Allen with blood and splinters of bone. Three other men in Allen's division were wounded. Captain Gordon appeared through the chaos with a message from Barron—"For God's sake fire one gun for the honor of the flag, I mean to strike"— and asked Allen why they were not firing. Allen shouted that he needed powder to prime the guns, and Gordon himself ran to the magazine, on his way meeting a boy who at last was heading up with two filled horns. Gordon grabbed them, ran the length of the gun deck, and tossed them across the open main hatch to Allen. Allen got three of his guns primed and grabbed a loggerhead, but still the guns would not fire: the iron was not hot enough to ignite the powder. In desperation Allen finally seized a coal from the galley stove with his bare hands and fired off a single gun. At almost the same instant Barron shouted down the hatch, "Stop firing, stop firing! We have struck, we have struck."[59]

Three of the *Chesapeake*'s men lay dead, another eight seriously wounded. Another man would later die from his wounds.

Two boats from the British ship came over; a boarding party lined up the crew and interrogated them for three hours. Ratford was found hiding in the coal hold and, along with the Americans from the *Melampus*, was taken across to the *Leopard*, where they were put in irons.

Allen, to his eternal mortification, was sent across to the *Leopard* with a note from Barron formally surrendering the ship. He returned with the British captain's note refusing it: "Having to the utmost of my power fulfilled the instructions of my Commander in Chief, I have nothing more to desire; and must, in consequence, proceed to join the remainder of the Squadron . . . I am ready to give you every assistance in my power and do most sincerely deplore that any lives should have been lost in the execution of a service which might have been adjusted more amicably."

The *Leopard* blithely returned that night to take up her customary anchorage within the sovereign territory of the United States of America. The *Chesapeake*, her mainmast shot through in three places, seven of her main and fore shrouds shot away, her mizzen rigging entirely cut to pieces, two dozen round shot lodged in her hull, limped back to Norfolk, the next morning silently passing the anchored British squadron at Lynnhaven Bay.

A month later the prisoners taken from the *Chesapeake* were transported aboard the *Bellona* to Halifax. At 9:15 a.m. on Monday, August 30, 1807, having being convicted of mutiny, desertion, and contempt by a court-martial at which he was given no counsel and offered no defense, Ratford was hanged from the fore yardarm of the *Halifax*, the ship he had deserted from. The three others, "in consideration of their former good conduct," were sentenced "only . . . to Corporal Punishment" of five hundred lashes apiece.[60]

FOR WEEKS war seemed all but certain. "Never since the battle of Lexington have I seen this country in such a state of exasperation as at present," Jefferson wrote his friend Pierre-Samuel du Pont de Nemours, the French émigré economist and reformer, three weeks after the firing on the *Chesapeake*, "and even that did not produce such unanimity." Phineas Bond, Britain's consul in Philadelphia, had lived in the country for twenty years and had seen eruptions of democratic anger before, and he advised London that this one would die down in the usual manner after some venting of steam, but even he was taken aback by the "universal Ferment" the incident had provoked, with mass meetings in cities up and down the coast denouncing the British action.[61] Traveling through New York, Augustus Foster, who also knew something about American mobs, hastened out of his carriage and decided to proceed incognito as soon as he heard the news of the *Leopard*'s attack—just in time, as it turned out, for a crowd almost immediately congregated and threatened to throw his horse and curricle into the Hudson River.

In Hampton crowds of armed men boarded tenders that had come ashore from the British squadron and demolished two hundred casks of fresh water and burned one of the boats. The funeral for Robert Mac-Donald, the American seaman who died from his wounds after the *Chesapeake* returned to Norfolk, brought out four thousand citizens, officials, and dignitaries. "Their blood cries for vengeance, and when our Government directs, vengeance it shall have," declared a solemn toast to the wounded and dead proclaimed at a meeting attended by nearly seven hundred in Norfolk a few weeks later.[62]

Not even the new British minister in Washington, David Erskine, was sure if Berkeley's orders represented a new and more aggressive policy directed from London, but in Washington the administration frantically tried to rush plans into place to prepare for the worst. Jefferson issued a proclamation ordering all British armed ships out of American waters without delay and directed Madison that "the interdicted ships are *enemies*"; if the British should try to land any men, his orders were to "kill or capture them as enemies." On July 5 the cabinet called on state governors to make 100,000 militiamen ready; two days later the governor of Virginia was requested to mobilize troops to defend Norfolk and the American navy gunboats in the area against further British attack.[63]

Stephen Decatur was sent orders to relieve Barron. On July 1 he went aboard the wounded *Chesapeake* to assume command, and a few hours later Barron limped off past the assembled crew and officers. For the first time since the *Chesapeake* struck her flag, the colors of the United States broke out aloft, along with Decatur's broad pennant.

The next day a swarm of shipwrights from the navy yard in Washington arrived and set to work heaving out her wounded masts. Decatur immediately had the guns set right and put the crew to work exercising them relentlessly, sometimes firing them twice a day, working to make second nature the choreography of heaving in three tons of metal with the rope tail tackles; sponging out the sparking embers and ramming home the cartridge bag of powder, then shot and wadding; pricking the cartridge with a wire and pouring in powder from the horn; heaving the gun back out with the side tackles; shifting the aim with handspikes; firing and dodging the sometimes unpredictable direction of the gun's recoil, which could crush a man in a second; and then doing it again and again until they could do it like machines even when staring death in the face. No American captain ever neglected gunnery practice again.

The British squadron did not depart but neither did it make any aggressive moves, and slowly the sense of crisis began to ease. By the fall, word came that Berkeley's actions had been officially disavowed by the Admiralty and he was being recalled from Halifax to London. Humphreys too was soon back in England and placed on half pay. He would never again receive a sea command; a few years later he changed his name to Davenport, in acknowledgment, he said, of his "accession to a considerable property in right of his second wife," which may have been true but was also a convenient way to leave behind his considerable notoriety.

In disavowing Berkeley, the British government underscored that it was not disavowing impressment. The government offered to pay compensation to the families of the American seamen who were killed, and publicly acknowledged that it was contrary to British policy to stop national ships belonging to a neutral power. But it adamantly rebuffed attempts by Monroe in London to widen the discussion of the *Chesapeake* affair to include a comprehensive resolution of America's long-standing complaints about the British policy of stopping and impressing sailors out of American merchant ships. "*They* insist upon mixing two questions which *we* insist upon separating. We are ready to atone where we were wrong, but determined to maintain our rights," the British foreign minister, George Canning, told a colleague. Most British newspapers thought even that was going too far, and expressed satisfaction, as one put it, that American "arrogance" received "a severe rebuke" in the form of the *Leopard*'s broadsides.[64]

. . .

RECRIMINATIONS OVER the *Chesapeake* affair continued to reverber-
ate within the American navy for years. American public opinion in
1807 was already turning against what Jefferson once termed that "most
barbarous of appeals," the practice of challenging men to duels over
personal disagreements. In the aftermath of the sensational duel in
1804 that left Alexander Hamilton dead at the hand of Vice President
Aaron Burr, antidueling associations were formed, sermons were
preached, and editorials denounced the practice as a barbaric throw-
back. In 1806 Congress made it a criminal offense for officers of the
army to issue challenges.

But not for officers of the navy: Congress may have felt powerless to
stop dueling between naval officers both because many of their duels
were fought in foreign ports and because it had become a virtual epidemic in the service. One in twelve American navy officers who died on
active duty before 1815 were killed in duels, eighteen in all; easily twice
that number had fought a duel; and every officer lived with the knowledge that his reputation for courage was always liable to be tested on
the field of honor. Many of the duels were fought over ridiculous dis-
putes or slights, but the loss of respect that an officer faced from ignor-
ing even a slight was far from trivial. Midshipman Richard Somers
had once challenged the entire midshipmen's berth aboard the frigate
United States after they ostracized him for failing to properly defend his
honor—or so they felt—when fellow midshipman Stephen Decatur
had teasingly called him "a fool" and Somers had let the remark pass.
Actually, Decatur and Somers were close friends, had been since boyhood, and had thought nothing of the matter. But it was clear Somers
now had to defend his honor. Selecting Decatur as his second, Somers
exchanged shots with his first opponent and took a ball in his right arm;
switching to his left hand, he faced his second opponent and missed him
completely, taking a ball in his thigh this time; overruling Decatur's
insistence that he stop, he then took on his third opponent with Decatur
propping up his wavering right elbow and somehow managed to
slightly wound his adversary. At that point the remaining midshipmen
agreed that honor had been satisfied.[65]

It would have taken a miracle in the wake of the *Chesapeake*'s humiliation for men of this culture of honor to avoid trading accusations that
would lead to pistols at ten paces. If Barron thought that his officers

would close ranks around him as the wardroom of the *Philadelphia* had around William Bainbridge, he was disabused of the notion within minutes of striking the *Chesapeake*'s flag. While the British boarding party was still aboard carrying out their search for deserters and Barron was lying wounded in his cabin, a bloody rag tied around his leg, he had called his officers in, sent his servant out, ordered the doors shut, and asked for their views. Gordon hesitated and finally opined that Barron had "spared the effusion of blood, but it would have been better had we given her a few broadsides" before giving the order to surrender. Allen did not mince his words. "We have disgraced our flag," he said with unconcealed disdain.[66]

The next day the officers signed a letter to Secretary of the Navy Smith.

> The undersigned officers of the late U.S. Ship Chesapeake
> feeling deeply sensible of the disgrace which must be attached to
> the . . . premature surrender of the U.S. Ship Chesapeake
> without their previous knowledge or consent and desirous of
> proving to their country and the world, that it was the wish of all
> the undersigned to have rendered themselves worthy of the flag
> under which they had the honor to serve, by a determined
> resistance to an unjust demand, do request the Secretary of the
> Navy to order a Court of Inquiry into their conduct . . . and that
> an order may be issued for the arrest of Commodore James
> Barron on the charges herewith exhibited.[67]

Allen wrote his father a few days later, "You cannot appreciate you cannot *conceive* of my feeling at this moment, Was it for this I have continued so long in the service against your wishes—the wish of all my friends; to be so *mortified, humbled*—cut to the soul . . . I was near cursing him . . . give us a *Commander* give us a *man* to lead to us to glory."

Three weeks later he gave vent to more specific accusations. The half hour Barron had kept the British lieutenant waiting for his answer he spent "dictating, penning, and copying" when he could have used the time to get the ship cleared for action and the men to their guns, Allen told his father. "Now had the men been beat to Quarters . . . in 20 minutes they could have been in complete readiness for a fight (although we had on board a raw undisciplined crew, part of whom were never stationed at a gun in their lives before) *But NO it was the wish of the Commodore*." Questioned at the court of inquiry, Allen minced no words at all: "I do believe that the surrender of the *Chesapeake* was principally owing to Commodore Barron's want of courage and want of conduct."[68]

Barron, for his part, wrote to Dr. Bullus on July 3 blaming everyone but himself. "The gunners Worthless Cowardly trifling in the extreme . . . Allen . . . the most Vindictive Rascal of them all he came to that Ship with all the Prejudices that his friend Comdr R[odgers] could inculcate and I am induced to believe that all the Reports now in circulation Prejudicial to me have originated with him . . . about Striking the Colors, believe me, that there was no order of mine executed with one hundreth part of the Alacrity that this was."[69]

A relative of Barron's called out Gordon over his implied criticism of his commander and they exchanged seven shots; an argument over whether Gordon's challenger fired too soon on the last shot led to another duel, between Gordon and the man's second, in which both men were wounded. Two of the *Chesapeake*'s midshipmen disagreed on whether Barron was a coward and fought a duel in which Barron's accuser was wounded in the thigh. Gordon fought yet another duel in which he was seriously wounded in the lower abdomen, an injury that left him with "an air hole in his side" that never healed. Finally, Secretary Smith ordered Decatur to forbid any further duels among his officers. In all, nine duels were fought as a result of the *Chesapeake*'s surrender.[70]

Following the court of inquiry, Barron was brought up before a court-martial. Stephen Decatur was named to the court and tried to recuse himself, writing the secretary of the navy that as soon as the event occurred he had "formed and expressed an opinion that Commo. Barron had not done his duty," but the secretary waved that aside. The president of the court, Commodore Rodgers, Barron's old enemy, had no such compunctions. Barron would always claim that he had been made a scapegoat, but the most damaging testimony came from his own mouth. "What was my duty with the *Leopard*? My duty was defense; not attack—resistance, not assault. It was my duty to use my utmost exertions to keep my ship out of battle, not to bring her to battle with the ship of a friendly power." He was sentenced to suspension from the navy for five years.[71] The *Chesapeake*'s hapless gunner was dismissed from the service and the captain of marines given a reprimand for failing to see that his men had proper cartridges for their muskets. All the other officers were cleared of any wrongdoing.

As more distant repercussions from the *Chesapeake* affair rippled through the navy, it at times seemed a contest as to whether defiance or demoralization would have the upper hand. The *Chesapeake* was supposed to have relieved the *Constitution* on the Mediterranean station. The *Constitution*'s cruise had stretched on and on, to four years now; many of the sailors' two-year enlistments had long since expired; and as the weeks went by with no sign or word of their relief, discontent and restlessness had grown. By the time the *Constitution* finally received her recall orders on August 18, 1807, five of her men were in irons following a near mutiny.

Her commander, Commodore Hugh G. Campbell, had handled the incident with a judiciousness and tact that appeared to have defused the immediate crisis and regained the crew's respect, but still it was an ugly situation. The confrontation started when one of the ship's much-disliked lieutenants, William Burrows, had tried to have two men flogged for going too far from the ship when the crew had been allowed to go swimming one evening at anchor in Syracuse harbor. Burrows had shouted to the men to come back, but the men had not heard him at first; when they did come aboard, Burrows ordered the men to strip and told a boatswain's mate to take a rope to them. An angry knot of seamen immediately formed, one shouting to the men they were fools if they obeyed the order to remove their shirts; the boatswain's mate threw down his rope; and Burrows, in a rage, went for one of the delinquent men with a handspike.

Campbell had been ashore, and when he returned a little after eight o'clock, he found the marines and officers under arms and took in the situation at once. "Follow me to my cabin," he told the lieutenant on deck. "I fear me there has been some misconduct among the officers as well as among the crew." The next morning Campbell mustered the crew and asked those whose enlistments had expired to state their grievances. The men complained of the cruel treatment they had suffered under the harsh regime of the ship's lieutenants; they were especially resentful that men whose enlistments had expired months earlier should be flogged at all, which outraged their sense of justice. They said if the captain would sail for home at once they would quietly obey his orders; if not, they would take the ship home themselves. "Well," Campbell replied, "if you have a mind to take the ship, you may." He promised, however, that if they could wait for him to conclude his business he would sail for America as soon as possible and henceforth no man would be punished unless he deserved it. A short while later, when news of the *Chesapeake* affair reached the ship at Málaga, Campbell called the crew together and asked if they were ready to fight their way through the British navy back to America if war had broken out, as was rumored. The men had given three hearty cheers in the affirmative.[72]

The *Constitution* arrived in Boston in October 1807 after an ultimately uneventful crossing. Campbell recommended that five men be court-martialed, but Secretary Smith overruled him, ordered the men discharged from the service, and left it at that. The frigate was moved to the navy yard in New York, where more than year's worth of deferred maintenance lay before her; she needed a mainmast, an entire new set of sails, new topgallant masts and dozens of other spars, new rigging, boats, water casks.[73] America's naval presence was now confined to her own ports and yards.

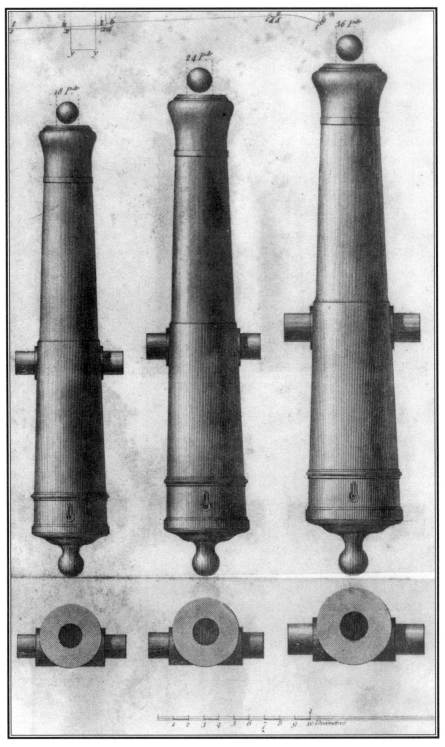

Iron guns of the American navy (Naval History & Heritage Command)

CHAPTER 3

"A Defence Worthy of Republicans"

A WOODEN ship began to rot the instant it touched water, rotted all the faster when it was laid up in port, as all the ships of America's small navy now were; but these were still fine ships, among the finest in the world. They were the offspring of an American shipbuilding tradition that went back to early colonial times, old enough to have gained much practical acumen but still too young and small to be afflicted with the pilfering, chicanery, corruption, bureaucracy, and conservatism that were the bane of the shipyards of as vast and venerable an institution as the Royal Navy of the last decade of the eighteenth century.

In early 1794, as Congress was moving to approve the construction of the first ships for the new United States navy—the capture of ten American merchant ships by Algerine corsairs the previous October had swayed even some of Secretary of State Jefferson's Republican followers to support the bill—Joshua Humphreys, a Philadelphia Quaker who had overseen the construction of several warships during the Revolution, set down his ideas about what those new ships would need to look like. He had written Robert Morris, one of the state's first two United States senators and an influential figure in naval matters ever since serving as agent of marine for the Continental Congress during the Revolution. Morris was also a fabulously wealthy man, or at least had been before issuing his own personal notes for $1.4 million to help finance the Yorktown campaign in 1781. "It is time this country was possessed of a Navy," Humphreys began, and immediately got to the point. "As our navy must for a considerable time be inferior in numbers," he wrote, its ships had to be individually more formidable than any enemy ships of the same class they were likely to encounter: "such

Frigates as in blowing weather as would be an overmatch for double deck Ships, & in light winds, to evade coming to action."

In other words, they had to be large enough to carry armaments that would outgun even a double-decker ship of the line when rough seas prevented the more powerful vessel from opening its lower gun-ports; they had to be fleet enough to outsail the larger ship in light breezes. And in an equal match, they should hold their own against any enemy frigate known, and even smaller ships of the line up to sixty-four guns. Humphreys thought the keel should be a minimum of 150 feet long, about 20 feet longer than the largest British frigates of the day. "Ships built on these principles will render those of an Enemy in a degree useless, or require a greater number before they dare attack our Ships," Humphreys argued.[1]

American shipyards up and down the coast turned out everything from fishing boats to four-hundred-ton merchant brigs; they had acquired a reputation for creating fast, sharp, weatherly ships, the schooner emerging in the eighteenth century as the quintessential American vessel possessing those characteristics in abundance. They also had acquired a surprising amount of knowledge of modern warship design, much of it coming directly or indirectly from the Royal Navy's practices. England's royal dockyards employed fifteen thousand workers, a third of them skilled shipwrights who had come to their trade in the only way possible, via a seven-year apprenticeship under another royal dockyard shipwright. As early as 1690 there were enough of those English dockyard-trained artisans living and working in America for the Royal Navy to issue a contract to a privately owned shipyard in Portsmouth, New Hampshire, for construction of a fifty-gun ship of the line, the *Falkland*.[2]

By the time of the Revolution, Philadelphia had become the largest shipbuilding center in America, owing less to its inconvenient waterfront, a hundred miles from the sea up the Delaware River, than to its proximity to huge stands of timber. Humphreys's business partner and cousin John Wharton was a close friend of Morris's, and when the Continental Congress voted in December 1775 to have thirteen small frigates built, Humphreys immediately submitted a proposed design. The draft of the thirty-two-gun frigate from Humphreys & Wharton followed the basic Royal Navy plan for ships of this class in its arrangement of decks and guns, but was uniquely American in its hull plan, a sharp, fast-sailing design. It was also bigger than its British counterparts, 132 versus

124 feet long on the berth deck. The *Randolph* would be completed at the Humphreys & Wharton yard in Philadelphia in 1776. That same year Humphreys was "disunited . . . from religious fellowship" with the Society of Friends for his participation in the work of war.[3]

A ship of war even more than any other sailing ship was a compromise between a series of utterly irreconcilable forces. A ship built massively enough to absorb enemy fire in her spars and hull and sustain the considerable shock of recoil from her own guns would necessarily ride low in the water from all the weight carried, limiting speed and maneuverability. For the guns to be usable when the ship heeled over in heavy seas, they had to be as high above the waterline as possible, resulting in a high center of gravity and poor stability. Trying to overcome the hull's resistance in the water with lofty masts and large spreads of canvas exacerbated instability still further. Extra ballast could counter this problem to some extent, but only at the cost of depressing the hull still deeper in the water. A hull with sharp, narrow ends yielded a ship that sailed faster and closer to the wind, but cut into the space available for stowing the large stocks of provisions a man-of-war had to carry for the large crews needed to fight the guns or board an enemy ship. Increasing the length of the hull made it possible to increase weight and storage capacity while still preserving comparatively sleek proportions, but the strains that constantly worked on the elastic wooden structure with every roll of the sea increased rapidly with length as well, causing frames and members to separate, leaks to open and expand, and bow and stern to sag, or "hog," along the length of the keel.[4]

By the late eighteenth century every European sea power had evolved its own basic designs for warships and the construction practices required to build them and was generally loath to deviate from what had been found through trial and error to yield a workable if often uninspiring result. Conservatism was built into the process. All the pressures of government policy and practice worked to standardize designs to minimize costs and risks—and to preserve the deeply vested interests of workers and suppliers, nowhere more so than in the Royal Navy's long-established shipyards, with their long-established traditions. Royal Navy officials regularly railed against the stranglehold the artisans held on the craft and against the corruption that drove up costs and stifled improvements, but nothing changed. One ancient privilege allowed shipwrights to take home "chips," supposedly small scraps of leftover wood good only for burning but in practice extending to substantial pieces of sawn timber that went out the door every day, a steady stream of legalized pilfering. Captain Thomas Troubridge, a lord of the Admiralty from 1801 to 1804, thought "all the master shipwrights should be hanged, every one of them, without exception." Lord St. Vincent, first lord of the Admiralty in the same period, more mildly proposed that all dockyard artisans be given a pension—on the condition that "they should reside fifty miles from any dockyard."[5]

IF AMERICAN shipbuilders were less experienced, they were also free of all those hindrances. And so the design that Humphreys drew up when the first frigates of the United States navy were to become a reality in 1794 was like none ever seen. With a nominal rating of forty-four guns, his frigate was not only longer but proportionately more slender than any other frigate of the day. The design also incorporated a number of striking structural innovations that liberated it from some of the constraints that had forced so many trade-offs on designers of warships in the past. A series of long, arcing diagonal braces, six on each side, three sweeping forward and three aft, hugged the inside frame of the hull and were tied to it every two feet with one-inch copper bolts. These "diagonal riders" were an entirely new idea, and they greatly improved the strength and stiffness of the entire structure while counteracting the tendency of the long ship to hog. The deck planking was pressed into service as a structural reinforcement too; four pairs of extra-thick planks ran fore to aft the length of the ship, each plank of the pair "joggled" into the other and to the beams below with interlocking cuts like a jigsaw puzzle. This also added to longitudinal stiffness. A series of mutually supporting stanchions and knees carried the weight from the top, spar deck to the gun and berth decks below, and finally onto the diagonal riders beneath, which made for a substantial boost in the gun-carrying capacity of the entire ship. The top deck of standard European frigates consisted of a quarterdeck aft and forecastle forward with only lightweight, narrow gangways running between them on each side and a large open hatch between them and the fore- and mainmasts. A total of about twenty carronades and chasers could be carried on the quarterdeck and forecastle of a typical British frigate. But Humphreys's bracing system allowed for a nearly complete spar deck running flush fore to aft, broken only by the main hatch, with room and support for as many as twenty-six guns along its entire length.[6]

Secretary of War Henry Knox showed the plan to another Quaker shipwright who had recently arrived in America and made an impression in Philadelphia, still the nation's capital at that time. Josiah Fox was born in England to a well-off family, served an apprenticeship to a master shipwright at the Royal Navy's dockyard in Plymouth, and then, having come into his inheritance, spent the following seven years traveling the world, visiting dockyards and educating himself on the design of ships across Europe. In the fall of 1793 he went to America to study timber and was introduced to Knox in Philadelphia.

Fox had several critiques to offer of Humphreys' plans; in particular, he objected to "any hollows in the Body; by no means to have any hollow in either her Waterlines or Timbers in the Fore Body."[7] He also strongly opposed the size of the ship and offered his own alternative plan for a more conventionally dimensioned frigate. After seeking a third opinion from John Wharton, Knox settled on a compromise: many of Fox's specific objections were addressed in a final redesign under Humphreys's direction, but the size of the final ship remained as Humphreys wished.

As work began in Philadelphia on the first of the forty-fours in the spring of 1794, copies of Humphreys's final drawings were prepared by Fox to send to the shipyards up and down the coast that had been contracted to build the other five frigates. The work had been distributed in an unfeigned bid to build political support for the program, and at each yard a private "Constructor or Master Builder" was hired at an annual salary of $2,000 to oversee the building. Humphreys was chosen in Philadelphia; yards in Boston and New York were selected to build the other two large frigates, while three smaller thirty-six-gun ships, built to a design Fox supervised, were assigned to Norfolk, Baltimore, and Portsmouth, New Hampshire.

To make patterns for the large riblike frames of the ship, a full-size plan was drawn in chalk on the floor of what was known as a mold loft. Humphreys found it would cost $2,000 to erect his own building large enough to house a mold loft for his frigate and was forced to rent space from another builder. Following the chalk outlines, thin battens of quarter- or half-inch wood were cut and nailed together to form flat templates for the curved shapes of the frames, and copies of these too were sent to the New York and Boston yards. In the summer of 1794 copies also went to woodcutters and ship's carpenters dispatched to the islands of Georgia to seek out large timbers of the right rough shapes.

They were looking for live oak, *Quercus virginiana,* a tree unique to the seacoasts of the southeastern United States. The name "live" came from its evergreen habit, and it was a beautiful tree, growing 40 to 70 feet high with a magnificent spread, 150 feet or more at the crown, usually draped with Spanish moss; a single tree could shade half an acre. Its attraction to shipbuilders, though, lay in its incredible density and resistance to decay. At seventy-five pounds per cubic foot, it was 50 percent denser than white oak. And its large angled branches offered ready-made timbers whose strong grain would follow the curve of each finished section of the frame without any weakening cross-grain angle cuts.

British surveyors had identified live oak as a promising wood for ships back in the 1770s. To build a single seventy-four-gun ship of the line required three thousand loads of six hundred board feet of oak, the equivalent of sixty acres of mature wood, and the Royal Navy was already importing oak from as far away as Spain and the Baltic to meet its burgeoning needs. But live oak was a difficult wood to harvest and work. On the Sea Islands of Georgia, where the trees grew in abundance, the local planters were making too much money growing indigo to be interested in going into the lumber business, and other places the trees were found tended to be wild and inaccessible. Many live oaks were afflicted with rot that spread from the taproot up into the heartwood and was only apparent after the tree had been laboriously felled. Ship's carpenters dreaded working with it; the wood was so hard that a nail driven in was impossible to remove, tools were instantly dulled, and augers had to be hammered in to start drilling a hole.[8]

But Humphreys had used live oak in the *Randolph* in 1775 and thought its value in the new big frigates was indisputable. His design called for abundant use of two other uniquely American woods that combined decay resistance with resilience, pitch pine and red cedar, but only live oak had the strength and density to form the backbone of what Humphreys envisioned as an enveloping cage that would not only support the ship's structure but provide a solid barrier to enemy shot. British ships had 6 or 8 inches between frames, but the new American frigates were designed to have frames butting flush together in pairs with only 2 inches of space between each pair, not enough room for a cannonball to penetrate. At the waterline, a ball would have to smash its way through 22 inches of wood formed in a three-ply sandwich: an outer layer of white oak planking, the live oak frame, and then another interior layer of white oak plank. Given the higher density of live oak, it was altogether equivalent to something closer to 30 inches of white oak, which was the typical thickness of the walls in a seventy-four-gun ship of the line. A thirty-two-pound carronade ball fired even point-blank at maximum charge would not have sufficient momentum to penetrate that.[9]

Humphreys confidently predicted that fifty-five men could cut all the live oak needed for one frigate—about five hundred trees' worth—in two months. But he utterly underestimated the obstacles involved in working in the inhospitable locales where it was found. Finding local labor, hacking out roads through the woods with teams of oxen and horses, and fighting torrential rains and sickness all but unmanned the supervisor sent to manage the business, a Boston shipwright named John T. Morgan. From Georgia he wrote Humphreys, "These Moulds frighten me they are so large," and cataloged all his woes. "I lost a fine lad, an apprentice last Saturday with fever, I have it now, everybody is sick here. If I am to stay here till all the timber is cut I shall be dead . . . I cannot stand it." When Humphreys tried to shame him for his slowness, Morgan replied, "You say that if I was there I should be mortified, if you was here you would curse live Oak."[10] Several more of the northern carpenters died, others deserted, but by the end of the year a shipment arrived in Philadelphia that was every-thing Humphreys had hoped for. "One cargo of live oak has arrived from Georgia . . . most of which is now under workmen's hands," Humphreys reported in late December 1794. "This timber is greatly superior to any in Europe, and the best which ever came to this place."[11]

The frigates were probably the most technologically complex pieces of machinery that existed in the America of 1794, with every part made by hand: iron bolts up to twenty feet long, forged one at a time by black-smiths; 150,000 treenails, wooden pegs as much as four feet long that were slowly hammered into augered holes to fasten planks together, their ends then split and wedged to hold them tight; more than a thou-sand pulley blocks of varying dimensions, their sheaves made of ultra-hard lignum vitae. Every plank was sawn over a sawpit, one man in the pit below and another standing on the timber above, each working one end of a two-man saw; large frames were roughed out with an ax, then finished with an adze, which when swung at arm's length by a skilled master shipwright could shave a whisker off a huge timber in exactly the right spot. Each of the longest of the hundreds of thousands of holes that needed to be drilled might take two men a week to complete by slowly working their way through twelve feet of solid timber, constantly backing the auger out to clear the chips, and finally running a heated iron through the finished hole to leave a smooth, hardened, and somewhat water- and decay-resistant surface. Copper bolts used below the waterline were not threaded but had to be secured by "upsetting" their ends, working them with hammers to form a flattened head.[12] Rope had to be spun and tarred, decks caulked with a ton of oakum and a dozen barrels of pitch, sails cut and sewn. The building of the ship went on outside, in all weather. Yet when all went well it could be done start to finish in a year, even a ship the size of one of Humphreys's large frigates.

But months and then years of delays ensued waiting on the shipments of live oak. By the end of 1795 five of the six shipyards still had only two-thirds of the live oak pieces they needed; New York had only a quarter, because a schooner carrying one of its large shipments was lost off Cape Hatteras.[13]

Another spring and fall went by before finally, in 1797, three of the frigates were done; the remaining three would follow over the next three years. Humphreys had submitted a long list of proposed names for the ships, mostly rather feeble imitations of Royal Navy names— *Ardent, Terrible, Invincible, Resolution, Tartar, Formidable*—but after much toing and froing, *United States, Constitution,* and *President* were chosen for the Philadelphia, Boston, and New York forty-fours; the thirty-sixes were given the names *Congress* (Portsmouth), *Constellation* (Baltimore), and *Chesapeake* (Norfolk).

It was always an unknown how a ship would perform when the forces of wind and water combined for the first time on a new design, not least because the sizing of the masts and spars of a sailing ship was more of an art than a science. Humphreys had in his possession a book containing long lists of rules of thumb, copied from a British handbook written out at the Royal Navy's Deptford yard in 1719, which specified numerical proportions for establishing the lengths and diameters of all the yards of a ship. The Philadelphia merchant captain William Jones sent Humphreys his own list of such rules, as did Captain Thomas Truxtun. Though inarguably the product of much trial and error, rules like these were equally obviously ad hoc; there was no law of physics behind them, no mathematical reason for the main topsail yard to be

$^{18}/_{25}$ the length of the lower yards or the mizzenmast $^{11}/_{13}$ of the main-mast.[14] The ultimate decision rested with the ship's captain, however, and so for months as his ships were being fitted out for sea, Humphreys had to sit uncomfortably on the sidelines, an idle spectator as crucial decisions were made that could make or break his reputation, fairly or unfairly.

Republican newspapers were waiting to pounce on any sign that the ships were a failure; they had already had a field day over the snags at the launching of the *Constitution* in September 1797. The previous May, at the launch of the *United States* in Philadelphia, the inclined ways that the ship slid down were set at too steep an angle, and the ship hit the water so fast that it struck the river bottom, doing serious damage to the keel. The *Constitution*'s ways had the opposite problem, sinking into the mud so that the ship came to a halt after sliding only twenty-seven feet. A large crowd had assembled to watch the launch, including President Adams. Two days later a second try sent the ship only a few dozen feet farther. The anti-Federalist newspaper *Time Piece* responded with a mocking ode that suggested the frigate was far better staying where she was, and singled out her builders for particular derision:

> When first you stuck upon your ways
> (Where half New England came to gaze)
> We antifederals thought it something odd
> That where all art had been display'd
> And even the builder deem'd a little god,
> He had not your ways better laid.[15]

The ship finally made it into Boston harbor on October 21, the third attempt.

With immense relief, Humphreys received a letter in September 1798 from Captain John Barry practically ecstatic with praise for the *United States*. She had finally made her way down the Delaware and out to sea after more than a year of additional delays from accidents, febrile illness that had swept Philadelphia, and problems in fitting out and recruiting a crew. "No ship ever went to sea steers and works better, and in point of sailing, I have every reason to believe, she is equal, if not superior to any I ever saw," Barry wrote. "I have seen nothing that I could not with the greatest ease outsail, and in a sea, an easier vessel perhaps never spread canvas."[16] The second of the frigates to be

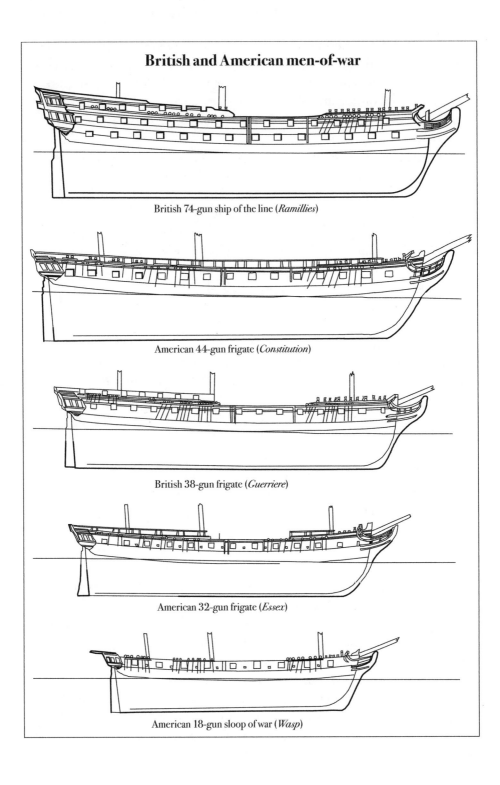

British and American men-of-war

British 74-gun ship of the line (*Ramillies*)

American 44-gun frigate (*Constitution*)

British 38-gun frigate (*Guerriere*)

American 32-gun frigate (*Essex*)

American 18-gun sloop of war (*Wasp*)

launched, Baltimore's *Constellation,* received equally high praise from her officers; she "steered like a boat," running ahead of everything as she dropped down Chesapeake Bay in a strong wind.[17]

In June 1798, during the Quasi War, Congress authorized the construction of several more warships, to be funded by public subscriptions in the leading maritime towns and repaid by government bonds yielding 6 percent interest. Five smaller frigates resulted from the effort: the thirty-six-gun *Philadelphia,* the thirty-two-gun *New York* and *Essex* (the latter the contribution of Salem), and the twenty-eight-gun *Boston* and *John Adams* (the latter from Charleston). None were especially innovative designs, hewing closely to contemporary Royal Navy models, but they were all well-built ships that helped spread the know-how of warship construction, not to mention support for the new American navy, along the American seaboard.[18]

THE LAST full year of Thomas Jefferson's second term, 1808, found William Bainbridge in Portland, Maine, assigned to oversee the building of gunboats and enforce a series of wildly unpopular measures that the president and the Republicans thought would force Britain to recognize American rights. Jefferson remained convinced that America possessed a powerful weapon in economic coercion; limiting or banning America's oceangoing trade would deliver British concessions without recourse to war.

John Randolph offered up his usual scorn. Supporters of trade restrictions, he said, wanted "to cure the corns by cutting off the toes." Subsequent events only seemed to confirm his cynicism. American exports and re-exports, which had reached $108 million in 1807, plummeted to $22 million in 1808 after Jefferson's embargo of all American oceangoing trade with Europe or European colonies went into effect. A few towns were especially hard hit; a fifth of the residents of Salem were said to be reduced to beggary and the pastor of the town's East Church, Dr. William Bentley, noted in his diary that more than a thousand of the town's citizens were being fed each day at a soup kitchen supported by public subscription.

To the American navy fell the unsavory task of stopping violations of the laws, halting and turning back American ships, and seeing through the myriad ruses that American ship's captains inventively created to get around the restrictions. This did not make Bainbridge a popular man in Portland. It would not have been the most lively place to live in the best of times, but his job added a social awkwardness and isolation to his stay there. He wrote to a friend begging for news and said he could "promise in return to keep you informed of the price of *codfish & potatoes.*"[19]

What made the duty all the more galling was that the trade restrictions were so shot through with loopholes and exceptions and hesitations, even as they gave navy and customs officers ever more coercive powers, that it all seemed an exercise in arbitrary futility; a few merchants were severely punished while others carried on better business than ever. One of the first measures banned British imports but then went on to exempt those items that America could not get anywhere else—in other words, precisely the things that Britain profited the most by in trading with America, such as Jamaican rum, coarse woolens, and Birmingham hardware. The subsequent embargo on American trade included an exemption that allowed any American merchant with property abroad to send a ship for it; that resulted in 594 departures from American ports. After that loophole expired, American coasting vessels kept showing up in Caribbean or even European ports, their captains maintaining with perfectly straight faces that they had been blown across the ocean by bad weather. Benjamin W. Crowninshield, who like his brother Jacob was prominent in the family shipping business in Salem, told Treasury Secretary Gallatin about several such incidents he had heard about. In one case the ship *Hope* put into Havana on the excuse that her mainmast had been split by lightning. The "lightning" turned out to have been a keg of powder set off in the mast, accidentally killing a crewman in the bargain.[20]

Meanwhile, foreign depredations on American shipping intensified. Despite endless diplomatic negotiations in London and Washington, Britain had only escalated its clampdown on American trade. Since 1807 a series of orders in council—proclamations issued by the British government through royal prerogative—had in effect abrogated Britain's adherence to the international law of neutrality by barring all neutral trade with the Continent. The only exceptions were for merchant ships that first put into a British port and obtained a British license to proceed. Napoleon retaliated with edicts banning neutral vessels from calling at French-controlled ports *if* they had touched first at a British port. American shippers were now damned if they did and damned if they didn't. Each of the warring European powers admitted that its act was contrary to the law of nations, but justified it as a retaliatory response to the other's illegal acts. By the end of 1811 the total number of American ships seized since 1803 was approaching the 1,500 mark, divided roughly two to one between Britain and France.[21]

What made it all the more obnoxious was that, in practice, the orders in council only seemed to reinforce the obvious conclusion that Britain's real aim was not so much to deny France trade but to make sure Britain benefited from whatever trade occurred. The British government sold as many as twenty thousand licenses a year to shippers who wanted to trade with the French Empire; bought and sold on the open market, they fetched up to £15,000 apiece. The blockade, justified as a military necessity, was looking an awful lot like a system simply of legalized extortion.[22]

In the 1808 U.S. elections the Federalists doubled their seats in the House of Representatives, and though still a minority, the party was riding a rising a tide of New England resentment over the embargo. Behind the parties' differing economic and regional interests lay a bitter class and cultural divide that gave their disagreements an increasingly ugly tone. Federalists looked at Jefferson's supporters and saw an irresponsible—and hypocritical—rabble that spouted stock phrases about egalitarianism while defending slavery, that was always willing to rattle the sabers toward Britain but never willing to raise taxes to pay for the navy, and that had replaced the virtuous selflessness of the Revolutionary generation with a politics of crude and self-interested demagoguery.

The Republicans for their part saw the Federalists as Anglophile elitists out to impose "monarchical" tyranny upon America, and could point to the Federalists' own glaring hypocrisies. Though they had borne the brunt of Britain's seizure and impressment policies, New England's merchants also had the most to lose from war with Britain and the total loss of trade that would result, and so were constantly making excuses for Britain's actions. Federalist writers even tried to claim that only a handful of American sailors had ever been impressed, or that it was the nefarious doing of a few American merchant captains who connived to have their sailors pressed toward the end of a voyage to avoid paying them.[23]

Still, between the Federalists who wanted a navy but not to oppose Britain with and the Republicans who wanted to oppose Britain but not with a navy, enough votes emerged between the two parties to override Gallatin's furious objections and approve a modest naval expansion. In January 1809 Congress passed "an act authorizing the employment of an additional naval force" that tripled the number of seamen to 3,600 and the number of midshipmen to 450, and ordered four of the frigates that had been in ordinary for years immediately fitted out and made ready for sea to join the frigates *Constitution* and *Chesapeake* in active service. Sixteen Republican senators and some forty House Republicans, largely from New England, joined the Federalists in passing the measure. Gallatin fumed about "the navy coalition of 1809, by whom were sacrificed . . . the Republican cause itself, and the people of the United States, to a system of favoritism, extravagance, parade, and folly."[24]

By a much wider margin Federalists and disaffected Republicans joined forces in both houses to repeal the ineffectual embargo. In an unmistakable parting shot, they chose to make Jefferson's by now much-hated law expire the same day as his presidency, March 4, 1809.

As ONE OF his first official acts, the new president, James Madison, named Paul Hamilton as his secretary of the navy. Hamilton was an unknown, a former governor of South Carolina, a man with no experience of ships or the sea. But one of his early acts was to order the four frigates and several smaller seagoing vessels now in service organized into a Northern Squadron under Rodgers and a Southern Squadron under Decatur and begin regular sea patrols. Their ostensible mission was to protect the American coastal trade, but Hamilton meant to send a more important message, and he did: the American navy was no longer going to be a passive bystander to British and French encroachments on American home waters.

Hamilton also began cautiously pointing out to Congress that a navy built around gunboats and always kept in port was scarcely a navy at all, nor could it even be the seed of one. In June 1809 he told the Senate:

> Much must depend on the species of policy which, in the event
> of war, may be adopted. If . . . a plan of operations merely
> defensive shall be pursued, there can be no doubt that gunboats
> will aid materially, if properly stationed; but, if, on the contrary,
> our marine should be directed against a foreign trade, and to
> the convoying and protection of our own, a system of well
> armed, fast sailing, frigates, and small cruisers, would, on every
> principle, be preferable in point of effect, and, comparatively

rated per gun and number of men to be employed, would be much less costly. It must also be observed that it is only on board vessels suited for sea service that good seamen are to be formed, and that those calculated merely for ports afford no opportunity for improvement in naval science.[25]

Whatever complex blend of circumstances and politics had led to it, American naval officers began to see a glimmer of light: the navy was back at sea at last. As William Bainbridge wrote David Porter later that year, "You may rest assured of one fact, that we have an excellent secretary and that he is a most zealous friend of the navy."[26]

No one wanted to be caught napping again, and all the American commanders took advantage of their patrols up and down the coast to drill their crews and inculcate in them a new, unmistakably aggressive posture. In March 1810 the *President,* under William Bainbridge's command, chased the British sloop of war *Squirrel* off Charleston bar. In June, Hamilton reinforced the navy's resolve to confront the British in American waters with an order sent to all his captains:

> You, like every other patriotic American, have observed and deeply felt the injuries and insults heaped on our Country . . . Amongst these stands most conspicuous the inhuman and dastardly attack on our Frigate the *Chesapeake*—an outrage which prostrated the flag of our Country and has imposed on the American people, cause of ceaseless mourning. That same spirit which has originated and has refused atonement for this act of brutal injustice, still exists with Great Britain. . . . What has been perpetrated may again be attempted. It is therefore, our duty to be prepared and determined at every hazard, to vindicate the injured honor of our Navy, and revive the drooping Spirit of the Nation . . . offering yourself no unjust aggression, your to submit to none, not even a menace or threat from a force not materially your Superiour.[27]

A summer cruise in 1810 uniting the entire American navy under Commodore Rodgers in a small show of force was planned, and Midshipman Henry Gilliam, aboard the *Constitution,* wrote his uncle that the secretary's orders had been read aloud to the frigate's assembled crew. Capturing the new spirit of determination that the *Chesapeake*'s surrender never be repeated, Gilliam said, "The General orders from the Navy department to Comr. R is not to suffer the smallest insult whatever to the Squaderon under his Command . . . but to resent it with all the force he can. . . . if so I am confident the Amer flag will never be struck until it has made a defence worthy of republicans." And Decatur, now in command of the frigate *United States,* promptly replied to Hamilton, "Your instructions . . . have infused new life into the officers. No new indignity will pass with impunity."[28]

The following May, in 1811, on a dark night off Cape Henry, Virginia, Commodore Rodgers in command of the frigate *President* encountered and exchanged shots with a strange warship. Rodgers had made it publicly known that he was on the lookout for the British frigate *Guerriere,* which had been reported stopping American ships and pressing American seamen. No one would ever agree who hailed first or who fired first, and while the evidence slightly favored Rodgers's account, it was also evident he was spoiling for a fight. When the firing was done, the small British sloop of war *Little Belt* had sustained heavy damage along with nine dead and twenty-three wounded.

Recriminations flew across the Atlantic, and British commentators emphasized the unequal odds of the fight, but in writing to Rodgers, Secretary Hamilton could not contain his satisfaction over the "chastisement, which you have very properly inflicted." He begged Rodgers to let him know the name of the one wounded boy aboard the *President* so that he might "hug him to my bosom (whatever may be his condition, or circumstance in life), while I made him an officer in the American Navy."[29]

Equally rapturous cheers echoed from American newspapers, exulting that the score with "the Leviathan of the deep" and the "mistress of the seas" had been evened at last, no matter the details and circumstances.

JAMES MADISON was an easy man to underestimate. At five foot four, the fourth president of the United States stood a foot shorter than Washington or Jefferson and weighed little over a hundred pounds. He habitually dressed in sober black, which made more than one observer think of "a schoolteacher dressed up for a funeral."[30] More comfortable in his own company than in society, given to hypochondriac anxieties about his nerves and health, he was forty-four before he again summoned his courage to approach a woman after having been jilted twelve years earlier on his very first attempt. Even on this second try he had sent Aaron Burr to act as an intermediary, to inquire if the twenty-seven-year-old widow Dolley Payne Todd might be interested in him. To his infinite relief she was, and they made a devoted if odd couple, she enthusiastically fulfilling the social duties that he always dreaded.

Madison had a thorough and logical mind; he was able to master the most complex subjects, develop ideas, invest countless hours writing and rewriting; but as the historian Garry Wills observed, he always preferred to let others get the attention: "He worked best not merely in committee but in secret." He was the anonymous voice of the most persuasive papers of *The Federalist* that rallied public opinion in favor of the Constitution, the unnamed author of pamphlets that bolstered Jefferson's presidency; he had even ghostwritten George Washington's first inaugural address, the House's reply to Washington's address, and then Washington's thank-you reply to the House. He had, said political friends and enemies alike, the naivety of a man who, unacquainted with the world, works out the perfect solution at his desk and is baffled when the world does not agree.

At his inaugural ball the new president looked "spiritless and exhausted," thought Margaret Bayard Smith, the wife of the editor of the *National Intelligencer* and a keen early observer of Washington society. Jefferson was beaming, happy to pass on the office to a trusted colleague, but even happier to be formally free of the burdens of the job he had all but abdicated since the election, letting decisions drift as his eight-year policy of economic resistance to British outrages collapsed about him. When the managers of the ball appeared at the new president's side to ask him to stay to supper, he wanly assented, then turned to Mrs. Smith and blurted out, "But I would much rather be in bed."

It was not just Madison's personality that was deceptive; everything about his political ideology seemed to point to a man who disparaged strong leadership and bold action. Madison had been the single strongest proponent of the embargo as an alternative to military confrontation; as secretary of state he had talked Jefferson into it, clung to it through all its inconsistencies, defended it even when the tide of Republican party feeling rose against it and repeal became inevitable. Even when Albert Gallatin had concluded that all America had accomplished with its weakly enforced trade restrictions was to parade its pusillanimity before the world—"I had rather encounter war itself than to display our impotence to enforce our laws," he had conceded to Madison in 1808—Madison clung to a belief that his policy of peaceful coercion would ultimately bring Britain to relent.[31] In his public writings he had always been true to the Jeffersonian article of faith on the inherent evil of war, not so much because of the destruction and killing that war entailed but because of the threat it posed to liberty at home. "Of all the enemies to public liberty war is, perhaps, the most to be dreaded," Madison wrote in 1795 in his *Political Observations.* "War is the parent of armies; from these proceed debts and taxes; and armies, debts, and taxes are the known instruments for bringing the many under the domination of the few."[32]

What friends and enemies alike failed to grasp was that the kind of man who quietly worked out solutions to complex problems in the privacy of his study and his mind could be a man of stubborn resolve once he determined what those solutions were. And the fact was that as early as the spring of 1811 he had concluded that peaceful means would never bring Britain to respect American sovereignty and independence; no option remained but war. His challenge now was to slowly, cautiously, and deliberately build the political case for what would inevitably be seen as a total about-face in a policy that for a decade had been most closely associated with no one but Madison himself.

On April 13, 1811, the president invited the editor of the *National Intelligencer* to a private dinner at the White House. The paper was the semi-official voice of the administration, and three days later it printed a lengthy editorial that named no sources but strongly suggested that diplomacy with Great Britain had run its course. Britain had repeatedly refused even to seriously discuss the three paramount demands that the United States could never concede: revocation of the orders in council, an end to blockades that contravened international law, and abandonment of "the practice of impressing whomsoever her commanders chuse to call British seamen." The editorial flatly predicted that talks with the newly appointed minister from Britain to the United States, due to arrive in Washington soon, would fail and that it would then be up to the people of the United States to "substitute . . . some measure more consonant to the feelings of the nation" than the peaceful measures so far tried.[33]

The new minister was Augustus J. Foster, who had served as secretary to the British legation from 1804 to 1808—and who had once declared that he would not take the job he was now undertaking for ten thousand pounds. When the British warship that brought him to America anchored off Annapolis on June 29, one seaman promptly deserted by leaping overboard and swimming three miles to shore, an ominous reminder of the flash points between the two countries.

But Foster swept into Washington all charm and goodwill. Thirty-three years old, handsome, well-bred, he struck a studied contrast to the prickly arrogance of his predecessors. His mother, herself the daughter of an earl, had married the Duke of Devonshire on the death of her first husband and had used her powerful connections to promote her son for the job. "I know you dislike that country, but it is a wonderful opportunity for future advancement," she wrote him. Foster arrived with the secure confidence of a man who felt himself so far above the taint of vulgarity that he could even rub shoulders with American republicans with natural ease. He brought with him seven servants and a lavish entertainment budget, and proceeded to exhaust his $50,000 expense account in six months, wooing congressmen, giving excellent dinners for as many as two hundred guests at a time three or four times a week, and confining his contemptuous observations about American crudity to his private notes. Even there he seemed more amused than affronted as he recounted the "droll, original but offending" characters he became acquainted with among the Republican members of Congress, such as the one who had been caught in the act of relieving himself into Foster's drawing room fireplace when he thought everyone had left the room for supper during a ball the minister gave for the queen's birthday, or the others, not knowing what caviar was, who mistook it for black raspberry jam and crammed in huge mouthfuls that they immediately spat out. He had moved the legation to a new location at the very heart of the city, taking three of the adjacent row houses that made up the Seven Buildings on the north side of Pennsylvania Avenue at Nineteenth Street, just three blocks from the White House. Foster immediately let it be known that he had come with instructions to settle the *Chesapeake* matter by offering compensation to the victims' families and returning the seized Americans, still prisoners four years after the event—their sentences of five hundred lashes having since been remitted to "temporary" imprisonment.

And when, as the *National Intelligencer*—or rather President Madison—had accurately foretold, Foster's charm offensive failed to distract his American hosts from the inescapable fact that Britain was as unmovable as ever on the central issues of impressment or the orders in council, Foster remained serenely unperturbed. Talk of war was simply electoral politics or bluff, he reported to London, and urged that Britain hold firm; an outward show of bland conciliation would soon enough soothe ruffled American spirits. He wrote a comforting reply to the embarrassed note of apology he received from his "poor Guest," the congressman who had committed the "act of great impropriety" in his drawing room fireplace. "I most graciously answered and hoped to have gained his vote for peace by my soothing."[34]

SECRETARY OF the Navy Hamilton took the unusual step of remaining in Washington through the steaming summer of 1811 when all other sane residents of the city fled for the mountains or home. The American navy's notably more aggressive stance in showing the flag and resisting British encroachments along the American coast had led to several brushes between the two navies since the *Little Belt* confrontation in May, and Hamilton wanted to stay on top of what could at any moment become a rapidly escalating situation.

On June 9, 1811, Decatur, in the frigate *United States,* was sailing from Hampton Roads to New York when he encountered two British warships. As the ships lay side by side the captain of the thirty-eight-gun British frigate *Eurydice* identified himself and said he was carrying dispatches to the United States government. At that moment a gun on the *United States* went off. "I am happy that a pause followed," Decatur reported to Hamilton, "which enabled me to inform her commander that the fire was the effect of accident." No one was injured, the captain accepted Decatur's apology, and the ships went on their way.

On August 30 a more serious confrontation was barely averted. Off Norfolk the British sloop of war *Tartarus* seized two American merchantmen—and then put into Norfolk, in violation of not only the order barring British men-of-war from American ports but plain common sense as well. David Porter, in command at the navy yard there, at once moved to carry out Hamilton's standing instructions of the year before and ordered a force of two gunboats, the brig *Nautilus,* and the ship's boats of the *Essex* to the roads "with an intention of driving her from that place." Meanwhile, the British consul at Norfolk caught wind of what was happening and sent the *Tartarus*'s captain an urgent message: "For God-sake if you are not already gone—get to sea as fast as you can." The ship cut her anchor cable and fled into the night just ahead of Porter's small flotilla, leaving a local pilot to retrieve her anchor later.

Two weeks later Hamilton reported to Madison that Decatur's and Rodgers's squadrons were again at sea continuing their patrols: "There have been three british Cruisers on the coast of New York besetting, for some time past, our commerce"; there were rumors that a British squadron sent to America following the *Little Belt* affair was planning to retaliate, and after Rodgers's full exoneration by a court of inquiry in September the rumors intensified. "As [Rodgers] will, no doubt, meet with the British squadron," Hamilton said, "it will be ascertained, probably, whether their views are hostile or not."[35]

Even members of Madison's own party and administration had been slow to detect the president's new militancy. His secretary of state, James Monroe, had at first been convinced that the April article in the *National Intelligencer* was a plant instigated by his predecessor Robert Smith, designed to embarrass and sabotage his upcoming negotiations with Foster, and Monroe furiously upbraided the editor for printing it. Meanwhile, from the small but vocal "malcontent" wing of the Republican party that had begun agitating for war, Madison was being openly attacked for "pusillanimous" conduct and a want of "spirit."[36]

But in fact he was working steadily to build a case, and a sense of crisis, that would bring his party and the public along with the momentous decision for war he had already made. In July 1811 he had issued a proclamation summoning Congress to meet November 5, a month earlier than customary. When the legislators arrived, Madison sent them as their first order of business a "war message" that called for raising ten thousand troops on a three-year enlistment and providing for fifty thousand volunteers. He summarized the failed negotiations with Foster, emphasizing the refusal of the British government to concede anything to American claims. He concluded, "With this evidence of hostile inflexibility in trampling on rights which no independent nation can relinquish, Congress will feel the duty of putting the United States into an armor and an attitude demanded by the crisis, and corresponding with the national spirit and expectations."

Although conspicuously deferring to Congress's constitutional authority to declare war, Madison followed up with behind-the-scenes lobbying. In a private letter to John Quincy Adams, he said, "The question to be decided therefore by Congress . . . simply is, whether all trade to which the orders in council are and shall be applied, is to be abandoned, or the hostile operation of them be hostilely resisted. The apparent disposition is certainly not in favor of the first alternative." He also treated Foster's concessions on the *Chesapeake* affair as the too-little-too-late window dressing they were: he passed the agreement on to Congress without any official comment, and to John Quincy Adams dismissed it with the observation that it merely "takes one splinter out of our wounds." On January 16, 1812, the president sought to keep the momentum moving toward war by releasing the full text of the letters exchanged between Foster and Monroe during their futile negotiations. As further evidence of "the hostile policy of the British Government against our national rights," they were damningly effective; even Federalists were astounded at the arrogance of Foster's insistence that the orders in council that barred American trade with the Continent would only be rescinded if Napoleon first opened his ports to British goods.[37]

John Randolph remained true to the old Republican antiwar faith, lambasting his fellow party members for apostasy and accusing them of wanting war with Britain only because they lusted after Canada's territory. But he was running against an unmistakable tide. The new Speaker of the House, Henry Clay, of Kentucky, was at the forefront of the war faction and filled key committee positions with like-minded allies. He also was the first speaker ever to dare tell Randolph to stop bringing his dog into the House chamber, a small but telling straw in the wind.

Clay and his fellow war hawks fully reflected the "national spirit and expectations" that Madison had alluded to. As tumbling farm prices drove home the connection between trade abroad and prosperity at home, the war spirit grew sharply even in the traditional frontier strongholds of Jeffersonian republicanism. Cotton prices had dropped two-thirds since 1808, along with an overall 30 percent decline in farm commodity prices, and newspapers in Kentucky, Tennessee, Ohio, and western Pennsylvania boldly declared that only war would free America from the British restrictions that had closed off markets to American farmers. "We have now one course to pursue—a resort to arms," asserted one Kentucky paper. The Ohio legislature adopted a resolution declaring that the report the House Foreign Relations Committee had just issued in response to Madison's message—and which focused exclusively on British violations of American maritime rights— "breathes a spirit in unison with our own."[38] In western Tennessee,

Andrew Jackson, commander of the militia, issued a call for volunteers that began, "For what are we going to fight?"

> We are going to fight for the reestablishment of our national charector, misunderstood and vilified at home and abroad; for the protection of our maritime citizens, impressed on board British ships of war and compelled to fight the battles of our enemies against ourselves; to vindicate our right to a free trade, and open a market for the productions of our soil, now perishing on our hands because the *mistress of the ocean* has forbid us to carry them to any foreign nation; in fine, to seek some indemnity for past injuries, some security against future aggressions, by the conquest of all the British dominions upon the continent of north America.[39]

If the conquest of Canada was not the reason for war against Britain, it was in the eyes of Jackson and most other war hawk Republicans the most effective means of waging that war. The bill expanding the army was quickly approved and signed into law by Madison on January 11, 1812; a militia bill followed on February 6.

The navy was another matter. Even the war hawks could remain true to the old Republican creed of antinavalism if the coming war was to be fought mainly on land. And then Albert Gallatin, appalled as ever at what the navy was doing to his budget figures—only once during his eleven years as Jefferson's and Madison's Treasury secretary had he managed to keep the navy budget under $1 million, as he hoped, and in 1812 it was running $2.5 million—had sent Madison a blistering dissection of the president's proposed war message to Congress in which he urged Madison to remove any mention of the navy at all. Gallatin argued that to pay for the war the country would have to borrow $6 million at 6 percent interest; adding the navy's $2 million would not only increase that principal but push the interest rate for the entire loan to 8 percent. The only other option would be to cut the army budget, which Gallatin warned would be a "fatal" misapplication of resources. "Unless therefore a great utility can be proven" for the navy, he admonished Madison, "the employment of that force will be a substantial evil. I believe myself that so far from there being any utility it will in its very employment diminish our means of annoying the enemy."[40]

Madison, carefully trying to thread political minefields left and right as he built the case for war, chose the prudent political course and ducked the navy issue altogether. He ended up devoting one sentence to the navy in his message to Congress: "Your attention will of course be drawn to such provisions on the subject of our naval force as may be required for the services to which it may be best adapted."

In December 1811, Secretary Hamilton had responded to a request from the House Naval Committee asking for an estimate of the expense of building, manning, and equipping for actual service those vessels "most useful and most usually employed in modern naval war." Hamilton stated that in the event of "a collision with either of the present great belligerent powers," a force of twelve 74-gun ships of the line and twenty "well constructed frigates" of not less than thirty-eight guns each would "be ample to the protection of our coasting trade" and also "be competent to annoy extensively the commerce of an enemy."

At $200,000 for each of the new frigates and a third of a million dollars for each of the ships of the line, the total cost of construction would come to a little over $7 million. Repairing the five smaller frigates currently in ordinary (*Chesapeake, Constellation, New York, Adams, Boston*) so they could join the two small frigates (*Essex* and *Congress*) and three large frigates (*President, United States, Constitution*) already in service would cost half a million dollars.[41]

The committee prudently scaled back its proposal to ten new frigates and no ships of the line. But even that set off all the old expressions of horror from the Republican faithful when it came before the full House. One alarmed Republican congressman declared that such a navy, once a war was over, "would become a powerful engine in the hands of an ambitious Executive." The "Navy mania," warned another, would lead to permanent internal taxes that would fall on the agricultural class while all the benefits would accrue to the mercantile class. Representative Richard Mentor Johnson of Kentucky ominously observed that of all the great naval powers of ancient times, Tyre and Sidon, Crete and Rhodes, Athens and Carthage, none had ever been able to confine themselves "to the legitimate object of protecting commerce in distant seas," but had been led inexorably to plunder, piracy, and depredations abroad, tyranny at home: "While their commerce and navy furnished a small part of the people with the luxuries of every country at that time known, the great mass of citizens at home were miserable and oppressed." Others decried the waste and extravagance of naval expenditures; there were stories of navy yard workers traveling at government expense in stagecoaches, of timber purchased at inflated prices, of ships no sooner built than needing repair, with the frigate *Constitution* alone running up repair bills of more than $43,000 per year ever since she was launched.[42]

And then Adam Seybert of Pennsylvania rose to point out that the British navy possessed 1,042 vessels, 719 of those in commission, 111 of those already on the American station; among those were 7 ships of the line and 31 frigates. The entire American navy, by contrast, consisted of 20 vessels carrying a grand total of 524 guns—in other words, half as many guns as the Royal Navy had ships. "We cannot contend with Great Britain on the ocean. It is idle to be led astray by misstatements and false pride—we have no reason to expect more from our citizens, than what other brave people have performed," Seybert asserted. "I fear our vessels will only tend to swell the present catalogue of the British Navy."[43]

Nearly every Federalist and two dozen Republicans supported the frigate bill, but it narrowly lost on a 59–62 vote in the House. A proposal to build a dry dock for repairing navy ships was voted down 52–56. The Senate also narrowly defeated the frigate bill, though the speech of Federalist senator James Lloyd of Massachusetts in favor of the measure was subsequently reprinted and sold twelve thousand copies in Boston. In the end, Congress would agree only to a small appropriation to purchase timber and fit out existing frigates. Most Federalists were so disgusted they abstained from voting on the final bill.

Representatives from the frontier had voted 12 to 1 against the frigate bill; six months later they would vote 12 to 1 in favor of the declaration of war against Great Britain. Representatives from Pennsylvania voted 17 to 1 against the naval expansion and 16 to 2 in favor of war. In all, 53 of the 79 House members who would eventually vote for war voted against preparing the navy to fight one.[44]

NEWS OF America's move toward war reached William Bainbridge in Russia. He had gone there to try his fortune once again as a merchant captain, having obtained another furlough from the navy, and had sailed twice to St. Petersburg; on the first voyage he made a considerable profit carrying a load of indigo, but by the time he arrived with a second shipment so many American merchants had the same idea that the market was flooded and prices collapsed. In the fall of 1811 Bainbridge took a house in St. Petersburg to wait for prices to recover as Russian re-exports slowly eased the glut.

Traveling in northern Europe in midwinter was a harrowing ordeal, but Bainbridge decided to return at once. With the northern harbors frozen, his only route lay overland across Finland to Sweden, where he hoped to get passage on a ship for England. Roads and facilities for travelers were equally nonexistent; in Sweden his coach overturned and fell down a thirty-foot embankment, killing the coachman and one horse, but Bainbridge emerged miraculously unhurt.

He arrived in Boston on February 9, 1812, and at once wrote Secretary Hamilton that the desire to serve his country alone had compelled him to take "a very fatiguing journey of 1200 miles on the Continent of Europe, and a dangerous passage of 53 days from Gothenburg." Hamilton appointed him to the command of the Boston Navy Yard to allow him some time with his family before assuming a sea command.[45]

The frigate *Constitution* was swiftly making her way back from Europe at the same time. She had been sent on a diplomatic mission to take to Paris the new American minister, Joel Barlow, deliver to the Netherlands debt payments of $220,000 in specie, and on her return drop the current American chargé d'affaires in France, Jonathan Russell, in England, where he was to take up the same post at the consulate in London.

In command of the *Constitution* was Isaac Hull, whose novel approach to being the captain of a ship of war was to take unfeigned delight in his job. He was the son of a Connecticut merchant captain and like many American naval officers had begun his career that way. He was short and pudgy where Decatur was tall and slim, kind and trusting where Bainbridge was rough and suspicious. When Gilbert Stuart was going to paint his portrait, he remarked to another artist who had earlier painted Hull, "You have Hull's likeness. He always looks as if he was looking at the sun and half shutting his eyes."[46]

The captain from Connecticut made a point of avoiding personal confrontations and never fought a duel; he disliked corporal punishment and rarely ordered men flogged; he wrote Bainbridge humorous letters about his tribulations over love as a thirty-eight-year-old bachelor and how much he wished he had money. Once, when away from the ship at Christmas, he returned to discover that some men had been flogged, and promptly wrote out an order addressed to all the officers of the ship: "It is my positive orders that they do not punish any seaman, marine, or any other person on board in my absence, and that the punishment for missing muster, or any other trifling offense, shall not exceed three lashes with a small rope over the shirt."[47]

There was no mistaking his bravery, though, or his seamanship. In the Quasi War he had led a daring cutting-out expedition that boarded and seized a French privateer in the Caribbean; in the Tripolitan war, as Captain Campbell's lieutenant on the frigate *Adams,* he had saved the ship from breaking up on rocks with his quick thinking and cool disregard of his captain's panicked indecision. Campbell was not known as much of a seaman, and when the ship missed stays while tacking in Algeciras harbor and began drifting rapidly aback toward the rocks of Cabrita Point, Campbell was momentarily struck speechless. Hull, who had run on deck wearing only his nightshirt and carrying a pair of striped pantaloons, grabbed the speaking trumpet out of Campbell's hands, issued a quick series of orders to wear the ship, and seeing the furious astonishment on Campbell's face, turned to the captain and said, "Keep yourself cool, Sir, and the ship will be got off." And then he calmly pulled on his pantaloons. The crew kept a straight face, but a new catchphrase was soon being heard throughout the ship: "Keep yourself cool!"[48]

Like Bainbridge, he had once almost resigned his commission in anger at being passed over for promotion, and it was not until 1807 that he was made a captain, not until May 1810 that he received command of one of the navy's plum frigates. He had had the command of the *President* for scarcely a month when Rodgers, pulling seniority, ordered him to switch with him in the *Constitution,* which Rodgers thought a sluggish sailer.

But nothing now could dampen Hull's enthusiasm. Years later, David Porter would look back on his own long naval career and sourly remark, "During the whole thirty one years that I have been in the naval service, I do not recollect having passed one day, I will not say of happiness, but of pleasure."[49] Hull seemed to take pleasure in everything about his new command. "I have now one of the best ships in our Navy," he wrote his half sister from Boston, "and a crew of 430 men, which you will think a large family, it's true; but being a good housekeeper I manage them with tolerable ease. . . . Mary, I have not a word of news to tell you. Indeed, I am so much rapt up in my ship if half Boston was to burn down I should not know it unless I got a singe." Even when the ship sailed terribly on his first cruise, amply confirming

Rodgers's disdainful assessment, Hull remained exultant in his letters home. Divers inspected the ship's bottom and discovered "ten waggon loads" of mussels and oysters clinging to her copper sheathing: she had not had her bottom cleaned since Preble had had her careened in Boston in 1803. Hull was confident he could solve the problem by taking the ship up the Delaware River, where the fresh water would kill the clinging shellfish, or by scraping the bottom with an iron drag; then she would sail as well as she ever did, he told Mary, which "would give me great pleasure as she has always been a favourite of mine."[50]

There was also no mistaking that Captain Hull's officers and crew fully returned his devotion to them and to his ship. Charles Morris jumped at the chance to move with Hull to the *Constitution* as first lieutenant even though Rodgers asked him to stay with the *President*. "Rodgers is passionate, and we should soon disagree," Morris wrote his family. But "Captain Hull . . . gives his first lieutenant every opportunity of displaying taste or talent that they can desire." When three of the *Constitution*'s crew drowned in an accident, Hull learned that one of the men was the sole support for his widowed mother and called the crew together to suggest they take up a subscription for her; he told them that they must not put down more than they could afford, but if every man contributed even a small amount, say twenty-five cents apiece, it would come to a tidy sum. When the subscription was complete Hull was astonished to find it totaled $1,000—an average of $3 a man, or one to two weeks of a seaman's pay.[51]

On August 5, 1811, the *Constitution* rode at anchor in Hampton Roads preparing to sail for France, and there was no doubt in any American captain's mind now of the proper drill when passing a British warship: The ship was cleared for action, fully prepared as if heading into battle in earnest, her crew at quarters and guns run out, powder horns filled, slow matches smoking in tubs, the decks cleared from fore to aft, even the walls of the captain's spacious quarters at the stern of the gun deck knocked out by the carpenters and the furniture struck down to the hold below so that guns which occupied the captain's dining cabin could be freely worked. The marines manned the tops, muskets and cartridges at the ready, fire hoses rigged to the pumps, chains slung to the largest yards to hold them in place if their rigging was shot away. The surgeons were in the cockpit on the orlop deck down below the waterline, their knives and saws and other grisly instruments laid out. So prepared, the *Constitution* sailed out of Hampton Roads past the

British frigates *Atalanta* and *Tartarus*. The ships exchanged polite greetings; the band on the *Atalanta* even serenaded the American ship with "Hail Columbia."

Minister Barlow's widowed sister-in-law, Clara Baldwin, was traveling with the diplomat to Paris; Hull wrote his half sister Mary, "I find I am to take out a *buxom widow. Take care:* at sea is a dangerous place to be with ladies." The ship made nine, ten, eleven knots; day after day the crew exercised at the great guns, or at small arms and boarding, or at trimming the sails for battle maneuvers. Mrs. Baldwin's two pet mockingbirds and a raccoon and caged squirrels kept the wardroom entertained; David Bailie Warden, another member of the minister's retinue, who was going to take up the post of consul in Paris, each day took notes about the Gulf Stream, recording the color and temperature of the water. On the night of August 28 he noted a phosphorescent sea around the ship, and the next day they were surrounded by dolphins.

Just after noon on September 1 the lookout from the masthead sighted Lizard Point, the southernmost tip of England. For several days they beat up the Channel against contrary winds to Cherbourg, and on the afternoon of the fifth the ship was again cleared for action and at battle stations as they ran through the British squadron blockading Cherbourg, two ships of the line and two frigates. Again all was polite and correct.[52]

At Cherbourg, Hull had to wait two weeks for Russell to appear. He exchanged dinners with the French admiral, toured forts and the shipyard and the naval hospital, and went to Paris and played tourist, escorting the "buxom widow" to galleries, buying items friends had asked him to purchase, and speculating $3,000 of his own money on Parisian goods that were in demand at home owing to the British blockade—satins, laces, gloves, ribbons, watches, razors.

On the voyage to England they now beat down the Channel fighting contrary winds. Approaching Portsmouth on the night of October 9, they were followed by the British brig of war *Redpole*. Suddenly at 2:30 a.m. the British ship ran down on them and fired two shots, one striking the quarter and one amidships. "*What sloop is that?*" Hull furiously hailed, and once identifications had been exchanged, he ordered the British ship to send a boat aboard.

"How dare you fire on us?" Hull shouted at the officer as he came aboard.

"O!—we beg pardon. We mistook you for French."

"French! French! You've been in sight all night and yet can't tell who we are? I've a good mind to sink you on the spot."[53]

At anchor at St. Helen's Roads, another incident occurred to increase tensions. On the night of November 12 a British officer came aboard to report that a deserter from the *Constitution* had swum across to the British ship *Havannah*. Captain Hull was gone to London, accompanying Russell, and so Lieutenant Morris received the officer, thanked him for the information, and said a formal demand for the man's return would be made the next day. The next day, perhaps predictably, Morris was given a runaround reminiscent of the treatment the *Halifax*'s captain had been given in Norfolk four years earlier. Finally, Morris called on the port admiral, who refused to discuss the matter without first receiving an answer to the question of "whether we would surrender British deserters who reached our ship," Morris said.

The admiral got his answer four days later. Morris was wakened the night of November 16 by the sound of the sentries firing their muskets and the cries of a man in the water near the ship. When the man was pulled out and brought on deck, he identified himself as a deserter from the *Havannah*. "On being asked his country," Morris said, the deserter answered "in the richest Irish brogue, 'An American!' This was sufficient." A boat was immediately sent across bearing with excruciating politeness a reciprocation of the message the British had sent about *Constitution*'s deserter.

The humor of the situation was lost on the British, who the next day moved two frigates close to the American ship, making it almost impossible for her to get under way without running afoul of one of the anchored vessels. Morris nonetheless brought the *Constitution* to a new anchorage outside the British ships, slipping down with the tide and barely avoiding getting foul of the blocking ships. On November 20, cleared for action even before weighing anchor, the *Constitution* put to sea without further challenge.[54]

Back in Cherbourg again, this time to pick up dispatches for Washington from Barlow, Hull was for the first time beginning to feel vexed. The brushes with the British had given him only satisfaction: "I have again had my troubles in England but luckily got off with flying colors," he noted on his arrival in Cherbourg. "It was whispered about on shore that they intended taking [the deserter] out at sea, but they made no attempt of that sort. If they had, we were ready for them." But the wait for Barlow's dispatches dragged on for seven weeks, and every American in France who had something he wanted to send safely home was besieging Hull with requests for passage. Russell and Warden sent box after box of goods, "sufficient to load a ship of sixty tons," Hull fumed. "I find I am about to make many enemies by endeavoring to serve my friends." He flatly refused Russell's request to transport a flock of merino sheep, a gift to the United States from the empress of France, and further angered Russell by sending back to him dozens of boxes of stuff that kept arriving. Running a ship of war and facing down a hostile enemy were fine, but even Hull's normally relentless optimism was being beaten down by these troubles from friends. "I have everything to trouble me: detained far beyond my calculation; fifty men on the sick list; constant bad weather; a cold and unpleasant passage to make, &c. &c. &c. &c. If I get home safe you need not calculate on seeing me soon on a voyage of this sort," he wrote home. It was a sign of his uncharacteristic mood that on December 19 he ordered two men flogged for sneaking rum aboard.

Not until January 9, 1812, did the ship weigh anchor at last; once again the crew was ready for action as they bore down on the British blockading squadron, but the swift forty-day voyage was uneventful, despite tempestuous weather, and the *Constitution* anchored at Lynnhaven Bay at 11:00 p.m. on February 19. She had been away six months.[55]

Standing in the roads when she arrived was the British frigate *Macedonian*, Captain John Surman Carden. The British warship had come in nine days earlier and was permitted into American waters upon her informing the collector of the port that she was carrying diplomatic dispatches.

CARDEN HAD last been to America thirty years before. His family belonged to the minor Anglo-Irish gentry that conspicuously filled the ranks of the British army and navy of the era. During the American Revolution, while still a very young boy, he had been commissioned an ensign in a loyalist regiment raised in South Carolina by his father, a British army major. Three months after Carden's arrival in America in 1781 his father and uncle were killed at the Battle of Guilford Courthouse; another uncle was wounded in the same battle, and Carden had been allowed to accompany him on "a long & tedious Journey" by litter and cart to Norfolk and then on a transport home to Ireland. Carden's mother died ten days after he returned, overcome with the news he and his uncle had carried with them. Yet Carden's view of America was not black and white despite this melancholy history; in his memoirs years later he referred to the "blind Injustice" by which the war against American independence had been commenced on Britain's part.[56]

Whatever apprehensions Carden entertained about setting foot on American soil again, though, were maliciously inflamed by the local pilot who brought the *Macedonian* in. He gravely assured Carden that he and his officers could not possibly pass through the country to Washington safely; they would be insulted every step of the way, and most likely injured or killed. But the British consul in Norfolk laughed off Carden's fears, assuring him in any event that there was no need to send an officer to Washington to carry his dispatches since the United States mails were completely trustworthy. Meanwhile, Stephen Decatur put on a fine show of chivalrously welcoming his visitor, and Carden was soon a regular guest at Decatur's dinner table. On one occasion the two captains had a friendly debate over the relative merits of the twenty-four-pound long guns on Decatur's frigate *United States* versus the eighteen-pounders that the *Macedonian* and other British frigates carried. Carden maintained that the Royal Navy's superior experience proved the smaller guns more than made up for their shorter range by the efficiency and speed with which their crews could handle and fire them.

But Carden's visit to Norfolk would not end on so pleasant or convivial a note. A few days after sending his dispatches to Augustus Foster in Washington, Carden told his dinner companions of his outrage at what had happened: Foster had just written back to say that the dispatches had been opened in public and their contents made known. Decatur and Littleton Waller Tazewell, a local lawyer and a close friend of Decatur's, were among the company, and the Americans said they were much concerned by this reflection "upon the integrity of our public officers, if not upon the government itself," and promised to look into the matter. Tazewell asked the Norfolk postmaster to write his counterpart in Washington to inquire what had happened. On February 26 a reply came back that put an entirely different light on the story.

In fact, no one had tampered with Carden's package; rather, when the parcel arrived in Washington along with a $39 charge for postage, Foster himself had gone to the post office and told the postmaster that he thought the large packet must contain just newspapers, which carried a much lower postage rate. The postmaster offered to let him open the package and see if that was the case. When Foster did, he and the postmaster found themselves staring at a huge sheaf of bills of exchange, hundreds of thousands of pounds' worth.

When the Washington postmaster's explanation arrived in Norfolk, Tazewell called on Carden that same day to give him the news, whereupon Carden abruptly blurted out, "Then the cat is out of the bag at last," adding after a short pause, "I shall lose £1,800 sterling by the blunder."

Tazewell found this mystifying, to say the least, but after several questions Carden revealed the whole thing. The "sealed dispatches" he was carrying had indeed consisted of nothing but £600,000 in government bills of exchange, which Foster was to have sold to U.S. banks for specie, and which the *Macedonian* was then to have carried to Lisbon. The £1,800 Carden ingenuously referred to was the customary "freight money" the captain of a man-of-war received as a fee for transporting specie. It was a huge windfall he had lost, about a decade's regular pay for a frigate captain.

It was also a distinctly unfriendly business, not to mention a violation of the diplomatic privilege that permitted British warships to continue entering American ports to carry dispatches. Tazewell wrote to Secretary of State Monroe the next day relating the whole incident, and adding that it appeared the British government had been carrying on this kind of business for some time: manipulating the American currency markets with rumors designed to drive up the exchange rate of the pound against the dollar and then quickly distributing British government bills to agents who would exchange them for gold at banks across the country at the temporarily higher rate. In part, the British were trying to offset a huge drain of specie from Lisbon to the United States that had resulted from keeping Wellington's army on the Iberian Peninsula fed; a flotilla of American grain ships was plying the trade under British licenses, and with nothing worth purchasing in Lisbon to carry back to America, the ship captains insisted on payment in cash. Yet coming just at a moment when Congress had approved Gallatin's plan to borrow $11 million to finance anticipated war expenses, this undercover British scheme to drain American capital markets of $3 million of cash in a single blow was clearly an act of economic warfare as well.[57]

No official action was taken against Carden, but he did not wait to find out; two days later the *Macedonian* weighed anchor and was gone.

SECRETARY HAMILTON was caught by surprise by the vehemence of the attacks in Congress on the navy's expansion plans, and after the rejection of the frigate bill in January 1812 he retreated into vacillation, accompanied by bouts of defeatism. In February he suggested to Madison that perhaps it might be better to do as Gallatin wanted and keep the entire small navy in port in the coming war, rather than risk losing it all—possibly in one throw—to the British. The rest of the cabinet appeared inclined to agree.

William Bainbridge and his fellow captain Charles Stewart were in Washington at the time and caught wind of what Hamilton was saying and at once wrote an impassioned remonstrance to the secretary. Not only would such an order have a "chilling and unhappy effect" on the spirit of the officers of the navy, they wrote, but it would imperil the entire future of the service: the people of the United States would never again "support the expense of a navy which had been thus pronounced useless during a time of national peril." Frigates and smaller ships of war sallying out singly would be able to "materially injure the commerce of the enemy"; it was at least worth trying.[58]

Madison thought his aggressive-minded captains had the better of the argument and, overruling Hamilton and the cabinet, agreed the navy had to be used. Suggesting perhaps a bit facetiously that given how small the American navy was it was not risking much, he told Hamilton, "It is victories we want; if you give us them and lose your ships afterwards, they can be replaced by others."[59]

But there remained the question of *how* the ships ought to be used, and faced with such a momentous decision, the secretary became almost paralyzed with self-doubt as the nation inched toward war. The demands of his office, his inexperience in naval affairs, the difficulties of living in the half-built capital city, and his rapidly unraveling personal affairs were all taking a toll. For the last year and a half he had been helplessly reading notices in the Charleston newspapers of forced sales of his slaves by his creditors. "Nothing short of ruin can be the consequence to me," he wrote his son-in-law upon reading of "another sale of 22 of my Negroes"; "I do not now expect that I shall be left a shelter for myself and family, or a Servant to hand them a cup of water." At one point he thought he might be sent to jail if his creditors demanded security, as he had none to offer; at another point he spoke of resigning his office as soon as he could, "for I am too deeply wounded to remain here with any degree of ease. I shall then . . . wholly retire from the world." In the spring of 1812 he lamented, "To me and mine this place is unhealthy, for we have not had a week since November last in which I could say that every one of us has been well. . . . generally, this city is not favorable to health—and I believe it is to be ascribed to the circumstance that the whole extent of it has been cleared of Trees calculated to afford shade, while not one thousandth part is covered by buildings."[60]

On May 21 he finally roused himself to send a short note to Rodgers and Decatur seeking their advice:

> As a war appears now inevitable, I request you to state to me, a plan of operations, which, in your judgment, will enable our little navy to annoy in the utmost extent, the Trade of Gt Britain while it least exposes it to the immense naval force of that Government. State also, the Ports of the US which you think the safest as assylums for our navy, in time of war.[61]

The two captains each replied in early June with their plans to "annoy" the enemy. Over the years many historians, following the lead of the late-nineteenth-century American naval strategist Alfred Thayer Mahan, would characterize their views as sharply diverging on fundamental strategy, Rodgers advocating operating the navy in a concentrated force while Decatur wanted ships to disperse in ones or twos. But in fact the two captains agreed much more than they disagreed. Both saw that the only way to overcome Great Britain's huge numerical advantage at sea was to divide the small American force and send it far and wide to attack British merchant shipping in a manner calculated to be "the most perplexing," as Rodgers put it, and so keep the British navy chasing in multiple directions after this hydra-headed annoyance.

Decatur argued that cruising in ones or twos played to American strengths and minimized the small navy's obvious weaknesses against the British:

> Two Frigates cruising together would not be so easily traced by an enemy as a greater number, their movements would be

infinitely more rapid, they would be sufficiently strong in most instances to attack a convoy, & the probability is that they would not meet with a superior cruising force; If however, they should meet with a superior force & cannot avoid it, we should not have to regret the whole of our marine crushed at one blow.

Rodgers similarly underscored the importance of splitting the American force. While "such dispersion" might seem counterintuitive, he wrote, it was in fact the most effective way to tie up a hugely disproportionate number of British warships. "It would require a comparatively much greater force to protect their own trade . . . than it would to annihilate ours," he told Hamilton. The Royal Navy would be so distracted swatting at this swarm of gnats that it would not be able to turn its might against American shipping and the American coast. Rodgers allowed that there might be limited circumstances when very slightly larger squadrons might come together, such as two or three frigates and a sloop of war to maraud against the English coast; but the only time he foresaw all the American frigates operating together in a single powerful force would be to stage a single strike against Britain's large East India convoys. He added with pugnacious relish that he was looking forward to playing the role of "Buccaneer"—a title, he observed, he had already been honored with by the British "in their lying naval chronicle."[62]

In fact, Rodgers was never the Mahanian proponent of unity of force that Mahan tried to make him out to be. Mahan was writing at a time when American navalists were trying to make the case for a large blue-water fleet, and a central tenet of Mahan's sea power theory was that a navy was most effective when structured to threaten the enemy's navy—and the best way to do that was to sail in powerful squadrons or fleets. Dispersion of force was by the same reasoning a fundamentally unsound military strategy. In his analysis of the War of 1812, Mahan insisted that had the American navy followed Rodgers's views on concentration of force—or rather what Mahan *said* were Rodgers's views—Britain would have been forced to keep her warships sailing in company for self-protection and so been unable to spread out along the American coast to prey on American commerce.[63]

But Rodgers and Decatur had a keener grasp of the hit-and-run strategy they needed to adopt, and the David-and-Goliath odds that dictated it. The fact was that in a fleet action even the whole American navy operating together would not stand a chance against a concentrated force of the vastly more powerful and vastly more experienced Royal Navy. Decatur pointed out that what mattered above all was to draw the British off, and distant cruising by small detachments was perfectly well suited to attaining that end. The effect, he told Hamilton, "would be to relieve our own coast by withdrawing from it a number of the hostile ships, or compelling the enemy to detach from Europe another force in search of us," and probably also drawing off the greater part of the British cruisers that were at the moment lying wait in Bermuda, ready to go pounce on American commerce with the start of hostilities.[64]

If America did have an advocate for the concentration of its naval force in June 1812 it was Albert Gallatin, but his ideas of naval strategy remained strictly defensive. Gallatin pointed with alarm to the revenues that stood to be lost if American merchant ships returning to port were captured after war was declared. He began urging that the frigates all be sent to sea off New York to protect them. "On the return of our frigates, keep them on our coast, which will best promote our commerce and prevent any but properly defensive engagements with enemy," Gallatin argued to Madison in a memorandum a few weeks later.[65]

For nearly two weeks Rodgers's and Decatur's letters sat on Secretary Hamilton's desk unanswered. But everything about the move toward war seemed enveloped in hesitation and uncertainty, if not outright confusion. Even many Republicans in Congress still confidently predicted that talk of war was merely saber rattling. As late as May, Augustus Foster reported that he was at a total loss as to what to make of the contradictory signals coming from various officials in Washington.

On June 1 Madison finally issued what was at last an unmistakable call for a declaration of war; in a secret message to Congress he reiterated America's long-standing grievances against Britain and asserted that British actions already constituted a state of war against America. But his timing in many ways could not have been more off. Throughout the spring, acting under new orders to avoid any clashes with the American navy, British warships had been staying well clear of the American coast. Rumors of impending British concessions arrived almost daily. In place of the war fever that had swept the nation in the wake of the *Leander* and the *Chesapeake–Leopard* incidents, the march to war, now that it was finally happening, was bloodless and even at times surreal, unimpelled by any immediate air of crisis.[66]

For the next two weeks Congress met in secret session to debate a declaration; still Hamilton delayed making a decision on deploying the navy. Finally, he took the temporizing step of ordering Decatur to sail for New York to join Rodgers and await further instructions there. Decatur left Norfolk on June 16, with the frigates *United States* and *Congress* and the brig *Argus*.

More days passed but still no orders came to put to sea. On June 20, two full days after Congress had passed and Madison had signed the declaration of war, Gallatin complained to Madison about Hamilton's incomprehensible dithering. The Treasury secretary calculated that a million to a million and a half dollars' worth of shipping a week would arrive from foreign ports for the next four weeks. Orders sending the combined American squadrons off the coast to protect these ships "ought to have been sent yesterday, & that at all events not one day longer ought to be lost."[67]

On Monday, June 22, after a cabinet meeting hastily called to render a decision on the matter, Hamilton sent an express rider galloping to New York with as confusing a set of orders as probably ever came from the pen of a military commander. Hamilton instructed Rodgers that the two squadrons should focus on protecting returning commerce, as Gallatin wished, but operate independently—Rodgers off the Chesapeake eastward, Decatur southward—not as a single large squadron, as earlier implied by the decision to send Decatur to New York. But the two squadrons could come together whenever the captains thought it "expedient"; on the other hand, when "a different arrangement may promise more success," they could detach their vessels "either singly, or two in company"; it also "may be well for all vessels occasionally to concentrate—& put into port, for further instructions," and to that end he would direct his letters to New York, Newport, Boston, "& sometimes Norfolk."

"May the God of battles be with you," the secretary concluded, "& with all our beloved Countrymen."[68]

It was all so contradictory and vague and confusing that perhaps it was just as well Rodgers never received it. On June 20 news of the declaration of war reached New York. The next day Rodgers put to sea with his combined squadrons, the large forty-four-gun frigates *President* and *United States,* the smaller thirty-six-gun frigate *Congress,* the eighteen-gun sloop *Hornet,* and the sixteen-gun *Argus.* He had his sights on a large convoy of 110 merchantmen reported to be sailing from Jamaica for

Britain. Left behind were the frigates *Essex* (in New York) and the *Constitution* (in Washington), both undergoing frantic last-minute repairs that were still expected to take a few more days.

As he waited through the ensuing days to learn the fate of the force under his care but now beyond his control, Hamilton wrote his son-in-law, "In our Navy Men I have the utmost confidence, that in equal combat they will be superior in the event, but when I reflect on the overwhelming force of our enemy my heart swells almost to bursting, and all the consolation I have is, that in falling they will fall nobly."[69]

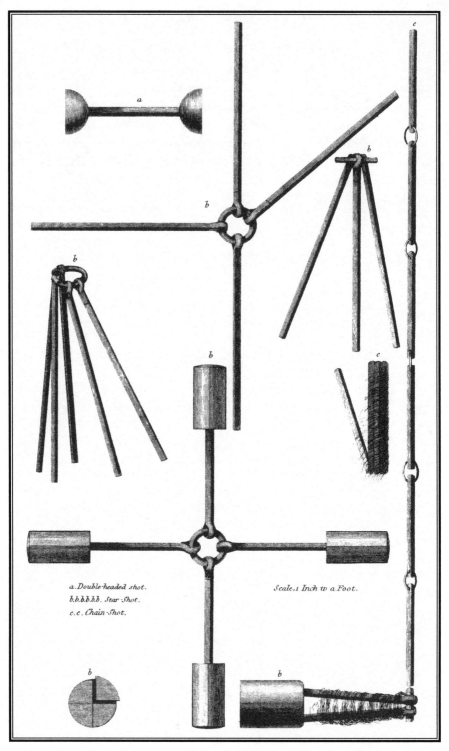

a. *Double-headed shot*.
b.b.b.b.b. *Star-Shot*.
c.c. *Chain-Shot*.

Scale, 1 Inch to a Foot.

American dismantling shot (James, *Full and Correct Account*)

CHAPTER 4

"The Present War, Unexpected, Unnecessary, and Ruinous"

EVEN A DECLARATION of war could not immediately persuade British officials that America was in earnest. Augustus Foster thought that 80 percent of Americans opposed the war and that the declaration was mostly bluff. Every single Federalist and 20 percent of the Republicans in Congress had voted against it; the 79–49 margin in the House and 19–13 in the Senate would forever remain the closest vote on a formal declaration of war in American history. On June 20 the British minister had gone to Monroe's office, and the two had "endeavoured to frighten one another for a whole Hour by descanting on the Consequences of War," Foster informed London.[1]

Since the spring of 1812 a powerful movement had been growing in Britain in favor of repeal of the orders in council, but it had almost everything to do with the effect the orders were having on the British economy and almost nothing to do with fear of war with America. The loss of the American trade as a result of the orders had been devastating. Seven thousand firms had failed; the production of textiles in Lancashire was down 40 percent; fifteen thousand paupers were receiving relief in Liverpool. So sharply had public feeling turned that when Spencer Perceval, the British prime minister who had been the chief architect of the orders, was assassinated by a deranged gunman on May 11 in the lobby of Parliament, the news triggered public rejoicing in Britain's industrial towns. A week later, huge crowds shouted "God bless you!" as Perceval's murderer was led to the gallows at Newgate. Repeal now seemed all but certain.

But even Henry Brougham, who led the repeal campaign in Parliament, ridiculed the idea that those seeking to abolish the orders were out to appease America. "Jealousy of America!" he mockingly exclaimed in the House of Commons. "I should as soon think of being jealous of the tradesmen who supply me with necessaries. Jealousy of America! . . . whose assembled navies could not lay siege to an English sloop of war!"[2] There was no sense of urgency as the question of repeal worked its way for the next month and a half through a special parliamentary committee that had been authorized to investigate the state of trade.

And so, with exquisite mistiming, Parliament found itself voting on June 23, five days after America's declaration of war, to repeal the orders in council that the United States had so bitterly resented for five long years.

Almost alone among the voices of the British establishment, the *Naval Chronicle* had been cautioning its readers for months not to underestimate American determination. "A large portion of the daily press of England has been engaged in promulgating errors with regard to America," the *Chronicle*'s editor asserted. "We have been persuaded to believe that our hostile system was useful, and that the American government had not the power, if it had the spirit, to resent provocations." These political miscalculations, he lamented, had now brought England to "war against the descendants of Englishmen . . . against the seat of political and religious freedom." Yet even now the same delusions were still at work: most British newspapers were confidently predicting that no real war would ever materialize, that as soon as word of the repeal of the orders in council reached Washington it would be over before it had ever begun. But, the *Chronicle*'s editor cautioned, "it is the people, and not merely the government of the United States, who have declared war." And the American people, he predicted, were not going to stop fighting now that they had begun until a treaty satisfying all their grievances was agreed to.[3]

In sweltering Philadelphia, where the shipping merchant and former Republican congressman William Jones had stayed through the summer to tend to his business while his family went to visit friends in the country, Jones noted that some Americans were making the same mistake—believing that forthcoming concessions by the British government would bring about a swift restoration of peace. Speculators had briefly driven up the prices of goods following the declaration of war. But, he wrote his wife, Eleanor, in early July, prices had been rapidly falling in the past few days on as yet unconfirmed rumors of the revocation of the orders in council. Jones contemptuously dismissed what he called "these coffee house politicians" who "think that the character, Independence and policy of this country hang upon the breath of a British Minister." The state of war, he told Eleanor, "has totally changed the political relations of the two countrys." Now that it had begun, the war could only be brought to an end by "an ample and final settlement of all sources of difference."[4]

On July 10 a British schooner arrived in Boston from Halifax under a flag of truce in an even more poignant piece of bad timing. The ship carried John Strachan and Daniel Martin, the two surviving crewmen taken from the *Chesapeake* five years earlier. The third of the *Chesapeake* seamen who had been imprisoned in Halifax, William Ware, had died in captivity in the interim.

At a ceremony the next day aboard the *Chesapeake* at Charlestown Navy Yard, the two men were formally returned under the settlement Foster had offered, and Madison had wordlessly accepted, the previous November. The commander of the British sloop came aboard, and an American lieutenant read a statement that Bainbridge, the ranking American naval officer in Boston, had prepared: "Sir I am commanded by Commodore Bainbridge to receive those two American Seamen on the *very* deck from which they were wantonly taken in time of Peace by a vessel of your Nation of Superior Force." On the quarterdeck Bainbridge then added a few of his own slightly graceless words to the two freed men. "My Lads, I am glad to see you. From this Deck you were taken by British outrage. For your return to it you owe gratitude to the Government of your Country. Your Country now offers you an opportunity to revenge your wrongs, and I cannot doubt but you will be desirous of doing so on board this *very* Ship." It apparently did not occur to Bainbridge that men just released from five years' imprisonment, some of that time spent with a sentence of five hundred lashes hanging over them, might want to see friends or family or old homes again upon returning to freedom and their native land, or for that matter might never want to see a ship or the sea again. But having invited the two men to show their gratitude by immediate reenlistment in the United States navy, he dismissed them from the quarterdeck and his mind, did not even mention them by name in his subsequent report to the secretary of the navy, and invited the British officer to lunch, which he accepted.[5]

Sails and wind

Sails carried in varying winds, strong to progressively light

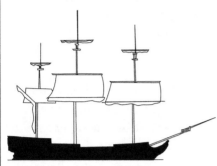

1 Reefed topsails, in strong winds

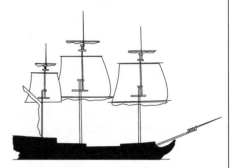

2 Topsails only, but without reefs

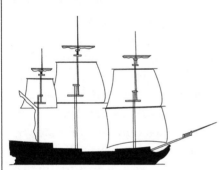

3 Foresail set

4 In fair weather: topgallants set

5 In squally weather: main course set

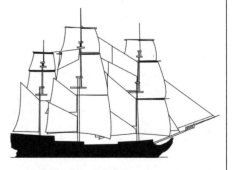

6 All sail set, in light breezes

. . .

Isaac Hull's orders were to get to New York as quickly as possible and report to Rodgers, but on the day war was declared, June 18, the *Constitution*'s crew had just begun the tedious ritual of moving a large warship down the shallow Potomac. At the Washington Navy Yard "Jumping Billy" Haraden had been on hand again to manage her repairs, and the work had proceeded at his usual breakneck pace. In two months the shipyard workers had hove her down to clean and patch her coppering, ripped out and replaced her decks, and shipped a new bowsprit and foremast. To answer Hull's complaints about her poor sailing, Haraden had overhauled her rigging and taken off a third of her ballast. Hull also wanted sky poles rigged to carry an extra set of sails above even the royal poles that topped the topgallants to get every ounce of thrust in light winds. The ship had been towed to Alexandria when the work at the yard was done. Then came the choreographed reloading of all her heavy fittings and stores over the course of several days as she made her way down the long looping fishhook of the river to deeper waters and the Chesapeake beyond: the lighters coming alongside and transferring iron shot and casks of provisions and the new battery of two dozen thirty-two-pounder carronades for the spar deck, a ton and a half apiece.[6]

At Annapolis, Hull shipped more men and stores and, after firing the eighteen-gun national salute (one for each state of the union) at noon on the Fourth of July, headed down the Chesapeake Bay the next day. He wrote a short note to his father, a farewell in case:

> My Ship is now underway from Annapolis and standing down to the Bay. you will ere long hear from me some where to the North[d] unless I fall in with superior force in that case you may Probably hear of my being in Halifax or Bermudas . . . Should anything happen [to] me I leave but little but it may be sufficient to make you comfortable during your stay in this Troublesome world.
>
> be pleased to make my love to all the Family and accept for them & your self my most fervent Prayers for your health & long life.
>
> your Son
> Isaac Hull[7]

The passage down the Chesapeake was constant drilling even as more men and supplies kept coming aboard. Though many of her crew had never served on a ship of war, "in a few days we shall have nothing to fear from any single-decked Ship," Hull promised Hamilton a few days before their departure. For the seven days it took to reach the Virginia capes, Hull had the crew at quarters nine times; 1,250 cartridges were filled for the guns, 7,000 for muskets and pistols; each day the gun crews blazed away at an anchored hogshead or other targets.[8]

On the twelfth they put off their Chesapeake pilot and stood for the sea. Hamilton's final instructions to Hull, written July 3, were again all caution: if Rodgers was not at New York upon his arrival, he was to remain there and await further orders. Hamilton added: "If, on your way thither, you should fall in with an enemy's vessel, you will be guided in your proceeding by your own judgment, bearing in mind, however, that you are not, voluntarily, to encounter a force superior to your own."

On their third day at sea, July 15, Hull ordered one of the new carronades tested by loading it with double charges and double shot and fired five times. "Found them to stand very well," he noted. That evening the ship spoke a merchant brig from New Orleans bound for Baltimore and warned her that war with England had been declared.[9]

At two o'clock the next afternoon the *Constitution* was off Egg Harbor, near present-day Atlantic City, when four ships were sighted far off to the north and inshore. Hull was uncertain whether they were Rodgers's squadron come south from New York to rendezvous with him or whether they were the enemy; the winds were now light from the northeast, and Hull ordered all sail made to close with the strange ships.

At four o'clock the lookout at the masthead hailed the deck: another ship was in sight off to the northeast, standing for them under all sail. The inshore ships were now visible only from the tops of the masts, and toward sunset the wind shifted around to the south, bringing the *Constitution* to the windward of the lone ship in the offing. Hull decided to head for her to get close enough at some point in the night, six or eight miles, to make a lantern signal and learn her identity. At 7:30 p.m. the crew went to quarters, and a half hour later Hull was standing on the forecastle staring ahead through the lowering twilight sky at the chase ahead, just off the starboard bow. He turned to the boatswain, one of a small group of officers and men who had, in the words of able seaman Moses Smith, "clustered respectfully around."

"Adams, what do you think of that vessel?" the captain asked.

"Don't know, sir. I can't make her out, sir. But I think she's an Englishman."

"So do I. How long do you think it will take to flog her, Adams?"

"Don't know sir! We can do it, but they're hard fellows on salt water."

"I know that. But don't you think we can flog them in two hours and a half, Adams?"

"Yes, sir! Yes, sir! we can do it in that time, if we can do it all."[10]

The *Constitution* closed slowly on the stranger for the next two hours. At 10:30 p.m. they were close enough to send up the private recognition signal; three-quarters of an hour later there was still no answer from the strange ship, and Hull ordered the lanterns hauled down. A quarter moon was just dipping below the horizon to the west. Hull ordered his ship at once to haul off into the wind, southward and eastward, and wait until morning. The stranger, by now almost certainly an English frigate, did the same, dogging their course about two miles off their lee side.

Through the night the men remained at quarters, the gun crews allowed to sleep by their battle stations, though there was little sleep to be had. "That night every man on board the *Constitution* was wide awake," said Moses Smith, who was on the crew of gun number 1, closest to the bow. Smith lay next to his gun, stretched out on the bare deck, his sponger and rammer at his side "ready for use at a moment's notice." At 4:00 a.m. the quiet of the sleepless night was broken by two signal guns being fired from the enemy ship and then a rocket arcing into the sky. And then the faint predawn light disclosed their companion of the night just within gunshot, still on their lee quarter. Directly astern, strung out in a line from six to ten miles behind, were a ship of the line, three frigates, a brig, and a schooner. All were flying English colors, and all were coming up very fast on a fine breeze that filled their sails.

The closest British frigate would turn out to be the *Guerriere*, whose captain, James R. Dacres, had become notorious for his zeal in pressing sailors out of merchantmen up and down the American coast. As Lieutenant Charles Morris was taking in the helplessness of the situation from the *Constitution*'s deck, he watched to his surprise as the *Guerriere* first tacked away, then apparently reversed her decision and wore around to her original course to continue in pursuit. The maneuver wasted ten minutes; it would later come out that Dacres's signals to the other British ships had gone unanswered, and he had momentarily feared he had stumbled into Rodgers's squadron instead of his own.[11]

Then the breeze began to fall away entirely from the *Constitution,* even as it perversely continued to favor the ships astern. As she lost even the two knots' steerageway needed for her helm to answer, she began to fall off helplessly from the wind, her head slowly turning toward her pursuers. Hull immediately ordered the ship's boats lowered to tow the ship's head around into the wind, directly southward, and with the men straining at the oars, they began to inch the ship forward. The *Guerriere* and two of the other British frigates, *Shannon* and *Belvidera,* did the same. On the *Constitution* two 24-pounder guns were run out through the stern windows of the captain's cabin while on the deck above carpenters quickly sawed through the taffrail to make openings for two more guns to fire straight aft; the bow chaser, the sole long gun mounted on the spar deck, was run aft while Moses Smith's twenty-four-pounder from the gun deck, all six thousand pounds, was hoisted up to join it. At 7:00 a.m., as Smith stood a few feet away, Hull himself took the match in his hand, ordered the quartermaster to hoist the American colors, and fired the first shot from the number 1 gun.

Neither *Constitution*'s shot nor the return fire that quickly came from the British frigates hit its mark, but it was clear that the American ship's situation was desperate. *Shannon,* the foremost of her pursuers, had nearly all the boats of the squadron now towing her while the men aboard the ship manned sweeps out the ports. "It soon appeared that we must be taken, and that our Escape was impossible . . . and not the least hope of a breeze to give us a chance of getting off by out sailing them," Hull recalled. He was ready to turn the ship broadside and make a last stand against the entire squadron when Morris recollected a technique he had frequently been obliged to perform as lieutenant on the *President*—owing "to the timidity of my old commander," who was reluctant to sail into and out of harbors. The technique, called kedging, involved rowing out an anchor ahead of the ship on a long line, dropping it, and then having the men haul in the line to propel the ship forward by brute force. Morris said they had been able to get speeds of three miles an hour this way. Hull immediately told him to try it— though not without adding, in Seaman Smith's recollection, "But I imagine you'll fail."

Kedging generally only worked in shallow water, and a sounding revealed they were in twenty-four fathoms, 144 feet, which was pushing their luck; but the launch and first cutter were immediately sent ahead with the anchor, and every piece of line five inches and upward was bent on, making nearly a half mile of cable. It was a superb piece of seamanship, the anchor tripped up as the ship passed over it while a second anchor had meanwhile been carried ahead on a second line. Soon the distance from their pursuers began to widen. When a small breeze sprang up, the *Guerriere* ranged up on the American's lee quarter and fired a broadside, but all the shot fell short, evoking a derisive cheer from the *Constitution*.

Aboard the *Shannon*, James Brown, an American merchant captain whose ship had been taken and burned a few days before, watched what was happening on the American frigate through a spyglass and realized at once what the crew was up to. The *Shannon*'s captain, Philip Broke, was the senior officer of the squadron, and he chatted confidently with his officers about the certainty that the *Constitution* would soon be theirs; Broke had even already appointed a prize officer and crew to man her. But Brown, now with equal confidence, announced to the British officers, "Gentlemen, you'll never take that frigate."[12] He kept the reason to himself, and it would be two hours before the British at last recognized, and tried to imitate, the "Yankee trick" that was beginning to unfold ahead.

All day the slow-motion chase continued to the southwest. At ten o'clock in the morning Hull sent men down to the hold to start two thousand gallons of water from the casks, ten tons let flooding into the hold and then pumped out, enough to raise the ship one inch out of the water.

A light wind played teasingly like a cat's paw from the southeast. Whenever it sprang up, the *Constitution* called in her boats, hauling them up on temporary tackles suspended from spars boomed out over the water, the men still in their places, leaning on their oars, "ready to act again at a moment's notice," said Morris. At two in the afternoon *Belvidera* was now leading the pack of pursuers, and the boats from all four British frigates and the ship of the line, eight or ten of them, converged on her, towing to get her to windward and in range to fire a few crippling shots that would halt their quarry while the rest of the squadron came up. The ships exchanged shots with their chasers, the four stern guns on *Constitution* firing back at maximum range. From the deck, the *Constitution*'s surgeon, Amos Evans, was watching

Belvidera through a spyglass when he saw one of the *Constitution*'s all-but-spent shot come aboard and scatter a group of officers crowded on the forecastle.

All through the night the chase went on. The first half of the night the boats were out again, kedging and towing, four more hours of back-breaking work.

Dawn of the eighteenth came to reveal the *Belvidera* on *Constitution*'s lee bow, *Guerriere* and *Shannon* nearly abeam, and the smallest of the frigates, the thirty-two-gun *Aeolus,* to the eastward, on her weather quarter. The ship of line, brig, and schooner followed two miles astern. The winds were now steady though still light, and at around four in the morning *Belvidera* tacked eastward on a course that would intercept the *Constitution*'s current course in less than an hour. Hull's choice was to let that happen or tack and risk the fire from *Aeolus,* and as the lesser of the evils Hull tacked. *Aeolus* hauled as close to the wind as she could to try to outreach *Constitution* and cut off her escape. It was now a slow-motion race to see which would cross the other's track first. For the next half hour the bearings of the enemy ships on each side of *Constitution*'s deck slowly edged aft. As the *Constitution* slipped past the *Aeolus,* the two ships passing on their opposite tacks just within gunshot, *Aeolus* did nothing—perhaps, said Hull, out of fear that firing her guns would stun her wind and becalm her in the light breeze—and the *Constitution* weathered her, the British ship tacking in her wake to follow.

Now all of the *Constitution*'s pursuers were astern or on her lee quarter, and it was a pure sailing match. In another tour de force of seamanship, the launch and first cutter were hoisted on board while the ship was under way, not pausing a second, "with so little loss of time or change of sails that our watching enemies could not conceive what disposition was made of them," according to an account Morris later heard from an American lieutenant who was a prisoner in the British squadron and saw it all. The skysails Hull had specially requested were now set, the pumps were at work spraying jets of sea water through the fire hoses to keep the sails wetted and drawn tight, and all the efforts put into improving the *Constitution*'s trim and sailing abilities now told. At nine in the morning an American merchant ship appeared on *Constitution*'s weather beam, and immediately the nearest British frigate hoisted American colors to decoy her in; Hull responded with the perfectly matched ruse de guerre of hoisting British colors, and the merchantman hauled wind and quickly made her escape. By noon the *Constitution* was making ten knots in the freshening breeze, by two o'clock twelve and a half knots, with the wind abeam. "Our hopes began to overcome apprehension," said Morris. A squall tore through at six in the evening, and when it passed, the *Constitution* had gained a mile; she was now eight miles ahead.

Another night passed with the men and officers still at quarters. At dawn the next day only three of the British ships could be seen from the masthead, the nearest twelve miles off. All hands were again set to manning the pumps and wetting the sails, and at 8:15 a.m. the lead British ship hauled her wind to the northward and gave over the chase. In a few minutes all were out of sight. The men of the *Constitution* had been at quarters for sixty hours straight.

The next day Captain Hull sat down in his cabin to write Secretary Hamilton a long explanation of why he regretfully could no longer obey his orders for New York, concluding:

> . . . the Enemy's Squadron stationed off New York, which would make it impossible for the Ship to get in there, I determined to make for Boston to receive your further orders, and I hope that my having done so will meet with your approbation. My wish to explain to you as clearly as possible, why your orders have not been executed, and the length of time the Enemy were in chase of us with various other circumstances, has caused me to make this communication much longer than I would have wished, yet I cannot (in justice to our brave Officers, and crew under my Command) close it without expressing to you the confidence I have in them, and assuring you that their conduct whilst under the Guns of the Enemy was such as might have been expected from American Officers and Seamen.
>
> I have the Honour to be &c. Isaac Hull[13]

THE UNITED States frigate *Constitution* made her way against a contrary wind, beating up tack on tack for Boston lighthouse. The night had been cold, foggy, and wet, but it was now a clear, bright Sunday morning, the twenty-sixth of July, and from her deck surgeon Amos Evans noted with pleasure the "very romantic and picturesque" country surrounding the bay: round smooth hills, small villages, neat farms. In the distance the church steeples of Boston and the dome of the statehouse marked their destination.

The next day Evans went into town; the ship's purser had gone ahead in the pilot boat to arrange for provisions, and news of the *Constitution*'s safe arrival had already spread like wildfire. "The people of Boston with whom the Constitution and her Commander are both favorites, appear overjoy^d at our arrival, as they had confidently expected we were taken by the British squadron," Evans wrote in his journal that day. "So confident were the people of this place that we had been taken and carried to Halifax that a friend of one of our officers had forwarded letters of credit for him to that place. . . . They cheered Capt. Hull as he pass^d up State Street about 12 o'clock."

The surgeon hired a hack and toured Harvard College and Bunker Hill and thought the two-story frame farmhouses in the countryside handsomely painted and nicely planted with gardens and English walnuts and poplars, and the females of Boston he passed on the streets "rosy and healthy, and their countenances, features, sprightly and animated," though with "more *mind* and less *grace*" than the southern ladies of his native Cecil County, Maryland, on the upper Chesapeake.[14] He established himself for a few days at the Exchange Coffee House, which was the wonder of America. Built in 1808 at the fantastic cost of a half million dollars, it was the largest commercial building in the nation, seven stories tall, surmounted by a thirty-foot-wide dome that offered a commanding view of arriving shipping in the harbor. "I slept last night in the room No. 190 something," Evans remarked in wonderment at the hotel's size. Its ambitious proprietors had devoted the entire first story to an exchange floor, but the Boston merchants insisted on keeping their customary habit of meeting outside on the sidewalks of State Street from noon to two each day to transact their business, even in winter. The Coffee House also let space to Topliff's News Room, which was always jammed; it was furnished with all the latest foreign and American papers, and its famous register books recorded the shipping news and other events of interest and served as a sort of local commercial and topical bulletin board.[15] Hull handed in a message he asked to be placed on the books:

> Capt. HULL, finding his friends in Boston are correctly informed
> of his situation when chased by the British squadron off New
> York, and that they are good enough to give him more credit for
> having escaped them than he ought to claim, takes this
> opportunity of requesting them to make a transfer of a great part
> of their good wishes to Lt. MORRIS, and the other brave
> Officers, and the Crew under his command, for their very great

exertions and prompt attention to orders while the enemy were in chase. Capt. HULL has great pleasure in saying, that notwithstanding the length of the chase, and the officers and crew being deprived of sleep, and allowed but little refreshment during the time, not a murmur was heard to escape them.[16]

Surgeon Evans filled a couple of mornings browsing the bookstores, "of which there are a great number in this place. In all of them I found plenty of sermons in pamphlet form, & pieces against 'Maddison's ruinous war,' as they call it." The sight of several old fortifications around the city dating from the Revolution sent him into a gloomy reverie.

Will the United States receive any assistance from the eastern states in the prosecution of the present war? Judging from present symptoms, I fear not. Good God! Is it possible that the people of the U.S. enjoying the blessings of freedom under the only republican government on earth, have not virtue enough to support it! Well might Horace say—'all men are mad.'[17]

BOSTON CHEERED Isaac Hull, but there were few cheers for the war. Not without justice, New Englanders saw themselves as bearing almost the entire economic brunt of a war they had opposed. "Time *was* (and might still *be* had we had a correct administration) when our ports were thronged with shipping, giving full employ to the merchants, mechanic and laborer—exchanging the products of our country for the commodities of every section of the navigable world," declared Boston's *Columbian Centinel* on the same day it published Captain Hull's generous praise of his crew from the Exchange Coffee House books, and then continued in verse:

Yes—time *was*—but *that* time hath fled. . . .
Sad, on the ground, all ranks and callings bend
Their alter'd looks—and evil days portend—
And fold their arms, and watch with anxious stand,
The tempest blackening o'er their sinking land![18]

The printed sermons that filled Boston's bookstores were not content with scraps of doggerel to make their point: they shook with all the moral certainty of the New England Puritan church to denounce the war as an abomination, a reckless and wicked adventure, a transgression against the will of God. At Boston's Second Church, where Increase Mather and Cotton Mather had preached a century before, pastor John Lathrop ascended his pulpit on Thursday, July 23, to deliver a sermon with the title "The Present War Unexpected, Unnecessary, and Ruinous." War, said Dr. Lathrop, is one of the great evils under which the sinful children of men have been doomed to suffer. "When the chief ruler of a nation signs a declaration of war, he . . . signs the death warrant of thousands of his fellow creatures. The business of war is the business of destruction." Yes, there might be times when to retain their liberty a people would be justified in the eyes of God in resorting to war, even a people as unprepared for war as Americans were now, even when fighting an enemy "much stronger, and much better provided." Yet no such circumstances attended the present case. The very divisions of the country proved that there was no such inescapable urgency to righting the wrongs America had recently endured— endured as a result of actions by both Britain *and* France, he noted. "Good rulers will not suffer war to be proclaimed until every possible method be attempted to bring an offending nation to make satisfaction; because, when war is commenced, no mortal can tell *when* or how it will end," Lathrop warned.

He added: "Our republick, I fear is corrupted; it is awfully divided, and if no means can be devised to heal the division, we need not the spirit of prophecy to predict its ruin."[19]

Many Republicans had optimistically believed that the coming of war would unite the country, or at least silence opposition, but precisely the reverse had happened in the weeks since the declaration on June 18. The Massachusetts House passed a resolution calling it an act of "inconceivable folly and desperation."[20] Within days of the declaration, the Federalists in Congress came together to issue a widely publicized address reiterating their attack on the Republican war policies. "It cannot be concealed, that to engage in the present war against England is to place ourselves on the side of France, and expose us to the vassalage of States serving under the banners of the French Emperor," they said. And, they asked again, "How will war upon the land protect commerce on the oceans?"[21]

Republican efforts to paint opposition to the war as unpatriotic or even treasonable created an instant backlash that only inflamed opposition all the more. Federalists in the House denounced the tactics employed by the Republican majority to silence dissent—secret sessions, refusal to consider motions offered by the minority, calling the previous question to cut off debate—as an attack on representative government and liberty.[22] When Republican newspapers printed none-too-veiled threats of violence against "tories" and "traitors" and warned, "Whoever is not for us, is against us," the *Boston Gazette* retorted: "Agreed, if you say so. The States of New-York and New-England are against you . . . and the opposition to you will increase through every stage of your madness."[23]

More ominously, even respected Republican political leaders began coyly referring to mob violence as the right way to deal with "signs of treason" from the opposition. Robert Wright, a Republican congressman from Maryland and former governor of the state, declared on the floor of the House that the proper remedy for traitors was "hemp and confiscation"—hanging and loss of property. Jefferson wrote to Madison a week after the declaration of war, "the federalists indeed are open mouthed against the declaration. but they are poor devils here, not worthy of notice. a barrel of tar to each state South of the Potomac will keep all in order & that will be freely contributed without troubling government. to the North they will give you more trouble. you may there have to apply the rougher drastics of Gov. Wright."[24]

Sarcastic blasts from the leading Federalist newspaper in the South, Baltimore's *Federal Republican,* had long infuriated local Republicans; they referred to it as "His Majesty's paper." With the coming of war there was talk around town that unless the paper changed its "obnoxious" tone, some of the local toughs were going to put them out of business. Toughs were one thing Baltimore had in abundance. The youngest and fastest growing of the cities on the East Coast, it had a large Irish and French population, a shortage of females, a history of political street brawls, and a good many taverns and beer gardens.

Two days after the declaration of war, the *Federal Republican* vowed it would employ "every constitutional argument and every legal means" to oppose the war. Two nights after that, a mob of several hundred laborers from Fell's Point, the notoriously rough end of town, marched to the newspaper's offices, pulled down the building, and destroyed the printing press and everything else inside.[25]

A month later the undaunted editors leased a new building on Charles Street. In preparation for a renewed sarcastic assault on

Republican war policies, one of the paper's engravers had produced an "excellent caricature of a democratic officer, making 'A Rapid Descent upon Canada,' mounted on a terrapin."[26]

On July 27 the paper came out with a defiant edition heaping scorn on the "rabble" that had attacked their previous offices. Early that evening a mob of boys began throwing stones at the paper's new building, and they were soon joined by a crowd of laborers that by morning reached two thousand. At one point in the night the editor of the rival *Baltimore Sun* had appeared along with a cannon that some men had dragged to the scene and, said one witness, "appeared almost deranged" as he urged the men to fire it. Only the hesitant intervention of a militia officer stopped that.

Among the defenders of the newspaper's building was General Henry "Light-Horse Harry" Lee, a Revolutionary War hero and stalwart Federalist, in town from his native Virginia to arrange for publication of his war memoirs. The mayor and other town officials finally arrived at dawn and urged the Federalists to surrender to protective custody with the promise that they and the newspaper building would be protected. Lee accepted. The mob immediately destroyed the newspaper offices as they left.

That night the mob returned, stormed the jail, and beat and tortured Lee and the others, dripping hot candle wax in their eyes and stabbing them with penknives to see if they were still alive, leaving most of them for dead in a heap in front of the jail. General James M. Lingan, an elderly veteran of the Revolutionary War, was killed, stabbed in the chest after his pleas for mercy were ignored. Lee never recovered from his injuries; his face was swollen for months afterward, his speech halting the rest of his life, and he died an invalid six years later. Another of the mob's victims, John Thomson, was stripped, tarred and feathered, and dumped in a cart; one of the mob tried to gouge out his eyes, and another tried to break his legs with an iron bar; another threw some flaming tar and feathers on him, and he was severely burned; then they threatened to hang him if he did not give them the names of everyone in the house who had tried to defend it against the attack.

The newspaper's editor survived and, setting up offices in Georgetown in the District of Columbia, published an edition on August 3 and sent it to Baltimore by mail, setting off a third riot when a mob tried to storm the post office to seize the papers. The Baltimore postmaster sent an express rider to Washington with an urgent plea for assistance; President Madison replied that he did not think "any defensive measures were within the Executive sphere."

But support poured in from Federalists around the country. To keep the paper going, hundreds of new subscribers signed up from as far away as Boston, $2,000 was raised within a few months, and the *Federal Republican* continued its thrice-weekly invectives against the folly of Mr. Madison, the incompetence of his generals, and the imbecility of his policies.[27]

ONE NEW Englander and Federalist who did support the war was old John Adams, the cantankerous second president of the United States, who had seen his proposals for a strong navy rejected again and again but who saw war with Britain as inevitable and the cause as just. A Federalist who supported the war and a war supporter who supported the navy, he was an odd man out in every sphere. But even Adams despaired of the impossible odds America faced against the Royal Navy. "Our navy is so Lilliputian," the former president wrote his grandson John Adams Smith a few days before the declaration of war, ". . . that Gulliver might bury it in the deep by making water on it."[28]

The Royal Navy was the size of all the rest of the world's navies combined.[29] From the majestic Admiralty building in Whitehall—the nerve center of the Royal Navy where the Lords Commissioners of the Admiralty met every day, Sundays and Christmas included, surrounded by maps and charts of all the world's seas, linked to the dockyards and anchorages by a semaphore telegraph on the roof that relayed reports and orders—a vast bureaucratic network of administration, training, supply, and repair spread out across the globe. Just feeding its seamen cost Britain about $10 million a year, five times what America spent on its navy in total. Victualing yards at Deptford, Plymouth, and Portsmouth employed three thousand men to bake biscuits, brew beer, and put up salt meat to keep the fleet fed; the bakehouse in Portsmouth produced ten thousand pounds of biscuits a day, and at Plymouth's warehouses three million pounds of them were stacked up in wooden casks.[30]

By 1812 the Royal Navy was an institution as well as a fighting force; it had 187 admirals, 777 captains, 586 commanders, 3,100 lieutenants, and all the corruption and inefficiency of a long-established government organization with favors and spoils to dispense.[31] Samuel Pepys, who would later be far better remembered for his remarkable private diary of life in Stuart England than for his attempts at reforming the navy, had done what he could; as secretary to the Admiralty Board in the 1670s and 1680s, he had tried to ensure that officers were selected for promotion at least partly on merit, that they knew something about ships and the sea and not merely influential and powerful personages.

But becoming an officer in the Royal Navy in the first place was almost entirely a matter of having the right connections. Captains of each ship appointed their own retinues of "young gentlemen" as captain's servants and midshipmen, who then rose through the ranks. Pepys managed to loosen the grip of patronage a bit by giving the Admiralty the power to directly appoint a few midshipmen whom the captains were then forced to take on board, but mainly he sought to exert control with regulations that established professional requirements for promotion to the rank of lieutenant. Under Pepys's reforms, a candidate for lieutenant had to be at least twenty years of age and have served at least three actual years at sea, at least one of those as a midshipman; pass an oral examination in navigation, seamanship, and command of a warship; present certificates from his previous commander attesting to his sobriety, diligence, and ability; and produce his logbooks as proof he had done the required service and knew how to take navigational observations and keep competent records.

The reforms were aimed not only at limiting influence and patronage but also at addressing an old problem that the Royal Navy had never quite known how to deal with. As Pepys put it, a gentleman was not a seaman and a seaman was not a gentleman. Almost nobody questioned the idea that an officer had to be a gentleman: only members of the gentlemanly classes possessed the natural courage, leadership, and sense of honor that military command required. The problem was that commanding a ship also required the mastery of manual skills that were equally universally held to be demeaning to a gentleman. Under Pepys's system, the rank of midshipman was meant to be the key bridge between these two worlds; it was a formal stage of apprenticeship, which ensured that even the most gentlemanly future officers had spent some time getting their hands dirty, learning the ropes, and climbing the tops before actually assuming full command responsibility for a ship of war.[32]

But none of this could compete with the old power of influence. While a few "tarpaulin" captains did rise on sheer ability from the lower classes and the lower decks thanks to Pepys's rules, and while the

Admiralty always would look favorably on promotion for an officer who had distinguished himself heroically in battle, family and political patronage remained deeply ingrained in the system.[33] There were all kinds of ways around the rules, and by the early 1800s the ways around them were so much the norm that few naval officers gave them a second thought. Admirals on station were allowed to commission their own candidates as lieutenants or commanders to fill vacancies, and could always stall if subsequently overruled by the Admiralty. A prominent politician or peer might exert his influence directly with the Admiralty on behalf of a relative or protégé. One young man whose father was a minor government official with many useful connections was taken aside at age fourteen by one of his father's noble friends, who told him, "When there is a general naval promotion, I am always allowed to provide for one friend, to get him made either a lieutenant, a commander or a post captain. Therefore, when your time is up, let me know and you shall be my lieutenant. In short, you are as sure of the commission as if you had it in your pocket."[34]

But most of all there was a constant trade of mutual backscratching among old navy families. To get around the rule of three years' service for promotion to lieutenant (subsequently increased to six), it was routine for captains to enter a friend's son or nephew on their ship's books without his having served at all. A crown piece handed to the Navy Office porter on the way in to the lieutenant's examination ensured that the age requirement would be ignored as well, which in the early 1800s resulted in many eighteen-, seventeen-, and even sixteen-year-old lieutenants (there was even one thirteen-year-old).

Three captains were required to conduct the examination for lieutenants, and some took the job seriously enough to prepare lists of questions they intended to ask covering an array of technical knowledge about seamanship, fitting and rigging a ship, and naval warfare. But for favored candidates the fix was always in. "Well, well, a very creditable examination," one new lieutenant was told by his examiner, a friend of the boy's two naval uncles. He had not been asked any questions at all, and when one of the other examiners, who had just walked in the door at this point, tried to ask one, the first captain cut him off, humorously threatened to have him arrested for showing up late, and turning to the successful candidate said, "*That* is not the way to pass, to linger there when you are told you will do!" "So out I bolted like a hunted rat," the boy recalled.[35]

Those who tried to buck the old system found it nearly impossible. Admiral Lord Collingwood, who as Horatio Nelson's second in command at Trafalgar in 1805 commanded one of the two British lines of battle that smashed the French fleet, was asked the following year by a fellow admiral to make a protégé of his a lieutenant. "He is 18 years old and as dull a lad as I ever saw," Collingwood privately observed. "It is this kind of person that causes all the accidents, the loss of ships, the dreadful expense of them, mutinies, insubordination and everything bad. . . . If the Country is to depend on the Navy, it must be reformed and weeded, for a great deal of bad stuff has got into it, and hangs like a deadweight where all should be activity." Collingwood was by then a national hero, made a baron and granted a £2,000-a-year pension by Parliament for the victory at Trafalgar; still he could not turn down an old friend and patron to whom he felt he owed a favor: "My conscience reproved me when I promoted him, which I made two or three attempts to do before I could bring myself to do it. Nothing but it's being Adml. R's request could have induced me."[36]

Since 1793 the Royal Navy in its encounters with the French had lost 10 ships to the enemy's 377, which spread a layer of complacency over any deficiencies in its commanders. Nelson made a point of playing to Britain's heroic image of herself in the tactics he pursued, and the image and results had reinforced one another: there was little finesse and a lot of bloodshed in the way the British took on their opponents at sea. Most battles of the Royal Navy were fought at extremely close range, where there was little choice but to kill or be killed and where seamanship and accurate gunfire mattered far less. The French, having guillotined most of their corps of professional sailors during the Revolution, took a similar view that zeal could substitute for skill and so were largely willing to fight on the same terms. The mayhem reached its zenith in the occasional but absolutely brutal boarding actions, which were hand-to-hand combat on a confined battlefield with no escape. Pistols, cutlasses, long-poled pikes, even fire axes, crowbars, clublike wooden belaying pins, and other tools at hand were used as weapons in what were basically free-for-alls for control of the ship. Casualties in single-ship engagements were known to reach the hundreds, and the bloodiness of such actions was spurred all the more by the Admiralty's practice of judging the worth of a captain's action by how many of his own crew were killed or wounded. On more than one occasion, an officer's claim for promotion for victory in battle was turned down on the grounds that his "butcher's bill" was not long enough.

The lopsided casualty figures in most of the Royal Navy's encounters with the French were largely due to the fact that the French sought to disable and capture their enemy's ships, while the British sought to kill and maim as many of their opponents as they possibly could. French crews were taught to fire as the ship began its up roll, and they tended to shoot high to disable spars, masts, and rigging. British crews fired on the down roll, straight into the hull. While enough shots low to the waterline could eventually sink a ship, that was not the purpose: it was to send cannonballs crashing directly into the gun crews of the ship lying a dozen yards away. In fourteen major engagements between 1794 and 1806, French losses totaled twenty-three thousand killed and wounded versus seven thousand for the British. One in four British casualties was fatal: more than half of the French sailors' were.[37]

The enthusiastic British adoption of the carronade added to the destructive effects of the British blood-and-guts approach to naval warfare. Developed by the Carron Company of Scotland in 1776, these were short-barreled, thinly molded guns that weighed about half as much as a long gun of the same caliber and could accordingly fire a much larger round for their weight. Carronades had an effective range of only about four hundred yards, a third that of long guns, but at those short ranges they were appallingly effective: the British called them "smashers," and placed on the upper deck of a frigate that could normally support only a twelve-pounder or smaller long gun, carronades sent their twenty-four- or thirty-two-pound balls hurtling forth to do horrific execution. The force of a shock wave from a large cannonball passing inches away was said to be able to kill a man, but what multiplied the destructive radius of each six-inch-diameter carronade ball many times over was the avalanche of jagged oak "splinters" unleashed when it crashed into a ship's planking or frames; "splinters" was a bit of bravura understatement, since they were often several feet long and weighed several pounds, with edges as sharp as a battle lance.

So confident of its success, or perhaps complacent, had the Royal Navy become that gunnery practice came to be officially discouraged as a needless waste of shot and powder: a thirty-eight-gun frigate like the *Guerriere* was allowed to fire a total of seven practice rounds a month in its first six months at sea and ten a month thereafter. In 1801, when Nelson was shown a proposal for a gun sight to improve the accuracy of fire, he dismissed it, saying, "The best and only mode I have found of hitting the enemy afloat is to get so close that whether the gun is pointed upwards or downwards forward or aft . . . it must strike its opponent."[38]

By 1812 an aura of invincibility suffused the Royal Navy, bedazzling the British public and naval commanders alike. Neither skill in seamanship nor skill in gunnery was necessary—just pluck, dash, courage, and British moral superiority.

IF THERE was one advantage to being as small as the American navy of the first decade of the 1800s, it was that its secretary could become acquainted with the merits of every officer, and possessed the authority to act on that knowledge. The result was that the American navy, as young and inexperienced and untested as it was, quickly attained a level of professionalism that probably surpassed any navy's in the world.

Robert Smith had in many ways been a lackluster secretary of the navy for the eight years he served in the post under Jefferson. He was a frankly political selection made after Jefferson acknowledged that he was seeking "what cannot be obtained . . . a prominent officer equal and willing to undertake the necessary duties." No one with expertise in naval matters was interested in presiding over the Jeffersonian program of retrenchment, and Smith's major qualifications were a willingness to oblige his colleagues and being the brother of an important Republican senator from Maryland whose support Jefferson needed.[39]

But Smith had proved a quietly steady force for improving the standards of the officer corps throughout his tenure. His office files were filled with copies of letter after letter to parents, congressmen, senators, even the president himself, steadfastly declining their entreaties to promote officers who Smith felt were not yet qualified. "A lieutenant having the charge of a watch is often entrusted with the entire command of the vessel—hence that absolute necessity of his being an experienced seaman," Smith wrote one would-be benefactor of a midshipman seeking promotion. "The meritorious midshipmen must rise agreeably to their rank. This is a principle which I shall invariably adhere to," he told another. When President Jefferson sought the promotion of a midshipman who had served only two years, Smith answered, "He cannot possibly have acquired in this short time that knowledge of seamanship which would justify the placing him in a situation where a public vessel, with the lives of all on board, might depend upon his skill as a seaman."[40]

Smith thought it took a minimum of four or five years of actual service at sea for a midshipman to gain the required experience, but he also made clear that he would weigh promotions to lieutenant, and all higher ranks as well, on the basis of merit as well as seniority. He routinely asked captains to submit brief evaluations of their officers at the end of a cruise, and received apparently frank responses:

> Lieut. Gordon, an excellent officer
> Lieut. Jacobs, a good officer but unaccommodating
> Doctr. Taylor, an excellent surgeon
> Doctr. Kearney, his mate, worthless and indolent
> Mr. Garretson, purser of the first rate
> [Midshipmen]
> Edward Nicholson, well disposed but dull and inactive
> Hazard, a smart young officer
> Travis, middling
> Rice, unfit for naval service[41]

Most naval officers would have been content with a system of promotion strictly by seniority and frequently complained about being passed over, but Smith and his successors were stonily unmoved by these appeals and regularly passed over dozens of officers in the same rank with greater seniority when selecting officers for promotion. Experience, Smith explained to one aggrieved midshipman, was not just a matter of serving time but of embracing the opportunities that had been provided him; his failure to acquire professional knowledge during that time was "unfortunate" but "attributable entirely to himself."[42]

"If seniority of date was the absolute rule, the task would be very simple and less irksome to the secretary," acknowledged one of Smith's successors a few years later. "But it never has been—*it never ought to be*—except where merit and knowledge are equal in the candidates." Promotion on the basis of seniority alone, he said, "I pray may never become the absolute rule; for I should, from thence, date the decline of our infant naval Hercules":

> . . . genius, valor, talent, and skill would be leveled to the dull
> equality of the humblest pretensions; and, instead of those
> brilliant feats which adorn our annals, every commonplace
> automaton who performed the ordinary acts of duty with
> sufficient prudence to avoid court martials would rise, by the

mere lapse of time and the casualties of mortality, to the highest honors of his profession.[43]

The constitutional requirement that military and naval commissions be confirmed by the Senate gave the whole promotion process in the American navy an openness and a gravity that served as a check on the kind of winking regulation-bending and favoritism so rampant in the Royal Navy at the time. Since the Quasi War, when some lieutenants had been appointed directly to meet the sudden need for experienced officers, all new officers entering the American navy had begun as midshipmen. Though not subject to Senate approval, even midshipmen were all appointed directly by the secretary; an equivalent policy would be adopted in Britain only in 1815.

There was no formal application process, but there were always many more candidates than openings, and Smith on several occasions showed he was looking for young men of good character, ambition, and zeal, regardless of their social or economic standing. Most were distinctly middle class, sons of master craftsmen or small merchants seeking a career to support themselves. "They are poor; their characters are good; it is from this class of society that we are to expect to find the real defenders of our country," wrote the mayor of Annapolis in recommending two brothers from his town for midshipmen's warrants.[44] To the extent politics intruded in the selection of midshipmen, it was largely confined to ensuring that all the states were fairly represented in reasonable proportions.

The emphasis on making sure midshipmen mastered seamanship was an incessant theme in the American navy of the early 1800s. Thomas Truxtun, who was captain of the frigate *Constellation* in the Quasi War, set down his views on the subject in 1794. He was still enough of a product of the American navy's British heritage—and the aristocratically tinged, antirepublican Federalist political leanings of so many American navy officers—that he felt he needed to warn midshipmen against the moral "contagion" they were liable to fall victim to when associating with common sailors, especially while learning to extend or reduce sails in the tops. But he nonetheless stressed that seeing things from the seaman's vantage was as vital a lesson as the practical skills of seamanship acquired in the process. "The midshipman who associates with these sailors in the tops till he has acquired a competent skill . . . will be often entertained with a number of scurrilous jests at the expense of his superiors," Truxtun said, especially the sailors' mercilessly deadpan practice of showing up a less than fully competent officer by "punctual obedience" to his incorrect commands. The real lesson from this for the young officer-to-be was that to "prevent him from appearing in the same despicable point of view" he had better become a thoroughgoing seaman himself: nothing less would command true respect from the crew.[45]

There were plenty of American captains who resorted to brutal floggings to maintain control over their men, meting out sentences of dozens of lashes at a time through the legal fiction of dividing a single infraction into multiple offenses (such as drunkenness, neglect of duty, and insolence) in order to get around the regulation, copied from the Royal Navy, that limited punishment on captain's authority to a dozen lashes; but there were also more than a few who embraced Truxtun's much more enlightened view that authority was more effectively maintained by example and an easy air of command than by flaying a man's bare back into ribbons of flesh. "Consider men in an inferior station as your fellow creatures . . . always remembering that rigid discipline and good order are very different from tyranny," Truxtun advised his midshipmen. "Good order can be maintained without much whipping on shipboard; and I can assure you that the worst-disciplined ships I ever saw in our or the British navy was those renowned for severe punishment."[46]

An American man-of-war was no less a ranked society than was any navy's in the world, but the moral distance between officers and men was closer on many scores—a difference that on repeated occasions would prove a hidden strength in the fighting ability of the American navy. Half the men on a typical British warship of the year 1812 had been impressed, and another eighth were the none-too-voluntary "volunteers" who had chosen service in the navy over rotting away in the county jail or worse; in all, probably only a quarter of the crew of a British ship were there in any sense of their own free will. The "quota men" delivered up from the county jails were said to be the worst of them all, demoralizing the rest of the crew with their shirking and thieving, breeding seething resentments over the bounties of as much as £70 apiece they had received, bringing harsh discipline down on the whole ship for their misdeeds. "Them was the chaps as played hell with the fleet!" said one old British tar. "Every grass-combing beggar as chose to bear up for the bounty. . . . Every finger was fairly a fish-hook:

neither chest nor bed nor blanket nor bag escaped their slight-of-hand."[47] The lists of punishments aboard British ships on the American station for two months in the summer of 1812 go on page after page: striking the sergeant of marines, 48 lashes; desertion and running away with the boat, 36 lashes; pissing in the manger and skulking, 24 lashes; theft and mutinous behavior, 36 lashes; contempt, 24 lashes; striking his superior, 36 lashes; drunkenness, 42 lashes; mutinous behavior, 60 lashes; neglect of duty, 36 lashes.[48]

By contrast the men of an American warship were all genuine volunteers, enlisted freely for a term of two years. An able seaman was paid $12 a month in the American navy versus $8 in the Royal Navy. Charles Morris noted that many American recruits brought with them practical skills in carpentry or blacksmithing or other trades, along with a general air of self-reliance.

Nearly all the captains of the American navy of 1812 were under age forty. All had done something to earn their rank beyond the circumstances of their birth or their family influence. All knew how to handle a ship.

ON THE first day of August 1812, a damp and foggy Saturday morning in Boston, the *Constitution* awaited only a fair wind to proceed to sea. Isaac Hull had spent the week completing his supplies and growing anxious over the absence of any orders from Washington. Rumors were swirling over the whereabouts of the British squadron: the frigate *Maidstone* was said to be capturing fishermen off Cape Cod; another report claimed a frigate had been seen off Cape Ann just to the north; yet another placed two frigates in the bay itself, where they would be in a position to seal Boston harbor shut.

Hull had sent to New York for any letters that might have been directed to him there, but neither Rodgers nor Hamilton had apparently left him any instructions. On July 28, Hull wrote Hamilton explaining his haste to get to sea again while there was still a chance, and hoping again that he was not exceeding his authority:

> Should I not by the time she is ready get instructions from New
> York, or find some at this place . . . I shall proceed to Sea and run
> to the Eastward, and endeavour to join [Rodgers's] Squadron,
> and if I am so unfortunate as not to fall in with them I shall

continue cruising where (from information I may collect) I shall
be most likely to distress the Enemy. Should I proceed to Sea
without your further orders, and it should not meet your
approbation, I shall be very unhappy, for I pray you to be assured
in doing so I shall act as at this moment I believe you would order
me to do so.[49]

Hull's letter crossed in the mail with one from Hamilton written the
same date. "On the arrival of the Constitution in port, I have ordered
Commodore Bainbridge to take command of her," the secretary
instructed. "You will accordingly deliver up to him the command and
proceed to this place and assume command of the frigate Constellation."[50] Whether Hull had an inkling of what was in the wind or not—
and given Bainbridge's seniority, his presence in Boston, and his
repeated demands for the command of one of the three large frigates,
it was unlikely Hull did not—he weighed anchor on Sunday, August 2,
taking advantage of the wind that hauled around to the west to run out
of the harbor. He wrote a final hasty note to Hamilton, expressing the
hope that the ship's boat that was even at that moment at the post office
might come bearing orders; "but to remain here any time longer I am
confident that the Ship would be blockaded in by a Superiour force,
and probably would not get out for months."[51] To add to his unease,
Hull had just learned that his brother was dangerously ill and not
expected to live. Hull wrote to his father the night before sailing, urging
him to take heart but ending, "Indeed my mind is in such a state I
hardly know what I am writing—nor will it be at Ease until I hear from
you and god only knows when that will be as I sail in the morning."[52]

The harbor was filled with small vessels, fifty sail in view as they
stood out from the lighthouse a little past six in the morning. By afternoon the land was lost to sight.

Surgeon Amos Evans recorded in his journal on the eleventh of
August that he had caught a redheaded woodpecker aboard, 150 miles
from land. On the fourteenth a sailor fell from the main chains and
struck the water; the topsail was instantly backed, the stern boat lowered, and the man pulled out two hundred yards behind the ship
unharmed but considerably shaken: "The blood . . . appeared to have
forsaken his cheeks. The tenure of a sailor's existence is certainly more
precarious than any other man's, a soldier's not excepted. Who would
not be a sailor? I, for one." The same day a fire broke out in the cockpit

when one of the surgeon's mates left a candle burning in his room with the door locked; trying to break open the door with a crowbar, Evans smashed his hand but the fire was quickly extinguished. The surgeon's mate was arrested for negligence. Evans feared the injury to his hand would "terminate in *Tetanus*," and brooded about the folly of war:[53]

> What an anxious uncomfortable life is ours! What a pity that people cannot live in peace. . . . In this enlightened era . . . oceans of blood are spilt and numberless throats cut to retrieve their honor! "Can honor heal a wound or set a leg?" said Shakespeare. . . . Honour in the present expectation of the word, at least, is no surgeon.[54]

On the seventeenth, about four hundred miles southeast of Halifax, they tacked ship to investigate what appeared to be the wreck of a capsized vessel, but as they approached, it proved to be a dead whale, the oil from the carcass covering the water for some distance around, the stench unbearable.

It was at 9:30 the next night that the ship was called to quarters, the lookouts having spotted a vessel nearly ahead standing before the wind. The *Constitution* gave chase and came up to her an hour and a half later. She was an American privateer brig out of Newburyport, the *Decatur*. During the chase the privateer had thrown overboard twelve of her fourteen guns; convinced it was a British frigate that had brought them to, the *Decatur*'s crew had actually been getting their bags together to come aboard as prisoners, "and were overjoyed when undeceived by our boarding officer," Evans recorded.

The privateer's captain told Hull that the day before he had seen a large ship of war standing alone to the southward and that she could not be far from them. At midnight Hull ordered his ship to make sail to the southward.[55]

HULL HAD already decided to head for the south, and Bermuda, at the first chance: a few days earlier the *Constitution* had scattered a group of sail eastward in a long chase beginning at sunrise that had carried them within forty miles of Cape Race, Newfoundland. A British sloop of war ran free, but in midafternoon the *Constitution* caught up with an American brig that had been taken a prize by the sloop, with a British master's mate and five seamen aboard. From the prisoners they learned that the British squadron was just to the east, on the edge of the Grand Banks. "I determined to change my cruising ground," Hull noted; it was time to keep the enemy guessing again about his whereabouts.

In fact, the British squadron had sailed east for three weeks after giving up its chase of the *Constitution* off New Jersey; they had gone to escort a homebound West India merchant convoy and only a few days earlier had finally turned back for New York. On August 10 an American merchant brig, the *Betsey*, bound for Boston from Naples with a load of brandy, had fallen in with a lone British frigate on the Western Banks. The *Betsey*'s master, William B. Orne, was taken aboard as a prisoner and his ship sent on to Halifax as a prize.[56]

The cruising frigate was the *Guerriere;* she had gone with the rest of the squadron halfway across the Atlantic but then been detached and ordered to Halifax, the first in a regular rotation that would send one ship of the British cruising force at a time into port to replenish her stores and refit while the others maintained a constant presence off the American coast. On her way in to Halifax the *Guerriere* had already encountered several American merchant ships, better luck than the squadron had had in its weeks of blue-water sailing. The day after taking the *Betsey* the *Guerriere* halted and boarded the brig *John Adams*, bound for New York. Finding that the ship was sailing under a British license, Dacres told her captain he could go on his way, but not before he first wrote an entry into the merchant ship's register:

> Capt. Dacres, commander of his Britannic Majesty's frigate Guerriere, of forty-four guns, presents his compliments to commodore Rodgers, of the United States frigate President, and will be very happy to meet him, or any other American frigate of equal force to the President, off Sandy Hook, for the purpose of having a few minutes tête-à-tête.[57]

At two o'clock on the afternoon of August 19, after a day's sailing southward in pursuit of the privateer captain's report, the *Constitution* spotted a sail in the far distance off the larboard bow. Hull was on deck instantly, followed quickly by nearly every man on board. "Before all the hands could be called, there was a general rush on deck," said able seaman Moses Smith. "The word had passed like lightning from man to man; and all who could be spared came flocking up like pigeons from a net bed. From the spar deck to the gun deck, from that to the berth deck, every man was roused and on his feet. All eyes were turned in the direction of the strange sail, and quick as thought studding-sails were out, fore and aft."[58] The *Guerriere* spotted the American almost simultaneously. On her deck Dacres handed Orne his glass and asked if he thought she was an American or a French frigate. Orne said he thought American for sure, but Dacres replied that she "acted most too bold to be an American." Dacres paused, then added, "The better he behaves, the more honor we shall gain by taking him," even remarking to Orne that he would "be made for life" by being the first British captain to capture an American frigate. The British crew facetiously hung up a barrel of molasses in the netting for their soon-to-be prisoners; Yankees were said to like a drink of molasses and water known as switchel. Ten impressed Americans in the crew were allowed by Dacres to go below, and Dacres turned politely to Orne and asked if he would like to go below as well and assist the surgeon in the cockpit in case any of the men were wounded in the battle—"as I suppose you do not wish to fight against your own countrymen." Just before he left the deck, Orne saw the main topsail backed, the yard rotated around so the sail caught the wind and checked the ship's forward motion, as the *Guerriere* prepared to stand to and face the rapidly approaching American. An English ensign broke out at each masthead, and the drum began to roll to bring the men to quarters.[59]

As the *Constitution* came up, her crew could see another bit of English facetiousness; on one of the ship's topsails painted in large letters were the words NOT THE LITTLE BELT, a sarcastic allusion to Rodgers's mistaken encounter with the *Little Belt* when he was seeking to intercept the *Guerriere* off Cape Henry the year before. If there had been any doubt as to the ship's identity, it was now gone.

Since the *Constitution* was to windward, she held the weather gauge, and with it several theoretical advantages in a ship-on-ship engagement. A ship to leeward, heeling away from the wind, exposed a portion of her hull below the waterline to the enemy's shot; in a close action the smoke from a windward ship's guns might envelop an opponent, obscuring the aim of her gun crews; the sails of the ship on the weather side could block the wind and becalm the leeward ship, hindering her maneuverability. But most of all, the commander of the ship that held the weather gauge held the power of decision; he could haul away and avoid a fight, and an equal opponent to leeward could never

Stephen Decatur's daring raid of February 16, 1804, on Tripoli harbor to burn the captured American frigate *Philadelphia* made the twenty-five-year-old lieutenant a national hero and helped salvage the honor of the embattled young navy. (Painting by Edward Moran, Naval History & Heritage Command)

For three days at the outbreak of the war the *Constitution*
eluded a pursuing British squadron off the coast of New Jersey;
at a crucial moment when the winds died the ship was towed
forward on anchor lines carried ahead by the ship's boats.
(Painting by F. Muller, Naval History & Heritage Command)

Isaac Hull, the *Constitution*'s
first wartime captain, a
kind but thoroughgoing
seaman who commanded
the almost worshipful
loyalty of his crew.
(Painting by Samuel L.
Waldo after a portrait by
Gilbert Stuart, Naval
History & Heritage
Command)

"The birth of a world power" was how Charles Francis Adams Jr. described the moment the *Constitution* claimed the first American naval victory of the war: the defeat of the British frigate *Guerriere* on August 19, 1812. (Painting by Michel Felice Corne, Naval History & Heritage Command)

William Bainbridge had three times struck the flag of the United States in prewar commands and was possessed with jealousy, resentment, and self-pity; he also fought one of the most tactically brilliant engagements of the war, defeating the British frigate *Java* on December 29, 1812. (Painting by John Wesley Jarvis, Naval History & Heritage Command)

The *Shannon* leads the ill-fated American frigate *Chesapeake* into Halifax harbor, June 6, 1813. (Naval History & Heritage Command)

A weapon more of intimidation than military effectiveness, the British Congreve rocket caused only a single known fatality during the war—but it would be immortalized in Francis Scott Key's verse describing "the rockets' red glare." (Congreve, *Details of Rocket System*; courtesy National Maritime Museum, U.K.)

British admiral George Cockburn, probably the most hated man in America for the raids he carried out along the Chesapeake Bay in 1813 and 1814, was depicted in his portrait standing against a backdrop of the White House in flames. (Painting by John James Halls, National Maritime Museum, U.K.)

The secretary of the British Admiralty was the conservative politician John Wilson Croker, who raised the withering of opponents and subordinates to an art form. (Painting by William Owen, National Portrait Gallery, London)

A man ahead of his time: Croker's American counterpart,
Secretary of the Navy William Jones, keenly grasped the importance
of keeping a much more powerful enemy constantly off balance.
(Painting by Gilbert Stuart, Naval History & Heritage Command)

Stephen Decatur was the quintessential American naval hero,
whose "sense of honor too disdainful of life" brought him wartime
fame and later tragedy. (Painting by John Wesley Jarvis, Naval History
& Heritage Command)

Opposite: The funeral of James Lawrence in Salem on August 13, 1813,
brought out the vice president of the United States and a host of other
dignitaries to honor the slain captain of the *Chesapeake*. (Belcher, *Account of
Funeral Honours*; courtesy U.S. Naval Academy Nimitz Library

ORDER.

Officers of the Navy of the United States.
Masonic Societies.
Ciergy.

CAPTAINS.		CAPTAINS.
HULL,		STEWART,
BAINBRIDGE,		BLAKELY,
CREIGHTON,		PARKER.

LIEUTENANTS.		LIEUTENANTS.
BALLARD.		WILKINSON.
HOFFMAN,		NICHOLSON.
REILLY,		NORRIS,

Relatives.
Capt. CROWNINSHIELD, and ten Masters of ships, who accompanied him in the Flag.

Marshal of the District and his Deputies.
Vice-President of the United States.
Members of Congress.
Judges and other Civil Officers of the United States.
Officers of the Army of the United States.
Ministers and Consuls of Foreign Powers.
Committee of Arrangements.
Hon. Joseph Story and the officiating Clergymen (in a carriage.)
Members of the State Legislature.
Civil Officers of the State.
Military Officers of the State, in Uniform.
Principal Municipal Officers of the town.
Salem Marine Society.
East-India Marine Society.
President, Directors and officers of the respective Banks.
President, Directors and Officers of the respective Insurance
Offices.
Citizens in general.

British commander in chief John Borlase Warren, an experienced naval man and diplomat, was hampered by contradictory orders and a lack of support from London as he tried to enforce the blockade of America. (Painting by James Fittler, National Maritime Museum, U.K.)

Warren's replacement, Alexander F. I. Cochrane, had the aggressive instincts the British government was seeking—as well as a visceral hatred of Americans. (Painting by William Beechey, National Maritime Museum, U.K.)

By the Honorable Sir ALEXANDER COCHRANE, K. B.
Vice Admiral of the Red, and Commander in Chief of
His Majesty's Ships and Vessels, upon the North Ameri-
can Station, &c. &c. &c.

A PROCLAMATION.

WHEREAS it has been represented to me, that many Persons now resident in the UNITED STATES, have expressed a desire to withdraw therefrom, with a view of entering into His Majesty's Service, or of being received as Free Settlers into some of His Majesty's Colonies.

This is therefore to Give Notice,

That all those who may be disposed to emigrate from the UNITED STATES will, with their Families, be received on board of His Majesty's Ships or Vessels of War, or at the Military Posts that may be established, upon or near the Coast of the UNITED STATES, when they will have their choice of either entering into His Majesty's Sea or Land Forces, or of being sent as FREE Settlers to the British Possessions in North America or the West Indies, where they will meet with all due encouragement.

GIVEN under my Hand at Bermuda, this 2nd
day of April, 1814.

ALEXANDER COCHRANE.

By Command of the Vice Admiral,

WILLIAM BALHETCHET.

GOD SAVE THE KING.

A day after assuming command, Cochrane gave notice of Britain's intensifying economic warfare against America with a proclamation encouraging slaves to flee their owners. (The National Archives, U.K.)

David Porter sketched this view of his ship *Essex* with her prizes in the harbor of Nuku Hiva in the Marquesas Islands: a respite in his remarkable cruise against British commerce in the Pacific in 1813. (Porter, *Journal of Cruise*; courtesy Charles E. Brodine Jr.)

David Porter (Painting attributed to John Trumbull, Naval History & Heritage Command)

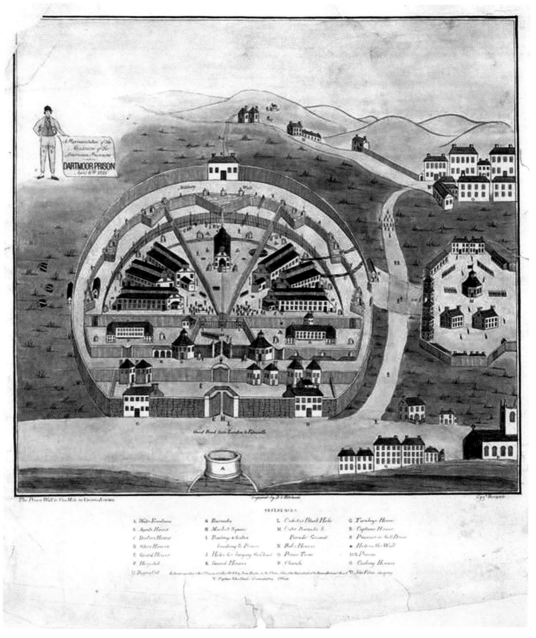

More than six thousand captured American seaman were held in the notorious Dartmoor Prison, a veritable fortress surrounded by eighteen-foot-high solid granite walls and miles of uninhabited moorland in southwest England. (Library of Congress)

SOME AMERICAN CAPTAINS OF NOTORIETY AND FAME

William Henry Allen
(Naval History & Heritage Command)

Oliver Hazard Perry
(Library of Congress)

James Barron
(Naval History & Heritage Command)

Thomas Macdonough
(Library of Congress)

GRAND VICTORY ON LAKE CHAMPLAIN.

[TENTH NAVAL VICTORY---" COM. MACDONOUGH obtained a glorious victory, over the British Fleet, on Lake Champlain Sept. 11. The Squadrons were nearly equal in force, and the carnage is reported to have been very great. The vessels captured were a Frigate of 32 guns, mounting 37---a Brig of 22 guns---2 Sloops of 10 guns each, and several Gallies ;---indeed the whole British force on the Lake,---3 Gallies excepted which escaped." The action lasted 2 hours 15 min.---Loss on board their Ship 106 men---The Growler had but 5 men left alive---their commander Downie killed at the first fire.---Our Com. Macdonough is safe !---HONOR TO THE BRAVE !---]

The Old-War Proverb still holds good ; " There's VIRTUE, in the YANKEE blood."

TUNE---" Hark ! hark ! the joyful news is come."

THE triumphs of your country sing,
  And hail the *Fidettes*, as they bring,
  From *North* and *South*...Good News :
'Our ranks have *Heroes*...not a few,
All *British* foes they WILL subdue !
  No more shall they abuse !
Rise *PATRIOTS, rise !...Obey your Country's call ;
  ...D we all stand !...Divided FALL !!
  ...Britain's vengeful Clans,
  ...rojected plans,
  ...n to destroy ;
  ...terans, in train,
  ...m off all *Europes* main,
  ...try to annoy.
  ...IOTS, rise ! &c.
  ...forces thus arrang'd,
  ...and from home estrang'd,
  ...owd around your shores ;
  ...esolate and base,
  ...of devil, in ev'ry place,
  ...pointed cannon rears.
  ...PATRIOTS, rise ! &c.
  ...and Carnage...Ruin...all,
  ...ympathetic heart appal,
  And stagger our belief ;
  ...hey swear your cities all shall flame,
To blast your *Hopes*,your *Rights*,your *Fame*
  In unavailing grief.
  Rise ! *PATRIOTS* rise ! &c.
Cities and *Villages* are fired,
Your *Nation's CAPITOL's*...not spared,
  Nor *Alexandria* sav'd ;
The *ENEMY* your strength defies,
Your brave *Militia*, they despise,
  With blood, your streets are pav'd !
Rise ! *PATRIOTS* rise ! &c.
Alas ! how fills th' eventful year...
Their *Troops* are round our whole *frontier*,
  With *Instruments* of Death !
Their *Savage Allies* all in arms,
Thro' all our country, spread alarms,
  As rapid as their breath.
Rise ! *PATRIOTS*, rise ! &c.
Ross was the greater *Savage* far ;
BROCK was the *Gentleman* in war,
  And lean'd to *Virtue's* side !
But *Ross* and *Cochrane* fruitless beast,
To make us...*Sacrifice and Cost* !
  We *SPURN* their daring pride,
Rise ! *PATRIOTS*, rise ! &c.

Our troops are brave...nor yet despair ;
For all their *Threats*, we neither care ;
  Nor feel ourselves afraid :
Our vast *Munitions*, we retain,
We'll give them ALL,and draw our *Gain*,
  In th' YANKEE " *mode of Trade*" !
Rise ! *PATRIOTS*. rise ! &c.
Good-News now circulates around,
Our hearts, with grateful hopes abound,
  ...All *Baltimore* is *BRAVE* !
Smith, *Winder*, and a powerful force,
" *Repulse the enemy with loss*,"
  They...ALL their country, *SAVE* !
Rise ! *PATRIOTS*, rise ! &c.
But mark, kind reader, *Patriots* say,
" Rejoice triumphantly...THIS DAY...
  The *Eleventh* of *September* ;"
A *Tenth GRAND VICTRY*, is obtain'd,
Immortal trophies you have gain'd,
  PERRY'S Compeer remember.
Rise ! *PATRIOTS* rise ! &c.
The far-fam'd *Plattsburgh* and *Champlain*,
New honorary triumphs, gain,
  MACDONOUGH's *Brave in War*,
He leads the *New-York VETRANS* on,
Vermont unites,...the *Vic'try's* won,
  " Green Mountain boys,"...*Huzza* !
Rise ! *PATRIOTS*, rise ! &c.
Sir George Prevost directs his bands,
And makes *INVASION*, on our lands,
  To multiply our fears ;
But *HE*, nor *Downie*, nor *O'Brien*,
Can " *lather Yankees*"...after trying,...
  We " *shave close*"...English Peers !
Rise ! *PATRIOTS*, rise ! &c.
With but one hundred *Guns and six*,
One hundred twenty-five, we fix,
  In silence, most complete !
Our brave *MILITIA* stand *their fire*,
Their *FLEET's* " cut up"...their *TROOPS*
  retire,
  And *Thousands* we defeat !
Rise ! *PATRIOTS*, rise ! &c.
Army to army...fleet to fleet,
In all their pride and spirit meet,
  In rivalry and ire ;
The *Yankees*, " in close action," move,
And to the *Enemy*, they prove...
  An opposing *wall* of *Fire*.
Rise ! *PATRIOTS*, rise, &c.

Wildly the *Drum*...the *Cannons* roar,
The echoes tremble round the shore,
  Thick clouds of smoke arise ;
Clangor of arms, and shouts, and groans,
...The mingled sacrifice atones !
  ...There many a *HERO* dies !
Rise ! *PATRIOTS*, rise ! &c.
Broadside and broadside close they run,
MACDONOUGH conquers,...man for gu
  On board the *Frigate Royal* ;...
To prove true *Bravery* is ours,
To prove our *Eagle* never cowers !
  To prove our hearts are *loyal*.
Rise ! *PATRIOTS*, rise ! &c.
" *The agony is over*"...THERE,
But still we pledge our hearts and swear...
  Our country to defend :
Then give us " *Honorable Peace*"
We're " Enemies in War," for this,
  With this...we're all...the FRIEN
  Rise *PATRIOTS*, rise, &c !
Your hopes, ye *Britons*, all are vain,
You never can the *War* maintain,
  When all OUR hearts UNITE ;
Our *hearts-blood* is refin'd and pure,
Nor will we *Insolence* endure,
  For RIGHTS AND LAWS,...WE
  fight !
Rise ! *PATRIOTS*, rise, ! &c.
Then cease your efforts to subdue ;
We'll yield to no pow'r ;---nor to YOU ;
  Ye vet'ran *Barb'rous* Clans ;
Withdraw your troops and send them home
Or give them *Freedom*, when they come ;
  And so change all your plans.
Rise ! *PATRIOTS*, rise, &c.
For *Freedom* and for *Rights* contest;
Like *YANKEES*, may you then be blest,
  Beyond all other powers ;
For *US*---may all our Blessings be---
Enrich'd with Fame and Liberty,
  And be they always OURS.
Rise ! *PATRIOTS*, rise !---Obey your Coun-
  try's call ;
UNITED we all stand !---Divided *FALL*! !
  Full Chorus.
Huzza ! Huzza ! for FREEDOM RIGHTS
  and HONOR !
Huzza ! Huzza ! for COM. M'DONOUGH.

☞ Printed by N. COVERLY.

The Battle of New Orleans was one of the most lopsided engagements
ever fought, affirming America's ability to hold off the disproportionate
might of the British empire. (Library of Congress)

intercept and catch him, or he could use the wind to steer a direct course to come up as quickly as possible to close with the enemy. That posed its own risks, though: the more direct the angle of approach, the more exposed the approaching ship was to the enemy's broadside while unable to answer with her own. But that was the course Hull now chose to take.

Several times Dacres wore his ship and fired broadsides as the American came up. The first fell short, and others went too high, and each time Hull ordered his ship to yaw slightly to larboard and windward to take the enemy fire on the side of the bows and avoid being raked from stem to stern down the vulnerable length of the deck. Ships usually went into battle with topsails only to avoid the danger of sails catching fire from their own cannons' flaming wads and to keep the number of sail trimmers needed to a minimum, but Hull now ordered the main topgallant sail set to close rapidly and bring his ship right alongside the enemy. The crew broke out with three cheers.

With the *Constitution* coming up on her windward quarter the *Guerriere* could now bring her sternmost guns to bear and some of her shots started to tell. Several men on the *Constitution* were mowed down, and Lieutenant Morris impatiently asked Hull for permission to fire.

"No, sir," Hull replied.

A dead silence hung over the ship. "No firing at random!" Hull shouted into it. "Let every man look well to his aim." At 6:05 p.m. the *Constitution* was directly alongside the *Guerriere,* less than a pistol shot, or two dozen yards, away. Then came the first crashing broadside from every gun on *Constitution*'s starboard side, double-shotted and fired right into the deck and gunports of the enemy.

To Orne, crouching in the cramped cockpit below the *Guerriere*'s waterline, it sounded like "a tremendous explosion . . . the effect of her shot seemed to make the Guerriere reel, and tremble as though she had received the shock of an earthquake." Almost instantly came an even more tremendous crash. And then as the smoke from the last shot cleared, the men on the *Constitution* were cheering like maniacs: *Guerriere*'s mizzenmast had gone by the board. "Huzzah boys! We've made a brig of her!" one of the *Constitution*'s crew shouted. "Next time we'll make her a sloop!" shouted another voice. Hull, who had literally split his dress breeches excitedly leaping atop an arms chest on the deck for a better view, exclaimed, "By God that vessel is ours."[60] The cockpit of the *Guerriere* was instantly filled with wounded and dying men, barely leaving room for the surgeons to work at the long table in the center that they kneeled or bent over. From the decks above, Orne said, blood poured down as if a washtub full had been turned over.

Most of the *Constitution*'s sails and spars were still undamaged, and now she began to forge ahead. Hull ordered the helm put to port to bring the ship to starboard and cross the *Guerriere*'s bows. The English ship attempted to turn in parallel to foil the maneuver, but the drag of her fallen mizzenmast in the water prevented her from answering her helm, and the *Constitution* began to pour a murderous fire, two full broadsides, into the enemy's larboard bow. Grapeshot, clusters of balls weighing a couple of pounds apiece that separated like a shotgun's blast when fired, swept across the decks and mowed men down while round shot continued to take a toll on the *Guerriere*'s masts.

To keep the *Guerriere* from passing across her stern and raking the *Constitution* in turn, the American ship bore up, but the *Guerriere*'s bowsprit and jibboom crossed her quarterdeck and became entangled in the mizzen rigging. Men crowded on the forecastle of the *Guerriere* preparing to board or repel boarders, and Morris quickly suggested to Hull that he call the *Constitution*'s boarders too, then joined the men running for their ship's stern preparing to board the enemy. As Morris began to wrap a few turns of the mainbrace over the enemy's bowsprit to hold her fast, a musket ball tore into his abdomen, knocking him to the deck grievously wounded. Lieutenant William S. Bush, the captain of the ship's marines, leapt on the taffrail at almost the same moment, sword in hand, shouting, "Shall I board her?" when he was drilled through the cheek by a musket ball that tore through the back of his head, shattering his skull and killing him instantly.[61] The facetious barrel of molasses hanging over the *Guerriere*'s deck was riddled with holes and molasses poured over the deck. During the closest part of the battle the *Constitution*'s gunners fired a hundred rounds of canister shot—cylinders packed with bullets, nails, bolts, and scraps of old iron—which was even more deadly than grapeshot at short range.[62]

Although only a few of the *Guerriere*'s forwardmost guns would bear, the British sailors ran one of the guns almost into the window of the captain's cabin of the *Constitution* and a flaming wad came aboard, starting a fire, but the American sailors quickly put it out. Marines in *Constitution*'s mizzentop kept up a steady barrage of musketry, shooting down over the head-high breastwork of hammocks packed into the netting over both ships' rails that offered some protection for the crews on the deck, clearing the forecastle of the enemy and wounding Dacres in the back as he stood on the piled hammocks to get a better view of the situation. Hull was about to climb back atop the arms chest when a sailor grabbed him by the arm and, pointing to the epaulets on his shoulders that made him an equally prime target for the enemy's sharpshooters, said, "Don't get up there, sir, unless you take them swabs off!"[63]

Boarding would still have been an extremely dicey move at this point, the boarders having to make their way in a heavy running sea single file over the bowsprit of the *Guerriere*. But in rapid sequence the ships now tore away, the foremast of the English ship fell in a cascade of spars and rigging over her starboard side, and then her mainmast went too. Not a spar was left standing on the *Guerriere* but the bowsprit. Hull immediately ordered his sails filled and hauled off.

For half an hour the *Constitution* stood off nearby, repairing her rigging. The sun had gone down, and it was hard to see if any colors were still flying from the enemy, though her guns had fallen silent. William Orne made his way up on deck. The scene was "a perfect hell." Blood was everywhere, like a slaughterhouse. The men who were still sober were throwing the dead overboard, but many of the petty officers and crewmen had broken into the spirit locker and were screaming drunk. The mastless ship, with nothing but a jury-rigged scrap of canvas flying from the bowsprit, lay "rolling like a log in the trough of the sea," her main deck guns rolling under water. Water also poured in from thirty holes smashed through her side below the waterline. A British ensign was still flying from the stump of the mizzenmast, but with a crack the spritsail yard carried away, taking with it any hope of bringing her before the wind and fighting on.

The American ship now wore back and stood across the *Guerriere*'s bow, completing her picture of helplessness. From the *Constitution* a boat rowed over under a flag of truce, and Lieutenant George Read hailed the ship: "I wish to see the officer in command." Dacres stood on the deck appearing slightly dazed. Read hailed again: "Commodore Hull's compliments and wishes to know if you have struck your flag."

The British officers had already held a council and agreed that further resistance was futile, but Dacres seemed to make an effort to utter the fateful words. "Well, I don't know," he finally said, "our mizzen-mast is gone, our main-mast is gone—and upon the whole, you may say we have struck our flag." Read asked if they could send their surgeon to lend assistance. "Well, I should suppose you had on board your own ship business enough for all your medical officers," Dacres replied. "Oh, no, we have only seven wounded, and they were dressed half an hour ago." Dacres then turned to Orne and said, "How our situations have suddenly been reversed: you are now free and I am a prisoner."[64]

The British captain came across in the boat to present his sword to Hull and formally surrender. "Your men are a set of tigers," he said to Hull in wonderment. Not a single shot had hulled the *Constitution;* her casualties were seven dead and seven wounded. The British ship officially reported fifteen dead and sixty-two wounded, but Orne was certain that at least twenty-five more of her crewmen were dead, their bodies dumped over the side or the men swept to their deaths with the falling of the masts.[65] The American victory had taken twenty-five minutes, and the accuracy of American fire had been decisive. Hull would later single out for praise his black sailors: "I never had any better fighters than those niggers,—they stripped to the waist, and fought like devils, sir, seemingly insensible to danger, and to be possessed with a determination to outfight the white sailors."[66]

All night *Constitution*'s boats went back and forth removing the prisoners. Hull later told a friend, "I do not mind the day of battle, the excitement carries one through: but the day after is fearful." Midshipman Henry Gilliam was aboard *Guerriere* the whole night, and the scene of her decks "were almost enough to make me curse the war," he admitted to his uncle in a letter a few days later; "pieces of skulls, brains, legs, arms & blood Lay in every direction." Morris had pulled himself off the deck and gone back to his station after being shot, but once the action was over he found he could not speak and the pain began to overwhelm him; he was carried down to the cockpit and spent an agonizing night. "The pain nearly deprived me of all consciousness," Morris said. But Evans was amazed by the fortitude of the wounded men; Orne had had the same reaction in the cockpit of the *Guerriere,* almost doubting his own senses as he witnessed men making jokes as they were having an arm amputated. Evans had no sleep at all, working through the night assisting the *Guerriere*'s surgeon to dress the wounds of the British injured. The next day Evans amputated the leg of Richard Dunn, one of the *Constitution*'s men. Dunn muttered, "You're a hard set of butchers," and then stoically submitted to his fate.[67]

With dawn the condition of the *Guerriere* was clearly hopeless; she was, said Hull, "a perfect Wreck," and he hastened to get the remaining wounded men off before she sank. Six feet of planking had been completely shot away in one place below her waterline, there was five feet of water in the hold, and the pumps could not keep up. At three o'clock in the afternoon the two captains watched wordlessly from the *Constitution*'s quarterdeck as Lieutenant Read's boat began to row back across for the last time, and minutes later the English frigate was ablaze from the scuttling charge Read had set, her guns discharging in succession as the heat of the flame reached them; then there was a momentary silence followed by a deafening roar. It was like waiting for a volcano to erupt, Moses Smith remembered; then the quarterdeck, immediately over the magazine, heaved skyward in a single piece and broke into fragments; then her whole hull parted in two. Seconds later the entire ship disappeared beneath the sea's surface. "No painter, no poet or historian could give on canvas or paper any description that could do justice to the scene," Evans said, "a sight the most incomparably grand and magnificent I have experienced."[68]

That evening the bodies of Lieutenant Bush and one of the *Guerriere*'s men who had died from his wounds were committed to the deep.

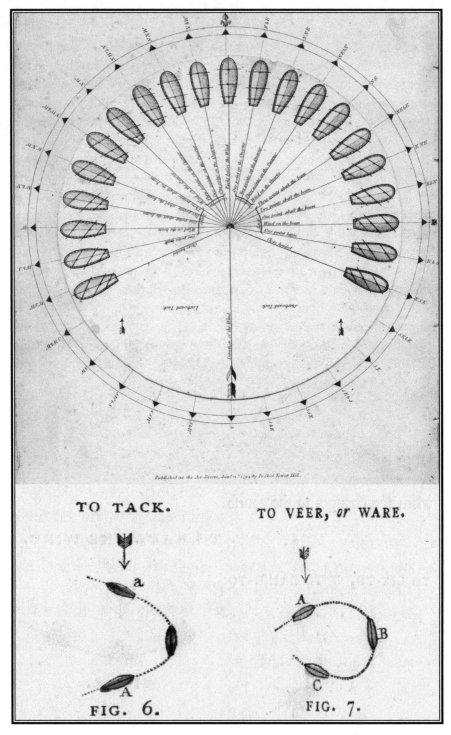

Sailing points and maneuvering in the wind (*Elements and Practice of Rigging and Seamanship; System of Naval Tactics;* courtesy Charles E. Brodine Jr.)

CHAPTER 5

Love of Fame Is
a Noble Passion

THIS TIME a whole procession made its way up the harbor, *Constitution* in the lead, the *Guerriere*'s flag flying beneath the Stars and Stripes from her peak, then the frigates *President, United States,* and *Congress,* then *Argus* and *Hornet* taking up the rear. Word had spread through Boston from the moment of the *Constitution*'s arrival in the outer harbor the day before, anchoring at the lighthouse in the early hours of Sunday, August 30, 1812. Now, as the ship passed Long Wharf, chorus upon chorus of huzzahs echoed from a huge crowd gathered there, repeated by each of the merchant ships in the harbor.

Earlier in the morning, having anchored in Nantasket Roads overnight to await a favorable wind to carry her into the narrows, the ship had been sent tearing to quarters when her lookout spotted five unidentified armed vessels nearing Boston light. At 6:30 a.m, roused from his first peaceful night's sleep in weeks, Hull gave the order to cut the two anchor cables and make all sail to try to get under the protection of the harbor forts before their last chance of escape was cut off. Hull had already decided to "sell our lives as dear as possible" in what he expected to be a last stand against the entire British squadron when he made out the American flag on the leadmost of the approaching men-of-war and recognized the outlines of *Constitution*'s half sister the *President.*

All day, boats surrounded the frigate at her anchorage at the navy yard, cheering the victorious crew; Bainbridge went aboard, as did Decatur from the *United States* and James Lawrence, now a master commandant and captain of the *Hornet.*

Rodgers's squadron had returned with little to show for its ten-week cruise but an outbreak of scurvy that had left scores of his men dangerously sick. On June 23, two days out of New York, they had chased a lone British frigate, the *Belvidera*, off Sandy Hook, but Rodgers had bungled the engagement from the start. Rather than bring the out-numbered and outmatched enemy to close action as quickly as possible, Rodgers had repeatedly yawed to bring the *President*'s broadside to bear, hoping to cripple her with a long-range shot. Some of the *President*'s shots struck home, but each time he turned his ship, the chase got far-ther ahead. Ill luck added to miscalculation: ten minutes after the *President* began firing, one of her bow guns burst, killing and wounding sixteen men including Rodgers, whose leg was broken, and setting off the powder box with an explosion that destroyed both the main and forecastle decks around the gun. The *Belvidera* dumped fourteen tons of drinking water and threw her boats, anchors, and spare spars over-board to lighten ship and two and a half hours from the start of the action had run out of gunshot; in another few hours she had disap-peared into the vast stretches of the Atlantic.

Back on the trail of the Jamaica convoy, Rodgers had sailed for three weeks across the Atlantic until he was within a day and a half of the English Channel before abandoning the futile chase. Twice the Ameri-cans had come within a whisker of their prize: on July 1 they had sailed into a floating sea of coconut shells and orange peels, and on July 9 they had taken a British merchant brig whose crew told Rodgers they had seen eighty-five sail the night before. Rodgers disconsolately wrote Sec-retary Hamilton on his arrival at Boston that his had been a "barren" cruise; they had taken only six British merchant ships and had also recaptured the *Betsey*, William Orne's schooner that had been snapped up by the *Guerriere* and ordered to Halifax just before her battle with the *Constitution*. (The *Betsey* was recaptured yet again five days later, by the British frigate *Acasta;* two other of Rodgers's prizes were also recaptured before they could make their way to an American port.) The "only con-solation" Rodgers said he could take was "derived from knowing that our being at Sea obliged the Enemy to concentrate a considerable por-tion of his most active force and thereby prevented his capturing an incalculable amount of American property that would otherwise have fallen a sacrifice." But even that was mostly wishful thinking; knowing that Rodgers had taken nearly the entire American navy on a wild goose chase far to the east had allowed Captain Broke to separate the ships of his squadron in the meanwhile, returning to the American coast with all but the sixty-four-gun *Africa,* which he left with the Jamaica convoy, and proceeding in Rodgers's absence to send in a stream of prizes to Halifax.[1]

The next morning, September 1, Hull stepped ashore at 11:00 a.m. to more cheers and a seventeen-gun salute from an artillery company, returned by the *Constitution*'s guns. The captain "had barely room to plant his feet on the stone" as he clambered onto the pier from the boat that had rowed him ashore, said Moses Smith, so dense were the throngs; Smith estimated that thousands were there. From adjacent buildings women waved handkerchiefs and threw flowers. A letter awaiting Hull at the Exchange Coffee House carried the news of his brother's death two weeks earlier.[2]

On Saturday night, the fifth, a huge dinner was held at Faneuil Hall for the *Constitution*'s officers, five hundred guests, and all of Boston's leading citizens, with magnificent wreaths of flowers adorning the walls and a model of the *Constitution* in the gallery above with colors flying as they were during the battle. John Adams was unable to attend, pleading his age and the inclement weather, but he sent a couple of barbed toasts to be read on his behalf, each punctuated by an artillery salute from the street:

> May every Commodore in our American Navy soon be made an Admiral, and every Captain a Commodore; with ships and squadrons, worthy of their commanders and worthy of the wealth, power, and dignity of their country!

> *Talbot, Truxton, Decatur, Little and Preble*—Had their country given them the means, they would have been *Blakes, Drakes* and *Nelsons!*[3]

For weeks Federalist Boston celebrated in spite of itself. The manager of Boston's Federal Street Theater hastened into production a new addition to the bill:

> A new naval Overture composed by Mr. Hewett
> To which will be added, the first time,
> A New Patriotic Effusion, called the
> CONSTITUTION AND GUERRIERE; or
> A Tribute to the Brave!
> written to commemorate the late brilliant Naval
> Victory.

Amos Evans went to the theater to see it on opening night; "a very fool-
ish, ridiculous thing," he said in his diary, remarking too that the actors
of the serious works on the program needed to study Hamlet's advice to
the players, so awfully had they "butchered" and "murdered" their
parts with overacting.[4] But the manager knew his business: the house
was packed. The dramatization of the naval battle ended with a song,
"Huzza for the Constitution," with the chorus, "With our true noble
Captain we fought on the main . . . And we hope that with him, we'll
soon conquer again."[5]

A raft of other odes to Hull and the *Constitution* appeared on broadsides around town.

> They met with a Warrior, by name and by nature,
> That had challeng'd the whole Yankee fleet,
> Our sailors, they stood, every man at his station.
> The Briton disdain'd to retreat.
>
> In a broadside or two, not a mast was left standing,
> The deck it was cover'd with slain;
> So Hull gave the Guerriere a good reprimanding
> For disturbing the rights of the main.[6]

And, to the tune of "Yankee Doodle":

> Come, come my lads, the glasses raise;
> Let's drink to gallant Hull, Sir,
> For well, our Constitution, he
> Sustain'd against John Bull, Sir.
>
> Where's now the Guerrere? Deep she sinks
> Beneath old Neptune's Acres;
> Hull, Hull's the lad, will make them glad
> To bear away with Dacres.
>
> Our good *Live Oak* 'gainst *British Oak*
> On Ocean shall maintain, Sir,
> With Yankee balls and *Hearts of Oak*
> Its claims to Ocean, vain, Sir.[7]

A few of the more skillful editorial writers for the Federalist papers twisted themselves into logical knots trying to explain the contradiction of celebrating victory in a war they opposed. Boston's *Repertory* newspaper opined that the pleasure to be derived from Hull's success came chiefly from the proof it offered "that in this disastrous war which will terminate most certainly in our ruin on the ocean, we shall have the consolation of shewing that it is neither through want of naval skill, or courage, or good conduct in our officers or men, that we shall not succeed, but to the imbecility, or treachery, or lukewarmness of our administration." The editor added that the town's Republican newspaper, the *Chronicle,* which "has uniformly been the zealous opponent of a naval establishment, . . . to be consistent ought to lament Hull's victory."[8]

But those barbs cut two ways; part of the glee that Boston took in the first triumph at sea was undeniably due to news arriving at the very same instant of the first disaster on land. William Hull—Isaac Hull's uncle, no less, a Revolutionary war officer who was leading the western prong of what was to be a three-pronged attack on Montreal, Niagara, and the Detroit frontier—had already become the butt of a relentless series of facetious barbs for his disorganized and hesitant start. In the same issue that lauded the *Constitution*'s victory, the *Repertory* ran an item under the headline PROGRESS OF THE WAR that was par for the treatment he had been receiving from the war's critics: "The news from Gen Hull's army is that he has taken 836 Merino SHEEP, which will probably be detained till a cartel is arranged for exchange of prisoners."[9]

Two days later, on September 3, news arrived in Boston that General Hull and his entire army had been taken prisoner on August 16. Evans noted that at the dinner at Faneuil Hall one of the guests had said he couldn't resist observing that "we had a Hull Up and a Hull Down," but the news at the Exchange Coffee House a few days later added details that stilled the humor, even as they fed Federalist schadenfreude. General Hull had apparently surrendered Fort Detroit without any resistance at all, panicked by rumors that a vast band of Indians was preparing to descend on the fort and massacre all the women and children. The rumors were actually a hoax planted by the British army commander, Isaac Brock: he had written a letter addressed to a fellow British general at a nearby post asking that no more Indians be sent to reinforce his position because he already had five thousand and was running short of provisions. Brock arranged for the letter to fall into American hands, then sent Hull a surrender demand stating, "It is far from my inclination to join in a war of extermination, but you must be aware, that the numerous body of Indians who have attached themselves to my troops, will be beyond controul the moment the contest commences." And so without consulting any of his officers Hull had waved a white flag, surrendering his twenty-five hundred men without firing a shot.[10]

Evans noted in his diary that two of the *Guerriere*'s officers, free to move about town on parole while waiting to be exchanged as prisoners of war, had come by to see him and reported that they were delighted with the attention paid to them by the citizens of Boston, and had been overwhelmed with invitations to dine.[11]

"WITH OUR true noble Captain we fought on the main . . . And we hope that with him, we'll soon conquer again": on the stage of the Federal Street Theater the chorus of officers, sailors, and marines of the *Constitution* had marched up State Street in the final scene, colors flying, after singing that refrain; but it was not to be. The same day Isaac Hull set foot ashore and received the news of his brother's death, he had closed himself in his room at the Exchange Coffee House and written to Secretary Hamilton asking to be relieved of his command:

> Having had the misfortune to lose a brother since my departure
> from this place, on whom depended my father's family, and with
> whom all my private concerns have been left ever since I joined
> the Navy, makes it absolutely necessary that I should take a short
> time to make provision for my younger brothers, and to see my
> father placed in a comfortable situation. I have therefore to
> request that you will be pleased to order a commander to the
> Constitution to take my place.[12]

His family obligations were real enough, but so too was his manifest desire for some tranquillity; Hull never had the killer instinct or the boastful drive of a Decatur or Bainbridge or Rodgers. "It is so dreadful to see my men wounded and suffering," Hull confessed to a friend, and Moses Smith recalled that his captain "even looked more truly noble, bending over the hammock of a wounded tar, than when invading and conquering the enemy." Beyond offering praise for the bravery of his crew, Hull never once afterward spoke or wrote—even privately to friends—of his part in the taking of the *Guerriere.* He even sent Hamilton a second, much shorter account of the action a few days after his first report, fearing the first would sound too vain; he told Hamilton, "As it's my opinion that the less that is said about a brilliant act the better, I have therefore given you a short sketch which I should prefer having published."

Bainbridge, who had missed by a day or two getting the command of the *Constitution* when she was in port a month earlier, wrote Hamilton hard on the heels of Hull's letter, offering what he saw as the perfect solution: he would take the *Constitution,* but without giving up his claim to the Boston Navy Yard whenever he wanted it back. "Captain Hull could be appointed to the command of this Navy Yard, during my absence from it," Bainbridge proposed. Agreeing to the switch and no doubt feeling he had enough troubles without worrying about hypothetical future assignments, Hamilton replied on September 9, ordering the change of commands and not addressing Bainbridge's "during my absence" proviso.[13]

At four in the afternoon of September 15 Commodore William Bainbridge went aboard the *Constitution,* hoisted his broad red pennant, and found himself with a mutiny on his hands before he could even open his mouth.

Breaking ranks, the crew swarmed around Captain Hull, begged him to stay, gave him a thundering three cheers, and swore they would sail out and take the British flagship, the sixty-four-gun *Africa,* with him as their captain. But if they had to serve under Captain Bainbridge, they demanded to be transferred, at once, to *any* other vessel. In the midst of the uproar the ship's armorer, Leonard Hayes, was placed under arrest and hauled off onto one of the nearby gunboats "on the charge of insolent and mutinous language."

Finally Bainbridge addressed the crew. He demanded to know whether there were any among them who had actually sailed with him before and refused to go with him now: "My men, what do you know about me?" It was the wrong question: they knew plenty. One after another of the men spoke up to say that they had indeed sailed with him and would not do it again if they could help it. One man declared he had been with Bainbridge on the *Philadelphia* "and had been badly used." Though the man allowed "it might be altered now," he would still prefer going with Captain Hull, "or any of the other commanders."[14]

Eighteen sentries were posted all over the ship that night, but that did not prevent two of the crew from slipping over the side and stealing the cutter to try to make a break for it. They were quickly caught when they floated past an anchored gunboat nearby and were returned to the *Constitution* in the morning.

All hands were called aft, and Bainbridge for the first time in his career decided that he might gain more by not flogging a recalcitrant crewman. Addressing the assembled crew, Bainbridge proposed a deal: "I will not punish these men as they deserve if you will consent to go in the ship." Moses Smith recalled that "this was appealing to our best feelings," and "nearly every man consented, to save his brother sailors from punishment." The only punishment recorded aboard the *Constitution* for the next two and a half months occurred a week later, and even that won Bainbridge support from the crew: a seaman named George Mitchell, ashore on liberty, was returned to the ship one afternoon by an army recruiting agent. If Mitchell had just run away he probably would still have had the crew's sympathy, but attempting to enlist in the rival service, and pocketing the eight-dollar bounty for it, was another matter. "No one could justify him," Smith said. He got twelve lashes, probably the mildest sentence Bainbridge had ever awarded for such an offense, too mild as far as most of the crew was concerned.[15]

Hull spent the rest of the fall settling his brother's estate and quickly proposing marriage to, and equally quickly being accepted by, a lovely, intelligent, and much-sought-after young woman from his home state of Connecticut. Ann Hart was twenty-one, just over half his age. One of her male acquaintances reported with ill-concealed jealousy that "Miss Ann Hart bestowed her hand . . . on Victory as personified by our little fat captain, Isaac Hull, who is now reposing in the shade of his laurels"; and Hull himself could not resist gloating in a letter to John Bullus, "I find the last frigate I had the good fortune to capture as tight a little boat as I could wish . . . I only wish you could have seen more of her before I took my departure. Had you I am sure you would have liked her construction." Ann, for her part, told a friend, "What a delightful thing it must be to be the wife of a hero."

The only sour note to the beginning of what would prove to be thirty years of happy marriage was predictably provided by William Bainbridge. On the newlyweds' return to Boston from New York, where Hull had been temporarily assigned for a few months before taking up his post at the Boston Navy Yard, they discovered that Mrs. Bainbridge and her children were still occupying the commandant's house and refused to move out. The Hulls had to rent lodgings. Mrs. Hull and Mrs. Bainbridge hated each other at first sight.[16]

ON SEPTEMBER 26 a report on the Exchange Coffee House books in Boston noted that Sir John Borlase Warren, Baronet, Knight of the Bath, Admiral of the Blue, had arrived in Halifax to assume command of all of His Majesty's naval forces in the northern half of the American hemisphere. The Admiralty had decided to consolidate all four stations in British North America and the Caribbean into a single unified command; besides the 32 ships of the North American station based in Halifax, Warren was to have at his disposal the 28 ships of the Leeward Islands station based at Antigua, the 18 of the Jamaica station based at Port Royal, and the 12 of the Newfoundland station based at St. John's—some 90 ships in all, among them 18 frigates and 5 ships of the line. Warren arrived on the seventy-four-gun *San Domingo,* accompanied by a second ship of the line, the seventy-four-gun *Poictiers,* plus two sloops of war and a schooner; two more frigates were to follow as soon as possible.[17]

Warren was fifty-nine, a man of good looks and smooth manner, former ambassador to Russia, former member of Parliament; all in all, more a diplomat and politician than an admiral. He had previously served as commander in chief of the Halifax station from 1807 to 1810, sent out at that time to smooth things over with the United States after the British government had recalled Admiral Berkeley in the aftermath of the *Chesapeake* affair.

Warren was the epitome of the aristocrat who had made an effortless ascent in the Royal Navy. Entered as an able seaman on the books of the ship of the line *Marlborough* in 1771 when he was eighteen—and actually attending Cambridge University—he did not begin serving on a naval vessel until six years later. Within a year he was a lieutenant, three years after that a captain. Warren had, however, gone on to distinguish himself as a squadron commander, in 1798 intercepting a French flotilla off the coast of Ireland that was carrying five thousand troops, a feat for which he was voted a gold medal by Parliament. But he had never commanded a force larger than a frigate squadron and had never had to deal with larger questions of naval strategy.[18]

Warren came bearing both carrots and sticks. Empowered to open negotiations with the American government, he wrote at once to Secretary of State Monroe proposing an immediate cessation of hostilities based on Britain's revocation of the orders in council.[19]

He was also immediately inundated with the administrative responsibilities of managing four stations: ninety ships and twelve thousand men to supply and keep fed, complaints from merchants to be answered, chronic shortages of dockyard supplies to deal with. Then there was the avalanche of forms that the Admiralty bureaucracy constantly demanded: statistical compilations of punishments inflicted on each ship; weekly returns of the sick and wounded on His Majesty's vessels itemized by number on the sick list, number confined to bed, number in hospitals, number discharged back to duty, and then broken down by cause—intermittent fevers, continued fevers, catarrhs, pneumonic inflammation, consumption, rheumatism, venereal disease, scurvy, ulcers, wounds and accidents, dysentery, diarrhea; preprinted grids two pages wide to be filled in for each ship listing how much bread, beer, brandy, wine, rum, beef, pork, pease, oatmeal, flour, suet, fruit, butter, cheese, rice, sugar, oil, vinegar, and water was on board, how many men short of complement each was, what condition each ship was in.[20] Adding to all the paperwork was an accounting task that unmistakably occupied a good deal of Warren's attention, filling ledger after ledger with meticulous entries tracking the value of every prize brought in to the vice admiralty courts at Halifax and Bermuda, calculating the one-twelfth share due the flag admiral, converting Halifax and Bermuda currency to sterling, deducting the prize agent's 5 percent commission and the 5 percent of the remainder assessed to support the naval pensioners at Greenwich Hospital, and subtracting miscellaneous advances the admiral had had his prize agent in Bermuda make for house rent, printing bills, twelve dozen bottles of Champagne, a pianoforte, hire of a horse and gig, two rounds of beef, a sheep, his annual subscription to the Halifax Bible Society, pocket money. He was said to employ one clerk full-time just keeping track of his prize money accounts, and by the end of his first year of managing Great Britain's war with America on the high seas the admiral's take, even after deducting all those living expenses his agent had advanced, was 15,238 pounds, 16 shillings, and 2 pence—about $60,000 in 1812, the equivalent of something like $1 million today. He would receive another £13,602 in prize money a year and a half after that.[21]

When the admiral turned his attention to running the war, he found that much of the strength of his force was illusory and many of his options were distinctly limited. His predecessor in Halifax, Vice Admiral Herbert Sawyer, had done almost nothing to prepare for war. Sawyer had waited until June 22 to return to Halifax from Bermuda, where the squadron had spent the winter, and most of his ships arrived home in a state of disrepair and well below their complement owing to sickness and desertions and a severe shortage of naval stores and trained shipwrights in Bermuda. The Halifax dockyard was in a shambles too. A proclamation offering a full pardon to any naval deserters in the Maritime Provinces who returned to duty brought few takers. Then a series of mishaps in August and September wreaked more havoc. The brig *Emulous* ran aground in a storm off Nova Scotia; the schooner *Chub* was fired on and damaged beyond immediate repair in a case of mistaken identity during a foggy night; the frigate *Barbadoes* struck a notorious shipwrecking bar off tiny Sable Island two hundred miles southeast of Halifax, and although her crew and £60,000 she was carrying for the dockyard payroll were saved, the ship was bashed to pieces on the beach; and a severely undermanned sloop of war, the *Laura*, was taken by a French privateer in a battle that left almost half the British crew dead. The small squadron that had put to sea under Broke in July—the four frigates plus the sixty-four-gun *Africa* that had chased the *Constitution* off New Jersey—represented almost the entire serviceable portion of the station's paper strength for most of the summer.

Hundreds of American privateers were already swarming the waters off the Maritime Provinces, and Halifax itself remained woefully undefended, but a request from Sawyer to the Newfoundland station for reinforcements was rebuffed; most of its ships were busy protecting the fishing fleet on the Grand Banks. The Caribbean stations had their own problems, not least that their available ships were similarly committed to escorting convoys and few could be spared to initiate offensive operations on the American coast.[22]

In early October Warren issued a flurry of sailing orders, trying to cover as many contingencies as possible: The flagship *San Domingo*, in which Warren had just arrived, would cruise the Grand Banks with the *Africa* for the "succor and protection" of several valuable British convoys. A squadron consisting of the ship of the line *Poictiers*, two frigates, two sloops of war, and a schooner was ordered to the capes of the Chesapeake to protect British trade passing to and from the West Indies and gather intelligence on American naval movements. The frigates *Shannon*, *Nymphe*, and *Tenedos* and the brig sloop *Curlew* were to cruise the North Atlantic "for such time as circumstances of Wind and Weather or information may tender expedient, but taking care to return here by the 15th of November" while looking out for the convoys from New-foundland that Rodgers's squadron was believed to be pursuing. Several frigates and smaller ships were to bottle up Charleston harbor; the frigate *Belvidera* to cruise the mid-Atlantic coast of America for six weeks for "the destruction and annoyance of the Enemy"; a powerful squadron of nine ships to patrol the coast and harbors of Nova Scotia and New Brunswick and "in the event of invasion" to "proceed forth-with to the point of attack with the whole of your squadron to cooper-ate with and aid and assist the Army."[23]

At the same time he sent his own urgent plea to the Admiralty in London for reinforcements "to enable me to meet the exertions of the Enemy, who seem to be determined to persevere in the annoyance and destruction of the commerce of Great Britain."[24] He enclosed a copy of an American privateer's commission found on the prize master of a captured British ship retaken by the *San Domingo;* it was numbered 318, which seemed to fully confirm his worst apprehensions about the size of the problem he had on his hands protecting British convoys and guarding against surprise attacks on the Maritime Provinces.

Warren's orders authorized him to "attack, sink, burn or otherwise destroy" the commerce and navy of the United States but also instructed him to "exercise all possible forbearance" while the prospect of negotiations remained alive.[25] In many ways, both sides were still treating it as a short, civilized war in the early fall of 1812. Amid all his preparations for belligerency, Warren casually dispatched the frigate *Spartan* to the island of Madeira in November to pick up a shipload of wine to keep the squadron supplied in its accustomed fashion.[26] Mon-roe took an early opportunity of writing to Warren that "it is the sincere desire of the President to see (and to promote, so far as depends on the United States,) that the war which exists between our countries be con-ducted with the utmost regard to humanity." And officers on both sides had gone out of their way to make honorable, even chivalric gestures to one another: Dacres's magnanimous act of allowing the impressed Americans in the *Guerriere*'s crew to go below during the battle was widely noted, as was his praise of the treatment the British had received aboard the *Constitution* after being taken prisoner. "I feel it my duty to state," Dacres wrote Vice Admiral John T. Duckworth in Newfound-land, "that the conduct of Captain Hull and his Officers to our Men has been that of a brave Enemy, the greatest care being taken to pre-vent our Men losing the smallest trifle."[27]

Arrangements for exchanging naval prisoners of war were quickly agreed to, with cartel vessels chartered to carry prisoners back to their respective countries. The agreement stipulated that prisoners on both sides would be returned without delay and established relative values for officers of different ranks: one admiral was worth 60 men, a commodore 20, a captain of a line of battle ship 15, a frigate captain 10, a lieutenant 6, a midshipman or the master of a merchant vessel 3. If the balance sheet did not even out on both sides, prisoners would still be returned promptly, in the meantime giving their parole of honor that they would not resume any naval or military duty until regularly exchanged.[28] In August, when David Porter in the frigate *Essex* captured the British sloop of war *Alert* in the middle of the Atlantic about five hundred miles west of the Azores, the two captains quickly reached a gentleman's agreement skipping the formality of having to take the British prisoners back to America at all. Porter put the *Alert*'s crew back on their own ship, threw their guns overboard, and accepted their parole for themselves and their ship. The agreement transformed the prize directly into a "sea cartel" that would sail to St. Johns, put the prisoners ashore, and then proceed to New York with any American prisoners released in exchange. A single lieutenant from the *Essex* was placed aboard the *Alert* to command the ship.[29] This was actually playing fast and loose with the laws of war, and such a procedure was definitely not to the strategic advantage of a naval power like Britain that enjoyed such a huge numerical advantage of force: Admiral Duckworth wrote to Secretary Hamilton protesting the arrangement "in the strongest manner," pointing out that it not only relieved the capturing vessel of the burden of her prisoners without having to break her cruise or even diminish her crew by manning the prize, but also secured the prize against recapture, since it was now effectively sailing under a flag of truce. Duckworth noted that to be properly recognized as a cartel, a ship first needed to enter a port of the nation by which she had been captured.

Nevertheless, the admiral continued, he was prepared to honor the agreement as a token of British goodwill:

> I am willing to give proof at once of my respect for the liberality with which the captain of the Essex has acted, in more than one instance towards the British subjects who have fallen into his hands; of the sacred obligation that is always felt, to fulfill the

engagements of a British officer; and of my confidence in the disposition of his royal highness the prince regent, to allay the violence of war by encouraging a reciprocation of that courtesy by which its pressure upon individuals may be so essentially diminished.[30]

The *Alert* subsequently arrived in New York as agreed, carrying 232 released American prisoners.[31]

But even in the first months of the fighting, humanity was already beginning to fray against the inevitable rough friction of war. On September 11 a cartel arrived in Boston with the crew of the brig *Nautilus,* which had been captured July 16 off New Jersey, the first American navy ship taken in the war. They had several stories to tell of the less-than-chivalric treatment American prisoners had received in Halifax. One midshipman, manning a prize that was recaptured by a British frigate, had his sword taken from him by the captain, who then stamped on it, threw it overboard, and said, "There's one damn Yankee sword gone." Both sides traded accusations of attempts to "seduce" their prisoners to desert and join the other's navy.

Much more seriously, six of the crew of the *Nautilus* had been detained in Halifax and were not returned with the other exchanged Americans. Claiming that the men were British subjects, Captain Broke ordered them sent to England for examination and possible trial on a charge of bearing arms against the king, which was treason, punishable by death.[32] Commodore Rodgers learned of this just as the cartel ship was leaving Boston harbor on its way back to Halifax with the prisoners of the *Guerriere;* he sent a boat to halt the ship and took off twelve of the British prisoners in retaliation, announcing that they would be held hostage and subjected to whatever fate the Americans were.

The British chargé d'affaires protested this "outrage," and Warren sent a warning of his own directly to Monroe threatening retaliation against any repetition of Rodgers's "extremely reprehensible" conduct.

The admiral added, however, that it was "still very much my wish . . . during the continuance of the differences existing between the two countries to adopt every measure that might render the effect of war less rigorous."[33]

IN LITTLE over a month of solo cruising, the *Essex* under David Porter's command had taken eight enemy merchant ships and a sloop of war, amply affirming the wisdom of dispersing the small American naval force for maximum "annoyance" of the enemy. Porter estimated that along with the 424 prisoners he captured, he had taken or destroyed property worth $300,000.[34] In taking the *Alert* he had been able to decoy the smaller British ship by a ruse de guerre of discreetly throwing out two drags astern while sending a few men aloft to put on a disorganized show of trying to shake out the reefs in the topsails, looking for the world like an undermanned merchantman trying to make a desperate getaway. The crew went to quarters and cleared for action but kept their gunports closed until the *Alert* came within range, whereupon Porter ran up the American ensign, the gunports flew open, and the *Essex* fired a broadside, shooting the tampions out of the end of the guns along with the first round. The *Alert* struck in eight minutes. Of course it was an uneven contest, but it also showed what a single frigate sailing alone could do.[35] Upon his arrival at the mouth of the Delaware in early September, Porter wrote Bainbridge, "I hope however to have another slap at them ere long that will gall them still more."[36]

With the example of *Constitution* and *Essex* before them, both Bainbridge and Rodgers wrote Secretary Hamilton reiterating the advantage of having the American frigates sail singly to strike most effectively at the enemy's commerce. "It will at the same time afford now and then an opportunity to our Frigates and theirs, of falling in singly, to our advantage," added Rodgers. Bainbridge promised the secretary that by ordering the ships to venture out individually "you would occasionally hear glad tidings of us," whereas "if we are kept together in squadron . . . the whole are scarcely of more advantage than one ship would be." Rodgers thought that there might be a benefit in keeping in small squadrons while leaving port and separating once at sea to confuse the British as to the disposition and intentions of the American force, and Hamilton agreed to that suggestion. He ordered Rodgers in the *President*, Bainbridge in the *Constitution*, and Decatur in the *United States* to form their squadrons by selecting, in order of seniority, one of the smaller frigates from among the *Congress, Chesapeake,* and *Essex;* each would also be assigned a small brig to complete his squadron.[37]

But Hamilton left it entirely up to the three senior captains to decide where they would cruise, which while satisfying their personal inclinations for independence abandoned any attempt at strategic planning or coordination of the fight at a higher level; Hamilton did not even suggest that the captains consult with one another to make sure their plans did not conflict. And so each absurdly kept his intentions a secret from the others.

While the *Constitution* awaited the completion of her repairs at the Charlestown Navy Yard, Bainbridge wrote his old friend William Jones of Philadelphia asking for advice on where the best pickings might be had. Jones replied with a long letter, promising to forward a copy of *Elmores Indian Directory,* which included details on the sailing schedules and routes of the British East India trade, and drawing on his own expertise as a shipping merchant and captain to recommend six cruising grounds best suited "for intercepting the British trade." Jones thought Rodgers had erred in his recent cruise by being too far north along the meridian of the Azores; the West India fleets tended to pass to the south of the tail of the Grand Banks to avoid the fog and pass near the Azores before turning to the north after passing east of the islands, and "from one or two degrees North" of the Azores "is an excellent position." Other promising spots were along the coast of Portugal, on the track of convoys between Britain and Gibraltar; off Cape Canaveral, where "in the outer verge of the Stream you intercept to a certainty everything from Jamaica through the Gulph and have the ports of Georgia and the Carolinas near you"; the Crooked Island passage in the Bahamas, "to intercept trade from the East end of Jamaica"; and the coast of Brazil, "with which the British drive a valuable trade and the returns are very frequently in a very convenient Commodity Viz Gold Bars and Coin and other compact valuables." Jones added that "a Brilliant Cruize ought no doubt be made in the Indian seas, but for the distance and absolute deprivation of a Single friendly Port to refit in Case of Accidents to which you would be much exposed"; on balance there was probably "too much of chance and responsibility to warrant the enterprize with so important a part of our Gallant little Navy."[38]

The *Constitution* had sustained significant damage to her spars and rigging that needed the full attention of the navy yard, but all the ships that had come into Boston needed resupplies of provisions and stores as well. Complete supplies for even one of the smaller frigates included twenty tons of bread in a hundred casks, ten tons of beef and ten tons of pork in another hundred barrels each, three thousand gallons of rum, two tons of cheese, six tons of flour and cornmeal, two tons of rice, and eighty barrels of potatoes. There was coal for the galley stove and forge, five hundred pounds of musket balls, a thousand flints, a hundred pounds of slow match, seventy cartridge bags and like numbers of round shot and grapeshot or canister shot and several hundred pounds of powder for every gun. There were huge lists of supplies and spare parts that every ship needed to keep on hand and well stocked at all times to deal with the emergencies that arose at sea, everything from fifty pounds of 20d nails to caulking mallets and rasps and hundreds upon hundreds of gallons of paint and turpentine and varnish, spare pump chains and bolts, sewing twine and iron bar stock, fishing lines and fire buckets, barrel hoops and soldering irons.[39]

The simultaneous arrival of Hull and Rodgers nearly drove the navy's Boston agent, Amos Binney, to despair. He also had no money. By the third week in September the warehouse at the navy yard that could hold 1,200 barrels of salt provisions was empty. On October 7 Binney wrote Hamilton that he had actually advanced $52,501.96 on his own account, borrowing from banks and even personal friends to meet the navy payroll, procure medicines and provisions, and proceed with repairs of the battle damage sustained by the *Constitution* and the *President:* "I have exhausted every resource within my controul, and am paying interest on the most of this sum. I have been induced to make these extra exertions that the Squadrons should not be detained in port one moment on my acct at a crisis like the present." [40]

The *Constitution* needed all new lower masts, many other new spars, patches to the outer layer of her hull, an entire new set of standing rigging. Bainbridge wrote Jones that he was even working Sundays to get the work done: "So you'll perceive, that I dare even break the Sabbath in this Religious Land." He was also so envious of Rodgers's having the *President* that he offered him $5,000 to switch ships. Rodgers declined, and both Rodgers's and Decatur's squadrons got under way October 8, "whither bound, I know not," Bainbridge said.[41] It was actually Decatur's ship that was now considered the poorest sailer of the three large frigates: the *United States* was known derisively as the "Old Wagon."

The *Constitution* followed them out to sea three weeks later. Passing a fort in the harbor, the ship was hailed with three cheers from the soldiers. Before they sailed, Amos Evans noted in his journal that the congressional elections in Maryland had just gone strongly in favor of the Federalists. "What miserable dunces the people are to be so easily gulld!" Evans fumed. Widespread revulsion over the Baltimore riots had cost the Republicans their majority in the state, and among those newly elected to the House was Alexander Hanson, the editor whose newspaper, the *Federal Republican,* had been the chief target of the mob.[42]

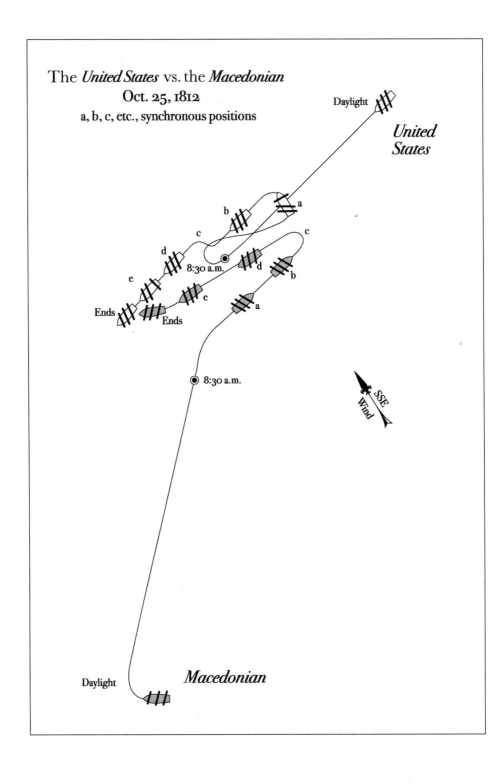

The *United States* vs. the *Macedonian*
Oct. 25, 1812
a, b, c, etc., synchronous positions

Daylight

United States

a

b

c

c

d

8:30 a.m.

d

b

e

e

e

a

Ends

Ends

8:30 a.m.

SSE
Wind

Daylight

Macedonian

. . .

HIS BRITANNIC Majesty's frigate *Macedonian,* Captain John Surman Carden, had been assigned to the Lisbon station since leaving Norfolk the previous winter, and among its tedious tasks was to carry home from the Peninsula the invalided Marquis of Londonderry, Charles William Stewart. Stewart had been serving as Wellington's adjutant general in the campaign against Napoleon's army in Spain, and when the nobleman arrived at Spithead, he expressed his "gratification of the Comforts & attentions he had receiv'd" on the voyage, Carden recalled, and asked the captain "what in the way of the Naval Service he could do for me." Carden replied that the command of a frigate was all he could wish for, but ventured to suggest that the "only possible" addition to his ambition would be "a Cruise on the Western Ocean, where chances would be more favourable to my future prospects." It was a wish, Carden later ruefully recalled, which only went to prove "how short sighted are the Creatures of this World."[43]

In the ways of the Royal Navy and the influence of the well-connected, Carden received orders on September 29, 1812, to convoy an East Indies merchantman past Madeira, at which point he would be free to sweep the Western Ocean, hunting any French or American prizes he could find, for as long as his water and provisions held out.

The *Macedonian* had a reputation as a "crack ship"; she was also as unhappy a ship as there was. Carden was, to be sure, an experienced captain who appreciated the value of a well-trained crew, and he constantly exercised his men at the guns. He even encouraged incompetent men to desert with the winking assurance that he would not try to pursue them. The captain would eye a man with a meaningful look and order him to go ashore "to cut broom." The "broomers" would not return, and nothing more was ever said about them. But Carden was also an unflinching disciplinarian, regularly meting out sentences of three dozen lashes; punishing a man who was accused, probably falsely, of stealing a midshipman's handkerchief with three hundred lashes; and teaching a lesson to the ship's drummer who dared to demand a court-martial over a trivial offense by making sure he received a sentence of two hundred lashes through the fleet, a warning to any other men who had the insolence to question the captain's authority to order punishment.

The real trouble was Carden's first lieutenant, David Hope, a man who was not only a disciplinarian but a sadist, and especially enjoyed watching the ship's boys being whipped. Since Hope joined the ship, punishments had become "an almost every-day scene," said seaman Samuel Leech, who remembered the "gleam of savage animation" that would come over the lieutenant's face when one of his victims was stripped and seized to the grating in preparation for a flogging.[44]

On Sunday morning, October 25, the *Macedonian* was about halfway between the Azores and the Cape Verde Islands, having parted company with the Indiaman three days earlier. For several days a shark, with its attendant pilot fish, had accompanied the ship: an ill omen that more than a few of her crew declared to be a presentiment that they would never see England again. The Sunday morning had brought a stiff breeze from the southeast. Just after breakfast the crew was mustered on the spar deck in their customary Sunday dress clothes—blue jackets, black glossy hats with black ribbons bearing the name of the ship painted on them—when the lookout on the masthead hailed the deck: "Sail ho!"

Since leaving Madeira, Carden had been more anxious than usual, on deck nearly all the time, constantly hectoring the man on the masthead to "keep a good look-out." Carden came on deck in a flash, hailing, "Mast-head, there, where away?" The lookout reported that she was a large, square-rigged ship, on the lee beam. Then a few minutes later he added, "A large frigate, bearing down upon us, sir!" The crew was murmuring its own views of the stranger's identity when Carden interrupted with "Keep silence, fore and aft!" and then "All hands clear the ship for action!"[45]

Eight impressed Americans were on the crew, and one of them, John Card, ventured to approach the captain and declare his objections to fighting against his own countrymen, should the ship prove to be an American. Carden was not the man to make the kind of magnanimous and chivalrous gesture Dacres had when he allowed the Americans on the *Guerriere* to go below. Erupting in fury, he ordered Card to his station and threatened to shoot him if he made the request again.[46]

At around 8:30 a.m. the approaching frigate was about three miles away when she suddenly wore around in the opposite direction, revealing the Stars and Stripes flying from her tops. Lieutenant Hope had just been urging Carden to steer directly for the enemy's bows and risk taking a raking fire during the approach in order to close as quickly as possible; he brushed aside the captain's concern about keeping the weather gauge, saying it did not matter whether they engaged from windward or leeward "as long as we went close alongside of the enemy."[47] Carden proposed keeping to windward and using that advantage to get past the enemy's broadside at a safe distance and then wear around on to her stern, so he could then close the gap between the ships without being exposed to raking fire while also taking advantage of the apparently superior sailing speed of his ship. But the enemy's maneuver seemed baffling on all counts. The British officers at first thought it must mean that she had thought better of seeking a fight and was fleeing. Carden ordered his ship brought closer to the wind to keep the windward position and the possibility of carrying out his original intention. The ships were now on a parallel course, sailing in the same direction, a lateral distance of about half a mile separating their tracks.

Then the enemy wore again, back on to her original course, though a bit farther off. As the two ships passed on opposite tacks, at about 9:00 a.m., the enemy's entire lower gun deck erupted in a billow of flame and smoke. All the shot fell short, but Carden now knew he was up against one of the large American frigates, armed with a broadside of fifteen 24-pound long guns. A few minutes later he wore in pursuit.[48]

With the battle joined, Carden no doubt felt honor bound to close as rapidly as possible in the traditionally aggressive British fashion, but having let himself be baffled by the enemy's initial maneuvers had placed him in the least favorable position to do so. A substantial lateral distance still separated them, and Carden was now facing a long, angling approach that exposed him to constant fire from the broadsides of an enemy whose guns substantially outranged his own eighteen-pounders. Overconfidently he pressed on; almost at once the American frigate's fire began doing horrific execution. Samuel Leech had the job of powder boy, running filled cartridges from the magazine up to his gun, and all around him men were dropping. On one trip up from the magazine he suddenly saw blood flying from the severed arm of one of the men at his gun; he had seen nothing strike the man, just the instant effect of an incoming shot. A Portuguese boy stationed on the quarter-deck was carrying powder when it ignited, searing most of the flesh off his face. The boy "lifted up both hands, as if imploring relief, when a passing shot instantly cut him in two," Leech said. Another man had his hand cut off by a shot, and then almost at the same moment a ball tore through his guts. Two seamen nearby caught him by the arms and, seeing the hopelessness of his situation, simply threw him overboard to a comparatively merciful death. Another man was carried past with the blood coursing out of him. "I distinctly heard the large blood-drops fall pat, pat, pat on the deck," Leech recalled; "his wounds were mortal." The goat kept by the officers to supply the wardroom with milk had her legs shot off and was thrown overboard. "The work of death went on in a manner which must have been satisfactory even to the King of Terrors himself," Leech wrote.

At one point the American frigate made a sharp jog to starboard, then back on course, increasing his range, drawing out the British frigate's ordeal. A little over an hour into the battle, when Carden finally succeeded in getting within half a musket shot, one hundred yards, it was over. All three of the *Macedonian*'s topmasts were gone, the main yard shot through and hanging in the slings that were rigged to hold up the spars during action. All the quarterdeck carronades on the starboard side were disabled, crippling the only weapons that offered a justification for closing to short range in the first place.[49] The American ship backed her mizzen topsail to keep from shooting ahead and continued to pour on her broadsides, now bringing her spar deck carronades into play as well.

And then the American filled her mizzen topsail and majestically pulled ahead across the *Macedonian*'s bows, momentarily holding her at mercy; then, without firing a shot, the American frigate pulled off. Some of the *Macedonian*'s men broke out in cheers, thinking the American was abandoning the fight, but all the officers except for Lieutenant Hope knew better. Hope himself had been wounded, and when he was brought below to have his wound dressed, Leech said, "there was not a man in the ship but would have rejoiced" had he never risen up off the surgeon's table. Hope was soon back on deck, urging the fight to continue. But at that moment the mizzenmast, "in a toppling state," fell by the board. Once again a British frigate was described by her captain as "a perfect wreck, an unmanageable log."[50] An hour later the American ship came up again, having repaired her minor damage, and took up a raking position as the *Macedonian* hauled down her colors.

A boat came across from the American ship, and Carden was rowed back to deliver his surrender and found himself facing his old acquaintance from Norfolk, Stephen Decatur. "I am an undone man," Carden said. "I am the first British naval officer that has struck his flag to an American." Decatur smiled and, returning Carden's proffered sword, replied, "You are mistaken, sir; your Guerriere has been taken by us, and the flag of a frigate was struck before yours." And then he jokingly turned to his marine officer and said, "You call yourselves riflemen, and have allowed this very tall and erect officer, on an open quarterdeck to escape your aim?" But Carden thought Decatur might have spared the attempt at levity; of the fifty-two men and officers on his quarterdeck, he would later recall, forty-three had been killed or grievously wounded.

Decatur wrote his wife not long after, "One half of the satisfaction arising from this victory is destroyed in seeing the distress of poor Carden, who deserved success as much as we did, who had the good fortune to obtain it. I did all I can to console him." Decatur paid Carden $800 to purchase his personal stores, including several casks of wine and the musical instruments of a band of French musicians whom Carden had recruited out of a prison hulk in Lisbon, and who now gladly agreed to join the *United States*.[51]

Decatur's victory was as lopsided as Hull's had been. A third of the *Macedonian*'s crew were casualties, 43 killed and 61 wounded. Among the dead were two Americans—including John Card, the man Carden had threatened to shoot if he did not fight. The *United States* had suffered a total of 7 killed and 5 wounded. Each ship had fired about 1,200 rounds; the *Macedonian* had taken 95 hits in her hull to 5 in the *United States*.[52] But Decatur's aim all along had been to bring in his prize intact; a great deal of the American fire, especially at the start of the battle, had been aimed at the *Macedonian*'s spars, with devastating effect. Barrages of chain and linked iron bar and double-headed shot joined by rods sliced through the *Macedonian*'s sails and rigging while leaving her hull intact. Decatur unhesitatingly ascribed his victory to the accuracy of his own men's gunnery, and singled out for praise the efforts of his first lieutenant, William Henry Allen, in training the gun crews.

Even when it was all over, the British would never understand what hit them. The court-martial of the *Macedonian*'s officers focused on Carden's "over anxiety" to keep the weather gauge but showed no comprehension that he had been outmaneuvered from the start. Hope testified that he believed the key opportunity had been lost in not closing rapidly when they had a chance, and the fact was that Carden compounded his initial hesitation to risk a brief raking with his subsequent impetuosity in closing when it meant taking a long-drawn-out battering. Unlike Hull, who had used his windward position on the *Guerriere* to come up rapidly, but on a zigzag course that kept him from being raked each time the British ship fired and kept the enemy gunners guessing as to the proper lead to put on their aim, Carden had shown no finesse at all when he finally chose to close in on the *United States.* But the fact also was that Decatur's maneuvering had left Carden no good choices: by wearing twice at the start, he had forestalled Carden's plan to get past him and on his stern, and by keeping his distance during the heat of the battle, he had played to the advantage of his longer-range guns while forcing Carden to make that long, exposed approach.

A prize crew from the *United States* commanded by Lieutenant Allen quickly took charge of the British frigate. Lieutenant Hope was surly to the end, petulantly replying to Allen's polite invitation to get into the boat by saying, "You do not intend to send me away without my baggage?"

"I hope you do not suppose you have been taken by privateersmen?" Allen answered.

"I do not know by whom I am taken."

"Into the boat, Sir!"[53]

Allen put a guard on the officers' baggage and sent it over later in the day and set the prize crew to work at once fothering two large leaks below the waterline by working a sailcloth under the ship's keel. Seven feet of water was pumped out of the hold while the cloths temporarily held the sea from rushing back in. With that makeshift fix the carpenters could get at the holes from the inside to plug them more solidly, with wooden patches and oakum, while other work crews rigged jury masts. The work took five days; the whole time the two ships hove to along a well-traveled shipping lane. But Decatur's luck held; the only vessel that appeared was a Swedish merchantman bound for Cádiz. Decatur allowed Carden to put his purser aboard carrying his official dispatch for the Lords of the Admiralty in London that began, "It is with the deepest regret I have to acquaint you . . ."

And then the two ships sailed for home, 2,200 miles across strangely empty seas, the British captain each day scanning the horizon in vain for a British man-of-war.[54]

AGAIN THERE were dinners and celebrations, salutes and odes; the legislatures of Pennsylvania and Virginia voted Decatur ceremonial swords; and after two weeks at Newport and New London, where the *Macedonian* was given a quick sprucing up, the ships arrived in New

York, where the city presented Decatur with a gold box containing the Freedom of the City and still more honors, dinners, parades, theatrical tributes, everything else the city could think of to outdo what Boston had done to celebrate Hull's victory. Decatur had put his prisoners ashore in New London when he arrived there December 4, installing them in a not very well guarded barn, and about a hundred promptly ran for it so that they would never have to serve in the British navy again. Samuel Leech slipped into New York City a few weeks later with the all-but-open conniving of the Americans, having earned money in the meanwhile by giving tours of the captured frigate to throngs of gawking sightseers. Several more of the prisoners signed on to the *United States'* crew.[55]

One of Decatur's lieutenants was Archibald Hamilton, the twenty-two-year-old son of the navy secretary, and Decatur dispatched him directly to Washington with his official letter announcing the victory. The young lieutenant made a dramatic entrance at a "naval ball" that had already been arranged for the evening of Tuesday, December 8, in the capital to honor Hull, Morris, and other officers of the navy. Bursting through the doors of the hotel ballroom at 10:00 p.m. bearing the *Macedonian's* colors to a loud huzzah and the embraces of his mother and sisters, Lieutenant Hamilton knelt at the feet of Dolley Madison and laid the flag of the captured British frigate before her.

"This was rather overdoing the affair," thought one of the guests, Mrs. Benjamin H. Latrobe. She was the wife of the British-born architect responsible for much of the Capitol, and she wrote a long, vivid, and drily humorous description of the scene to a friend, concluding seriously:

> Now, between ourselves, I think it wrong to exult so outrageously over our enemies. We may have reason to laugh on the other side of our mouths some of these days; and, as the English are so much stronger than we are it is best to act moderately when we take a vessel; and I could not look on those colours with pleasure, the striking of which had made so many widows and orphans. In the fullness of my feelings, I exclaimed to a gentleman who stood near me, "Good Heavens—I would not touch that colour for a thousand dollars," and he walked quickly away, I hearing the gentleman say, "Is it possible, Mrs. Latrobe." I looked around and it was a good staunch Federalist from Rhode Island, Mr.

Hunter, the Senator, so that I shall escape hanging after so treasonable a speech. I came home at 12 with a raging headache.[56]

Along with the exultation over victory came an outbreak of squabbling and jealousy among American naval officers. In a burst of enthusiasm over the *Guerriere* victory, Secretary Hamilton decided to promote Charles Morris directly from lieutenant to captain, which brought the secretary a deluge of outraged letters from other officers objecting to the decision, especially to the fact that Morris was being advanced two grades in a single leap. One master commandant complained that "if *we* are to be over topt by every brave Lieut on whom fortune may smile, there will be no stimulus left *us*"; an aggrieved lieutenant added that he "cannot discover from the Official letters of Captain Hull" that Morris "particularly distinguished himself any Special Act of Gallantry." Bainbridge objected on behalf of several officers he wanted to see promoted, and Master Commandant James Lawrence threatened to appeal directly to the Senate to see his "legal rights" protected—and to resign from the navy altogether if he did not get satisfaction.[57]

The prize money that Decatur was due for bringing in an enemy ship of war was rapidly becoming another source of ill feeling. Under the navy department's regulations, the officers and crew of a ship capturing an enemy of equal or greater force were entitled to share the full value of the prize but were awarded only half the value of a captured ship of lesser force. Two referees were named, one by Hamilton and one by Decatur, and they promptly decided that the *Macedonian* was worth $200,000, which was fair enough, but also that she was of greater force than the *United States*, which could only be described as a bald-faced lie. Like all British thirty-eights, she was a smaller ship than the American forty-fours, armed with fewer and lighter guns. The captain's share, three-twentieths, put $30,000 in Decatur's pocket.

It was up to Congress to decide whether to grant Hull and his crew a reward in lieu of prize money for having destroyed the *Guerriere*, and the House Naval Committee at first reported a resolution authorizing $50,000 total. Hull and Hamilton testified to the committee that $100,000 would be a fairer compensation, and the bill was accordingly altered. But faced with having to come up with $200,000 for the *Macedonian*, the House cut the award for the *Constitution*'s crew back to $50,000, leaving Hull $7,500.[58] Hull, normally a modest man, was bitter and incensed and even two years later was still fuming about it, writing Connecticut's senator David Daggett:

> There has not been an action fought since, even by a sloop of war, but the commander has shared equal honors and more money. Look at the U States and Macedonian,—there Commo Decatur shared upwards of thirty thousand dollars, and for what? Because he was not so *unfortunate* as to shoot away her masts and got her safe in, for which he was allowed the whole of the ship, when the world knows that the Guerriere was a much heavier ship and the U States full as heavy, indeed heavier than the Constitution. Why such things are, I know not; but they are facts. . . . when I am led to think on the subject of the Navy I cannot but feel hurt at many things relative to myself that have taken place.[59]

Decatur meanwhile backed out of a gentleman's agreement he had made with Rodgers to "share and share alike" in all their prize money. Rodgers's prizes about equaled Decatur's by that point thanks mostly to Rodgers's capture of a British post office packet ship, the *Swallow,* on October 15 near the Grand Banks, just a few days after he sailed from Boston in the *President* on his second cruise of the war. On board were eighty-one boxes filled with gold and silver specie, tons in all, worth $150,000 to $200,000. But Rodgers had little else to show for his considerable efforts, and for a second time he was left expressing his sheepish frustration to Secretary Hamilton. On this cruise he made only two prizes in two and a half months at sea, an even poorer showing than the six merchant ships he had taken in July and August on his first cruise of two months' duration. "It will appear somewhat extraordinary," Rodgers wrote Hamilton, "when I inform you that in our late cruise we have sailed by our log nearly 11'000 miles, that we chased every thing we saw, yet that we should have seen so few Enemies Vessels." Decatur did not explicitly state to Rodgers the reason he now "would prefer going on our own accounts for the remainder of the war," but he probably did not have to: fortune had chosen to favor him and not his comrade.[60]

Meanwhile, jockeying for the best ships only grew more intense as the tantalizing lure of glory grew brighter with Hull's and Decatur's victories. David Porter grumbled to Hamilton that the *Essex* was the worst frigate in the service due to her bad sailing and the idiosyncratic decision to arm her completely with short-range carronades, and insisted that he had a claim to exchange his command for the *Adams:* "An Officer junior to myself has command of a 36 Gun Frigate," he complained to Hamilton. Lieutenants assigned to shallow-draft boats in out-of-the-way stations inundated the secretary with pleas for transfers to cruising vessels, citing years of service and the hardship "of my being Kept on a Station, where no opportunity could be afforded me to distinguish myself for want of proper vessels," as one lieutenant wrote from New Orleans.

Hamilton had for so long been in the habit of deferring to his officers and letting slide the mounting administrative demands of his office that when he now occasionally tried to put his foot down it only led to derisive hoots from the press and contempt from his subordinates. The secretary petulantly replied to Lawrence's threat to resign with a curt note that was widely reprinted in Federalist newspapers: "If (without cause) You leave the service of your Country, there will still remain Heros & patriots to support the honor of its flag."[61] Porter, who had sparred with Hamilton for months over his demands for promotion and choice of ships, had already turned against the secretary back in February 1812 when he wrote a colleague, "The secretary is unpopular here with the cloth, from the *highest* to the lowest he is disliked; it is supposed he has been too long in the habit of driving slaves to know how to regard the honorable feelings of gentlemen, added to his propensity to 'toss the little finger,' it is believed disqualifies him for the station."[62]

There were indeed increasing rumors and stories that the secretary was spending most of his day drinking. In October a Boston newspaper ran a short item:

THE SECRETARY OF THE NAVY

It is said, is fond of a glass. . . . would it not be better, that the department of the navy should be furnished with a secretary who likes business more than drinking? The tune of the cabinet seems to be:

> Let the drums rattle,
> We'll drink and prattle;
> Let the cannons roar,
> Give us one bottle more.

Hamilton was reported to have been intoxicated at the naval ball in Washington in December and also two weeks earlier at a celebratory gala held aboard the frigate *Constellation* in the Potomac, attended by the president and the cabinet. The New York congressman (and physician) Samuel Mitchill commented in December 1812 that Hamilton suffered from "the too free use of stimulant potation" and was usually to be found asleep at his desk by noon each day.[63] But it was Hamilton's disinclination for business more than his inclination for drink that was the real problem. With the coming of war not even the surprising successes of the American navy could conceal the secretary's fundamental incapacity for his job.

The presidential election in the fall of 1812 was a drawn-out affair, the results drifting in over the course of two months as each state voted according to its own rules. Madison's chief opponent was a fellow Republican, New York City mayor DeWitt Clinton, whom the Federalists decided to support on the basis of his promise to promote commerce and end the war. Clinton ran a frankly disingenuous campaign, his northeastern followers vowing that their candidate would negotiate with the British for a quick settlement, his supporters in the pro-war southern and western states attacking Madison for not prosecuting the war vigorously enough.

Madison, for his part, was prepared to stake everything on the war. In late October, Secretary of State James Monroe replied to Admiral Warren's armistice proposal by firmly shutting the door on any face-saving compromise that fell short of the aims the United States had gone to war to attain. Monroe stated that the president could not accept any peace terms that did not include a resolution of the issue of impressment. He proposed that the differences between the countries could be resolved by the United States' agreeing to forbid by law the employment of foreign seamen in its merchant marine in exchange for a British agreement to cease its practice of impressing men from American merchant vessels. But he also insisted that any armistice, pending negotiation of a final treaty, had to include a British pledge to halt impressment immediately in the interim. Monroe insisted that the citizens of the United States could never appear to acquiesce in "a practice, which while it degrades the Nation, deprives them of their rights as freemen, takes them by force from their families and their Country, into a foreign service, to fight the Battles of a foreign power, perhaps against their own kindred and Country."[64] Though couched in diplomatic language, Monroe's reply was clearly less an offer for negotiation than a pronouncement of American resolve aimed at domestic consumption.

"Day after day, like the tidings of Job's disaster," wrote Samuel Mitchill to his wife in late November, news of both military and electoral setbacks reached the "thin and solemn" gatherings in the president's drawing room.[65] On the Niagara and Montreal fronts, equally humiliating failures followed General Hull's ignominious defeat at Detroit. Henry Dearborn, Jefferson's secretary of war, was named to head the assault on Quebec, but he was fat, slow, sixty-one years old; his own troops called him "Granny." The commander on the Niagara campaign was Stephen Van Rensselaer, a forty-eight-year-old militia officer with no previous military experience, a Federalist chosen by New York's governor entirely in the hopes of shoring up political support for the war. In October and November, Dearborn and Van Rensselaer both launched attacks across the Canadian border with superior forces only to withdraw in failure.

By December it was clear that Clinton had carried four New England states, New York, New Jersey, Delaware, and part of Maryland, but Madison took Pennsylvania and the entire South, delivering a 128 to 89 electoral vote margin. In late December, with his victory secure, Madison summoned Hamilton to the White House and told him that unless he resigned, Congress would never vote future appropriations for the navy. On December 30 Hamilton bowed to the inevitable and submitted his resignation, asking the president to state whether there was "anything in the course of my conduct, in that station, reprehensible." The president's reply the next day praised Hamilton's "patriotic merits," "faithful zeal," and "unimpeachable integrity," earning Madison a scornful editorial in the *Federal Republican* that mocked him for praising the virtues of a man he had just compelled to resign for his manifest want of them.[66]

ON DECEMBER 2 the *Constitution* had put in at Fernando de Noronha, a Brazilian island two hundred miles off the coast and one of several planned rendezvous points where Captain Bainbridge hoped to meet up with David Porter in the *Essex*, which had sailed from Delaware Bay on October 28. The *Constitution* had passed only a few ships on her way from Boston. A few days out, flying English colors, she had halted an American merchant brig, the *South Carolina*, bound from Lisbon for

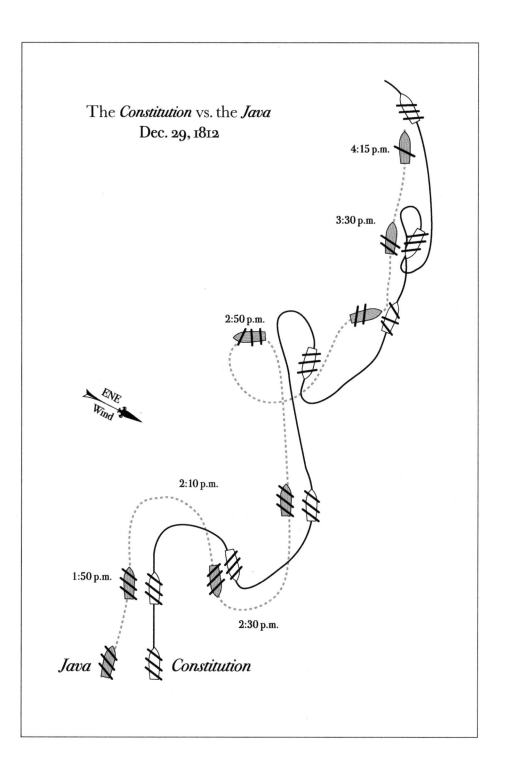

The *Constitution* vs. the *Java*
Dec. 29, 1812

4:15 p.m.

3:30 p.m.

2:50 p.m.

ENE
Wind

2:10 p.m.

1:50 p.m.

2:30 p.m.

Java   *Constitution*

Philadelphia, and the boarding party kept up the ruse, telling the master they were going to send him into Halifax. At that point the American merchant captain produced a British license—and the *Constitution* took possession and ordered her into Philadelphia as a prize. The brig's master "appeared much chagrined," noted Amos Evans, and "said we had worked windward of him this time but he be damn'd if we ever did it again."[67]

William Jones had suggested Fernando de Noronha to Bainbridge as a good resupply point if he decided to head for the coast of Brazil for his cruise: "It has a good Harbor on the NW side . . . Here you will find wood water and refreshments particularly turtle." Jones also noted that no women were allowed on the island; it served as a Portuguese penal colony for "*male* exiles and convicts, who for their sins are deprived of all Sexual Intercourse."[68] The *Constitution* sent her boats ashore with water casks to be filled and the men returned with eggs, melons, coconuts, bananas, cashew nuts, and pigs. There was no sign of Porter, and so Bainbridge, pretending to be the captain of the British frigate *Acasta*, left a note with the island's governor addressed to "sir James Yeo, of His Majesty's frigate *Southampton,* to be sent to England by the first opportunity." It read:

> My dear Mediterranean Friend, Probably you may stop
> here . . . I learnt before I left *England,* that you were bound for the
> Brazil coast; if so, perhaps we may meet at St. Salvadore or Rio
> Janeiro; I should be happy to meet and converse on our old
> affairs of captivity; recollect our secret in those times.
>   Your friend, of HM.'s ship Acasta.
>   KERR

The "secret" he was referring to was their use of invisible ink while prisoners in Tripoli back in 1804, and a postscript to Bainbridge's letter that could be revealed only when heated read "I am bound off St. Salvadore, thence off Cape Frio, where I intend to cruise until the 1st of January. Go off Cape Frio, to the northward of Rio Janeiro, and keep a look out for me. Your Friend."[69]

Every few days the crew of the *Constitution* exercised the great guns, or the marines practiced firing at marks, or the boarders exercised with small arms. There was no punishment recorded until December 6, when five seamen received a half-dozen to a dozen lashes apiece; then three days later a marine private convicted by a court-martial that Bainbridge had convened on board received fifty lashes for threatening the life of a midshipman. "Altho' very young he bore it much better than many hardy veterans would have," Evans observed.

On December 18 the *Constitution* rejoined the sloop of war *Hornet* in company off São Salvador, Brazil. James Lawrence was her captain, and he had just come from the port, where he had called on the American consul to gather what intelligence he could on British naval activity in the area. There were several British merchantmen in the harbor and a British sloop of war, the *Bonne Citoyenne;* the consul said that a British seventy-four was at Rio. He also said that the *Bonne Citoyenne* was rumored to be carrying $1.6 million in specie and was planning to sail in the next ten to fifteen days. Lawrence tried to goad the *Bonne Citoyenne* into a fight, sending her captain a challenge offering to meet him outside Brazilian territorial waters and pledging his and Captain Bainbridge's honor that the *Constitution* would not interfere in their duel. The British captain prudently declined, replying in a note to Lawrence that were he to prevail, the *Constitution*'s captain would not be able to avoid the "paramount duty he owes his country" and remain "an inactive spectator, and see a ship belonging to the very squadron under his command fall into the hands of an enemy." Bainbridge fumed about the insult to his own "sacred pledge" that was implied.[70]

The next day the *Constitution* and the *Hornet* again parted company, Lawrence remaining off São Salvador to keep an eye on the British ships. At nine in the morning on December 29 two sail were spotted off the weather bow. While one of the ships made for São Salvador, the other steered offshore for the *Constitution*. A little before noon the *Constitution* and the strange ship each hoisted signals that the other could not read and went unanswered, and fifteen minutes later they were close enough to see their respective English and American ensigns flying. The ships made straight for each other with no preliminaries, and the action that began a little after 2:00 p.m. would be the bloodiest yet between a British and an American frigate, a battle of close maneuver for two hours as the ships ranged alongside each other and each sought again and again to cross the other's bow or stern to raking position. The British ship held the weather gauge from the start and twice in the first thirty minutes tried to pull across the *Constitution*'s bows; Bainbridge responded each time with a broadside and then suddenly wore away under the cover of his own smoke.

It was immediately apparent that the British frigate was a faster sailer, and Bainbridge took the risk of setting his main course and fore course to compensate. Almost at the start of the battle a musket ball struck Bainbridge in the left hip, but he later said he did not even feel the pain until nine hours later. At 2:30 a shot entirely carried away the wheel of the *Constitution* and a flying bolt struck Bainbridge, this time in the right thigh. A line of midshipmen was quickly assembled to relay his steering orders down to men hauling the tiller's huge tackles in the steerage space behind the wardroom two decks below.

The two ships were side by side running east, and now the British frigate tried to tack to larboard, preparing to make a three-quarter circle to cross behind the *Constitution*'s stern. But her jibboom had been shot away, and without her head sails she hung agonizingly in stays; with her head to the wind and her stern fully exposed, she took two full broadsides before finally coming around. Again Bainbridge wore away, turning back to the west; again the British ship kept the weather gauge and this time headed right at her, obviously intending to run her aboard and take her by storm. But the British captain misjudged his timing, and the remains of his bowsprit skewered the *Constitution*'s mizzen rigging, almost exactly as the *Guerriere*'s had, pinning the British ship under the full weight of the *Constitution*'s broadside and musket fire. Her fore-mast was cut in two, then plunged straight down, spearing right through two decks before coming to a stop. Then the ships broke free and again were sailing side by side to the east, again the British frigate to the windward; Bainbridge wore to starboard and crossed the enemy's stern twice, each time pouring in a devastating raking fire. "At 3.55 Shot his mizzen mast nearly by the board," read the *Constitution*'s "Minutes Taken during the Action." They continued:

At 4.5   Having silenced the fire of the enemy completely and his colours in main Rigging being down Supposed he had Struck, Then hawl'd about the Courses to shoot ahead to repair our rigging, which was extremely cut, leaving the enemy a complete wreck, soon after discovered that The enemies flag was still flying hove too to repair Some of our damages.

At 4.20   The Enemies Main Mast went by the board.

At 4.50   Wore ship and stood for the Enemy

At 5.25   Got very close to the enemy in a very *rakeing* position,

athwart his bows & was at the very instance of rakeing
him, when he most prudently Struck his Flag.[71]

All but one of the *Constitution*'s eight boats had been reduced to
splinters during the action, shot to pieces on their davits. The lone
remaining boat was sent across and returned at 7:00 p.m. with Lieutenant Henry D. Chads, second in command of the frigate *Java*. Her
captain, Henry Lambert, lay in his ship mortally wounded. The *Java*
had been on her way to Bombay, carrying the new governor general of
India, Lieutenant General Sir Thomas Hislop, and a hundred other
passengers. Chads maintained that the *Java*'s casualties were 22 dead
and 102 wounded, but a letter accidentally dropped on the *Constitution*'s
deck by one of the British army officers taken prisoner told of 65 killed
and 170 wounded, and when Bainbridge examined the British ship's
muster roll and compared it with his list of prisoners, there were at least
53 who had not been accounted for.[72] At 3:00 p.m. on New Year's Day
the *Java* was set on fire and blown up, not nearly as spectacular an
explosion as the *Guerriere*, Evans observed, owing to her smaller quantity
of powder in the magazine.

The *Constitution* had suffered severely too. There were 12 killed and
22 wounded. In his official report Bainbridge tried to downplay the
damage his ship had received, but he wrote his old friend Dr. Bullus a
far more candid account a few weeks later:

U.S.F. Constitution 23d Jany. 1813
At Sea Lat 4.20 N°. Long 36 W.
Homeward Bound

Dear Bullus.
Knowing the interest you take in the success of our navy, I am
confident the enclosed paper, will afford you pleasure.
    The damage the Frigate Constitution received in the action
with the Java and the decayed state in which she is in made it
necessary for me to return to the U. States for
Repairs—Otherwise I should beyond doubt, by following my
intended plans, have made a most successful Cruise against the
Enemies Commerce and thereby have made the fortune of
myself & Crew. . . .
    The Constitution was a good deal cut. Some Shott between

wind & water. Her upper bulwarks considerably Shott. Foremast
& mizzen mast Shott through. Main & mizzen Stays Shott
through, Eight lower shrouds cut off. Fore top, mast Stays, &
every back Stay and all the Top Sail eyes Shott of. And almost
every Topmast Shroud. All the Braces standing and Preventers,
and Bowlines, were three times Shott away during the Action.
But rove again the very heat of it. 7 Boats out of 8 destroyed by
Shott. Our Sails extremely cut to pieces. The main Topmast,
Main Topsail yards, Jib Boom, Spanker Boomb Gaft & Try Sail
mast were all so Shott as to render them unserviceable. Yet this
damage, is incredibly inconceivable to the wreck we made the
Enemy. The Sea was smooth, that havock could not been
otherwise than great.[73]

His long-looked-for victory made Bainbridge exultant but not magnanimous, almost oblivious to his own wounds and eager for more
glory, yet ungenerous even in triumph. "I was wounded in the early part
of the action by a musquet Ball in my Hip and a piece of langrage in
my Thigh," he told Bullus. "But did not feel the inconvenience so great
as to cause me to quit the Deck to have it dressed until 11 oclock at
night, after which, returning on Deck and remaining on my Legs nearly
3 days & nights, brought on such inflammation & violent pains in my
wounds as to heave me on my *Beam ends* for some time. Ten days after
the action, the Surgeon extracted the piece of langrage by operating at
the wound. And I am now I thank God almost perfectly recovered. And
ready to hazard again a leg and an arm for such another victory."

And then he added with his usual sourness, "My Crew owing to the
constant Exercise we give them, are very active & clever at their Guns,
but in all other respects they are inferior to any Crew I ever had."

The crew had, though, apparently let off some unauthorized steam;
after the prisoners were put ashore at São Salvador on parole, Lieutenant Chads wrote to London, "I am sorry to find that the Americans
did not behave with the same liberality towards the crew that the officers experienced on the contrary they were pillaged of almost every
thing." He also reported the names and descriptions of four of the
Java's men who had entered on board the *Constitution*.[74]

Bainbridge spent the trip home writing other letters carefully
designed to burnish his stature and milk the maximum benefit from his
accomplishment. One, to a "friend" but obviously intended for

publication—it was widely reprinted in American newspapers almost as soon as he got home—modestly abjured any interest in prize money for himself while making the strongest possible case for a large cash award for the capture of the *Java*. For officers such as himself, of course, "patriotism and laudable thirst for renown" were motivation enough; "the applause of my countrymen has for me greater charms than all the gold that glitters." But his "poor fellows" the crew, alas, required the stimulus of prize money to keep up their spirits and ardor. "For if it is, as I hold it, the indispensable duty of the commander to destroy the captured vessel, on account of the gauntlet he would have to run with both the prize and his own ship—and the captain to receive *all the honor, and otherwise no compensation*—is it not natural to suppose that the ardent desire which our seamen at present so strongly manifest to get into battle would diminish?"[75] Like Hull, Bainbridge would eventually receive $7,500 of a $50,000 payment voted by Congress in lieu of the prize money that would have been awarded had he brought the enemy frigate home intact; each sailor and marine aboard the *Constitution* got about $50.

Porter had shown up at Fernando de Noronha on December 15, ten days after Bainbridge passed through, retrieved the letter to "sir James Yeo," and sailed immediately for Cape Frio. But he was far to the east on a futile chase of a small five-ship British convoy when Bainbridge passed north along the Brazilian coast heading for home.

Porter waited until January 13 before turning west for St. Catherine's, five hundred miles down the coast from Rio, one of the two final rendezvous points Bainbridge had set for the squadron.

By the *Right Honourable* SIR JOHN BORLASE WARREN,
Bart. K. B. *Admiral of the Blue, and Commander in Chief
of His Majefty's Ships and Veffels employed, and to be employed,
on the American and Weft Indian Station, &c. &c. &c.*

A PROCLAMATION.

WHEREAS His Royal Highnefs the Prince Regent hath caufed his pleafure to be
signified to the Right Honourable the Lords Commiffioners of the Admiralty, to
direct, that in confequence of the American Government having refufed to conclude a
ceffation of Hoftilities by Sea and Land, I fhould inftitute a ftrict and rigorous Blockade
of the Ports and Harbours in the *Bay of Chefapeake* and of the *River Delaware*, in the
UNITED STATES OF AMERICA, and maintain, and enforce the fame, according to the ufages
of War in fimilar Cafes. And likewife that the Minifters of Neutral Powers fhould be duly
notified that from this time all the meafures authorifed by the Law of Nations will be adopted,
and exercifed with refpect to Veffels which may attempt to violate the faid Blockade.

I DO, therefore, hereby require and direct you to pay the utmoft regard and attention to
His Royal Highnefs the Prince Regent's Commands as before mentioned, and by every means
in your power to maintain and enforce the moft ftrict and rigorous Blockade of the Ports and
Harbours in the *Bay of the Chefapeake* and of the *River Delaware*, in the UNITED STATES
OF AMERICA, accordingly.

GIVEN under my Hand, on Board His Majefty's Ship SAN DOMINGO,
at Anchor in Lynn Haven Bay, in the Bay of Chefapeake, in
the United States of America, this fixth day of February, 1813.

JOHN BORLASE WARREN,
Admiral of the Blue and Commander in Chief, &c. &c. &c.

To
*The Refpective Flag Officers and Captains, Commanders
and Commanding Officers, of His Majefty's Ships and
Veffels employed, and to be employed, on the American
and Weft Indian Station, and all others whom it may
concern.*

By Command of the ADMIRAL,

GEORGE REDMOND HULBERT,
Secretary.

GOD SAVE THE KING.

Proclamation of blockade, February 1813 (The National Archives, U.K.)

CHAPTER 6

Walls of Wood

IT TOOK at least forty days for news of each of the British defeats to reach London, the delay only adding to the sense of unreality and stunned disbelief that each left in its wake. British commentators found themselves literally at a loss for words, or at least rational words, to explain how the world could have been turned so upside down. "Another frigate has fallen into the hands of the enemy!—The subject is too painful for us to dwell on," was all that the editors of the *Naval Chronicle* could at first find to say at the news of the *Java*'s defeat.[1] The *Times* found it simply incredible that such things could be: "The public will learn, with sentiments which we shall not presume to anticipate that a *third* British frigate has struck to an American." The news came atop a report that Lloyd's had just listed five hundred British merchantmen captured by the Americans in the first seven months of the war:

> *Five hundred merchantmen, and three frigates!* Can these statements be true; and can the English people hear them unmoved? Any one who had predicted such a result of an American war, this time last year, would have been treated as a madman or a traitor. He would have been told, if his opponents had condescended to argue with him, that long ere seven months had elapsed, the American flag would be swept from the seas, the contemptible navy of the United States annihilated, and their maritime arsenals rendered a heap of ruins. Yet down to this moment, not a single American frigate has struck her flag. They insult and laugh at our want of enterprise and vigour. They leave their ports when they please, and return to them when it suits their conve-

nience; they traverse the Atlantic; they beset the West India Islands; they advance to the very chops of the Channel; they parade along the coasts of South America; nothing chases, nothing intercepts, nothing engages them but to yield triumph.[2]

Many British commentators noted that one, or even three, frigates amounted to a trivial material loss to the Royal Navy. But the symbolic consequences were positively incalculable. "It is not merely that an English frigate has been taken," the *Times* averred after the very first British defeat, "but that it has been taken by a new enemy, an enemy unaccustomed to such triumphs, and likely to be rendered insolent and confident by them. He must be a weak politician, who does not see how important the first triumph is in giving a tone and character to the war." And to Britain's aura of invincibility throughout the world: "We have suffered ourselves to be beaten in detail by a Power that we should not have allowed to send a vessel to sea," the *Times* added as the losses mounted. "The land-spell of the French is broken; and so is our sea-spell"; just a few more years like this would "render our vaunted navy the laughing-stock of the universe." Above all, it was now essential that no effort should be spared to achieve the one essential object, "the entire annihilation of the American navy."[3]

Stunned disbelief among the British public was equaled by frantic efforts by British officialdom to explain away the defeats. A perfunctory court-martial of Captain Dacres was quickly convened in Halifax upon his arrival there and promptly concluded that the loss of the *Guerriere* was simply due to bad luck, a result of "the accident of her masts going, which was occasioned more by their defective state than from the fire of the enemy." Dacres, and his officers and men, were "honourably acquitted" of any blame.[4] The *Macedonian*'s court-martial sat for four days and took much more extensive testimony, but focused almost entirely on demonstrating that there was not "the most distant wish to keep back from the engagement" and that the captain and his officers "behaved with the firmest and most determined courage," as the court concluded in its final judgment.[5] Exactly why the *Macedonian* was defeated was never particularly examined, discussed, or considered.

Letters poured into the *Naval Chronicle* and other publications indignantly defending the honor of the defeated British ships' officers and crews. Several writers went so far as to insist that not only was there nothing shameful about the British defeats, there was actually something contemptible about the American victories. "Not a tarnish is to be found on the trident of the seas," declared one correspondent after the *Guerrière*'s defeat. Another writer to the *Naval Chronicle*, signing himself "An Englishman," opined that "the Americans are welcome . . . to amuse themselves for three *wonderful* victories over the haughty Britons; it is a triumph worthy of themselves, a success which would disgrace an honourable foe, and cause no emotion but regret in the bosom of a high spirited enemy, in having gained success only by an unequal con- test." "America, like an ungrateful and malignant minion, turns upon her benefactor," said the London *Evening Star.* "Is Great Britain to be driven from the proud eminence which blood and treasures of her sons have attained for her among the nations, by a piece of striped bunting flying at the mastheads of a few *fir-built frigates,* manned by a *handful of bastards and outlaws?*"[6]

Many suggested it was little more than a dastardly trick for "a navy so small we scarcely know where to find it," as one writer put it, to call such large, powerful, and heavily manned ships frigates. "Is not the term frigate most violently perverted when applied to such vessels?" asked the *Evening Star.*[7] British writers repeatedly referred to the "over- grown American frigates," those oversize vessels that "the Americans choose to call frigates," those "disguised ships of the line" that had enticed brave British captains into believing they were challenging an equal foe, only to be surprised by overpowering force. By the traditions of naval honor there was nothing shameful in declining combat with a superior enemy; the Americans had thus resorted to dishonorable deception to secure their victories.

That face-saving excuse was picked up with alacrity by the defeated British captains, who made a point of calculating the relative weight of metal thrown by the broadsides of their respective ships, stressing the relative sizes of their crews, and concluding that the Americans had a 50 percent or greater advantage. "On being taken onboard the Enemys Ship," Carden wrote after his loss of the *Macedonian,* "I ceased to won- der at the results of the Battle; the *United States* is built on the scantline of a seventy four gun Ship . . . with a Complement of four Hundred and seventy eight pick'd Men."

It also quickly became an article of faith in British naval circles that a vast proportion of the crews of American men-of-war were British themselves, which helped to explain the American successes as well: the British navy was actually facing its own best men, trained by British captains, enticed into dishonorably taking up arms against their own country by the machinations of an unscrupulous foe. "I have no hesitation in believing that their crews are three-fourths composed of deserters from our own navy," declared "An Englishman" in the *Naval Chronicle*. Defending himself at his court-martial, Dacres asserted, "I felt much shocked, when on board the *Constitution*, to find a large body of the ship's company British seamen, and many of whom I recognized as having been foremost in the attempt to board." By contrast, he declared, the *Guerriere* had been "considerably weakened" by his own chivalrous conduct in allowing the ten impressed Americans of his crew to sit out the fight.[8]

As THEODORE Roosevelt would later wryly observe in his history of the war, Dacres's argument taken to its logical conclusion meant that the *Guerriere* was defeated because the Americans in her crew were *not* willing to fight against their own country while the Britons in the *Constitution*'s crew *were*. But the fact was that only a handful of British subjects were still serving on American ships of war once the war began.

Almost all the assertions by British writers about the relative firepower of the two navies' frigates were equally hyperbolic. All warships carried more guns than their nominal ratings, and while there was no doubt that the large American forty-fours were more heavily armed than the British thirty-eights they had defeated, the disparity was not that great. The American ships mounted a broadside of twenty-seven guns versus twenty-five on the British ships, and while the American guns were heavier in caliber, the Americans' solid iron shot was less dense by about 7 percent due to defective casting; the result was that the total weight of metal in the broadside of the *Constitution* was only about 10 or 20 percent greater than the *Guerriere*'s or the *Java*'s. The *United States* mounted massive forty-two-pounder carronades on her spar deck, which theoretically increased the weight of her broadside to 40 percent over the *Macedonian*'s, but nearly all of that battle was fought out of carronade range, and the difference in weight of broadside from the two ships' long guns was at best 30 percent.[9]

Although the "disguised ship of the line" charge would become an enduring part of British lore of the war, in fact a British seventy-four threw a broadside with twice the weight of metal of even the large American frigates. Even some in England mocked that face-saving excuse at the time. William Cobbett, an English journalist who began his career as a fire-eating Tory, spent several years in the United States in the 1790s propagandizing for Britain, and in the early 1800s called for an unremitting stance against American maritime pretentions, had since done a complete about-face and become a thoroughgoing radical and supporter of America; just a few months after his release in June 1812 from a two-year sentence in Newgate Prison for treasonous libel, he published in his *Cobbett's Political Register* some sarcastic doggerel in response to the shilly-shallying excuses being offered for the British naval setbacks:

> For when Carden the ship of the Yankee Decatur
> Attacked, without doubting to take her or beat her,
> A FRIGATE she seemed to his glass and his eyes:
> But when *taken himself,* how great his surprise
> To find her a SEVENTY-FOUR IN DISGUISE!
>
> If Jonathan thus has the art of disguising,
> That he captures our ships is by no means surprising:
> And it can't be disgraceful to strike to an elf
> Who is more than a match for the devil himself—[10]

Once the initial shock began to wear off, a number of more thoughtful correspondents to the *Naval Chronicle* began to assess the situation more objectively, suggesting in effect that it might be more productive to figure out how the British navy could start winning again rather than invest so much energy defending its losses as honorable ones. To be sure, defending British courage and honor was not merely a matter of national pride: much of Britain's real deterrent power upon the seas rested on its captains' undimmed reputation for courage. Yet it was clear to more than a few navy men that it was time to worry less about honor and more about practicalities. "It is not in our national character to despond, let us rather endeavour to trace the evil, that a remedy may be found," wrote "A Half-Pay Officer," who wondered whether the Americans had different equipment for their guns that enabled them to "have astonished us, not merely by taking our ships . . . but by taking them with such little comparative loss, and in so short a time."[11] Several noted the decisive advantage of the longer-range twenty-four-pounder guns employed by the American ships and recommended that British frigates needed to emulate this innovation.

One of the few signed letters, from Captain William Henry Tremlett, asserted that while "much has been said about their superior weight of metal, and size of the vessels," it was the Americans' superior handling of their guns that was infinitely more important. The long neglect of gunnery in the Royal Navy was at last coming home to roost: "The first and *grand* cause is, that the American seamen have been more exercised in firing at a *mark* than ours—their government having given their commanders leave to exercise whenever they think proper, and to fire away as much ammunition as they please." It would eventually come out that in their six weeks at sea, the crew of the *Java* had fired a total of only six broadsides before meeting the *Constitution,* all of them blanks. And Captain Tremlett noted that the damage done and the loss inflicted by American gunnery in all the battles was three to one, in one case ten to one, as great as what the British crews had been able to do, far beyond what any difference in the relative size and force of the ships could explain.[12]

A number of writers to the *Naval Chronicle* even dared to offer blunt criticism of the most time-honored practices of the Royal Navy, suggesting that it had grown too large, too dependent on the dregs of society to man its ships, too addicted to brutal punishment of a kind long abandoned by the rest of civilized society. "The absurdity of our antiquated naval institutions and 'customs,' " declared "Albion," had produced a "dread of the service of their country among sailors." That had made impressment a necessity to fill the navy's ranks—which in turn both weakened the quality of the service and helped contribute to the very causes of the war that was now going so badly against Britain. "A Naval Patriot" agreed; the navy was manned by a very small number of real seamen and the rest the "good, bad, and indifferent, viz. ordinary seamen, landsmen, *foreigners,* the sweepings of *Newgate,* from the *hulks,* and almost all the prisons in the country." With "such a motley crew," he wrote, it was no wonder it was so hard to produce a well-disciplined and efficient fighting force.

Another writer, denouncing the "system of coercion" that was equal to "the meanest capacities to execute," called for an end to flogging and its replacement with a "system of attachment" that would inspire British seamen to work together for reward rather than punishment. "Want of feeling and sense generally associate," he observed; "the wise and good" must take a stand against brutality, which had only weakened Britain's claim to mastery of the seas.[13]

. . .

IN PARLIAMENT, the wrath of criticism fell squarely on the government. Speakers berated the Admiralty for failing to issue proper orders to its admirals in North America, failing to equip the navy with frigates equal to the Americans', failing to send enough ships to the American coast, above all failing to emphasize sternness over forbearance in its prosecution of the war. "The arm which should have launched the thunderbolt was occupied in guiding the pen," declared George Canning, America's old nemesis. He took the government to task for sending out "not an Admiral, but an Ambassador; with instructions to carry, not fire and sword along the enemy's coasts, but a flag of truce into his harbours; and instead of sinking, burning and destroying the American Navy, His Majesty's ships were cooped up in the Halifax harbour, humbly awaiting the event of these overtures and negociations."

All agreed it was time for vigorous measures to teach the Americans a lesson for the "insolent spirit" they had shown. Britain had made magnanimous concessions only to have them spurned, had now suffered mortifications and insults intolerable to a nation that commanded Britain's place in the world. Britain had not sought war, but now had no choice but to crush American recalcitrance and reassert British military ascendency, all the more so because of the danger that continued American resistance posed to Britain's ability to concentrate its might on the more important struggle against France. "The paramount duty of British Ministers," asserted the *Times*, "is to render the English arms as formidable in the new world as they have become in the old."

Lord Liverpool, the prime minister, struck a tone of aristocratic regret at the necessity of chastising Britain's wayward offspring, but he left no doubt he meant to see the war through. While America might have legitimate grievances, he told Parliament, "she ought to have looked to this country as the guardian power to which she was indebted not only for her comforts, not only for her rank in the scale of civilization, but for her very existence." Augustus Foster, who had been elected to the House of Commons upon returning from Washington, completed the picture of wounded British pride by observing during the debate on the war that Americans "generally speaking . . . were not a people we should be proud to acknowledge as our relations." The debate concluded with an unopposed vote in favor of vigorous prosecution of the war, though not without a few opposition members cautiously suggesting that Britain would ultimately have to give way on impressment if the war was ever to end. But for now the government had the solid backing of British opinion for its policy of strong military action.[14]

The attacks on the Admiralty's management of the war, however, had hit home politically. In the first two weeks of January 1813 the London newspaper the *Courier* ran a series of daily letters "on the subject of the naval war with America" under the pen name "Nereus." They were a thinly veiled counterattack from the government, trying to undo the political points that had been scored against the Admiralty. Their author coyly disavowed any inside knowledge of government policy, but with all the mastery of a practiced parliamentary debater, he mercilessly skewered the government's critics and the jingoistic newspapers that had been so loudly denouncing the government for its supposed missteps and incompetence. Nereus mocked the very idea that Admiral Warren had been dispatched in the "character of a nautical negociator." Admiral Duckworth in Newfoundland had been given positive orders to "attack, take, sink, burn, and destroy all American ships" as soon as war was declared. Far from having an "inadequate" force on the American station, the navy had positioned there at the outbreak of the war "a total of 85 sail, to oppose 14 American pendants." Since then at least two more ships of the line and other additional ships had been dispatched. It was "mere accidents" that had caused the *Constitution* and the *United States* to fall in with lone British frigates rather than one of the five line-of-battle ships that were present on the station and which could easily have defeated them. And it would have been an absurd misallocation of resources for the British navy to have built and manned all of its hundreds of frigates with forty-four guns and five hundred men apiece just on the off chance that one of them might fall in singly with one of the large American ships, of which there were *three* to be found in the entire world. "Though the plodding pedantry of the *Times* should coalesce against me with the flippant ignorance of the *Morning Chronicle*," Nereus asserted, he was confident the facts would show that there had been no negligence of any kind on the part of the government nor any hesitation on the part of its admirals to do their duty.[15]

The *Morning Chronicle* for its part had a pretty good idea who it was dealing with. In an editorial replying to Nereus, the *Morning Chronicle* referred to him as "a poet," "a lawyer," "an Admiralty scribe"—and also as Harlequin, since he wears a "half-mask." In fact, Nereus was none other than John Wilson Croker, secretary to the Admiralty Board. Croker (pronounced "Crocker") was a young, ambitious, Irish-born lawyer, already a rising literary and political star when elected to Parlia-

ment at age twenty-six in 1807. The author of lyrical poems, anonymous satires about the Dublin stage and Irish society, and a serious and
influential pamphlet on the state of Ireland, he was a mercilessly partisan debater and polemicist, famous for vituperative personal attacks on
political opponents both on the floor of the House and on the pages of
literary reviews. One victim of his literary criticisms called him "the
wickedest of reviewers," claiming he took morbid delight in inflicting
pain on fellow authors.

But Croker was also deservedly known as an indefatigable administrator. Shortly after being appointed secretary to the Admiralty in 1809
he had courageously exposed a senior naval accountant, a personal
protégé of the king's, who Croker discovered from a close examination
of the files had embezzled more than £200,000. "I am almost always to
be found at my desk," Croker wrote an acquaintance. He told his wife
not to bother writing "private" on any letters she sent him at the office,
"as I open *all* letters myself." Years later, looking back on the two
decades he had continuously held the post at the Admiralty, he
remarked, "I never quitted that office-room without a kind of uneasiness, like a truant boy."[16]

The secretary was nominally no more than a staff assistant and
administrator to the Lords of the Admiralty, who determined policy
and issued orders to captains at sea, but in practice when the secretary
wrote "My Lords Commissioners of the Admiralty command me to
acquaint you" or "My Lords have thought fit to" or "Their Lordships
are not prepared to," it was John Wilson Croker and not their lordships
at all who had often made the decision. So firmly had Croker taken
control of the office in three short years, and so widely regarded—or at
least mythologized—was his power among naval officers, that John
Surman Carden was convinced to his dying day that the reason he
never received another sea command after losing the *Macedonian* was
not that he had lost a ship but that he had put his foot wrong with the
secretary by incautiously referring to "their Lordships of the Admiralty's" wishes in a way that suggested they, and not Croker, held the
power to make decisions. "Woe to him who did not pay homage to this
Tyrant," wrote Carden.[17]

Nereus may have been supremely confident of the conduct of the
naval war with America and the complete correctness of the government's handling of it to date, but Croker and the Admiralty privately
were unmistakably alarmed by the unexpected turn the war had taken.

At the very same moment Nereus's letters were appearing in the *Courier,* the secretary was hurriedly ordering new strategies, weapons, tactics, and commanders into place. Among the steps were some of the very ideas Nereus heaped scorn upon in public. The Admiralty immediately commissioned a private yard to build five large forty-gun frigates as soon as possible to meet the threat posed by the more powerful American ships, and ordered the eighteen-pounder main guns of the Royal Navy's one existing frigate of this class, the *Endymion,* replaced with twenty-four pounders during the extensive repair she was currently undergoing at Plymouth, expected to be completed in mid-1813. To reduce the weight and construction time of the new frigates, the Admiralty ordered them built of softwood rather than wait for increasingly scarce supplies of oak to become available—the jibes about America's supposed "fir-built frigates" notwithstanding. A design for an even larger fifty-gun frigate of about fifteen hundred tons was produced in three days, and orders for two were placed. And as a stopgap, three old seventy-four-gun line-of-battle ships—the *Majestic, Goliath,* and *Saturn*—that were about to be taken out of service and converted to prison hulks were ordered to be cut down instead as "razees" and sent to the American station: stripping off their top decks would quickly produce something that approximated the sailing qualities and firepower of the American forty-fours.[18]

While Nereus was expressing indignation at the suggestion that Britain's naval commanders on the scene had been lax, Croker was hectoring Warren with a series of increasingly impatient instructions, along with blasts of reproof for his lack of accomplishment and energy to date. The secretary was thirty-two now, just a little over half Warren's age, and he had all of three years' experience in naval affairs. But with the withering superiority that had become a deadly weapon in his hands, he proceeded to let Warren know exactly where he stood, instructing him on his defects in everything from his requests for additional force to the choice of words used in his dispatches, and warning him that the Admiralty now expected quick results.

"My Lords Commissioners of the Admiralty," Croker wrote on January 9, 1813, "had hoped that the great force placed at your disposal . . . would have enabled you to obtain the most decided advantages over the Enemy, and to blockade their Ships of War in their Ports, or to intercept and capture them at Sea if they should escape the vigilance of your blockading Squadrons. In this expectation their lord-

ships have been hitherto disappointed."[19] Warren's unaccountable failure to keep their lordships apprised of Rodgers's and Bainbridge's
movements, Croker told the admiral in a subsequent message, "has
obliged them to employ six or seven sail of the line and as many frigates
& sloops . . . in guarding against the possible attempts of the Enemy."
These deployments had required pulling ships from other vital duties to
patrol the seas around Madeira, St. Helena, and the Azores. "My Lords
cannot but hope that the reports which you state of *swarms* of American Privateers being at Sea, must be, in a great degree exaggerated,"
the secretary continued, "as they cannot suppose that you have left the
principal Ports of the American Coast to be so unguarded as to permit
such multitudes of Privateers to escape in and out unmolested." Their
lordships were surprised to learn that the *Spartan*—this was the frigate
Warren dispatched to Madeira to pick up a shipment of wine for the
squadron—"was seen on the 28th Novr. in Latitude 39°.41.—North
Longitude 25 West," near the Azores, in spite of their understanding
that she had been specifically instructed to sail in company with the
Africa and in spite of the admonition from the Admiralty that frigates
should not sail singly and be exposed to the superior force of the enemy.
Their lordships desired that the logs of the *Spartan* be transmitted at
once, as "they cannot suppose that with a knowledge that Commodore
Ro[d]gers and Bainbridge with their respective Squadrons were likely
to be at sea, you could have authorized the Captain of the *Spartan* to
expose himself to the danger of meeting them, unnecessarily and out
of your Station."[20]

And in a final, unmistakable slap at Warren's authority, the secretary
informed him that "my Lords have thought fit to appoint a Captain of
the Fleet to serve with your Flag"—but without consulting Warren on
the choice of the man to fill the post. As their lordships "were not aware
of any individual" whom the admiral might prefer, they were naming
Captain Henry Hotham to serve under him. Although Hotham was
able to relieve Warren of much of the weight of his administrative
duties in the coming months, he was also unmistakably the Admiralty's
man, sent to light a fire under the commander in chief while also keeping an eye on him and reporting back directly to the Admiralty in a
series of private letters describing the true state of things on the North
American command.[21]

Still, despite their lordships' considerable disappointment in Warren's failure to use the considerable force at his disposal, Croker

informed him, "as it is of the highest importance to the Character and interests of our Country that the Naval Force of the Enemy, should be quickly and completely disposed of, my Lords have thought themselves justified at this moment in withdrawing Ships from other important services for the purpose of placing under your orders a force with which you cannot fail to bring the Naval War to a termination, either by the capture of the American National Vessels, or by strictly blockading them in their own Waters." The additional forces nearly doubled the number of large warships on the American stations, giving Warren a total of ten ships of the line, thirty frigates, and fifty sloops of war.

On December 29, 1812, Warren had sent another plea for reinforcements, complaining that many of the promised ships had not yet arrived on station, and when that message arrived in London in early February 1813, it triggered an even more withering response from Croker. "Under these circumstances," the secretary wrote, "their Lordships are not only not prepared to enter into your opinion that the force on your station was not adequate to the duties to be executed, but they feel that . . . it may not be possible to maintain on the Coast of America for any length of time a force so disproportionate to the Enemy as that which, with a view to enabling you to strike some decisive blow, they have now placed under your orders." If some of the additional ships had not yet joined Warren's flag owing to their being detained on convoy duty, that was entirely the admiral's own fault for failing to do his job of blockading the American coast: "the necessity of sending such heavy Convoys arises from the facility and safety with which the American Navy has hitherto found it possible to put to Sea."

Croker's orders left no doubts about what was now expected. As instructed in a secret order dated November 27, 1812, to be carried out in the event the American government rejected the British proposal for a cessation of hostilities, Warren was to immediately institute a complete blockade of all American ports in the Chesapeake Bay and Delaware River. He was to destroy the American navy and as soon as the job was done return some of the extra line-of-battle ships to England.[22]

Their lordships had also decided to send the admiral some energetic assistance in the business of waging war. His new second in command, already sailed for Bermuda with a reinforcing squadron, was to be Rear Admiral George Cockburn. Sixteen years earlier, as a twenty-four-year-old frigate captain, Cockburn had distinguished himself by capturing a more heavily armed Spanish ship in an action that had so impressed Nelson he had awarded the young captain a gilt-handled sword he personally ordered made for him.[23] Admiral Cockburn's name was pronounced "Coburn," but Americans would soon be taking grim, sarcastic pleasure in pronouncing it as written, and with the stress on the second syllable.[24]

WARREN WAS in fact neither as hesitant nor as bereft of success in his first few months as Croker implied in his verbal keelhaulings of the admiral, nor were his excuses for his failure to seal off the American coast without some justice. By the end of 1812, the force under Warren's command had already sent 120 prizes in to Halifax, 50 to Bermuda, 40 to the Leeward Islands, and 30 to Jamaica—some 240 ships in all.[25] Besides taking the American navy brig *Nautilus* at the outbreak of the war, British warships had since captured two other American men-of-war, the eighteen-gun *Wasp* and the fourteen-gun *Vixen*.

Yet defeat seemed to stalk even British victories. The *Wasp* was taken on October 18, 1812, about 350 miles north of Bermuda by a British seventy-four, the *Poictiers*, that appeared on the scene only after the American ship had already triumphed two hours earlier in a savage forty-five-minute battle against a slightly more powerful British brig, the *Frolic;* in an action fought in a heavy sea, the Americans' deadly accurate gunnery left only 20 of the *Frolic's* 110-man crew unharmed.

The *Vixen* was also taken by a vastly superior British warship, the thirty-two-gun frigate *Southampton;* the American brig was captured on November 22 in the West Indies, but five days later, as the frigate and her prize were making their way through the Crooked Island passage bound for Jamaica, both struck an uncharted reef in the night. Daylight found the *Vixen* a total loss, her bows penetrated by a rock and her bilge filled, the *Southampton* impossibly wedged between the rocks and a leak sprung. "Lives were the only possible things that could be saved," wrote one of the *Vixen's* men in an anonymous published account that described the harrowing shipwreck, the rescue of the two ships' crews on Conception Island, and the Americans' subsequent tormenting imprisonment packed belowdecks in sweltering and airless prison hulks on Jamaica.[26]

Capping the ill-omened mischances that seemed to plague the British command that first year of the war were a series of disasters, natural and unnatural, that struck in December. The brig *Plumper* hit the ledges off Dipper Harbor, New Brunswick, sinking instantly and taking fifty men and £70,000 in specie down with her. And in a simply bizarre incident that same month on Cape Breton Island, Nova Scotia, a British captain went berserk, challenged town officials to a duel, and engaged in a three-day standoff with the local authorities and soldiers of the British army garrison, at one point ordering his marines to open fire on the townspeople, before he was finally subdued and arrested.[27]

And though the Royal Navy was the world's unquestioned master of the naval blockade, it was never so simple or straightforward a tactic as Croker implied in his impatient letters to Warren demanding results. That was especially so when it came to trying to seal off a coastline as long as America's, and so punctuated by a myriad of creeks, bays, inlets, and rivers.

The blockade was a natural recourse for a superior naval power, a way to replace the chance and fortunes of war with the methodical application of overwhelming force to strangle an enemy, and two crucial innovations of the previous two decades had made it possible for British ships to stay on station for the months at a time that blockade duty required. One was the Royal Navy's belated recognition, in 1795, of British scientific discoveries made a half century earlier regarding the cause and prevention of scurvy. As late as the 1780s a single six-week cruise of the Channel Fleet resulted in 2,400 cases of scurvy among the crews, and at one point in that decade nearly a quarter of the entire 100,000-man force of the Royal Navy was on the sick list from the disease. The subsequent addition of lime juice and fresh fruit to the shipboard diet alone greatly extended the time that British warships could remain at sea. The other almost simultaneous innovation was the use of copper cladding to protect the wooden hulls of warships. In warm waters, boring worms could do enough damage to an unprotected hull in just a few years to require a ship to be taken out of service for a nearly complete rebuild. In all waters, seaweed, barnacles, and other crustaceans accumulated so fast that in as little as six weeks the speed of an unclad ship was noticeably reduced, and in as little as six more weeks the ship might have to be careened, scraped, and recaulked to remain seaworthy at all. By taming the ravages of scurvy and weed, a ship could stay at sea for as much as four to six months, if resupplied with water and provisions, before accumulated wear finally required putting into port for a refit.

Still, blockade duty was a voracious consumer of ships and men. To be recognized and enforceable by admiralty law, a blockade had to be maintained continuously and with sufficient force to be effective. A blockade was a complete interdiction of all seagoing traffic in or out of an enemy port, neutral vessels included; and a blockading force had to match its words with actions, otherwise every belligerent could simply proclaim a blockade as a pretext for seizing any neutral vessels it happened upon in the vicinity of an enemy's coast. Maintaining a blockade on a port was debilitating, boring, but exacting work: the blockading squadrons sailing back and forth, tacking again and again across the same stretch of water day after day, the danger of a lee shore constantly looming and the chance for glory or even a respite from the tedium nil.[28]

And even with the ships' extended sea time, probably a third of the blockading fleet at any given moment would be undergoing repairs or traveling to or from the yard. Warren looked at the previous British experience blockading the American coast, during the Revolution, and found that in 1775 his predecessor had calculated he needed fifty ships for the job. But even that did not take into account the need to rotate ships on and off station; factoring that in increased the number to around ninety—in other words, virtually the entire nominal force under Warren's command. When Warren attempted to point this out, it predictably earned him another stinging rebuke from Croker, who replied that the comparison was "by no means just; you will recollect that at the former period the fleets of France were actually in the West Indies and American waters, and it was chiefly to oppose them that so great a force was necessary."[29]

But the Admiralty itself kept up a barrage of maddeningly contradictory instructions to Warren that kept tying up his ships for other duties—or potential duties. Both Warren and his masters in the Admiralty had a long list of contingencies they constantly worried about, chief among them the nightmare scenario that the French navy would indeed take advantage of the moment to strike a blow at the otherwise preoccupied British naval force on the North American station. The Royal Navy's blockade of France, involving hundreds of ships constantly patrolling the coast and adjacent waters of the Atlantic and Mediterranean, had managed to keep Napoleon's naval power almost completely at bay in the years since the defeat of the French fleet at Trafalgar in 1805; French warships all but abandoned any further attempts to put to sea, and Napoleon began reassigning thousands of sailors to infantry duty as the decisive struggle between France and her enemies shifted to a series of climactic land campaigns, on the Peninsula, the Continent, and Russia. By the start of the war with America, the Royal Navy had seized all of France's colonies and secured unchallenged control of the sea lanes needed to ferry troops and supplies for Wellington's campaign on the Peninsula.[30] Though the French navy never did succeed in breaking out and joining the battle in American waters, its mere existence was a danger that could not be ignored; sheltered within fortified ports, the French fleet was an ever-present threat that might take advantage of bad weather or good luck to allow a powerful squadron to slip out and fall on the back of Warren's force.

Meanwhile, the first lord of the Admiralty, Lord Melville, was privately cautioning Warren against withdrawing any of his ships from the Caribbean stations for offensive operations against America, given the political clout of the West Indian merchants and the "clamour" that they had created in London over fears that their merchant vessels might be left unprotected against the ravages of American privateers. Though these fears were "apparently unfounded," Melville conceded, it would be best not to upset such a powerful constituency. In frustration, Warren replied that since the addition of the West Indies stations to his command had only increased his administrative burdens without augmenting his useful force, the Jamaica and Leeward Islands commanders ought to be placed under his direct orders only if the French appeared. This earned him still another barbed reply from Croker. "If you should find that you are unequal to the management of so extensive a duty," the secretary sniffed, then their lordships would prefer to have three distinct and fully responsible commanders in chief under them, rather than the "divided authority and mixed responsibility" that Warren proposed.[31]

But Warren got the message. In early February 1813 he arrived at Lynnhaven Bay aboard his flagship *San Domingo,* issued a formal declaration of blockade of all ports and harbors on the Chesapeake Bay and Delaware River, and, leaving five frigates, returned to Bermuda and immediately dispatched Cockburn, who had arrived there in mid-January aboard the seventy-four *Marlborough,* with a huge additional force to the Chesapeake. Along with the ships already in place at Lynnhaven Bay and the *Marlborough,* Cockburn had at his command three other seventy-fours (*Poictiers, Victorious,* and *Dragon*), two additional frigates, a sloop of war, and a schooner.[32]

A few weeks later Warren issued a new standing order to all his captains conveying their lordships' admonition to increase gunnery practice, even if it meant forsaking some of the painting, shining, scrubbing, and polishing that was so ingrained in the traditions of the service. "Upon . . . the expert management of the Guns the preservation of the high character of the British Navy most essentially depends." Those endless spit-and-polish tasks "on which it is not unusual to employ the Men are of very trifling importance, when Compared with a due preparation (by instruction and practice) for the effectual Services of the day of Battle." Blockade duty was notorious for magnifying the obsession with appearance, with the ships constantly under the bored and disapproving eye of the admiral; even running out the guns in dumb show tended to mess their polish, and so gun drill was often abandoned altogether during the months ships spent at sea blockading an enemy coast. But scouring iron stanchions and ring bolts was now to be gradually phased out, the Admiralty reiterated in a subsequent circular message to the admirals, and "the time thrown away on this unnecessary practice be applied to the really useful and important points of discipline and exercise at Arms."

Warren concluded: "The issue of the Battle will greatly depend on the cool, steady and regular manner in which the Guns shall be loaded, pointed & fired."[33] Tradition was one thing, winning wars another. The Americans had already changed the traditional rules of what it took to win.

IN JANUARY 1813 the headquarters of the United States Department of the Navy consisted of three not very large rooms in a two-and-a-half-story brick building located about two hundred yards west of the White House, which it shared with the State and War departments. The four clerks were crowded into one room on the second floor, the secretary of the navy had another, downstairs the nine men of the navy accounts department filled the third, and everywhere hung an air of disorganized neglect. Secretary Hamilton's successor arrived in Washington at three o'clock in the afternoon on January 23, and the friends he ran into that very first day, he wrote his wife that evening, mainly "commiserate me on the Herculean task I have to encounter."[34]

The new man was William Jones of Philadelphia, whose Republican credentials, knowledge of ships and the sea, and experience in running an efficient and businesslike operation were matched only by his extraordinary reluctance to face the ordeal of public office. He had been one of the four men to turn down Jefferson's offer of the navy post in 1801, and had turned down two approaches by Madison for positions since, one to be consul in Denmark, the other to take on the job of commissary general of the army, a post newly created in the spring of 1812. Jones had considered taking the latter position until he read the statute governing it and realized it would be an unremitting nightmare, a figurehead fully responsible for the purchase of military supplies for the entire army but without any real authority to keep the process honest.[35]

On December 28, 1812, Pennsylvania congressman Jonathan Roberts wrote Jones to advise him that Hamilton was about to be dismissed and that Jones was Madison's first choice to replace him. "The vacancy about to occur has not been effected thro a hope of getting your services but from the impossibility of proceeding with Mr. Hamilton," Roberts wrote. Nonetheless, he begged Jones not to say no this time. "The Nation and the Navy point to you as the fittest man we have & what is to become of us if the fittest man will not come forward in a moment of public danger."

Besides having run a shipping business for decades, served as a member of Congress from 1801 to 1803, and sailed around the world from 1805 to 1807, Jones had seen the face of war firsthand. As a fifteen-year-old volunteer during the Revolution he had fought at the battles of Trenton and Princeton; later in the war he had served under Thomas Truxtun aboard an American privateer, then joined the Continental navy and been wounded and taken prisoner. In 1795, while living in Charleston where his merchant shipping business had taken him, he was elected captain of a local militia unit, the Charleston Republican Artillery Company, and during that time he wrote a manual for artillery drill.[36] In January 1813 he was fifty-one, had the substantial air of a prosperous merchant of the previous century, and was happily married to a wife to whom he wrote long, affectionate letters notable not only for their kindness but for the way he addressed her as a complete equal in business and political matters. He and Eleanor were childless but he was the guardian of Eleanor's nephew, whose father had died impoverished, and they had a comfortable and extensive social life among friends and family in Philadelphia.

Jones hated Washington society, dreaded the political attacks and slanders that he knew were to be his inevitable lot, missed his wife and home, but threw himself into the job with the encouragement of the many naval officers he knew and with a sense of urgency that the full discovery of the disorganized state of the office only galvanized all the more. "I can scarcely believe that you would have been drawn into Public life, knowing how little ambitious you are in that pursuit," his old friend William Bainbridge wrote. "Yet it was what I most sincerely wished . . . You mention the inorganized state of your department. I well know it. And without reflecting on the former head of it (the last a person I sincerely esteem for the goodness of his heart) I can say there never was any system in it, and for the want of it great abuses have crept in. And you will find, my dear sir, that even with your capability & exertions, it will take some time before you can fully correct them." Lieutenant George Read wrote from the *United States* in New York, "I see by the papers you are to be our secretary and permit me to say it is the best news not only to me but to all my profession, we have heard for some time."[37]

The mess that Hamilton left had settled deeply into the working of the office. The chief clerk, Charles W. Goldsborough, had let things slide as had his boss, and Jones decided immediately to get rid of him. "It required some little address to remove him from office without exciting his resentment," Jones wrote Eleanor, but "I effected my purpose" by appealing to the "no small share of pride" he had detected in his character, allowing Goldsborough to present his departure as his own decision and letting him stay on "until it had the public appearance of his own act and convenience." Jones dismissed another clerk whom Hamilton had apparently hired more out of pity for his impoverished state than for any ability he had; Jones informed the man, an unsuccessful physician named James Ewell, that "the necessity of substituting . . . an accurate and well qualified accountant and good hand writer" left him no choice.

Jones's new chief clerk fully confirmed the "exceptionally disordered and confused state" of the office that their predecessors had left them. Benjamin Homans was an experienced clerk as well as a former merchant captain; he had gained a good reputation for straightening out the office of secretary of the Commonwealth of Massachusetts when he held that post from 1810 to 1812, but even he seemed overwhelmed by "finding an office in such a state" as the Navy Department was. It was impossible to tell the state of supplies in the navy stores or gunpowder in the magazines. There was no regular system for resupplying each ship. "The Captains in the Navy have not made regular

returns of their Muster Rolls on Sailing, and of their Prisoners on arriving in Port." The wooden cases in the office are "*almost useless* for filing
away letters & papers." He discovered in the attic a room "filled with
Books, old Letters & papers of various kinds (some important) in great
disorder & dirty." Most of the really important papers, though, were in
the hands of the accountant, who jealously guarded them and made
difficulties whenever Homans tried to examine them or ask a question
about office matters. The constant stream of visitors through the clerk's
room made it hard to get any work done, and Homans wanted the
clerks moved to a quieter room but told Jones he dared not propose
"any innovation" himself as it "would be illy received and add to the
jealousy and ill-will that appear to prevail against me."[38]

Jones for his part began to send out a veritable gale of orders and
correspondence in his first few weeks, going over lists of officers for promotion or transfer, reducing and redeploying the infamous Jeffersonian
gunboats—Jones told his brother that they were "scattered about in
every creek and corner as receptecles of idleness and objects of waste
and extravagance without utility"—demanding that "*trees be cut down
immediately*" for needed timber, asking Congress for reforms in procure-
ment procedures and authorization to hire two more clerks, appointing
a competent physician to take charge and straighten out the haphazard
system of naval hospitals, which offered equally haphazard care in
inadequate temporary buildings scattered around the various ports. He
ordered a systematic review of every officer's fitness, requiring commanding officers to report on each of their officers upon their return
from each cruise, or once a year on July 4 for those on shore duty, and
developed a form for personnel files that listed mental and physical
qualifications; proficiency in mathematics, grammar, and nautical
astronomy; and "moral and general character." He instituted a general
order forbidding squadron or station commanders from making any
more acting appointments as they had long been accustomed: that
power was henceforth to be exercised solely by the secretary, and Jones
rebuffed a protest on this point even from his old friend Bainbridge. He
ordered junior officers to correspond with the Navy Department only
through their superiors and stop bombarding his office with personal
requests and complaints. The new secretary was on the job scarcely
a month before he reprimanded or cashiered several officers who,
through incompetence or corruption, had spent large sums without
department approval. To a lieutenant who had purchased an unsea-

worthy hulk without authorization Jones wrote a blistering dismissal: "Your irregular and extravagant conduct . . . prove you utterly unfit for the station with which you have been honoured. You are, therefore, dismissed from the service of the U.S."[39]

Every few weeks or sometimes every few days he wrote Eleanor, addressing her as "My dear wife," "My beloved wife and friend," signing his letters "Your affectionate friend," "Your ever affectionate husband, W. Jones." A few weeks into the job he described to her his new routine: "As to exercise, it is out of the question except the head and hands. I rise at seven, breakfast at nine, dine at half-past four, eat nothing afterward; at dinner take about four glasses of good wine, but have not drank a drop of any kind of spirit since I have been here. I write every night till midnight, and sleep very well when I do not think too much." His doubts about his fitness for the job and the social role he had to fulfill, receiving and returning formal calls throughout official Washington, nagged at him. "I perceive that my domestic habits have utterly unfitted me for a courtier for all this gives me pain instead of pleasure."[40]

He found, though, that "the terrors" of the job "appear to diminish with the serious contemplation I have given the subject. Having accepted the trust with reluctance, but with the purest motives and most ardent zeal for the sacred cause of our Country why should I despair? My pursuits and studies has been intimately connected with the objects of the department and I have not been an inattentive observer of political causes and effects." He tried to steel her for the "calumny" and "lashing" that he knew he must expect in public office. "If I am faithful and reasonably competent the consciousness of virtue and fidelity I hope will sustain me. . . . I have only to request you not to mind it when it does occur."[41]

To help smooth over his dismissal of Goldsborough, Jones agreed to his former clerk's request to take over his $300-a-year lease on a house in Washington that Goldsborough could no longer afford, and to buy some of his furniture as well; the house, he told Eleanor, was located in the best situation in the district, halfway between the Six Buildings, on Pennsylvania Avenue at Twenty-first Street, and the Potomac River, with a fine view across to Alexandria. It was two stories tall, forty-four feet wide across the front, with a two-story piazza all along the back; an ell with storeroom, dairy, bathhouse, and library; a dry well in the cellar that went down forty-five feet with a windlass to lower meat and butter to keep them cool; and a garden with a variety of "choice vegetables, fruit trees, grapes," stabling for a cow, and two fine clover lots.

He was looking forward to having her "snugly located here" with him before long. He asked after their old dog: "Shake Bibo by the paw for me, but I suppose he is going the way of all flesh—*and we must soon follow.*"[42]

AMONG THE inheritances left by Paul Hamilton to his successor was the ironic one of having finally persuaded Congress to approve the first new warship construction in a decade. Hamilton and his captains were keenly aware that their sudden successes at sea had produced a political opportunity that needed to be turned to advantage at once. Hull, in Washington for the opening of the congressional session at the end of 1812, made the rounds lobbying with all the power of his new celebrity. "The Navy is now up," Hull remarked, "and if nothing is done this session it never will be worth remaining any longer."

The first weeks of the session were filled with a furious debate on the war that brought all other business to a standstill. In June 1812, when the declaration of war was being considered, Federalists in the House had refused to participate in that debate as a protest against the Republicans' insistence on a secret session; now, as war hawk John A. Harper of New Hampshire complained, the Federalists were taking the "opportunity to *deliver* themselves of their war speeches with which they were pregnant last session." In long tirades, members of each party accused the other of exploiting the war for political ends. Josiah Quincy of Massachusetts, charging that for twelve years the country had been mismanaged by "two Virginians and a foreigner"—meaning Jefferson, Madison, and the Swiss-born Gallatin—said that the real purpose of the war was to ensure that the Virginian dynasty remained unbroken with Monroe ("James II") succeeding Madison ("James I"). Republicans in turn accused Federalists of secretly plotting a treasonous separate peace between the New England states and Britain, and argued that if Federalists really wanted peace the best way to bring it about would be to wholeheartedly support the war, so as to bring it to a quick and favorable conclusion.

Another lengthy debate was occasioned by Madison's proposal to enact into law the American bargaining position on impressment that the British had already rejected, namely that the United States would bar foreign sailors from the American merchant service in exchange for an end to the British practice of stopping and searching American ships and removing those it claimed as British subjects. More an effort at public relations than diplomacy, it was clearly an attempt to justify the war in the wake of the British repeal of the orders in council, and Federalists denounced it as a meaningless gesture while some of the war hawk Republicans opposed it as craven; but as Madison shrewdly calculated, it put the Federalists in a corner and enough members of both parties found it impossible to oppose the bill, which was passed and signed into law.[43]

A surprisingly large number of Republicans still saw no inconsistency in opposing new appropriations for the navy even as they denounced opposition to the war as tantamount to treason. But on December 23, 1812, enough broke ranks with the party's solid anti-navalist tradition to join every Federalist in passing a naval expansion bill; by a 70–56 vote the House approved the construction of six new forty-four-gun frigates plus four of the long-planned and long-delayed seventy-four-gun ships of the line. The Senate passed the bill on an unrecorded vote a week earlier. The total construction costs were estimated at $2.5 million, and the increased annual expense for the new ships was $1.5 million. Treasury Secretary Gallatin's budget estimates for 1813 projected a $19 million shortfall even without any increases for the army or navy, and with Congress stubbornly refusing even to consider reviving the hated internal taxes of the Adams administration and the prospects of raising a loan of that size seemingly unattainable, Gallatin wrote to Jones in February proposing that the new shipbuilding program simply be scrapped. But as Hull had correctly observed, the navy was "up," and Jones ordered work on the new frigates and seventy-fours to begin without delay.[44]

In one sense this was all well and good, but the new navy secretary had another idea entirely about the best way to counter the Royal Navy on the high seas, and that was not to try to beat them at their own game. The American navy could never win a sustained war of attrition against the British, fighting warship to warship, "man to man and gun to gun," as Jones would later put it, no matter how thrilling and encouraging the three single-frigate victories had been.[45] Nor could America directly oppose the British blockade or protect American commerce from the overwhelming might the enemy could bring to bear upon the coastline.

On February 22, 1813, Jones sent a circular to all his captains in port, laying down the strategy of hit-and-run raiding the American navy would henceforth pursue. Rather than strike the enemy where he was strongest, the American navy would seek to draw away as much of his force as possible by striking him where he was weakest, going after British commerce on the high seas, from the southern tip of Africa to the southern tip of Ireland:

> There is good reason to expect, a very considerable augmentation of the Naval force of the enemy on our coast the ensuing Spring; & it will be perceived that his policy will be to blockade our Ships of War in our own harbors; intercepting our private cruisers, prizes and trade, and Harass the seaboard.
>
> Our great inferiority in naval strength, does not permit us to meet them on his ground without hazarding the precious Germ of our national glory.—we have however the means of creating a powerful diversion, & of turning the Scale of annoyance against the enemy. It is therefore intended, to dispatch all our public ships, now in Port, as soon as possible, in such positions as may be best adapted to destroy the Commerce of the enemy, from the Cape of Goodhope, to Cape Clear, and continue out as long as the means of subsistence can be procured abroad, in any quarter.
>
> If any thing can draw, the attention of the enemy, from the annoyance of our coast, for the protection of his own, rich & exposed Commercial fleets, it will be a course of this nature, & if this effect can be produced, the two fold object of increasing the pressure upon the enemy and relieving ourselves, will be attained.
>
> Cruizing singly, will also afford to our gallant Commanders, a fair oppertunity of displaying distinctly their Judgement, skill & enterprize, and of reaping the laurel of Fame, and its solid appendages.[46]

While the secretary said he would welcome the commanders' proposals for where they would wish to cruise, he also made it clear that unlike his predecessor he intended to issue the final orders, to coordinate the effort and cover as wide a range of the seas as possible. The very same day, Jones wrote the chairman of the Senate's Naval Committee, Samuel Smith of Maryland, asking for an additional appropriation for eighteen-gun sloops of war—which the new secretary argued would be the most effective weapons in the coming commerce war that he envisioned as America's best riposte to British naval power. These were like smaller versions of a frigate; strongly built, ship-rigged with three masts but barely half the length and a third the tonnage of the *Constitution* and her sister ships, sloops of war could be built in as little as three or four months, much more quickly than the new frigates and seventy-fours, and would deliver much greater results for the price, about $75,000 apiece including construction costs, four months' provisions, and two months' wages in advance for the crew.

"Their force is inferior only to a frigate," Jones wrote the senator, "their cost and expenditure only about one third in actual Service; and in pursuit of the Commerce and light cruisers of the enemy three Sloops of the class proposed may reasonably be expected to produce a much greater effect than a single Frigate. . . . Aided by these vessels our Frigates would be enabled to take a wider range in pursuit of higher game."[47] Less than two weeks later Congress approved the construction of six additional sloops of war of the type Jones requested.

ON THE FIRST day of February 1813, with ice making fast in Annapolis harbor, the frigate *Constellation* got under way, heading down the Chesapeake for Hampton Roads. Three days later, approaching the capes that flanked the entrance to the Atlantic, the American ship ran straight into two British ships of the line, three frigates, a brig, and a schooner just entering the bay. Charles Stewart, the *Constellation*'s captain, made a quick decision to make a run for Norfolk, and the winds being calm, he ordered the boats out to kedge the ship to safety.

The tide was running out and so was Stewart's luck, it seemed, as the ship stuck on the mudflats at the mouth of the tidal James River. There the ship was held fast throughout the day as the crew labored to lighten her by starting her water and removing stores as the British squadron hovered cautiously off, out of gunshot and facing a contrary wind and unfamiliar shoal waters. By seven o'clock in the evening the rising tide lifted the *Constellation* off the flats, and the boats were able to tow her under the guns of Fort Norfolk. "From the first I was desirous of avoiding this place," Stewart reported to Secretary Jones; it was too easy to be trapped by the enemy. That same evening the British ships dropped down and anchored at Lynnhaven Bay, effectively sealing off the *Constellation*'s escape route to the sea.

Jones sent hasty orders to shore up the defenses of Norfolk, close off the entrance to the harbor with a line of gunboats, and dispatch a fast-sailing pilot boat to warn incoming merchant vessels of the British blockade.[48]

To Eleanor he wrote a few weeks later:

> There is great anxiety for Norfolk. The force of the Enemy is very great and may probably succeed in their main object the destruction of the Frigate and Navy Yard, but they will pay dearly for it. All that could be done on our part has been done—it has been impossible to get men sufficient for the Gun Boats there but if they were all manned and the enemy is determined to make the sacrifice it would make no difference.

He added the following day:

> No news from Norfolk today . . . My letters by mail to day from N York announce the appearance of the Enemy Squadron. Whether a new force from Europe or that which was off the Delaware I know not but hope it will be found to be the latter I have been urging the Dispatch of our Frigates from New York and Boston but the weather and the slowness of recruiting has retarded their departure. I am extremely anxious, lest they would be Blockaded.[49]

On March 3, Cockburn's squadron arrived at Lynnhaven Bay and dropped anchor, and nineteen days later Warren in the *San Domingo* joined him. In support of the far more aggressive approach to making war that the government was now expecting, Cockburn was advised he was being sent an expeditionary force of 2,300 men, including two battalions of Royal Marines, each with 842 men and a company of artillery; a detachment of 300 regular infantry from the 102nd Regiment in Bermuda; and two "Independent Companies of Foreigners," consisting of 300 French prisoners of war who had agreed to fight for Great Britain as "Chasseurs Britanniques" in exchange for their freedom.

To "effect a diversion" that would draw American troops away from the renewed campaign against Canada that was fully expected with the coming of spring, the British expeditionary force was issued orders to capture or burn naval or military stores along the Chesapeake, levy ransoms against civilian property by threatening its destruction, and generally "harass the Enemy by different attacks." While on "no account" were the British naval and military commanders to foment a general slave uprising—"The Humanity which ever influences His Royal Highness" must oppose a "system of warfare which must be attended by the atrocities inseparable from commotions of such a description"—they were authorized to enlist and guarantee the freedom of any "Individual Negroes" who offered their assistance to the British cause.[50]

CHAPTER 7

"You Shall Now Feel the Effects of War"

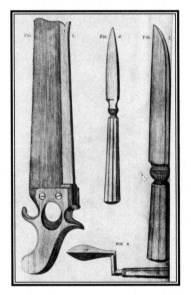

Knives and saw for amputations
(National Library of Medicine)

WITH HIS usual paternalism, William Bainbridge summoned the men of the *Constitution* in Boston harbor on the morning of April 9, 1813, and gave them a lecture. "Sailors, in the action with *Java* you have shown yourself men. You are this evening invited to partake of the amusements of the theater; conduct yourself well. Suffer me not to experience any mortification from any disorderly conduct on your part. Let the correctness of your conduct equal your bravery, and I shall have additional cause to speak of you in terms of approbation." And then the men marched off to Boston's Federal Street Theater for a Friday night performance, impressing the rest of the audience with their "decent mirth and jollity" and the thundering cheer they gave Bainbridge, Rodgers, and other officers when they arrived in the stage box that had been specially "fitted up" for them with patriotic decorations, and impressing at least one newspaperman on the scene for simply making it back to their ship in one piece. "Among the 'thousand ships' of England, there probably is not a single crew, three-fourths of whom would not have deserted, had they been allowed an opportunity like this," declared the New York *Statesman*.[1]

Bainbridge had been asked by Secretary Jones what he wanted to do next, command a frigate for another cruise or superintend the construction of one of the seventy-fours with the command going to him upon its completion, and Bainbridge replied immediately with a letter to the secretary "asking your advise" on which to choose but making perfectly clear which he preferred:

> You ask me my dear Sir what are my intentions—wether to pursue the fickle Jade fortune, or ride under the lee of a 74 until she is in Commission. . . . I will merely state that in 16 years, I have spent very little time with my family—And when honored with the command of the navy yard here & the Station, the Government was so indulgent as to leave me the choice of remaining where my services I trust were useful, or to embark on the Ocean in pursuit of honor & danger—having been the Child of adversity I did not hesitate a moment in preferring the latter—I left my comfortable home in hopes that the fickle Goddess was tired of her freaks. At all events I was determined to pursue her until she should smile. Good luck attended me in having an opportunity to gratify my ambition & fondest wish—By going again in a Frigate, I might reap similar honors, but, probably, not greater. But in a 74, I should expect and confidently trust to add much—A *British Admiral Flag*, would be a glorious inducement for great exertions.[2]

And so as Bainbridge had intended all along, Hull was bumped from the command of the Boston Navy Yard on March 15, 1813, and Bainbridge reclaimed the post he had come to view as his personal prerogative, taking up residence once again in the commandant's house that his family had never left in the interim. While Bainbridge oversaw the construction of the seventy-four-gun *Independence* in Boston, Hull was shuffled off to Portsmouth, New Hampshire, to take charge of the building of another of the new seventy-fours, the *Washington*. But Hull amiably went along with the arrangement, as did his new wife, who said she would be "satisfied with almost anything, provided he does not go to sea."[3]

The continued comings and going of American naval ships from Boston had earned Warren another withering from Secretary Croker; their lordships were quite aware that owing to contrary winds and fogs, "this Port cannot be effectually blockaded from November to March," but the *United States, Congress, President,* and *Constitution* had all managed to get out to sea in October. Even with bad weather, a sizable force could have been dispatched a reasonable and safe distance from the land to try to intercept some of the American warships that had then continued to traipse in and out of the port as if they had not a care in the world: *President* and *Congress* had gotten safely back into Boston on the last day of December 1812, the *Constitution* had returned from its victory over the *Java* on February 15, and the *Chesapeake* joined them April 9.

Then on April 25 Rodgers took advantage of a heavy fog, and squally weather that yielded a brief favorable wind, to slip out to sea right under the nose of the British frigates *Shannon* and *Tenedos,* which had been closely watching the port since arriving from Halifax in March. "It is with great mortification," Captain Thomas Bladen Capel wrote Warren on May 11, "I am to acquaint you that . . . two of the Enemy's Frigates (the *President* and *Congress*) have escaped from Boston." Capel, in the seventy-four *La Hogue* and accompanied by the sloop *Curlew,* scoured the Atlantic from Cape Sable to Georges Bank trying to intercept either of the American ships, but they escaped this dragnet as well.[4]

But the tightening British stranglehold on the American coast was telling everywhere. Two ships of the line and two frigates loitered off Sandy Hook and Montauk Point, sealing off Decatur in New York with the *United States* and his refitted prize the *Macedonian*. At Norfolk, the *Constellation* was for the moment safely holed up behind a floating gun-ship battery of thirty-four guns, a hastily erected artillery emplacement on Craney Island at the mouth of the harbor, and a line of blockships that had been sunk in the channel off Lambert's Point barring the entrance to the Elizabeth River; but the natural and artificial facts that made Norfolk hard for the British to get into made it equally hard for the *Constellation* to get out of, and ever escape to sea. The *Constellation*'s captain, Charles Stewart, reported to Jones that many residents of Norfolk had fled in anticipation of a British attack on the town, and that some of the local militia had deserted from an apprehension that they would be ordered to serve on the undermanned gunboats. Jones replied promising all assistance and authorizing a reasonable recruitment bounty to make up the deficiency of crews for the gunboats, but cautioning that defense everywhere against a superior force was impossible: "The presence of a powerful hostile squadron is naturally calculated to excite alarm, thus we have urgent calls from Maine to Georgia, each conceiving itself the particular object of attack."[5]

The blockade had almost completely shut down the coasting trade, forcing shipments to go by land and creating commercial gluts and shortages. Philadelphia was cut off from the lower Delaware, and Baltimore was completely isolated from the sea; flour from the mid-Atlantic states that sold for $10.50 a barrel before the war was now going for $18 in Boston and $6.50 in Baltimore, where fifty thousand barrels piled up in warehouses. Baltimore newspapers began facetiously listing the movement of wagons in the style of shipping news items, telling how many days they had been on their journeys and reporting "no enemy cruisers" sighted on the way, but the thin humor could not mask the grim reality that shipping by land was slow, laborious, and prohibitively costly. One item that was reported without any attempt at jocularity read "Four wagons loaded with dry goods passed to-day through Georgetown, South Carolina, for Charleston, *forty-six days* from Philadelphia."[6]

Jones wrote to Eleanor that the disruption of water transport was already playing havoc with supplying the navy too: "In my Department I shall feel serious difficulty as we cannot as hitherto transport our stores from the places of deposit to where they are wanted." In Boston the want of supplies had been responsible for the almost five-month delay in getting the *President* and the *Congress* back to sea after their safe return to Boston in December 1812. From Portsmouth, Hull wrote with the disturbing news that he could find only about two-thirds of the stockpiled pieces of live oak that had been cut for the frame of the seventy-four he was supposed to build; the rest had been cannibalized for repairs to other ships in the intervening years, which prompted Jones to reply in late April, "I can not but express my regret . . . particularly as the transportation by water is almost entirely cut off by the enemy." Hull wanted to substitute white oak, but Jones thought some extra live oak timbers ought to be available in Boston, where frames for two complete ships had been stockpiled. Hull accordingly sent Bainbridge a series of increasingly urgent requests for timbers from the Charlestown Navy Yard; Bainbridge sent grudging replies and finally and only with great reluctance turned over a few pieces.[7]

But throughout the difficult spring, Jones kept reminding his beleaguered commanders that retaliation, not defense, was the key to taking on a superior foe. "No reasonable man can suppose that our means are competent to the defence of the *all* against a superior force, which can be concentrated against any one point," he wrote to Stewart at Norfolk. The object was rather to tie up as many of the enemy's ships as possible by taking the offensive at every opportunity; as he wrote Stewart on March 27:

> It is some consolation, that while a strong squadron of the enemies Ships are employed in watching your little squadron & carrying out a Petty larceny kind of warfare, against the river craft & plantations, our gallant commanders are scouring the ocean, in search of a superior foe, & gathering laurels in such abundance, & in such rapid succession, as to afford the enemy scarcely time to soothe the chagrin of one defeat before he is subjected to the mortification of another.[8]

The same day's mail from New York brought news of the return of James Lawrence in the sloop of war *Hornet* from his cruise along the coast of South America. On January 24, 1813, the *Hornet* had been chased off the blockade of the *Bonne Citoyenne* at São Salvador by the arrival of a British seventy-four, but Lawrence had nimbly slipped away from the much more powerful enemy and stood out to sea. On February 4 he captured an English brig carrying $23,000 in specie. And then on February 24, nearing the mouth of the Demerara River, the *Hornet* fell in with the sixteen-gun British brig sloop *Peacock* and in fourteen minutes left her a sinking wreck, her captain dead along with thirty-seven other casualties to the *Hornet*'s three. The *Peacock* had been long known as "the yacht" for her resplendent appearance and immaculately polished fittings, and the accuracy of her crew's gunnery in the brief fight had been abysmal. Although a subsequent British court-martial ran true to form in underscoring that there had been no want of courage displayed by the *Peacock*'s officers and men, and "honorably acquitted" the survivors, the court frankly attributed her defeat to a "want of skill in directing the Fire, owing to an omission of the Practice of exercising the crew in the use of the Guns for the last three Years." It was the fifth American victory in a single-ship engagement.[9] Joshua Keene, the *Peacock*'s steward, kept a small notebook of clippings he saved while a prisoner in New York, and one included the words of a chantey that Keene noted was making the rounds "about the Streets of New York":

> Yankee sailors have a knack
> Haul away! yeo ho, boys
> Of pulling down a British Jack
> 'Gainst any odds you know boys.[10]

THE CLOSE proximity of the British blockading squadrons to the American coast presented irresistible temptations to both sides in an era of less than total war. Warren's orders to Cockburn instructed him to have as little communication as possible with the inhabitants of the coast "in order to avoid corruption, seduction, or the seeds of sedition being sown," but from Norfolk, Captain Stewart wrote Jones that a steady stream of British deserters was showing up daily. Others were dying in the attempt: "Their naked bodies are frequently fished up on the bay shore, where they must have drowned in attempting to swim."[11]

The British ships' need for provisions made it impossible to avoid contact with local citizens, who in many cases were all too happy to reap the benefits of trade with a cash-paying enemy. Cockburn encouraged local cooperation with the British force by offering to pay farmers along the Chesapeake well and in ready money for cattle and vegetables and other supplies they willingly provided, while seizing them by force if any resistance was offered to his foraging parties. And even as the war was becoming palpably more brutal and absolute, traditions of gentlemanly combat wove a crazy quilt of inconsistencies through the British blockade. The commander of an American militia regiment on Virginia's Eastern Shore sent Cockburn a formal request that the packet sailing between Norfolk and Northampton be allowed to continue its regular service unmolested by the British squadron, and Cockburn returned an equally formal reply magnanimously granting the favor.[12]

Secretary Jones complained bitterly about the "palpable and criminal intercourse held with the enemy's forces blockading and invading the waters of the United States," noting that both neutral foreign-flagged vessels leaving American ports and American coasting vessels "with great subtlety and treachery" were conveying "provisions, water, and succours of all kinds . . . direct to the fleets and stations of the enemy, with constant intelligence of our naval and military force." Block Island, at the end of Long Island Sound, and Provincetown, at the tip of Cape Cod, became virtual British ports, where ships of the blockading squadron regularly put in for water or other supplies. At Provincetown the squadron received fish, vegetables, and water, and the British captains furnished passes to several local owners of schooners allowing them to sail across Massachusetts Bay, through the British squadron to Cape Ann, to procure loads of firewood for them.[13]

Even many stalwart Republicans winked at the illicit commerce when they were the beneficiaries. One prominent Maryland Republican from the Eastern Shore, Jacob Gibson, engaged in a pugnacious public correspondence defending himself after selling cattle, sheep, and hogs to the British. It did not help his case when it also became known that he had personally entertained Admiral Warren to dinner at his plantation on Sharps Island in the Chesapeake, and had received in return a protection from the admiral safeguarding his property and slaves and allowing safe conduct of his wheat crop to the mainland. But Maryland congressman Robert Wright, the same who had demanded "hemp and confiscation" for traitors, loudly offered his support for Gibson's patriotism and assured him that "the enemies of your country" had signaled him out for attack only because of the conspicuous figure he cut in the Republican ranks. Other local Republicans acknowledged, however, that if Gibson had been a Federalist, "he would have been tarred and feathered and his house pulled down."[14]

Even harder to control was the illegal but absolutely booming commercial trade in British textiles, pottery, salt, sugar, and other goods smuggled in from Canada and the West Indies in exchange for cash, American produce, and naval stores. Congress banned all British imports in June 1812 with the advent of the war, but the huge profits to be made from smuggling led to widespread and often open defiance of customs officials who tried to enforce the law. A huge trade through Spanish-owned Amelia Island, in the mouth of the St. Marys River in Florida, kept Georgia and much of the South supplied with British manufactures and other goods throughout the war. An army officer in Eastport, Maine, estimated that two hundred merchants in that town were involved in smuggling; when he tried to halt the illegal trade, he was threatened with tarring and feathering, and when he persisted, he was thrown in jail for a fictitious debt. In Plattsburgh, New York, another federal officer was thwarted when he discovered that even the local judges had a share in the smuggling trade. In New Orleans smugglers killed a customs official and wounded two others in one altercation and staged a raid on the customs house to recover their seized property.

Merchants devised all manner of ingenious ruses to get around the law, including outfitting privateers that, sailing off the coast of Maine or on Lake Ontario or Lake Champlain or the St. Lawrence River, "captured" Canadian vessels filled with goods that had in fact been purchased by their own agents in Montreal or Halifax.

The lack of a coherent policy in Washington and a welter of contradictions in the Republican party's position on commerce made it difficult to marshal much public respect for the halfhearted government efforts to crack down on trading with the enemy. After initially seizing a flood of $18 million worth of British-made goods that were carried by returning American ships in the first months of the war, the Treasury first released them in exchange for penalty bonds put up by their owners, then offered to cancel half the forfeiture, then finally acceded to a congressional move to forgive the penalties altogether, in part to help bolster support for the war among the merchant classes.[15]

Congress had similarly balked at cutting off the British-licensed trade that even after the start of the war allowed American ships to continue carrying flour to the nominally neutral ports of Cádiz and Lisbon to keep Wellington's troops on the Peninsula supplied. Thousands of British licenses had been issued to American shippers since the start of the war between Britain and America; Augustus Foster had signed hundreds before he left the country, and British consuls and admirals in the region issued them too. The Baltimore mob attacked some vessels as they were being loaded with flour for Lisbon and threatened a rope around the neck for anyone sending "a Barrel of flour to the Enemy," but there were plenty of Baltimore merchants—not to mention the many good Republican wheat farmers across the mid-Atlantic and western states—who were eager to keep the business going, war or no war. For the first eight months of the war, until the blockade shut down Baltimore's access to the ocean, two-thirds of the sailings from the port were under British licenses. In both 1812 and 1813 licensed shipments of flour from American ports to the Peninsula totaled a million barrels a year, about 100,000 tons, ten times what it had been just three years before. In American port cities, signed British licenses—with spaces left blank for the name of the vessel and its master—fetched as much as $5,000 apiece.[16]

Jefferson repeatedly urged Madison not to interfere with such an important outlet for American farmers. He blithely explained the slightly cynical calculation behind keeping Britain well supplied with American wheat:

> If she is to be fed at all events, why may we not have the benefit of it as well as others? . . . Besides, if we could, by starving the English armies, oblige them to withdraw from the peninsula, it would be to send them here; and I think we had better feed them for pay, than feed and fight them here for nothing. To keep the war popular, we must keep open the markets. As long as good prices can be had, the people will support the war cheerfully.[17]

Madison decided to take action against the licensed trade only after it became clear that Warren and British officials in the West Indies had been specifically instructed to favor the New England states with licenses as part of the British strategy to encourage a separate peace with, or even secession of, the Federalist strongholds; that was the same reason the British blockade had so far spared the Northeast. The president sent a message to Congress on February 24, 1813, denouncing the British licensing policy as an "insulting attempt on the virtue, the honor, the patriotism, and the fidelity of our brethren of the Eastern States," and asked Congress to outlaw the acceptance of British licenses by any American vessel. The bill died in the Senate.[18]

American naval officers were generally furious over the continuing trade with the enemy, and relentlessly went after American merchant ships trading under British licenses on their own initiative, but it was a tricky business given that both the attorney general and the Treasury Department had issued rulings that the licensed trade was perfectly legal. Although common law forbade trading with the enemy in wartime, it was uncertain how American admiralty courts would rule in cases of American ships seized by their own navy as prizes for violating this traditional law.

Moreover, admiralty law laid down strict limitations on the right of ships of war to stop and search neutral or friendly merchant vessels, which often made it difficult to know if a ship was sailing under an enemy license. The basic rule was that a naval commander could halt any merchantman and examine her papers, but in the absence of clear indications of fraud or concealment in the representation of her cargo or destination, he had no right to search the ship for further evidence. Violating these rules was grounds for the court refusing to recognize the validity of the capture, potentially rendering the captor liable for considerable damages. All these rules were designed to regularize the capture of enemy shipping in wartime, to draw clear lines between the legitimate seizure of enemy property under the laws of war and the plunder of piracy, and to ensure fair treatment of innocent neutral parties. All of which meant that American shippers carrying British licenses took pains to present an innocent face and conceal their licenses from any American warships that stopped them, keeping the license to show only to British warships that stopped them.[19]

Approaching American merchantmen, American warships routinely followed the ruse Bainbridge had employed when stopping the brig *South Carolina:* hoist British colors, send over a boarding party that identified themselves as British, and otherwise keep up the charade to try to get the merchant captain to produce a British license. If the ruse worked, and a license appeared, the American ship would be seized and sent in as a prize to the United States. Given the similarity in warships, uniforms, and language between the American and British navies, it often worked. But in several early cases, federal district judges (who, under the Constitution, administer admiralty law) refused to go along with the condemnation of American ships thus seized. In February 1813 a federal judge in Philadelphia ordered the *South Carolina* restored to its owners and found Bainbridge liable for the damages they had suffered from their vessel's capture and detention; "this vessel is, indisputably, an American ship," the judge ruled, there was no intention to deceive, and her outward cargo of corn and flour carried to Lisbon was consigned to a Portuguese merchant.[20]

An even more draconian judgment was entered against John Rodgers in a ruling that threatened to make every American captain think twice about repeating the ruse de guerre of passing themselves off as British. Late on the night of October 16, 1812, the United States frigates *President* and *Congress* chased and halted an American schooner, the *Eleanor*, in squally weather off the Grand Bank. *Congress* sent over a lieutenant to fetch back the schooner's master and first mate. The lieutenant identified his frigate as "His Majesty's Ship Shannon," and an ironic dialogue ensued in which one of the schooner's men defiantly told the "British" lieutenant, "I wish the United States frigate President were along side" of his ship.

"Do you think she could do anything with her?" the lieutenant replied.

"Yes, I am sure of it."

But after the *Eleanor's* two top officers were rowed off, the crew, deciding they were about to become British prisoners, broke into the spirit locker and began to down as much liquor as they could hold. By the time the American officers on the *Congress* were convinced that the *Eleanor* was not sailing under a British license and dropped the charade, the damage had been done. The schooner's crew refused to believe that the American ship was not British, told the master he was being duped by the officers who now said they were in fact American, and refused to work the ship. At two in the morning a storm struck, the mainmast fell straight aft, and a few seconds later the foremast went too. The drunken crew managed to rig a jury mast and small sail and approach the two frigates, but the deck had been holed by the falling mast and she was rapidly taking on water; the next morning she was taken under tow, but even with men working the pumps around the clock she began to settle in the water, and three days later she sank.

The *Eleanor's* owner brought suit for the loss of the ship, and the district court agreed that Rodgers as squadron commander was responsible, at one point finding him personally liable for a $43,250 judgment. It was not until 1817 that the Supreme Court reversed the decision, unanimously holding that because the *Eleanor* had never been seized as a prize, her own crew had never been released from obligation to do their duty and that showing false colors was well within "the rights of war."[21]

Several of the district court rulings that found in favor of American owners whose ships were seized carrying British licenses were reprinted in a Federalist pamphlet published in Philadelphia, perhaps at British instigation. But both the political and the legal tides were turning by spring 1813. In June, Justice Joseph Story, writing a circuit court decision that would become the definitive ruling on the issue when the Supreme

Court affirmed it the following March, rejected an appeal by the owners of the brig *Julia,* which had been seized by the *Chesapeake* on December 31, 1812, on her return from Lisbon under a British license. Story, a
recognized authority on prize law, acknowledged that there was no
direct precedent of a ship ever having been lawfully condemned on the
basis of using an enemy license: "It is," he wrote, "one of the many
novel questions which may be presumed to arise out of the extraordinary state of the world." But Story found ample related precedents in
British and French prize law for concluding that "it is unlawful in any
manner to lend assistance to the enemy, by attaching ourselves to his
policy, sailing under his protection, facilitating his supplies, and separating ourselves from the common character of our country." Trading
with the enemy was prohibited under the law of nations not just for the
direct injury it caused but because it "contaminates the commercial
enterprizes" with purposes at odds with the policy of the nation,
exposes individuals "to extraordinary temptations to succour the
enemy by intelligence," and corrupts their loyalties by effectively turning them into neutrals.[22] With Story's ruling having paved the way,
Congress finally summoned the courage in the summer of 1813 to pass
Madison's requested legislation banning the use of all British licenses.

By that time Admiral Warren had also grown heartily sick of the
licensed trade and the crazy contradictory complications it created; not
least was the fact that under the cover offered by the dozens of licensed
vessels that sailed from New York every day through Long Island Sound
throughout the spring and summer of 1813, a steady stream of privateers and letters of marque slipped out past the British squadrons, and
out to sea, as well.[23]

FOR THE better part of a year Captain Philip Broke of His Majesty's
frigate *Shannon* had "sauntered about off Boston," as he at one point
described the endless and frustrating duty of watching an enemy port,
spoiling for a fight. He had been on the North American station since
August 1811, and success had eluded him. Broke was heir to an estate in
Surrey but far from rich; he was a navy man through and through, a
veteran of the Battle of Cape St. Vincent at twenty-one, a post captain
at twenty-five, commander of the *Shannon* ever since its commissioning
in 1806, but at thirty-six he was now thoroughly tired of the life of the
sea and longed for an honorable exit. He filled his hours writing letter

after letter, day after day, to his wife back in England, knowing he would not receive answers for months, if at all. His letters were full of sentimental dreams of flowers and life in the country and reading poetry to his wife, who was less a real person than just another prop in this domestic fantasy; she was "my dear little wife," "my sweet Looloo," "my gentle Loo," "my delightful angel," who would comfort him "with all her mild resignation" in his rural retirement.

Broke had all the English aristocratic disdain for the "savages," the "animals," the "reptiles" he had the misfortune to be fighting. He bemoaned his ill luck with prizes, but he would give them all up for one stunning, brilliant victory that would provide him the release he ached for:

> Shannon, off Boston,
> September 14th 1812.
> . . . I would give all our prizes for an American frigate, they are fighting in a bad cause my Loo, and I shall feel a satisfaction in beating them. . . . I see by the papers, our people at home have little idea of the bitterness and rancour with which the Americans have made war upon us; every overture of kindness we make to them, they consider as a submission, and become the more insolent to us: a year's war will tame them much, they have not yet felt our Naval power.

> Shannon, off Chesapeake,
> February 14th.
> . . . as to prizes I would never leave my lovely Loo for all our flag has ever taken: I have never been fortunate at all that way. . . . My being poor is no disappointment to me; to return without any successes to prove how we have been exerting ourselves so long and tiresome a pursuit (and which we feel conscious of deserving), is mortifying . . . Indeed you can't imagine the pains I have bestowed on this graceless wooden wife of mine . . . I am sure the other wife will make me happy if I quit this game of honor.

> Shannon, off Boston,
> April 14th, 1813.
> . . . Whilst we went (by order) to report our reconnaissance of Boston, one of their frigates (Chesapeake) got safe in, this is

mortifying. . . . 8 years of my youth, and all my plans of rural quiet and domestic happiness, have faded away, or been cruelly interrupted by this imperious call of honor, but surely no man deserves to enjoy an estate in England, who will not sacrifice some of his prospects to his countrys welfare.

Shannon, off Boston,
May 5th, 1813.
. . . The enemy have sent me no frigate yet . . . but they seem by their papers, to have been much annoyed at our being so familiar with their harbour lately. They may prove our best friends yet, and favor me with an opportunity of retiring with honor to my gentle wife (if the Admiralty do not remove me before they are decided upon meeting us). . . . I must get home indeed to my tender Loo, I am heartily sick of this sea life.

Shannon, off Boston,
May 9th, 1813.
. . . I feel much mortified at President escaping us after watching so long and anxiously for him; God send us better fortune to finish my campaign creditably. The day those rogues sailed it was thick weather, we must have been very close to them but they did not seek us. . . . I hope Boston will soon be added to the ports under arrest, and we will pinch them into repentance for this wanton war of theirs.

Shannon, off Boston,
May 28th, 1813.
. . . We sill haunt this tiresome place without any success to reward us, indeed I have been so particularly anxious to watch the great ships, that it has thrown us much out of the way of the smaller, tho' richer prizes. Since Rodgers escaped we have rarely hunted our game far from his den, which still contains another large wild beast; if all the nobler prey elude us, we must chace the vermin, but have great hopes yet of an honourable recontre.[24]

The "large beast" was the *Chesapeake,* which was undergoing a quick refit in Boston with orders that "not a moment should be lost" in getting to sea again for an independent cruise. Secretary Jones's orders were for her to proceed to the mouth of the St. Lawrence and intercept British troop and store ships heading to reinforce the army in Canada, and then to continue on to Greenland and destroy the British whale fishery.

Her new commander was James Lawrence, promoted to captain by the Senate in February as a resolution of the bitter controversy that Charles Morris's double promotion had engendered and then rewarded for his victory over the *Peacock* with the command of a frigate. On May 18, 1813, Lawrence arrived in Boston and found the ship in good order. But there was more than a little bad feeling in the air. Lawrence, in fact, had tried to decline the appointment, calculating there was more glory to be had in a smaller ship. Four of the lieutenants from the *Chesapeake*'s last cruise were sick or on indefinite leave. Many of the crew had reached the end of their two-year enlistments and had stayed on only because they had not yet been paid, their dissatisfaction made worse by the fact that they had not received the prize money they were due from their last cruise, either: all the prize money was frozen in a bank account because the ship's agent had just learned that Stephen Decatur was threatening a lawsuit to claim the one-twentieth share he said he was due as squadron commander, even though he and the *United States* had been thousands of miles away, already returned to New York harbor, when the *Chesapeake* had taken the most valuable prize of her cruise in January.

Lawrence himself had had an unpleasant interview with Bainbridge upon his arrival in Boston over a similar dispute. Bainbridge told Lawrence that as his squadron commander he was due one-third of the prize money Lawrence was to receive out of the expected $25,000 to be awarded for the capture of the *Peacock*. The very morning that the *Chesapeake* was preparing to stand to sea with her new captain of ten days' standing, the crew confronted Lawrence over their unpaid prize money; and Lawrence, no doubt displacing his own rancor over his contretemps with Bainbridge, furiously "damned them for a set of Rascals" and ordered them to their stations to weigh anchor.[25]

The day was June 1, a bright and clear morning sweeping across Boston harbor, and the entire town was aware that Lawrence was planning to make straight for the *Shannon* in a showdown that had far more in common with an affair of honor than a stratagem of war. Broke had sent away his consort, the frigate *Tenedos*, and had tauntingly run in alone into the harbor near Boston Light, showing his colors and heaving to. And as the *Chesapeake* got under way, the *Shannon* fired a single signal gun to punctuate the challenge.

Although Lawrence never received the letter Broke had written him the day before and dispatched to Boston with a released prisoner—a letter that would subsequently become famous in Britain and be reprinted over and over as a model of latter-day English chivalry—he had no doubt about Broke's intention to engage him in a single-ship duel. Broke had earlier sent similar messages by word of mouth to Rodgers; his written challenge to Lawrence was a final gamble to stake everything for the chance that had so far escaped him. "As the *Chesapeake* appears now ready for Sea," he began, "I request you will do me the favor to meet the *Shannon* with her, Ship to Ship, to try the fortune of our respective Flags." Broke offered to meet Lawrence anywhere within three hundred miles of Boston; he pledged to send every ship of his squadron far enough away that they would be unable to interfere; if Lawrence chose, he could keep Broke's challenge a secret and name the place of their meeting; the two ships could even sail together under a flag of truce to any place Lawrence felt safest from encountering another British warship. Broke appealed to his American counterpart:

> I entreat you, Sir, not to imagine that I am urged by mere
> personal vanity to the wish of meeting the *Chesapeake*, or that I
> depend only upon your personal ambition for acceding to the
> Invitation, we have both nobler motives,—you will feel it as a
> compliment if I say that the result of our meeting may be the
> most grateful Service I can render to my Country,—and I doubt
> not that you, equally confident of success, will feel convinced that
> it is only by continued triumphs in *even combats*, that your little
> Navy can now hope to console *your* Country for the loss of that
> Trade it can no longer protect.—favor me with a speedy
> reply,—we are short of Provisions and Water, and cannot stay
> long here.

"Choose your terms," Broke wrote in a postscript, "*but let us meet.*"

A small flotilla of boats followed the *Chesapeake* out of the harbor as she got under way from President's Roads at noon. Just before sailing, Lawrence went below to his cabin to write a short note to Secretary Jones. "An English frigate is now in sight from my deck; I have sent a pilot boat out to reconnoiter, and should she be alone, I am in hopes to give a good account of her before night." Huge crowds gathered every place in the town that commanded a view of the sea, but the two ships soon had dropped out of sight to the east, all their sails filled as they ran before a fair wind from the southwest.[26]

At 4:30 p.m., on a line between Cape Cod and Cape Ann, the *Shannon* hove to and waited for the *Chesapeake* to come up.

Broke was an exception to the Royal Navy's neglectful attitude toward gunnery; he may have grown weary of the sea, but he drilled the men of his ship incessantly. He trained his gunners to carry out concentrated fire, the crews of adjacent guns all angling their weapons to converge on a single aimpoint. At his own expense he had fitted the *Shannon*'s guns with quadrants, to mark the aiming angles at various distances to targets, and dispart sights, which corrected for the elevation error that occurred when aiming along the top of the gun owing to the fact that the barrel is thicker at the breech than the muzzle. The sights were simple metal wedges affixed to the top of the barrel, but they made all the difference; they were fashioned so that their upper edge ran parallel to the bore, so aiming along that surface provided a true line to the target.

Broke had also fitted his ship with two nine-pounders mounted on pivots on the quarterdeck and forecastle, raised so that they could shoot over the hammock nettings. As the *Chesapeake* closed the last distance between the ships, he ordered the men on the pivot guns to aim for the enemy's wheel. Anticipating a brutal close action, Broke had already ordered small arms and grenades issued to the men in the tops and the members of each gun crew designated as boarders; chests of canister shot were hauled into the tops for the small swivel guns, and tubs filled with boarding axes, bundles of long pikes, and cutlasses and pistols stood at the ready on the gun decks.[27] In the last few minutes of dead silence before the battle began Broke addressed the crew:

> They have said, and they have published in their papers, that the English have forgotten the way to fight. You will let them know today that there are Englishmen in the Shannon who still know how to fight. Don't try to dismast her. Fire into her quarters; maindeck to maindeck; quarterdeck to quarterdeck. Kill the men and the ship is yours. . . . Don't hit them about the head, for they have steel caps on, but give it them through the body. Don't cheer. Go quietly to your quarters. I feel sure you will all do your duty, and remember that you now have the blood of your countrymen to avenge.[28]

Whether out of an excess of reciprocal chivalry or an excess of concern to keep the weather gauge, which hardly would have mattered in the close action clearly in the offing, Lawrence declined to exploit the wide opening Broke had left him: *Shannon* lay with her head to the southeast, her main topsail braced so that it shivered to check the ship's motion, and Lawrence could easily have crossed her stern and delivered a devastating raking broadside. But instead he came up "in a very handsome manner," as Broke would later say, taking a parallel course fifty yards to windward, and at 5:45 p.m. the duel began.[29]

As the *Shannon*'s guns bore, they began to fire in turn and simply tore the men on the *Chesapeake*'s spar deck to pieces. The first broadside sent grape and canister sweeping across the decks, decapitating the *Chesapeake*'s sailing master and killing the helmsman and the fourth lieutenant at once, striking probably 100 out of the 150 men on the top deck. A second helmsman immediately sprang to take the wheel and instantly joined the growing ranks of dead. Lawrence, conspicuous in his full-dress uniform—tall cocked hat and high-collared coat with epaulets and gold lace shining in the afternoon sun—was struck in the right leg by a musket ball and was leaning against the binnacle for support when a round shot from *Shannon*'s nine-pounder pivot gun found its mark and blew the wheel to splinters, killing the third helmsman and barely missing Lawrence.

The *Chesapeake* had come on too fast initially, and now with the loss of her helm she forged ahead. The *Shannon*'s gunners had each fired three rounds in six minutes before their guns ceased to bear, and their fire had brought down the *Chesapeake*'s fore topsail yard and jib; now with her headsails gone she began turning helplessly into the wind, leaving her larboard quarter exposed to the *Shannon*'s mercy. Lawrence was struck by another musket ball, this time a mortal wound to the groin. Every man on the quarterdeck was mown down by grapeshot from the *Shannon*'s carronades and swivel guns in the tops. Lawrence was still conscious and called for his boarders, but the increasingly officerless ship was in a shambles. British grenades began pelting down and exploding on the deck. Lawrence was carried below, the first lieutenant was killed, the lieutenant of marines was killed, and then the *Chesapeake*, gathering sternway, crashed stern first amidships of the *Shannon* and Broke shouted for the boarders to follow him. George Budd, the *Chesapeake*'s second lieutenant, was at his station on the gun deck below, and several minutes passed before he received word that boarders had been called. The third lieutenant, William S. Cox, had left the deck to help carry Lawrence below, an act for which he would later be convicted by a court-martial eager to find scapegoats.

Still, the *Chesapeake*'s men put up a desperate if disorderly resistance. The *Shannon*'s boatswain was attempting to lash the ships together by passing a rope over the American frigate's taffrail when a crewman in the *Chesapeake*'s great cabin ran to the captain's quarter gallery and, reaching up with his cutlass, hacked the man's arm clean off.

Broke, waving the heavy Scottish broadsword he favored in battle, clambered over the hammocks onto the roof of the *Chesapeake*'s quarter gallery, stepped onto the muzzle of a carronade and gained the quarterdeck, dodged a pistol shot from the *Chesapeake*'s chaplain and hacked off his arm in return, then shouted to his men to follow him forward. In the tops a steady fire was still coming from the *Chesapeake*'s marines and topmen, and Broke shouted across to his topmen to turn their guns against them; from the main- and foretops of the *Shannon* several men crawled out to the end of the yardarms to pick off the Americans, and from the foreyard five of the Shannons then leapt, incredibly, across to the end of the *Chesapeake*'s yard and took the foretop by storm.

Broke arrived at the *Chesapeake*'s forecastle just as Lieutenant Budd appeared from below and tried to rally his remaining men; a furious musket blow from an American sailor left Broke momentarily stunned, and a second American then brought a cutlass down with full force, shearing off Broke's scalp and cutting through the skull to bare his brains; a British sailor then ran Broke's assailant through, and by that point the battle was essentially over, even if the blood-maddened fury continued for several minutes. The remaining Americans on the spar deck were herded down below, but some of the boarders fired down the hatches and others shot wounded Americans on the deck or threw them into the sea.

The action had taken fifteen minutes and left horrific casualties on both sides. Nearly half the American crew were casualties, sixty-nine dead and seventy-five wounded, but so were a quarter of the British sailors. Several of the boarders had been mauled by grapeshot mistakenly directed at them from their own ship; others were hacked or pistoled. The *Shannon*'s surgeon itemized the grisly particulars:

G. T. L. Watt, 1st Lieut grape carried away the top of his head
Wm. Birbles, A.B. grape lodged in back part of chest. Lived
    several hours

John Young, A.B. cut in two on board the Chesapeake
J. Hampson, A.B. musket ball through the hip, cutting though
    the urethra
James Wright, Ship Corpl. bayonet wound in the abdomen
Thos. Barr, Ordinary head shot off[30]

Five days later the *Shannon* led her prize into Halifax harbor, and the word quickly spread through the sleepy Sunday morning. At St. Paul's Church, a whisper went from pew to pew during the service, and "one by one the congregation left" to run to the waterfront to witness the scene.[31]

For a week Broke lay motionless, unable to speak in more than single syllables, shakily affixing his signature to a letter to Admiral Warren seeking to seize the moment to bestow some patronage upon his crew: promotions for his gunner and a carpenter who had served with him for seven years; an appointment as a cook for "my old coxswain Stark," who lost an arm; a "comfortable retirement" for Marine Corporal Driscoll, who "I fear . . . will prove a cripple" and who has "a decent respectable wife & family." Broke himself never fully recovered but was soon well enough to write his wife exulting over the release he had so honorably purchased, about the flower garden and greenhouse and new horse "we must have" with the £3,000 in prize money he would receive, assuring her that the celebrity and accolades would not turn his head: "I will be modest when I get to Suffolk and turn Farmer, renounce vanity with my laced coat."[32]

News of Broke's victory arrived at the Admiralty in London on July 8, and Secretary Croker was able to announce it theatrically in the House of Commons during a debate on naval policy that same night, relishing a chance to skewer the government's critics by pulling an account of British naval triumph out of his hat. Throughout England the exultation was hyperbolic bordering on manic. "Go, vain Columbia! boast no more," declared one of the many celebratory poems that were rushed into print. The normally sober *Naval Chronicle* declared Broke's triumph the "most brilliant act of heroism ever performed" in all of British history, hailed the rebuke to "American vanity" and the "unequivocal proof of their inferiority to us in fair and equal combat," and gloated more than once over the report that a grand victory dinner was actually being prepared in Boston for the *Chesapeake*'s officers at the moment of her surrender, running a slightly puerile poem that ended with the lines: "But for *meat* they got *balls* / From our staunch wooden walls, / So the dinner *Engagement* was BROKE." An action that in other circumstances would not merit more than recognition or promotion, much less so much as a knighthood, earned Broke a baronetcy. Both of his surviving lieutenants were promoted to commander, another highly unusual distinction.[33]

Beneath the hoopla Croker was able to issue an order that would have been humiliating under other circumstances, but which confronted the new reality of this new war. Two days after announcing Broke's victory in Parliament, Croker sent to all station commanders in chief a "secret & confidential" directive strictly forbidding any further single-ship combat with "the larger Class of American Ships; which though they may be called Frigates, are of a size, Complemant and weight of Metal much beyond that Class, and more resembling Line of Battles Ships." In the event of one of His Majesty's frigates falling in with such a ship, her captain was above all to "secure the retreat of His Majestys Ship."[34]

A subsequent American court-martial cashiered Lieutenant Cox for neglect of duty and un-officerlike conduct and sentenced the ship's black bugler, William Brown, who had been found cowering under the longboat when he was supposed to summon the boarders, to three hundred lashes, subsequently remitted by President Madison to one hundred lashes.[35] But William Jones used the opportunity to issue a directive to his captains to keep their eyes on the only strategy that mattered. His subsequent sailing orders to all of the American navy's vessels would contain the injunction "You are also strictly prohibited from giving or receiving a Challenge to, or from, an Enemy's Vessel."

As he would tell one of his captains: "The Character of the American Navy does not require those feats of Chivalry, and your own reputation is too well established, to need factitious support."

And he added: "His Commerce is our true Game, for there he is indeed vulnerable."[36]

ON THE same day the *Chesapeake* struck her flag, June 1, 1813, Stephen Decatur attempted to escape past the British blockaders that had been besetting the entrances to New York for most of the spring. For a week in early May he had waited in Sandy Hook Bay for a favorable wind that would carry the *United States*, the *Macedonian*, and the brig *Argus* past the British frigate and seventy-four that intermittently came into view to the south; a heavy sea would keep the seventy-four's lower gun ports closed and cut her thousand-pound broadside in half, giving the impromptu American squadron a decisive advantage. But the winds remained light and baffling, and a welter of fragmentary and contradictory intelligence reports of additional British warships made Decatur increasingly wary. On May 15 he gave up the attempt to reach the open sea by that route and returned to New York.

His new plan was to make the perilous passage through Hell Gate, the narrow channel from the East River that led to Long Island Sound. Decatur wrote Secretary Jones that he thought his chances that way were better on several counts; for one thing, the British ship of the line that was reportedly watching the end of the sound at Montauk, the *Ramillies,* was twenty-eight years old and "a much duller ship" than the *Valiant* off Sandy Hook. Moreover, there were reports that the frigate *Orpheus* that was in company with her had been making solo forays into the sound, so "it is not altogether improbable that I may fall in with her, out of the protection of the *Ramillies.*" On May 18, Decatur sailed up the East River, now with the sloop of war *Hornet* joining the two frigates. *Argus* stayed behind: she had just received new orders from Secretary Jones that "the President of the United States having in view a special service" for the ship, she was to remain in port, ready for "departure at a moment's notice," and await further instructions.[37]

Hell Gate was a narrow, rock-strewn tidal channel notorious for its swirling currents and the hundreds of ships that had been wrecked trying to make the passage; some two thousand ships would be lost there before the Army Corps of Engineers in the late nineteenth century demolished the rocks with hundreds of thousands of pounds of dynamite. On the approach to the channel the *United States* ran aground and stuck, but was undamaged and floated on the next tide. All the ships made it safely through Hell Gate a few days later. But on the twenty-sixth a freakish lightning strike disconcerted everyone, splintering the *United States'* royal mainmast and striking Decatur's broad pennant fluttering down to the deck; then, surging down the mainmast, the charge leapt down the side of the ship and through one of the main deck gunports onto a cannon, down the wardroom hatch, miraculously skirted the scuttle to the magazine below, and tore through the surgeon's stateroom, where it blew out a candle and destroyed the surgeon's unoccupied cot, then finally exited the ship below the waterline, blowing out several sheets of coppering as it went. The *Macedonian* was following in close order, and her officer on deck instantly shouted for all her sails put aback, convinced the *United States* was about to be blown to bits by her magazine detonating.[38]

Unbeknownst to Decatur, at that very moment both exits from New York were unguarded. Had he either turned back for Sandy Hook or pressed on toward Block Island, he would have made his escape free and clear at once. The senior British captain on the station was the *Valiant*'s commander, Robert Dudley Oliver, and seeing Decatur heading for Hell Gate, he had ordered the two small squadrons to switch posts. The *Valiant* was down to ten tons of water and her consort the *Acasta* had none, and they desperately needed to put into Block Island to replenish their stocks. But Oliver also clearly wanted a crack at Decatur himself, and when Sir Thomas Hardy, the *Ramillies*' captain, arrived off Sandy Hook in obedience to Oliver's orders and learned the real reason behind them he was livid. "It gives me a great deal of uneasiness to have quitted my Station just at this moment," Hardy wrote Warren, "but I still hope that Commodore Decatur will change his mind and come out my way."[39]

Oliver raced along the southern length of Long Island to reach its tip before Decatur arrived there on his parallel course along its north side, through Long Island Sound. But Decatur, for reasons never subsequently explained, bided his time now as he made his way east along the sound. It was a week later, on the morning of the first of June, that the *United States, Macedonian,* and *Hornet* passed between Block Island and Montauk Point at the end of Long Island, with the wind on their quarter and the two British ships in sight far to leeward. But unnerved by reports of other enemy vessels in the area, Decatur at that moment misidentified several other ships in the area as British men-of-war, and just as he was on the verge of making good his escape to the open Atlantic, he hauled his wind and beat back for the safety of New London. In the ensuing chase *Acasta* worked to windward and fired a ranging shot from her bow chasers, but still the American ships raced on, the *Macedonian* and the *Hornet* grounding in the mouth of the Thames River and the British ships abandoning their pursuit because they had no one aboard familiar with the tricky local channels.

Decatur at once got the ships lightened and moved up the river and unshipped two carronades and several of the large guns from his ship to fortify the point at Groton commanding the approaches across from New London. The next day Oliver "pressed a fishing smack" to carry an express order to Hardy to return with his two ships, and on the seventh they arrived to tighten the blockade of New London. British raiding parties landed at the point and carried off cattle and boasted that they planned to attack the American ships as soon as reinforcements arrived. Fearing that the British would go to any lengths to recapture the *Macedonian*—"even if they followed her into a cornfield," Decatur said—he ordered the ships lightened again and moved them eight miles up the river through shallow water and erected an earthwork fort that commanded the approaches by water and land. He had iron bolts driven into the rocks on either side of the river and a chain stretched across, and asked Secretary Jones to send some twenty-four-pounders from the navy yard in New York to reinforce the position. "At this point we shall be perfectly secure, as the channel is very narrow and intricate and not a sufficient depth of water to enable large ships to follow," Decatur reported.[40]

The American warships were secure: they were also impotent. New London's merchants had never been much in sympathy with the war, and now that their harbor was blockaded they were even less so. More than a few scornful comments about the erstwhile hero Decatur's newfound timidity began circulating. Decatur complained that the town was "utterly out of joint" with the war, the navy, and even his own predicament. At the end of the year he claimed he had been unable to escape to sea because traitorous citizens in New London had been making secret signals with "blue lights" to inform the British squadron of his planned movements, a charge that brought more derisive comments his way. Decatur admitted that other than having seen the lights—which he said had been burned from "both the points at the river's mouth"—he had been unable to substantiate the story that he was being betrayed, and there was much that was absurd about it on its face: it was the sort of hysterical wartime rumor that always circulates, and the fact was that the lights probably came from ordinary fishing boats. The two frigates would be trapped there for the rest of the war.[41]

THE BRITISH fixation was not just with the *Macedonian* but with all the American frigates that had come to seem a reproach to British honor, and honor along with other distractions kept playing havoc with Warren's efforts to implement the steady escalation of overwhelming force that the blockade strategy demanded through the spring and summer

Chesapeake Bay theater, 1813–14

Delaware R.

MARYLAND

Susquehanna R.

Frenchtown

Havre de Grace

Fredericktown

Baltimore

Georgetown

Sassafras R.

Delaware Bay

Washington   Annapolis

Alexandria

Bladensburg

DELAWARE

Patuxent R.

Benedict

Potomac R.

Rappahannock R.

Tangier
Island

York R.

Chesapeake
Bay

James River

N

Atlantic
Ocean

Hampton   Cape Charles

Hampton   *Lynnhaven
Roads*   *Bay*   Cape Henry

VIRGINIA

Craney Island

Portsmouth

Norfolk

Gosport navy yard

0	10	20	30

Miles

of 1813. Even Broke's morale-energizing triumph over the *Chesapeake* had come at a significant cost to the blockade: directly contravening the Admiralty's stern admonitions to Warren regarding Boston harbor, Broke had deliberately weakened his force to entice Lawrence into a duel, and then for two weeks afterward the station was abandoned altogether as the *Shannon* sailed to Halifax with her prize. American privateers and letter-of-marque traders used their absence to escape to sea while merchantmen and privateers' prizes rushed in—as did the American navy brig *Siren* from New Orleans. The day after news of Broke's victory arrived in London, Croker sent a scathing rebuke to Sawyer's successor in Halifax, Rear Admiral Edward Griffith, demanding to know in the name of their lordships why "the Shannon and Tenedos, and sometimes the former alone, have been employed in blockading the Port of Boston, when they had hoped that a Line of Battle Ship had been ordered to assist in performing that Service." Every blockading squadron was to have a ship of the line constantly attached to it, "it being of the utmost importance that the Enemy's Ships should be intercepted on their return." The admiral was to dispatch a ship of the line plus two or more frigates at once to Boston to be "constantly employed in blockading that port" and was to call on the captain of the seventy-four *La Hogue* "to account for not having done so, transmitting his report to me."[42] On June 8 the *Argus* had used the similar absence of the entire British blockading squadron from Sandy Hook to put out unmolested to sea, not sighting an enemy vessel at all until she was seventy miles off the coast, and then dodged those British warships—part of the reinforcements heading for the Chesapeake—by ducking into a fog bank and making good her escape.[43]

On the Chesapeake the *Constellation* remained a magnet for Warren's and Cockburn's attentions, even as the Admiralty ordered Warren to extend and intensify the blockade up and down the coast. An instruction had arrived from Lord Melville in May telling Warren to proclaim an extension of the blockade to include all ports to the south of Rhode Island, including the Mississippi River:

> We do not intend this as a mere *paper* blockade, but as a complete stop to all trade & intercourse by Sea with those Ports . . . If you find that this cannot be done without abandoning for a time the interruption which you appear to be giving to the internal navigation of the Chesapeake, the latter object must be given up,

& you must be content with blockading its entrance & sending in occasionally your cruisers for the purpose of harassing & annoyance. I do not avert to enterprizes which you may propose to undertake with the aid of the Troops.

Croker added one of his usual hectoring follow-ups. He stressed to Warren that while His Majesty's government had found it useful to publicly declare blockades "of certain Ports only, because it is considered that for these purposes your Force will be always adequate," that was in no way to be misunderstood by the admiral as relieving him of the obligation to do more; "their Lordships expect and direct you to maintain a blockade *de facto* of every Port to which your force may be adequate and which shall afford any facilities either to the Privateers or Merchant Ships of the Enemy." He was to crush any attempts by the enemy to evade the blockade by shifting activity to other ports. He was not to neglect the "still more important" point of "affording to the British Trade frequent and adequate Convoys." The secretary helpfully concluded by explaining to Warren, "By an attention to this point . . . the resources of the Enemy will be crippled and impaired and the Commerce of His Majesty's Subjects facilitated & protected."[44]

In March 1813 Cockburn had made three attempts to take the *Constellation* in boat attacks, all of them repulsed; the next month, while still awaiting the arrival of the two thousand troops that had been promised him, he launched a series of marauding attacks up and down the inlets of the Chesapeake. Leaving a small detachment behind at Norfolk to keep an eye on the *Constellation,* Warren in his flagship *San Domingo* led the entire fleet northward; off Annapolis, Warren dropped anchor with the main body of the force to threaten Baltimore as Cockburn proceeded farther up the bay in the seventy-four *Marlborough* accompanied by the frigate *Maidstone,* the brigs *Fantome* and *Mohawk,* and three tenders. Cockburn had earlier snapped up four privateer and letter-of-marque schooners, each armed with a half-dozen to a dozen guns, and then quickly manned them and sailed them into narrow inlets and in a few days took thirty-six more prizes from their unsuspecting crews, who recognized the schooners and did not realize until much too late their new character. As the bay grew shallower, the *Marlborough* could no longer proceed and Cockburn transferred to the *Maidstone.* At dawn on April 29 at the very top of the bay, Cockburn's men appeared off the town of Frenchtown, rowing for the shallow shore in launches, each mounted with a small swivel gun. Along with his ships' companies Cockburn had under his command the "naval brigade," a selected detachment of 180 sailors and 200 Royal Marines to carry out raids ashore, and as the launches began firing, a landing party got ashore and flanked a small Maryland militia unit manning a battery of six guns and quickly swept them aside. The British troops burned flour stocks and a few small arms caches and reembarked with total casualties of one man slightly wounded.

A few days later Cockburn's force was passing the mouth of the Susquehanna River when, as he reported to Admiral Warren, "I observed guns fired and American Colours hoisted at a Battery lately erected at Havre-de-Grace at the entrance to the Susquehanna River, this of course immediately gave to the Place an Importance which I had not before attached to it." Cockburn's whole attitude toward the Americans was as if they were already an occupied or subject people who had no legitimate right to resist British arms. Havre de Grace was a small town of no discernible strategic significance, but Cockburn at once "determined on attacking it" after this defiant show of American sovereignty. Having previously sounded the waters, he knew that only boats would be able to approach safely. At midnight on May 2, he sent 150 men into the boats to take up positions under cover of dark and be ready to attack at dawn.[45]

Again the fire from the British launches and a British assault party quickly silenced the American battery. Along with the small guns on the British boats was a "rocket boat" that carried Congreve rockets. They were remarkably inaccurate weapons, but Cockburn placed great faith in them. Propelled by black powder charges and carrying solid, shrapnel, or exploding warheads of twelve to forty-two pounds, they had a range of up to two miles and an undeniable terror-inducing effect as they hissed and whizzed along their arcing trajectories. But they were almost completely unpredictable and sometimes gyrated wildly or even reversed course, sending their firing crews fleeing for cover. At Havre de Grace a Maryland militiaman became the only known fatality from a Congreve rocket during the entire war.[46]

After being routed from the battery, the American militiamen kept up the fight, to Cockburn's outrage: "No longer feeling themselves equal to a manly and open Resistance, they commenced a teazing and irritating fire from behind their Houses, Walls, Trees &c." The British party chased the Americans into the woods but, having then "decided it would not be prudent to pursue them further," turned their attention to destroying the town: in order, Cockburn explained, that the townspeople might "understand and feel what they were liable to bring upon themselves by building Batteries and acting toward us with so much Rancor." The guns of the captured battery were turned on the town, and two-thirds of the sixty houses were then put to the torch. "You shall now feel the effects of war," one British officer told residents just before the orders were given to set fire to the houses.[47]

One of those was the home of Commodore Rodgers, who had been the British navy's bête noire ever since the *Little Belt* affair. According to a story that (true or not) circulated widely among British naval officers, Admiral Warren himself received some of the spoils of the plundering of Rodgers's home. Sir David Milne, a British admiral who would command a ship of the line on the American station in 1814, wrote a relation that he had heard that Rodgers's "pianoforte is in Sir John's house in Bermuda, and he was riding in his, the Commodore's, carriage at Halifax." Milne added: "What do you think of a British Admiral and Commander-in-Chief? This is not the way to conquer America."[48]

Cockburn reembarked his men and took a small detachment a few miles up the river to the cannon foundry at Principio, where "without difficulty" he destroyed forty-five guns, including twenty-eight fully finished thirty-two-pounders. Again total British casualties were one wounded: Cockburn's first lieutenant was shot through the hand.

Three days later, Cockburn returned to the top of the bay, planning to attack two more small towns, Georgetown and Fredericktown, located a short way up the Sassafras River—"being the only River or Place of Shelter for Vessels at this upper Extremity of the Chesapeake which I had not examined and cleared," Cockburn reported to Warren. Nearing the towns, the British flotilla caught a small boat carrying two local residents, and Cockburn used them to deliver an ultimatum:

I sent forward the two Americans in their Boat to warn their Countrymen against acting in the same rash manner as the People of Havre-de-Grace had done, assuring them if they did that their Towns would inevitably meet with similar Fate, but on the contrary, if they did not attempt Resistance no Injury should be done to them or their Towns, that Vessels and Public Property only, would be seized, that the strictest Discipline would be maintained, and that whatever Provisions or other Property I might require for the use of the Squadron should be instantly paid for at its fullest Value. After having allowed sufficient Time for this Message to be digested and their Resolution taken thereon I directed the boats to advance and I am sorry to say I soon found the more unwise alternative was adopted.[49]

The houses of the towns were burned, along with four vessels lying in the river and some stores of sugar, lumber, leather, and other merchandise.

The raids certainly had the effect of spreading panic and fury throughout the region. Cockburn became the most hated man in America. The *Weekly Register* in Baltimore reprinted a notice from one James O. Boyle offering a reward of one thousand dollars for the head of "the notorious incendiary and infamous scoundrel, and violator of all laws, human divine, the British admiral COCKBURN—or, *five hundred* dollars for each of his ears, on delivery."[50] Whether Cockburn's expedition up the Chesapeake had done anything to advance British strategic objectives was another matter, and despite Lord Melville's injunction to Warren not to let the summer campaign inside the bay interfere with the higher priority of enforcing the blockade, it had already done just that. The whole Chesapeake enterprise, in fact, was becoming a huge distraction and diversion of force and attention for the British commander in chief. Cockburn rejoined the fleet on May 7, and a week later the whole British armada was back at Hampton Roads, whereupon Warren decided that his first order of business was to sail with a powerful convoy to Halifax to deliver the forty prizes Cockburn had taken. He returned on June 19 with an even larger naval force, the long-awaited soldiers and marines from Bermuda, and a new plan to get the *Constellation*. It was a measure of how large the Chesapeake and the frigate it contained were looming in Warren's thinking that he had now amassed eight ships of the line, twelve frigates, eight smaller men-of-war, plus various other tenders and transports, some 70 percent of the entire British strength on the North American station, at Hampton Roads for the purpose. Commanding the ground troops was Colonel Sir Thomas Sidney Beckwith, an experienced army officer who had been sent earlier in the year to Canada to take on the post of assistant quartermaster general of British troops in North America.[51]

On June 21 a force of twenty British ships moved to the mouth of the Nansemond River, just west of Norfolk. Craney Island, guarding the mouth of the harbor, had been reinforced with three naval cannons (two twenty-four-pounders and one eighteen-pounder) along with 150 sailors from the *Constellation* and about 400 militiamen, including the Portsmouth Artillery Company, armed with four six-pounders. Midmorning on the twenty-second the Americans saw about 2,500 British marines and infantry landing on the beach of the mainland to the west of the island, which was separated by a narrow strip of water that could be forded at low tide. Then at eleven o'clock a flotilla of fifty barges began rowing toward the island from the seaward side in a second prong of the attack. At the lead was Admiral Warren's beautifully turned out personal barge, known as the *Centipede,* painted a rich green, rowed with twenty-four oars; in her bow was a brass three-pounder gun and Captain John M. Hanchett, captain of the ship of the line *Diadem,* who had volunteered to lead the boat attack.

On Craney a few Congreve rockets fell, fired from the British contingent on the mainland. The American artillery commander, an ex–merchant mariner named Arthur Emmerson, ordered his men to hold their fire until the boats were in range. "Now, boys, are you ready?" he called out. "Fire!" A hail of round shot, canister, and grape ripped diagonally into the *Centipede,* hulling the barge, carrying away both legs of a French mercenary soldier, and seriously wounding Hanchett in the thigh. Then the *Centipede* and four other barges grounded in the shoal water that stretched for half a mile in front of the island, never more than four feet deep even at high tide, but on the falling tide now considerably shallower. They stuck fast one hundred yards from the battery as the murderous fire continued to pour in. The officers of *Constellation* "fired their 18 pounder more like riflemen than Artillerists, I never saw such shooting and seriously believe they saved the Island yesterday," reported Captain John Cassin, the commanding naval officer at Norfolk. A British seaman sounding with a boathook found three feet of slimy mud, and the order was given to retreat. The American defenders waded out to the stranded boats and took about sixty prisoners as the other boats rowed back on the ebbing tide to the British ships. Sitting miraculously unhurt on the bow gun of the *Centipede* was a small terrier, a mascot of the British troops.

The British shore division had meanwhile abandoned their attempt as well; at least forty deserters seized their chance to come across to the American lines, but the rest were reembarking on the boats that had ferried them ashore.

The only casualty on the American side was a Quaker pacifist who had been given the task of watching over a tent on the island crammed full of reserve powder, which accidentally blew up that night, momentarily spreading a false alarm in Norfolk that the British had renewed their attack.[52]

Warren sent a completely dishonest report that wildly understated his casualties and the size of the fiasco, but in fact the whole operation had been a shambles. The boat assault needed high water to succeed and the land assault low water; the compromise of launching the attack on the ebbing tide simply made both impossible. "A large creek stopped our progress by land, and shoal water stopped the boats by sea. A sharp cannonade from the works on the island cost us seventy-one men, without returning a shot! We lost some boats also, and re-embarked in the evening with about as much confusion as at landing," wrote Lieutenant Colonel Charles Napier, the commander of the 102nd Regiment, in his journal the next day. "Our attack on Craney Island was silly," he went on to observe:

> Had Norfolk been decently attacked it would not have resisted ten minutes; had we landed a gun Craney was gone; had we attacked at high tide it was gone: still it was the wrong place to attack we should not have lost more men in striking at the town. But the faults of this expedition sprung from one simple cause—there were three commanders! It was a council of War, and what council of war ever achieved a great exploit?
>
> Had either Sir John Warren, Sir Sydney Beckwith, or Admiral Cockburn acted singly and without consultation, we should not have done such foolish things.

Napier thought British overconfidence was to blame as well: "We despise the Yankee too much."[53]

Four days after the failed attempt against Craney Island, the British force struck at Hampton, a town of about a thousand residents on the opposite side of the roads whose only appeal as a target for an amphibious assault was its great vulnerability to naval invasion: it contained nothing of military value. With Cockburn and Beckwith directing the attack ashore, the British troops brushed aside a few hundred militia and as usual started looting the town. But this time the plunder took on a wilder tone. The church was pillaged and its silver plate carried off;

the sails of windmills were torn to the ground; closets, trunks, and drawers were pulled open and plundered in private houses; and then the French chasseurs began brutalizing some of the townspeople, shooting and killing an elderly bedridden man, tormenting another old man by stripping him naked and stabbing him in the arms with their bayonets, and then carrying off and raping several women. One woman tried to run into a creek to escape and was dragged back to the house by her five or six assailants, among whom she said were soldiers "dressed in red and speaking correctly the English language," suggesting there were British troops joining in with the green-clad chasseurs. Napier wrote afterward that his men of the 102nd "almost mutinied at my preventing them joining in the sack of that unfortunate town." Only the marine artillery "behaved like soldiers," he said. "They called out, Colonel . . . we blush for what we see, depend upon us not a man of the marine artillery will plunder."[54]

At first Beckwith made no mention of the atrocities in his official reports. But when the Virginia militia commander, Brigadier General Robert Barraud Taylor, sent a formal protest, the British commander claimed that the "excesses of which you complain at Hampton" were a direct reprisal for atrocities committed on Craney Island by American troops who shot British troops in the barges after they had surrendered. But Beckwith privately admitted to Taylor's aide-de-camp Captain John Myers, who had been rowed out to the *San Domingo* under a flag of truce to present the American note, that the French troops were to blame and he had ordered them reembarked on their ships. "Appealing to my knowledge of the nature of the war in Spain, in which these men had been trained," Myers reported, "he told me they could not be restrained."

A few days later, Beckwith admitted in a memorandum to Warren that the "Two Independent Companies of Foreigners" had been "so perfectly insubordinate" even before arriving from Bermuda that it had been necessary to hold repeated courts-martial, one man actually being shot for mutiny, and that "their brutal Treatment of several Peaceful Inhabitants" of Hampton was the final straw. The men were shipped off to Halifax, where they continued to run wild, now with British civilians as their target. "The Inhabitants of Halifax are in the greatest alarm about these fellows," a British official reported a few weeks later.[55]

A subsequent American investigation rejected Beckwith's accusation of cruelty during the battle at Craney Island, which would hardly have been much of a justification for rape and pillage against noncombatants even if true; it concluded that one British soldier was shot when he attempted to escape after starting to wade to shore and surrender.

The atrocities at Hampton and the British officers' refusal to take responsibility for the actions of soldiers under their command seemed an ominous signal of a new and far less honorable phase of warfare. "Remember Hampton!" became an inevitable slogan for American supporters of the war. Lieutenant Colonel Napier was privately appalled at the British attempts to brush the matter under the rug. "Every horror was committed with impunity, rape, murder, pillage, and not a man was punished!" he wrote in his journal. General Taylor, in his protest note to Admiral Warren, had directly raised the question of whether respect for the laws of honor and chivalry was still to be expected: "We are, in this part of the country, merely in the noviciate of our warfare," Taylor wrote. "It will depend on you whether the evils inseparable from a state of war shall, in our operations, be tempered by the mildness of civilized life, or, under your authority, be aggravated by all the fiend-like passions which can be instilled in them."[56]

There were other signs by the summer of 1813 that the war had entered a new and much less genteel chapter. Beyond the inevitable brutalization that occurs in all wars in which easy victory proves elusive, the American–British conflict was shot through with the kinds of personal and emotional enmities that threatened to make the fighting especially ugly as each side retaliated in a chain of escalating violence. The British alliance with the Indians particularly inflamed American feelings, especially after several incidents in which Indian warriors massacred American militiamen after they surrendered to British-led forces. But the northwestern frontiersmen who flocked to the ranks of the United States land forces were no less barbarous in their accustomed treatment of Indians, often murdering, scalping, and mutilating any who fell into their hands. And while a few British officers respected and even liked Americans, others had personal scores left over from the Revolutionary War they still hoped to settle, and probably most regarded their foe as their distinct inferior in both martial prowess and personal honor—which in itself came to be a justification in the British mind for refusing to accord Americans the chivalric treatment due an equal.

British naval officers were especially outraged by a series of unconventional attacks launched against their ships by American civilians employing booby traps, floating mines, even submarines in June and July 1813. In March 1813 Congress had passed the "Torpedo Act," which authorized a bounty of one half the value of any British warship destroyed; inspired by that incentive, a number of inventors and dare-devils began hatching schemes. On June 5, 1813, the boats of the seventy-four *Victorious* picked up a "powder machine," consisting of a keg packed with gunpowder and a trigger designed to set it off on impact, floating toward their ship in the Chesapeake. Cockburn informed Warren of the development in a message sprinkled with sar-castic comments about official American publications "constantly harping" on the government's dedication to "Humanity" even as it was devising such "humane Experiments . . . to dispose of us by wholesale Six Hundred at a time, without further trouble or risk."[57]

Several attempts against the British ship of the line *Plantagenet*, guarding the mouth of the Chesapeake near Cape Henry, followed over the next weeks. On July 18 a Chesapeake mariner named Elijah Mix rowed an open boat he dubbed *Chesapeake's Revenge* to within eighty yards of his target under cover of night but rapidly withdrew when hailed by the ship before he could launch the homemade torpedo he was carrying. He tried again two nights later with the same result, this time getting within twelve yards and drawing musket and rocket fire and then an illuminating flare, followed by the ship opening up with its guns, slipping its cables, and filling its sails in flight. Mix again got away and returned once more on the night of the twenty-fourth. This time he succeeded in setting his torpedo drifting toward its target and was within a whisker of succeeding when it detonated just yards too soon, throwing a column of water forty feet in the air and cascading over the ship's deck but causing little damage.[58]

In New York some local civilians hatched even more audacious schemes to eliminate the line-of-battle ship *Ramillies* in Long Island Sound, and with her the blockade of the American frigates at New London. Outfitting a coasting schooner filled with naval stores as a tempting bait, they proceeded off of New London on June 25. British barges pursued, and the schooner's crew put up a show of firing some small arms in resistance, then fled to shore in a small boat. Below deck was a huge quantity of gunpowder and combustibles, set to go up when a hogshead of dried peas was shifted, which would pull a lanyard tied to a gunlock and fire a powder train. The captured vessel was anchored and a tender from the *Ramillies* sent alongside; the seventy-four herself was, however, a safe distance away when the booby trap exploded. A lieutenant and ten men from the *Ramillies* were killed and three seamen were wounded, "much scorched in the Face, Arms, & Legs," Captain Sir Thomas Hardy reported. Warren expressed fury and indignation, issuing a general order that as "it appears the Enemy are disposed to make use of every unfair and Cowardly mode of Warfare," no prize or boat was to be permitted alongside any of His Majesty's ships before a thorough examination had taken place. Hardy now kept his ship in almost constant motion, swept the underside every two hours to check for attached mines, and shifted his position away from the mouth of New London's harbor and closer to Long Island.[59]

The growing unconventional warfare in American waters led directly to a hardening of attitudes toward prisoners when Hardy learned in August of another plot to blow up his ship and sent a landing party to East Hampton to foil it. Joshua Penny, the civilian who was leading the attempt, was pulled out of his bed and carried aboard the *Ramillies,* where he was clapped in irons. When town officials protested, Hardy replied that Penny would be treated as a prisoner of war, if not a spy. President Madison personally ordered that a British prisoner of equal stature be put "in the same state, of degradation & suffering" in retaliation.[60]

A series of retaliatory actions over the treatment of prisoners, triggered chiefly by Britain's moves to bring to trial as traitors a number of American prisoners it claimed were British subjects, had already undermined the lenient rules the two nations had agreed to follow for exchanges. The men from the *Guerriere* whom Rodgers had pulled off the cartel in Boston harbor and held as hostages were released in June 1813 after word arrived that the British had dropped their plans to try the detained members of the *Nautilus*'s crew for treason, but tit-for-tat retaliations involving other prisoners immediately reinflamed the situation. In retaliation for the Americans' designation of several British seamen as hostages "to answer for the safety and proper treatment" of other Americans sent to England for trial, the British authorities in Halifax threw sixteen American seamen, including ten crewmen of the *Chesapeake,* into three dungeons each measuring nine by seven feet. In response, Madison ordered sixteen British seamen confined in similar conditions and also had another one hundred British prisoners held in close confinement as hostages for a like number of still more Americans just sent to Britain for trial. Twenty-three mostly Irish-born American citizens serving in the U.S. army were also in England facing charges of treason, and the American government designated twenty-three British officers as hostages to be "immediately put to death" if the Americans were; the British responded by designating forty-six American officers as hostages for them; the Americans ordered forty-six more British officers held as hostages; and by the end of 1813 all officers on both sides were being held in close confinement and under threat of death. Sir George Prevost, the governor general of Canada, vowed "to prosecute the war with unmitigated severity" if any of the British hostages were harmed.[61]

Meanwhile, local British commanders were starting to refuse to release any more prisoners on parole for future exchange. Cockburn issued orders that American prisoners taken in numbers beyond those that could be immediately exchanged for British prisoners would be sent straight to prisons in Bermuda. By the summer of 1813 the British were holding six times as many prisoners as the Americans were, and in August the British government stopped all releases of Americans from prison depots in England until the accounts were brought into balance. In England were 2,200 American seamen who had been impressed in the Royal Navy and who refused to fight when the war broke out and then were summarily held as prisoners of war; there were also a number of merchant sailors who had been trapped in Britain when the war began whom the British refused to exchange; the British also refused to release any crews captured from privateers that mounted fewer than fourteen guns.

After a year of escalating tensions, all the Americans brought to England as supposed British subjects charged with raising arms against their king were returned to the general prison population and none were brought to trial, and by April 1814 Secretary of State Monroe reported that most of the hostages on both sides had been removed from close confinement and the threats of retaliatory execution dropped. But the threats and counterthreats had left each side convinced that the other was prepared to abandon the laws of civilized war and humanity. And the collapse of the parole system made the consequences of being taken prisoner far greater than they had been for the combatants on both sides.[62]

On September 6, 1813, the British armada pulled out of Chesapeake Bay, Warren heading for Halifax with more prizes and several warships desperately in need of refit, Cockburn for Bermuda with other ships needing long-term repairs, and leaving behind the line-of-battle ship *Dragon,* two frigates, two brigs, and three schooners at Lynnhaven Bay for the winter. The coming of the autumn "fever season" was one consideration in Warren's decision to end the campaign, but so was the toll taken by constant desertions and the relatively poor return he had gained for all his troubles. Lieutenant Colonel Napier was dismayed by the ineptness of the campaign. "We have done nothing but commit blunders," he wrote in his journal. "Nothing was done with method, all was hurry, confusion, and long orders." Cockburn, he thought, "is no doubt an active good seaman, but has no idea of military arrangements; and he is so impetuous that he won't give time for others to do for him what he cannot or will not do himself. . . . Cockburn trusts all to luck, and makes no provision for failure: this may do with sailors, but not on shore, where hard fighting avails nothing if not directed by mind, and most accurate calculation.

"I have learned much on this expedition," Napier mused; "how to embark and disembark large bodies in face of an enemy; how useless it is to have more than one commander; how necessary it is that the commanders by sea and land should agree and have one view: finally never to trust Admiral Cockburn."[63]

"GREAT GOD when will the tide turn on Land," lamented the Philadelphia merchant Chandler Price to his old acquaintance William Jones. In the campaign against Canada, America's own blunders had continued at a steady pace through the spring and summer of 1813. On the Detroit frontier William Henry Harrison's army was thrown on the defensive, holed up in two forts on the southwest corner of Lake Erie. The Americans bravely held out against a series of British attacks— a 1,200-man relief force from Kentucky that arrived on May 5 suffered 50 percent casualties when it sallied out against some of the British and Indian troops besieging Fort Meigs—but Harrison's plans to take the offensive and recapture Detroit were completely stymied. On the Niagara front an American force of 1,700 raided York—present-day Toronto, the capital of Upper Canada—in late April but accomplished little. The Americans suffered 320 casualties, most when the retreating British set off the garrison's powder magazine, and among the fatally injured was General Zebulon Pike, one of the comparatively few capable officers the American army had in the field. Angered by the explosion, the American troops looted the town, burned public buildings, smashed a government printing press, and stole the books out of a subscription library before withdrawing, which did more to arouse British and Canadian anger than accomplish anything of military significance.

A month later an offensive by 4,500 American troops under Major General Winfield Scott pressed west into Canada from the Niagara River. Things began encouragingly enough with the capture of Fort George on the Canadian side of the river where it joined Lake Ontario, but within two weeks the campaign had turned into another American rout. Twice, outnumbered British units ambushed large American detachments that had pushed west trying to follow up the initial victories; the British captured two American generals and the collapse of the offensive forced General Dearborn to order the evacuation of all positions inside Canadian territory except for Fort George. When the news reached Washington in July, Republican war supporters forced Madison at last to relieve Dearborn of his command. "We have deposed Gen. Dearborn," said Pennsylvania Republican congressman Charles J. Ingersoll, "who is to be removed to Albany, where he may eat sturgeon and recruit."[64]

In the east, a disorganized plan to march on Montreal began late in the summer and almost immediately fell apart under the disastrous command of Major General James Wilkinson, whom one historian has called the worst general on either side in the war, and probably the worst general in all of American history. Winfield Scott thought Wilkinson an "unprincipled imbecile," and Major General Wade Hampton, who was supposed to cooperate in the invasion with a force of 4,500 men under his command, simply refused to obey Wilkinson's orders. During the campaign Wilkinson's officers observed with increasing alarm the general's attempts to treat his dysentery with massive doses of laudanum, which left him "very merry," singing and garrulously repeating stories but hardly inspiring confidence.[65]

The failure of the opening land campaigns had brought into sharp relief the crucial importance of controlling the lakes—Erie on the Detroit front, Ontario on the Niagara front, and Champlain on the eastern front—to secure the movement of men and supplies. Roads were extremely poor and exposed to attack, and initial British naval superiority on the lakes had given their forces a freedom of movement that had allowed them to take the offensive in what was increasingly becoming a slow positional war of maneuver, not the quick dash that Americans had confidently predicted. Securing American territory against further British advances, much less carrying out the still-hoped-for invasion of Canada, now hung on achieving control of the lakes. Right after assuming office, William Jones had assured Commodore Isaac Chauncey, who had assumed command of naval forces on Lakes Erie and Ontario in September 1812, that he recognized what was at stake: "It is impossible to attach too much importance to our naval operations on the Lakes—the success of the ensuing campaign will depend absolutely on our superiority on all the lakes—& every effort, & resource, must be directed to that object." Crash shipbuilding programs were begun on Lake Ontario at Sackets Harbor, New York, and on Lake Erie at Presque Isle (now Erie), Pennsylvania; 150 men from the *Constitution*'s crew and other men from blockaded or refitting warships were sent west; iron, cordage, and shot were hauled overland from Pittsburgh. Noah Brown, a master shipwright, took charge in March 1813 at Presque Isle, where two 20-gun brigs were under construction. That same month Captain Sir James-Lucas Yeo of the Royal Navy arrived in Canada to take charge of the British squadrons.[66]

Lake Ontario, which was the gateway to the settled areas of Upper Canada, would become a frustrating exercise in strategic stalemate to both navies, "a warfare of Dockyards," Jones would come to call it, as each side tried to outbuild the other; by the fall of 1814 the American navy would have 2,300 men on Lake Ontario, five times as many as were at sea at that point, and the British had by then launched from their harbor at Kingston a 104-gun vessel, among the largest warships in the world.[67] Neither side would ever gain decisive control, and Yeo and Chauncey, both cautious in the extreme, avoided a decisive confrontation that might have settled the matter.

Lake Erie was another matter, though. In September 1813 Commodore Oliver Hazard Perry, a twenty-seven-year-old officer who had begged to be transferred from the tedium of commanding gunboats at Newport, Rhode Island, sailed from Presque Isle with his two new twenty-gun brigs and seven schooners and other small vessels, most of them converted merchant vessels mounted with one or two 24- or 32-pound carronades. At daylight on September 10, near Put-in-Bay at the western end of the lake, he spotted the British squadron and signaled his other vessels to close with the enemy. Perry's flagship the *Lawrence* locked in a close-quarter carronade slugfest with the two largest British ships for two hours, fighting both sides of the ship simultaneously and taking 80 percent casualties until Perry was reduced to calling the surgeon's assistants one by one away from their post helping the wounded in the wardroom below and then calling down, "Can any of the wounded pull a rope?" Then Perry rowed through a hail of fire to the as-yet-undamaged *Niagara* as the *Lawrence*, reduced to fourteen sound men, struck her colors, and the commodore brought the second ship into close action and carried on the battle for another forty-five minutes until the British commodore surrendered.[68]

A month later Harrison's army, swelled to 5,500 by 3,000 more volunteers newly arrived from Kentucky, assembled at the west end of Lake Erie, retook Detroit, and pursued the retreating British into Canada. At Moraviantown, fifty miles west of Detroit, the British army of 800 regulars and 500 Indians, including the famous chief Tecumseh, turned to make a stand along the Thames River. The Kentuckians persuaded Harrison to adopt the almost bizarrely unorthodox tactic of staging a mounted infantry assault, and the shock of 1,200 backwoodsmen armed with muskets galloping out of the woods broke the British line. Tecumseh was killed and most of the Indians fled. The Americans tore clothing, and hair, from the Indian chief's body and then in a grislier spree of souvenir hunting skinned the corpse and carried off patches as trophies. Among the army's other prizes was a cannon that had been captured by the Americans at Saratoga in 1777 and lost by General Hull at the fall of Detroit in 1812.[69]

The naval contest on the lakes indirectly affected the broader naval war by cutting into the men, money, and materiel available to America's oceangoing navy, but Secretary Jones saw it was fundamentally isolated from the real fight he had to wage against the Royal Navy. Secretary of State Monroe would derisively refer to the "fish-pond war" of the lakes, which touched the heart of the matter: it was a war in a teacup, unable to directly tilt the larger strategic balance. Even the victory at the Battle of Lake Erie, though it secured the American frontier territories in the west, was primarily a defensive victory that could not translate into the kind of leverage that would change the thinking of the councils in London. By the end of 1813, unable to sustain an offensive campaign on the Niagara frontier, the War Department withdrew most of its regulars and sent them east; they arrived just in time for Wilkinson to call off his inept campaign against Montreal and retreat into winter quarters south of the St. Lawrence River, where many of the ill-provisioned and ill-clad men suffered frostbite or even froze to death.

"The difference between the Lake and the sea service," Jones would observe, "is that in the former we are compelled to fight them at least man to man and gun to gun whilst on the Ocean five British frigates cannot counteract the depredations of one Sloop of War."[70] It was still to the oceans that Jones was looking to force Britain to come to terms.

ONE OF THE most vivid and detailed accounts of the shocking devastation wreaked on human flesh by shot, splinters, and bullets in the course of naval combat came from the Battle of Lake Erie and the pen of Commodore Perry's surgeon, Usher Parsons. Like most American naval surgeons of the era, Parsons was young—he was twenty-four at the start of the war—but well trained and fully qualified as a physician if still inexperienced. Although not an M.D., he had done an apprenticeship under the renowned Dr. John Warren of Boston and was licensed to practice in 1812 by the Massachusetts Medical Society. Unable to pay off his debts and unsuccessfully trying to start a practice in New Hampshire, he had applied to the navy as a surgeon's mate as soon as war was declared and was practically overwhelmed with relief when he received his commission. "No one could imagine my joy, it was ecstatic, frantic," he said. The two other naval surgeons of the young American navy who left written accounts of their experiences in the war had similar backgrounds: Amos Evans of the *Constitution* was twenty-seven at the war's start and had studied in Philadelphia under Dr. Benjamin Rush, another celebrated physician of the period; James Inderwick of the brig *Argus* was twenty-three, had graduated from Columbia University, and was serving as the house surgeon at New York Hospital when he joined the navy in 1813.[71]

The carnage Parsons faced during the Battle of Lake Erie was compounded by the hellish conditions he had to endure. In a larger ship the surgeon worked below the waterline, in the cockpit of the orlop deck; it was a tiny space, about sixteen by nineteen feet in the frigate *Constitution*, and the overhead space was so low, about four feet five inches, that the surgeon and his assistants had to work on their knees; but it was the stablest part of the ship and well protected from enemy fire. Not so in the small brig *Lawrence*. "The vessel being shallow built, afforded no cockpit or place of shelter for the wounded," wrote Parsons; "they were therefore received on the wardroom floor, which was about on a level with the surface of the water." Several cannonballs barely missed Parsons as he worked in the cramped space:

> Being only nine or ten feet square, this floor was soon covered, which made it necessary to pass the wounded out into another apartment, as fast as the bleeding could be stanched either by ligatures or tourniquet. Indeed this was all that was attempted for their benefit during the engagement, except that in some instances division was made of a small portion of flesh, by which a dangling limb, that annoyed the patient, was hanging to the body. Several, after receiving this treatment were again wounded, among whom was midshipman Lamb, who was moving from me with a tourniquet on the arm, when he received a cannon ball in the chest; and a seaman brought down with both arms fractured, was afterwards struck by a cannon ball in both lower extremities.[72]

Parsons had already amputated six legs during the battle; he now faced ninety-six wounded, including thirty-six men brought aboard the *Lawrence* from the other ships of the squadron, and in the falling light Parsons decided not to attempt any more amputations until morning. He spent the evening tying off wounded arteries, administering opiates, and securing shattered limbs with tourniquets in preparation for the next day's surgeries. "At daylight a subject was on the table for amputation of the thigh," Parsons recounted, and he continued working nonstop, swiftly severing flesh and muscle with a sweeping motion of the large amputation knife, cutting through bone with saws, tying off severed arteries, moving on to the next patient. By midday all that grisly work was done, but it was not until midnight that he had finished tending to the fractures that could be set and the other lesser injuries.

Although injuries such as chest wounds that today could be treated were deemed inoperable and hopeless, and although amputation was the simple and drastic remedy for many injuries that in later years could have been treated in ways that saved the limb, the surgical techniques applied were generally remarkably successful in saving the lives of even grievously wounded men, at least if their injuries were confined to an extremity. The basic surgical tools of the day—probes, scalpels, knives, scissors, forceps—were not much different from those of two hundred years later; even so horrific-looking a device as the trepan, designed to cut a hole in the skull to relieve pressure on the brain from the life-threatening subcranial bleeding that often resulted from head injuries, was perfectly sound in principle and saved many a life. Only three of Parson's ninety-six patients subsequently died, an outcome he attributed to fresh air, boiled drinking water, wholesome food, and "the happy state of mind which victory occasioned." Parsons applied the $1,249 in prize money he received for the American victory to paying off his educational debts.[73]

Where naval surgeons of the first years of the nineteenth century were far more helpless was in the treatment of garden-variety disease; the standard-issue medicine chest contained upwards of two hundred drugs, nearly all of them worthless and most of them poisonous. The standard treatment for all manner of ailments included bleeding, emetics, purgatives, and compounds containing mercury, lead, antimony, and other toxic substances. A common prescription for headache and fever was Dover's Powders, a patent medicine combining the vomiting agent ipecac plus opium. For syphilis, which typically accounted for half the men out of action at any given time, the prescription was huge doses of mercury—the saying of the time was "seven minutes with Venus, six months with Mercury"—and the treatment was literally worse than the disease, causing first copious salivation, then ulcerations of the mouth, then loss of teeth and hair, and finally brain and kidney damage; only it was no treatment at all, having no effect whatsoever on the underlying disease itself.

The only drugs of the naval surgeon's armamentarium that actually had any beneficial value were opiates, which killed pain and stopped up the bowels of sufferers from life-threatening dysenterial illnesses, and Peruvian bark, which contained traces of antimalarial quinine. Forty percent of the *Constitution*'s recorded fatalities in the war were from disease. On the lakes the toll was far higher; "lake fever," probably malaria, struck in late summer and dysentery in winter; illness that swept through Sackets Harbor late in 1813 killed an average of one man a day and left hundreds debilitated.[74]

As in all wars, the greatest killer was one that took no human form at all, and was equally free of malice or chivalry.

CHAPTER 8

The Far Side of the World

Woman of Nooaheevah (Porter,
Journal of a Cruise; courtesy
Charles E. Brodine Jr.)

IN THE SUMMER of 1813 the first word reached America of the where-abouts of David Porter and the frigate *Essex*, not heard from since failing to make their rendezvous with Bainbridge off Brazil the previous fall. In August the *Weekly Register* printed a short notice of a report that had made its way to São Salvador stating the *Essex* had "certainly been in the South Sea," apparently having rounded Cape Horn into the Pacific at some point during the winter. A month later the newspaper carried a report from Rio de Janeiro, dated June 27, that the British frigate *Phoebe,* carrying forty-six guns, accompanied by the sloops of war *Cherub* and *Raccoon,* was about to proceed south to Cape Horn in chase of the elusive American.[1]

Porter's orders from Bainbridge had instructed him that if from "some unforeseen cause or accident" he was unable to make any of his rendezvous by April 1, 1813, he could act according to his own "best judgment for the good of the service."[2] David Porter had always been more than a bit impetuous; it was a trait that had more than once nearly ended his naval career, and it had on two famous occasions singled him out as one of the two American naval captains that the British press could never mention without an obbligato passage of derision. (Rodgers was the other.) In 1806 Porter had nearly triggered an international incident by hauling a drunken British sailor aboard the *Enterprize* in Valletta harbor in Malta after the man had rowed by shouting insulting remarks to the Americans, and when the sailor refused to apologize, Porter ordered him to be given twelve lashes on the spot. A tense exchange of notes between the British governor of the island and Porter ensued, the British threatening to fire on him if he attempted to sail before the matter was resolved, Porter defiantly responding that he had no intention of being detained and would fire back at any attempt to stop him when he departed as he planned to that night. Then he coolly carried out his declared intention, sailing past the silent forts "without molestation."[3]

The other incident was not so creditable. Right after the declaration of war, Porter had administered an oath of allegiance to his crew of the *Essex* in New York harbor, and one of the men, a sailmaker named John Erving, refused on the grounds that he was an English subject. The crew, in a burst of rough enthusiasm, decided to tar and feather him and Porter gave his consent. Erving, turned ashore in New York stripped to the waist and covered with tar and feathers, was pursued by a mob until a shopkeeper took pity on him and sheltered him; the police then arrived and took him into custody for his own protection, cleaned him up, and gave him some new clothes. Secretary Hamilton sent Porter a stern rebuke but nonetheless issued Porter's promotion to captain two days later. British writers never failed to bring up the incident; the *Times* referred to "Captain Porter (of tar and feathering memory)," and even years after the war he continued to be vilified in British accounts.[4]

But Porter's combativeness had none of the wounded or defensive self-justification that so ate at the spirit of his friend Bainbridge. Porter was as jealous for honor, rank, and money as any of his naval colleagues and carried on feuds with the best of them but seemed to find an outlet for his feelings in extroverted brashness rather than festering resentment. He thought dueling "a practice that disgraces human nature," and he had the energetic and at times fierce intellect of a self-educated man, which had served him well in his fourteen years since joining the navy in 1798 as an eighteen-year-old midshipman. He came from a seafaring family and had sailed with his merchant captain father out of Baltimore from an early age; keenly aware of his educational shortcomings, he had applied himself tirelessly throughout his life to make up for it. As a prisoner in Tripoli he had studied French well enough to read, write, and speak the language competently, had worked at drawing and become a talented pen-and-ink artist, and had read history. He would later write the finest literary work of the war, his account of his cruise in the *Essex,* a book whose unguarded openness gave ample ammunition to his English detractors for years afterward but whose vitality came directly from not only its guilelessness but its restless intelligence. Where Bainbridge was reduced to stuttering in moments of emotional upheaval, Porter poured out prose and hatched ideas. His marriage in 1808 to the seventeen-year-old daughter of William Anderson—he was the Pennsylvania tavern keeper who a few years later had the misfortune to become famous as the Republican congressman caught pissing in the British ambassador's fireplace—was marked by the same tempestuous energy; they had ten children, and many unhappy confrontations, over the years.[5]

His ideas were as busy and extroverted as his actions, and if he lacked Decatur's natural charisma or Hull's natural empathy, he succeeded in keeping a happy ship simply by adding human nature to the list of things he applied his impatient curiosity to intently studying. "My chief care was now the health of the crew," Porter noted a few weeks into his cruise on the *Essex,* and to that end he took a number of unconventional steps to improve the working conditions and routines of shipboard life. "Utmost cleanliness was required from every person on board," and each man was given a half gallon of water daily and advised to bathe at least once a day. Porter enjoined his officers to keep the men constantly employed during work hours but allow them time every day for recreation and amusement "and to be particularly careful not to harass them by disturbing them unnecessarily during their watch below." He allowed the men assigned to the main deck gun crews to sling their hammocks over their guns rather than in the overcrowded and airless berth deck below, insisting that it took no longer to clear for action and greatly improved health and comfort:

> What can be more dreadful than for three hundred men to be confined with their hammocks, being only eighteen inches apart, on the birth-deck of a small frigate, a space seventy feet long, thirty-five feet wide, and five feet high, in a hot climate, where the only apertures by which they can receive air are two hatchways of about six feet square? The situation must be little superior to the retches who perished in the black hole of Calcutta. . . . From the number confined in so small a space, the whole atmosphere of the ship becomes tainted, and . . . every person on board, is affected by the pernicious vapours arising from the birth-deck.[6]

At every port he could he took on oranges, lemons, plantains, onions, green vegetables, fresh meat, live pigs, fowl, sheep, turkeys, in what was practically a one-man crusade against scurvy. At the Cape Verde Islands he had cracked down on the huge trafficking in "bad rum" between the locals and the working parties sent ashore to fill the ship's water casks—one favorite dodge of the beach vendors was to fill hollowed-out coconuts with liquor—but allowed the men to furnish themselves with pet monkeys and goats, "and when we sailed from thence," Porter said, "the ship bore no slight resemblance . . . to Noah's ark." At the start of the cruise he had called the crew together and declared a general pardon for all offenses committed to date "and gave assurances that the first man I was under the necessity of punishing should receive three dozen lashes," but expressing the hope that punishment "would be altogether unnecessary." He was largely right: the crew returned the trust he placed in them and floggings were few and far between. He had a pet idea that fumigating the ship every day with vinegar poured over red-hot shot would have a salubrious effect, which probably had a talismanic influence at best; but his more practical notions about health had quickly reduced the sick list to 4 of the 319 men aboard. Even after a year at sea the *Essex* reported only four deaths from illness, one of them the ship's alcoholic surgeon, who succumbed to "disease of the liver."[7]

ON THE passage south through the Atlantic the *Essex* had marked the crossing of the Tropic of Cancer with the rough if time-honored ceremony much beloved of the common sailor, and prudently indulged by their captain as a boost to esprit de corps.

"Sail ho!" called the lookout at the masthead, at the appropriate moment.

"Where away?" replied the officer of the deck.

"Small boat on the lee bow."

"What boat is that?" hailed the officer.

"Neptune's, the god of the sea's; permission to come on board with his train."

"Granted."

Every man who had not before crossed the line had to submit to the initiation; King Neptune and Queen Amphitrite sat on their throne of boards lashed to an old gun carriage, a boat was placed on deck filled with water—and, as one seaman who went through the ritual at the time described the usual practice, "tar, slush, rotten onions and potatoes, stinking codfish, bilge-water, and various other nauseous ingredients improper to mention"—and the uninitiated were blindfolded and called up one by one to answer to Neptune and swear an oath never to leave the pump till it sucks, never to go up the lee-rigging in good weather, never to desert the ship till she sinks, never to eat brown bread when he could get white (unless he liked it better), never to kiss the maid when he could kiss the mistress. Then he was lathered by one of Neptune's barbers with a mix of paint, grease, slush, and tar and shaved with a rusty barrel hoop, dunked two or three times in the barge water, welcomed as a true son of the ocean, and cast loose.

Officers were allowed to buy an exemption with an allowance of rum; Neptune and his attendants, Porter recalled, "paid their devotions so frequently to Bacchus, that before the ceremony of christening was half gone through, their godships were unable to stand. . . . On the whole, however, they got through the business with less disorder and more good humour than I expected; and although some were most unmercifully scraped, the only satisfaction sought was that of shaving others in their turn with new invented tortures."[8]

On December 2, 1812, the *Essex* had taken a British packet ship, the *Nocton*, loaded with $55,000 in specie, a large portion of which was distributed to the crew; and with nothing immediately available to spend it on, the windfall set off a spate of gambling until Porter announced that any amount staked at games of chance would be forfeited to whoever informed on the transaction, the informer's name to be kept secret. There was also some incipient trouble over rations: Porter had kept the crew on two-thirds rations of salt meat and half rations of bread since leaving the United States to extend their time at sea, a privation the crew had cheerfully accepted in exchange for the shortfall being made up in cash. But when Porter ordered the grog ration cut to two-thirds to make sure it would last too, "every man in the ship refused to receive any . . . unless he could get the full allowance," Porter said. The captain tried to argue with them that two-thirds now was better than the "dejection and sickness" that would come later if it ran out altogether, but the crew was adamant. Porter handled the incipient rebellion by announcing that the grog tub would be put out with two-thirds of the rations in it and dumped upside down fifteen minutes later. Every man took his grog.[9]

On January 19, 1813, they arrived at St. Catherine's and waited a week for Bainbridge and the *Constitution*. "I was perfectly at a loss now where to find the commodore," Porter maintained. He called the purser to give him a report on the stores: there were 184 barrels of beef, 114 of pork, 21,763 pounds of bread, 1,741 gallons of spirits. That would suffice for three months, but Porter was itching for an excuse to carry out the dashing plan he had had his eyes on all along—to sail into the Pacific and cut a swath of destruction through the British whaling fleet. He now argued to himself that since Bainbridge had failed to meet him at four rendezvous, it was "absolutely necessary to depart from the letter of my instructions; I therefore determined to pursue a course which seemed best calculated to injure the enemy, and would enable me to prolong my cruise." To prolong his cruise he first needed supplies, "and the first place that presented itself to my mind, was the port of Conception, on the coast of Chili." With the possibility of additional British warships arriving along the Brazilian coast, which might trap him if he attempted to put into a port there, "there seemed no other choice left for me except capture, starvation, or blockade."[10] If it was self-serving it also admirably matched the strategic outlook of Bainbridge, fully shared by the new navy secretary, of keeping the British continually off balance, chasing over half the globe, never knowing where the tiny but highly annoying American navy would strike next.

On January 26, 1813, Porter set a course to the southwest, and three nights later the wind hauled around to south by east, sharp lightning began around midnight, and as the wind rose the crew went aloft in the storm to send down the royal yards and double reef the topsails. Woolen clothes that had been lying about the ship suddenly were being carefully guarded as temperatures began dropping. For the next week the winds would die to a dead calm, then spring back in heavy blows from every point of the compass, and Porter prepared the ship "to meet the worst," he said, sending down the royal masts, unreaving all unnecessary running rigging, removing every heavy or unnecessary article from the tops, striking down to the hold all the shot except six per gun, running the guns in from their usual positions at the side of the decks and securing them amidships, readying three anchors so they could be let go in an instant in an emergency.[11]

On February 3 the sun rose on a perfect clear day, the wind steadied from the northwest, and every sail was set for what promised to be an easy run to the straits. Porter issued a notice to the crew formally announcing what all had guessed by now but which sent spirits soaring with its promise of riches and South Seas girls to match the provident weather.

> Sailors and Marines:
> A large increase of the enemy's forces compels us to abandon a coast that will neither afford us security nor supplies . . . We will, therefore, proceed to annoy them, where we are least expected. What was never performed, we will attempt. The Pacific Ocean affords us many friendly ports. The unprotected British commerce, on the coast of Chili, Peru, and Mexico, will give you an abundant supply of wealth; and the girls of the Sandwich Islands, shall reward you for your sufferings during the passage around Cape Horn.
> D. Porter[12]

But by 2:00 p.m. the weather turned worse than ever, the wind head-on from their southwesterly course; then the next day the heaviest blows and worst sea yet, the wind boxing the compass and sending the sea pouring through the canvas shield around the rudder hole and flooding the wardroom. Whales appeared in the distance, and exhausted albatrosses rode on floating masses of kelp on the heaving sea.

The thirteenth found the ship driving south through a thick rain and haze, visibility down to a mile, Porter confident that the eastern end of Staten Island, the easternmost tip of land of the horn, lay thirty-five miles ahead. His plan was to bypass any of the inland passages by going completely around Staten. Late that afternoon a violent ripple appeared in the water close by along with great flocks of birds and masses of kelp. Porter ordered extra lookouts, took in the topgallant sails, double reefed the topsails, furled the mainsail, and instructed the officers to be ready to haul the wind if necessary. At half past six breakers were seen three-quarters of a mile to the southeast. A tremendous sea was running, plunging the forecastle completely under, and the ship was heading for the breakers with no hope now of weathering them and no sea room to wear away from the strong wind impelling the ship eastward. The only hope was to get the ship in stays and tack, and with the lead going constantly taking soundings the mainsail was set in a flash, the ship got around, but the jib was blown to pieces a moment later.

With night falling there was no choice left but to carry a heavy press of sail to keep off the lee shore, and Porter had her stand to the west-northwest for an hour when suddenly the water began to run smooth and a sharp-eyed lookout spotted land a mile ahead on the bows: it was now beyond doubt that they had gone to the west of Staten and were in the Strait of Le Maire. Porter ordered the helm put aweather and all sail made to southward, and with the tide mercifully with them, they hugged the coast of Tierra del Fuego, clearing the straits at nine o'clock that night.[13]

By the eighteenth they had made their westing and turned north into the Pacific. The fresh provisions from St. Catherine's were long gone, and now the pet monkeys vanished one by one, and even the rats that had overrun the ship began to be "esteemed a dainty," in Porter's words. Despite the assault of the rats on the bread rooms, the supplies of hardtack were still holding out and, even if full of weevils, were still edible; but the peas and beans proved to be nothing but "a mass of chaff and worms" when the casks were opened.

Once again the weather beguiled them; once again the worst was to come. On the last day of February, now well into the Pacific, the ship was in such a gentle sea and mild weather that Porter planned to get the guns back in position and the spars sent back up that day. By noon the wind "blew with a fury even exceeding any thing we had yet experienced," and it was touch and go whether they would be dashed to pieces on a lee shore or simply founder first. The ship rolled so violently that the shingle ballast choked the pumps, and so much water was coming in from the opening of the seams of the ship with each heave that she began to wallow like a bloated whale.

"The sea had increased to such a height, as to threaten to swallow us at every instant; the whole ocean was one continued foam of breakers; and the heaviest squall that I ever before experienced, had not equaled in violence the most moderate intervals of this hurricane," wrote Porter. For three days it blew, the ship able to change tacks but once the whole time; three times, Porter was hurled down the hatchways by violent jerks of the ship. The pumps had been cleared, but so much water had come aboard that everything was afloat between decks.

Then at three in the morning of March 3 an enormous sea broke over the ship that seemed to spell the end. The gun-deck ports were all broken in, the boats stove to pieces, the entire ship deluged. David Farragut, who had joined the ship as a twelve-year-old midshipman, said it was the only time he had seen "a regular good seaman paralyzed by fear at the dangers of the sea—Many of the marines & some of the seamen were sunk on their knees in prayer." Then through the chaos and wind came the roaring, commanding voice of boatswain's mate William Kingsbury, who had been the inebriated Neptune at the crossing-of-the-line ceremony. "Damn your eyes, put your best foot forward, there's one side of her left yet," he absolutely bellowed. The men at the wheel kept their heads and their station, the sky began to clear, and then the worst really was over.[14] On March 14 the *Essex* rounded the Point of Angels, and looking through his spyglass, Captain Porter saw a drove of loaded mules coming down a mountain on a zigzag path, and then in the next instant the whole city of Valparaíso was in view, the forts bursting out behind the rocks, the harbor crowded with shipping, colors flying. He was uncertain of his reception in Spanish territory, but before the *Essex* even got to anchor the captain of the port came aboard and to Porter's "astonishment" offered every assistance the city could offer: Chile was in revolt against monarchical Spain and welcomed the Americans as allies in the fight for republicanism, and liberty.[15]

A MONTH later, the *Essex,* sated with the provisions and almost exhausting hospitality of Valparaíso, rounded the point of Narborough in the Galápagos. Every yard aloft was manned by the officers and crew, every eye straining for the first glimpse of Banks Bay ahead and the crowd of British whalers they expected to see when they weathered the point and opened on the broad, thirty-five-mile-wide bay. The bay was said to abound every March to July in whales that came to feed on the cuttlefish the currents swept in, and if the British were anywhere, this was where they would find them.

Secretly, Porter had a "dread of disappointment": since leaving Valparaíso on March 23 he had been continually on the trail of his quarry and continually frustrated in his hopes. At Valparaíso the Americans had been feted at huge banquets and balls, stuffed with twenty-course meals, swiftly supplied with wood, water, and provisions "in the greatest abundance, of an excellent quality, and at a more moderate price than any port in the United States," Porter noted, and assured by all concerned that the coast of Peru and the Galápagos Islands were where all the British whalers surely were. But also in Valparaíso harbor when they had arrived were two Spanish ships that sailed for Lima during their stay, sure to spread the alarm to the British agent there of the presence of an American frigate in Pacific waters. And so the crew of the *Essex* worked nonstop amid their abundant social duties to get back to sea. "Perhaps no week of my life was ever more actively employed, both in labour and in pleasure," Porter wrote afterward; and in nine days they were away, soon making all sail northward.[16]

Two days out of Valparaíso they caught up with a Peruvian privateer, the *Nereyda;* flying English colors and ordering an American whaler he had fallen in with to hoist an English jack over an American ensign to make her look like his prize, Porter forced the privateer to heave to. He had gotten the officer of the *Nereyda* into his cabin, listened to his tale of the American vessels he had recently taken, offered to relieve him of his twenty-three American prisoners, and only when that was done did Porter strike the English colors, raise the American flag, and fire two shots over the Peruvian, who immediately struck his flag. Since Spain was neutral in the American–British war, the privateer was little better than a pirate, but Porter decided not to antagonize the royalist viceroy in Lima. Porter ordered the *Nereyda*'s guns, ammunition, small arms, and even the light sails thrown over the side, and allowed the crew to sail back to Lima carrying a note to the viceroy:

U S Frigate Essex
At Sea 26ᵗʰ March 1813

Your Excellency,
I have this day met with the Ship Nereyda mounting fifteen
Guns, bearing your Excellencies Patent and sailing under the
Spanish flag—

On examination of said Ship I found on her as prisoners the
Officers and crews of two vessels belonging to the United States
of America employed solely in the Whale fishery of those seas
captured by her and sent for Lima, after being plundered of
boats, cordage, provisions, clothes and various other articles . . .

I have therefore to preserve the good understanding which
should ever exist between the Government of the United States
and the provinces of Spanish America determined to prevent in
future such vexatious and piratical conduct, and with this view
have deprived the Nereyda of the means of doing the American
commerce any further injury for the present, And have sent her
to Lima in order that her commander may meet with such
punishment from your excellency as his offence may deserve—I
have the honor to be With the highest respect and consideration
Your Excellencies Obt. Huml. Servt.
    D. PORTER[17]

Flying fish appeared as they crossed the Tropic of Capricorn, and
the crew spent several days completely altering the appearance of the
frigate, painting a broad yellow streak around her hull, rigging false
waistcloths as high as the quarterdeck nettings to hide the gunports,
painting the quarter galleries different colors, and setting up a false
poop deck to make her look like a Spanish merchantman.[18] They had
heard that whaling ships left letters in a box at the landing place on
Charles Island, the southernmost of the Galápagos, and on the eighteenth of April, Porter sent his first lieutenant John Downes in a boat to
see what he could learn. Three hours later Downes returned with several not very recent letters from the box, which he had found readily
enough, nailed to a post with a painted sign atop it reading HATHAWAY's
POSTOFFICE. The most recent letter was dated the previous June, but it
listed six large British whalers on their way to the island of Albemarle,
and indicated that they intended to be there for at least a year filling
their holds with whale oil.[19]

And so the *Essex* headed for Albemarle, whose large crescent shape formed Banks Bay to the northeast of Narborough. And so every eye was straining as they weathered the tip of Narborough on the afternoon of April 23, and not a sail was to be seen across the entire bay.

With some difficulty Porter located a watering place on Albemarle, and on a rock were scratched the names of American and British ships; nearby were fresh ashes and the bones and shells of a recently butchered turtle and a leaf from an English political pamphlet. But the water source was little more than a damp rock where a few drops collected from a tiny spring. Water was already becoming a problem. The islands they had so far put in at teemed with giant land tortoises that the crew at once developed a passion for; their flavor was said to be like fine veal and their fat more delicious than olive oil. Iguanas by the hundreds were to be had too, and the crew set about clubbing them on the head. But water was barely to be found anywhere.

A few days later, as the *Essex* sailed north, the lookout's cry of "Sail ho" sent an electrifying surge coursing through the ship. But it turned out to be only two sand banks, "whose appearance had been so strangely altered by the intervention of the fog," wrote Porter, "as to assume precisely the appearance of ships under their top-gallant-sails." The false alarm broke the last dam that had been holding back the feelings of the crew. "The disappointment . . . occasioned no trifling degree of dejection and despondency," Porter said. "There were few on board the ship who did not now despair of making any captures about the Gallipagos Islands; and I believe that many began to think that the information we had received, . . . as well as the flattering expectations which this information had given rise to, had been altogether deception."

The current was now sweeping them to the northwest, and for several days they fought an unsuccessful battle against baffling winds and the running sea to work back southward, but Porter was determined not to leave the islands "so long as there remained a hope of finding a British vessel among them." On the twenty-eighth he passed a sleepless and anxious night. At daylight the next day, Porter was roused from his cot by calls of "Sail ho" echoing once again throughout the ship. In a moment all hands rushed to the deck, and there she was, a large ship bearing west, to which the *Essex* at once gave chase. In an hour, two more sail were sighted. At nine o'clock they came up on the first ship, the British whaler *Montezuma,* with fourteen hundred barrels of spermaceti oil. Porter put a prize crew aboard and made chase for the other two ships, but at eleven o'clock the wind fell calm with the whalers still eight miles off. Porter was concerned the ships might outrun him when the breeze returned, for the *Montezuma*'s captain had identified them as the armed letter-of-marque whalers *Georgiana* and *Policy*, both reputed to be fast sailers, armed with six to ten guns apiece.[20]

But this was the moment *Essex*'s crew had been waiting for. As David Farragut would later recall, "I have never been on a ship where the crew of the old Essex was represented, but that I found them to be the best swordsmen on board. They had been so thoroughly trained as boarders, that every man was prepared for such an emergency, with his cutlass as sharp as a razor, a dirk made by the ship's armorer from a file, and a pistol."[21] Porter ordered fifty-five men into seven boats, giving them "the most positive orders" to stay together and bring all the boats into action as a single force, and they pulled straight for the larger of the two ships. The boats were a mile away from their quarry when the ships hoisted English colors and fired their guns "to terrify them," as Porter would describe it, but still they pulled on, and when they were right under the muzzle of the guns of the *Georgiana*, Lieutenant Downes in the bow of the lead boat ran the American colors out on a pike and asked if they surrendered. The response was three cheers and a shout from many of the men on deck, "We are all Americans!" In fact, a good many of the British whalers were manned by Nantucket whalemen, and while some Nantucketers strongly sympathized with the British in the war, this crew clearly did not. The boats quickly took possession of the *Policy*, which lay a quarter mile away, and then in the afternoon breeze that sprung up, the sails of the two prizes filled and they majestically bore down for the *Essex*, greeted by her wildly cheering crew.[22]

"Fortune has at length smiled on us," Porter declared to the men of the *Essex*. "Continue to be zealous, enterprising, and patient, and we will yet render the name of the Essex as terrible to the enemy as that of any other vessel, before we return to the United States."[23]

EVEN MORE valuable than the two whalers were the stocks of water the *Essex* now took from them, and because whalers always counted on being at sea for well over a year, they were veritable floating warehouses of spare naval stores of all description: cordage, canvas, tar, paint, spars. The crew of the whalers had, to the great regret of the *Essex*'s men, thrown overboard fifty Galápagos tortoises in clearing for action, but a few days later they found them floating in the sea all about the ship, in the same place they had been dropped, and pulled them up. Porter refitted the *Georgiana* as a cruiser to serve as the *Essex's* consort; the men worked for days knocking out her heavy brickwork and iron boilers used for trying out the blubber, and put all sixteen guns aboard her. Five of her crew, all Americans, agreed to sign on as volunteers, and Porter willingly received them.

Back at Charles Island, Porter's growing squadron loaded two thousand gallons of water, a backbreaking exertion, each man making four trips a day lugging a ten-gallon keg from a spring three miles inland; the water smelled and tasted foul and was full of slime and insects, but "to us it was a treasure too precious to lose," Porter said. They tried digging two wells, but after getting down "a considerable depth" salt water flowed in. Sailors who frequented the Galápagos had learned that the huge tortoises could survive for a year or more without food or water, and four to five hundred were brought aboard and formed an extraordinary sight, piled on the quarterdeck under an awning to give them a chance to "discharge the contents of their stomachs" before being stowed away live below, "as you would stow any other provisions, and used as occasion required," Porter said.[24]

Over the next seven weeks the *Essex* and the *Georgiana* took six more letter-of-marque whalers, and by that point Porter had put so many of his officers aboard them as prize captains—he had even pressed the ship's chaplain and marine lieutenant into this duty—that the only officer left to take charge of an American whaler they had recaptured, the *Barclay*, was twelve-year-old midshipman David Farragut. The *Barclay's* master was an old and violent-tempered American mariner named Gideon Randall whose entire crew, except for the first mate, had jumped at the opportunity to abandon him and had entered as volunteers on the *Essex* the moment they were recaptured. A draft of men from the American frigate was sent back to work the ship with Farragut in their charge, and the arrangement was that Randall would continue to be in charge of navigating the vessel. But when, on July 9, Porter ordered four of the prizes plus the *Barclay* to be taken into Valparaíso for sale, Randall furiously came on deck muttering that he would shoot any man who dared to touch a rope without his orders. "I'll go on my own damn course," he said, and disappeared below for his pistols.

Farragut recalled, "I considered that my day of trial had arrived . . . But the time had come for me at least to play the man."

Mustering his courage, he politely told the first mate that he desired to have the main topsail filled. The man responded at once "with a clear 'Aye, aye, sir!' in a manner which was not to be misunderstood," said Farragut, "and my confidence was perfectly restored." Farragut sent word to the master that he was not to appear on deck with his pistols "unless he wished to go overboard; for I would really have had very little trouble in having such an order obeyed."[25]

Leading the convoy to Valparaíso was Lieutenant Downes in the *Atlantic,* the largest of the prizes yet; she was carrying one hundred tons of fresh water and eight hundred large tortoises when they took her on May 29, a godsend of a windfall; she was also faster than any of the others, so Porter decided to replace the *Georgiana* with the *Atlantic* as his consort, fitted her out with twenty guns and sixty men, and renamed her the *Essex Junior.* Over the next twelve weeks, while Downes sailed to Valparaíso and back, Porter took four more fat prizes, all British letter-of-marque whalers like the others. He had again shifted the appearance of the *Essex,* repainting her and adding to the possibilities of bafflement and ruses by repainting one of his prizes to look exactly like the *Essex* and one of the others to look like a sloop of war. One of the prizes in this final haul was the *Seringapatam,* which was a more than slightly fantastic vessel with an odd story on several counts. Originally built as a man-of-war for Tippoo Sahib, the maharaja of Mysore, she was constructed of beautiful teak and was reputed to be a very fast sailing ship. Although she had come to the Pacific on a whaling expedition, her master had spent all his time since arriving taking American whalers as prizes. But when Porter asked him for his privateer's commission, the man, "with the utmost terror in his countenance," informed him that it had not arrived yet but was no doubt waiting for him in Lima. Porter ordered him thrown in irons and said he intended to send him to America to be tried as a pirate. Porter put twenty guns on the *Seringapatam* and took her into service as another of his auxiliaries and a possible replacement for the *Essex* if a calamity befell her.[26]

Besides his piratical prisoner, Porter had been accumulating during their sojourn in the Galápagos a lot of other baggage he desperately wanted to be rid of, including $100,000 worth of whale oil and an increasingly unstable lieutenant, James Wilson. With extraordinary coolness Porter had faced Wilson down at one point when, inebriated and violently insolent, the lieutenant had grabbed for his pistol after Porter told him he was under arrest. Wilson subsequently insisted he meant only to kill himself, but either way he was hardly someone a captain of a man-of-war wanted to rely upon. Porter solved all three problems by putting the oil, the prisoner, and Wilson aboard the *Georgiana* with orders for America and hopes they would be able to run the British blockade of the American coast by timing their arrival to midwinter.

At the end of September 1813, Downes returned in the *Essex Junior* with the news that there was no market for the captured ships in Valparaíso, and he had had them laid up. He also brought a letter for Porter from the American consul in Buenos Aires. It reported that on July 5 the British squadron had sailed from that port in pursuit of him.[27]

The *Essex* had now been at sea a year. The rats had multiplied to the point that they were eating not just provisions but clothes, flags, sails, and gun cartridges, even endangering the planking of the hull with their gnawing. When the crew finally reached a sheltered port where they could completely empty the ship and smoke it with charcoal to fumigate the interior, they counted 1,500 dead rats in the basketfuls carried up and thrown overboard when the operation was complete.[28] But the copper sheathing was coming loose too, and the bottom was fouled with barnacles and sea grass, and the rigging was in need of complete replacement; and so on October 2, a few days after Downes's return, the *Essex,* the *Essex Junior,* and the three other remaining prizes set sail for the Marquesas Islands, a remote well-watered spot 3,500 miles to the west that had been frequented by American whalers from time to time since Captain Cook visited there in 1774.

"We are bound to the Western islands with two objects in view," Porter informed the crew in a written notice. "First, that we may put the ship in suitable condition to enable us to take advantage of the most favourable season for our return home: Secondly, I am desirous that you should have some relaxation and amusement after being so long at sea, as from your late good conduct you deserve it."

For the remainder of their passage, Porter said, the men "could talk and think of nothing but the beauties of the islands," and he was not talking about the scenery. "Every one imagined them Venuses, and amply indulged themselves in fancied bliss."[29]

IT HAD BEEN a long and trying summer of 1813 for William Jones.

In May his burdens had been doubled, more than doubled, when he was named acting secretary of the Treasury in addition to navy secretary. Secretary Gallatin was gone to Europe on what would prove a

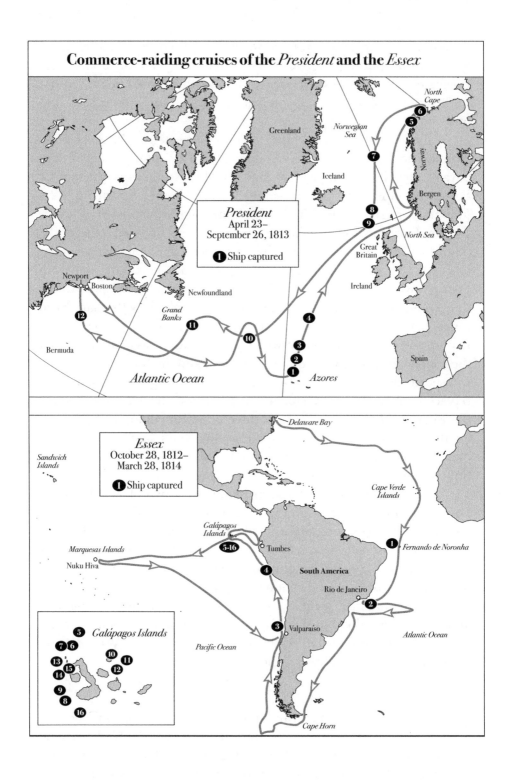

Commerce-raiding cruises of the *President* and the *Essex*

President
April 23–
September 26, 1813

1 Ship captured

North Cape
Norwegian Sea
Greenland
Iceland
Norway
Bergen
North Sea
Great Britain
Ireland
Newport
Boston
Newfoundland
Grand Banks
Bermuda
Spain
Atlantic Ocean
Azores

Essex
October 28, 1812–
March 28, 1814

1 Ship captured

Sandwich Islands
Delaware Bay
Cape Verde Islands
Galápagos Islands
Marquesas Islands
Nuku Hiva
Tumbes
Fernando de Noronha
South America
Rio de Janeiro
Valparaíso
Pacific Ocean
Atlantic Ocean
Cape Horn

Galápagos Islands

fool's errand, an attempt to open peace negotiations with the British under a Russian offer of mediation; the American peace commissioners sat in St. Petersburg for six months, until the very end of 1813, before finally learning that Britain had rejected the czar's offer. But before leaving Washington, Gallatin had written up a long memorandum of instruction to Jones that basically gave him all the responsibilities and no authority to initiate any actions on his own.

No one wanted to be in Washington in the summer, but especially not that summer of 1813. In June President Madison was struck ill with dysentery and for five weeks lay bedridden at his home, Montpelier, at times not expected to live; then for months afterward he recuperated slowly, trying to manage affairs of government by correspondence as he put off his return to Washington as long as he might. Secretary of State Monroe was in Virginia; Secretary of War John Armstrong was in upstate New York trying and failing to reconcile his warring generals Wilkinson and Hampton; and so William Jones was effectively left to run the whole government in Washington and push a desperately needed and desperately unpopular tax bill through Congress.

Even leading Republican newspapers were now at last acknowledging that there was no choice but to impose a new internal tax to pay for the war. The Treasury had just barely managed to raise a $16 million loan to cover the 1813 budget, but it had been touch and go; only by offering a discount of 12 percent was the loan finally subscribed, and two-thirds of the entire amount was taken by three wealthy merchants, John Jacob Astor among them. The punishing discount rate was a further reminder that there was little future market for United States government paper without some assurance that there would be at least some government revenues to eventually pay back investors.[30]

But financial reality was one thing, politics another. The Twelfth Congress had refused to even consider a tax measure all through the winter, then just before adjourning in March 1813 it had dumped the problem on its successor, passing a resolution summoning the new Thirteenth Congress to meet six months early, at a special session in late May, to take up the matter.

And so week after week the prematurely summoned congressmen met in their stifling chambers, getting nowhere. "Every one is for taxing every body," said John W. Eppes, Jefferson's son-in-law and the chairman of the House Committee on Ways and Means, "except himself and his Constituents." At the beginning of the special session it was "hotter, in this house, than purgatory," remarked one congressman, and by July it was more like hell: "the doors were closed and we were boiled and roasted three hours longer; almost to suffocation."

Finally, in July, the Republicans passed a $5.5 million tax bill, $3 million of that in the form of a direct tax on land, dwelling houses, and slaves. Still, putting off the evil day as long as possible, they voted it would not go into effect until January 1814 and would last only one year. The rest of the money was to come from excise taxes on stills, sugar, carriages, bank notes, auction sales, retailers' licenses, and other odds and ends.

Administering the new taxes was an enormous new duty that fell squarely in the lap of the acting Treasury secretary. Writing "to my beloved Wife and friend" in mid-July, Jones complained of the "multiplicity of details and arrangements to be made," not least the hiring of nearly two hundred revenue agents, one for each congressional district; even months later not only were more than a third of the positions vacant but no applications or recommendations had been received for filling them.[31] And almost as soon as the tax bill had passed, Jones had to go back to Congress with a new request for an emergency loan of $7.5 million to cover an unexpected shortfall in the current year and bridge the gap of the following year's expenditures until the tax revenues started to come in. The loan was approved, and eventually subscribed at an 11.75 percent discount, a small vote of confidence from the market compared with the mood in the spring.

Meanwhile, the normal vexations of public duty continued without relent. Jones told Eleanor that at his office he was "like a public pump kept constantly wagging by every one who thirsts after honors or emoluments which they run off with whilst I am left *dry*." With the passage of the tax and loan bills he hoped to beg off his double duty; but, he wrote, "A day or two since I expressed to the President my earnest wish to be relieved from the immense responsibility of the Treasury Department added to the laborious and highly responsible duties of the Navy, but he received it with so much repugnance . . . that I shall find great difficulty in renewing the attempt . . . No! There is no hope of Comfort or domestic peace, until Heaven shall turn the hearts or humble the pride and malice of our Enemy."[32]

Eleanor had come to Washington in May for a short stay before the worst of the Washington summer hit; her sister back in Philadelphia had written her shortly after her arrival, already missing her company, but adding, "Altho you have left your relatives and friends here, what sweet consolation you have in the society of your best and invaluable friend, in him you can find consolation in any situation in life." She returned to Philadelphia in July, leaving Jones again "a hermit & slave" in his lodgings, as he put it; but when she came again to Washington in September they at last would be able to move into their house. He figured it would save them $120 a year in rent and also allow them to save half what he was spending for the board of their three servants.

> Add to all this we shall both be infinitely happier. For *myself*—my wife my few *friends* and my home are the greatest solace that kind Heaven can bestow with the moderate means of enjoying those blessings. My spirit, naturally good and disposition cheerful (for Heaven and you well know that had they not my heart must have long since bowed down) has really had but little to preserve their natural tone. . . . The little recreation I get is a ride to the Navy Yard where I mount my hobby horse and feast my eyes upon the noble ships that are building and their little children the beautiful barges which I have constructed after my own fancy. These little excursions have in a great degree sustained my spirits and my health which is excellent.[33]

He indulged himself with a few visions of their domestic comforts to come, sending Eleanor a list of delicacies he hoped she could purchase in Philadelphia, or on her way through Baltimore: a hogshead of Snowden & Fishers pale ale ("particularly if they have any such as they put up for India"); a barrel of good last year's cider; a keg of nice pickled tripe; mustard, two bottles of cayenne pepper, spices, herbs; raisins, almonds, currants, filberts; twenty pounds of macaroni and a dozen pounds of vermicelli; a few pounds of good chocolate ("as we shall have a cow"). He hoped they could be moved in by October 1 so that they would have at least a month to be fully settled before they needed to plunge into their social duty of entertaining members of Congress returning to town for the regular session.

Before Eleanor could arrive, the "lashing" that he had told her she must be prepared for as his price of taking public office arrived first. "Before this reaches you in all probability as calumny travels fast," he wrote her in early September, "you will have seen your husband denounced as a 'Villain and base Coward' in the Georgetown Federal

Republican. Though I know this may wreck your heart for the moment your own experience independent of your love will pronounce it a base calumny. Let it not give you any moments thought."[34]

The incident bordered on the absurd but was nonetheless potentially deadly. To organize the harbor defenses of Baltimore, Jones had named Joshua Barney, a veteran of the Continental navy and a successful privateer captain, to take command and organize a flotilla of shallow-draft rowed barges that Barney himself had developed. After reading an announcement of Barney's appointment in the newspaper, an old Baltimore enemy of Barney's, Lemuel Taylor, sent Jones a letter denouncing Barney as "a most abandoned rascal, both as to politics and morals," and asserting that "he is despised by nine-tenths of all that have taken an active defence of Baltimore." After Jones showed the letter to Barney, to give him "the opportunity of vindicating his reputation," Taylor challenged the secretary to a duel, claiming he had committed a "flagrant breach of trust" in thus making the letter public. "As every man of honor and common sense in my position would have done," Jones replied, "I declined the invitation," sarcastically adding that since "*every* Editor in Baltimore" had shown the decency and good sense not to publish Taylor's subsequent public letter declaring Jones a coward, Taylor had had to deliver it "through the *common sewer*," meaning the anti-administration *Federal Republican*. But meanwhile Barney himself challenged Taylor to a duel and shot him in the chest, seriously wounding him, ending the episode. "It is very difficult for a public man to defend himself against calumny," Jones wrote Eleanor.[35]

It was also difficult to defend himself against the constant irritations of job seekers and others with claims to advance. James Barron—living in Denmark since his ignominious surrender of his ship in the *Chesapeake–Leopard* debacle, supporting himself with royalties from a few inventions, and working as master of a brig plying between Lisbon, Gothenburg, and Copenhagen—wrote Secretary Jones a strange and paranoid letter in July 1813 asking to be reinstated now that his five-year suspension was up. "I never can, nor never will, acknowledge that the sentence under which I have laboured was just, or that it was not the result of malice," he insisted. He said the officers who testified against him at the court-martial were guilty of perjury yet had got off scot-free. If the secretary would look into the mater fairly, "the strength of your mind and the justice & liberality of your disposition" would discover a matter "treated with as much Injustice & Inhumanity as any that ever came under your inspection." He did not wish to impose too much on the secretary's time, but "my only wish in life is to have an opportunity to prove to the world in general and my Country in particular that I have suffered without Just cause for there are circumstances known to those intimately acquainted with the particulars of that affair, that would in my humble opinion convince the world, that I was, to say the least of it, cruelly sacrificed."[36]

Secretary Jones declined to respond.

AFTER SLIPPING out of New York on June 8, 1813, and shaking off the British blockading squadrons in a fog bank off the coast, the United States brig *Argus* proceeded on "the special service" that the president had ordered her to stand at the ready to perform: she was to deliver the new American minister to France, William H. Crawford, to the first port they could make on the French coast, "without deviating for any other object." In command was Henry Allen, just promoted to master commandant for his part in the *Macedonian* victory, and he cracked on with all sail the small ship would carry, keeping his distance from the strange sails they passed, logging eight or nine knots, an escort of porpoises following alongside. For the first few days a variable and contrary wind kept the ship almost constantly tacking and running across the swell, and Minister Crawford observed in his diary that he "cascaded copiously."

But their wind and luck held; even a raging mid-Atlantic storm that forced them to scud on bare poles blew them in the right direction, propelling the *Argus* 525 miles in three days, and in four weeks they arrived at L'Orient, dropping anchor on July 11. A week later, ready for sea again, Allen called his officers together and read them the rest of Secretary Jones's orders now that the minister had been safely delivered:

> It is exceedingly desirable that the enemy should be made to feel the effect of our hostility, and of his barbarous system of warfare; and in no way can we so effectually accomplish that object, as by annoying, and destroying his commerce, fisheries, and coasting trade. The latter is of the utmost importance, and is much more exposed to the attack of such a vessel as the *Argus*, than is generally understood. This would carry the war home to their direct feelings and interests, and produce an astonishing

sensation. For this purpose the cruizing ground, from the
entrance of the British Channel, to Cape Clear, down the coast
of Ireland, across to, and along the N.W. Coast of England,
would employ a month or six weeks to great advantage.

Jones emphasized to Allen that destruction was his object; he was to
burn the prizes he took except in the most exceptional circumstances.
"There are very few cases that would justify the manning of a prize;
because the chances of reaching a safe port are infinitely against the
attempt, and the weakening of the crew of the *Argus*, might expose you
to an unequal contest with the enemy."[37]

This was the first solid test of Jones's strategy of striking at Britain's
commerce with small, fast, solitary-cruising vessels, and Allen proceeded to carry out his instructions with gusto. For four weeks, on the
very doorstep of the enemy, the *Argus* left a trail of burning hulks. At the
mouth of the English Channel, Allen took three homebound British
merchantmen, then repainted his ship to resemble a British man-of-war
with a broad yellow stripe along the gunports and shifted his ground to
the west and stood off the coast of Ireland. Slipping unnoticed in the
night within musket shot past a British frigate escorting a ninety-ship
convoy sailing home from the Leeward Islands, he dropped to the back
of the convoy and began picking off stragglers. By the time a British
warship finally caught up with the *Argus* in the early morning hours of
August 14, she had taken twenty prizes, twelve of them in just the last
three days.

Already exhausted from the rampage, Allen's crew had worked
through most of the night removing a valuable cargo, wine and fine
Irish linens, from the last prize they had taken and had not been in their
hammocks more than ten minutes when they were called to quarters at
4:00 a.m.; the *Argus* could easily have outrun the British brig *Pelican* that
now was approaching in the predawn gloaming, but this was where
Secretary Jones's pragmatic strategy and his officers' still-unsatisfied
search for honor parted company. Allen had told his crew that the *Argus*
could "whip any English sloop-of-war in ten minutes," and he gave the
order to shorten sail and let the enemy come up. In the short, murderous action that followed, Allen was struck by a thirty-two-pound shot
above the left knee just minutes into the battle as the ship's rigging was
cut to pieces. The *Pelican* was a larger and slightly more heavily armed
ship, but there was no comparison in the accuracy of her fire, which

was deadly. A quarter of the *Argus*'s crew was killed or injured. Lieutenant William Watson had his scalp taken off down to the skull by a grazing grapeshot and was knocked unconscious; Midshipman William Edwards's head was torn off by a round shot; a thirty-two-pound ball carried away both of Midshipman Richard Delphey's legs; and forty-five minutes after the battle began, as British boarders swarmed over the sides of the American ship, most of the *Argus*'s demoralized crew ran below while the one surviving lieutenant hauled down the colors. Surgeon Inderwick amputated Allen's leg at the thigh, and for a while it seemed he might survive, but gangrene set in and four days later he died ashore in a prison hospital at Plymouth.[38]

John Rodgers in the frigate *President* led the Royal Navy on a much longer wild goose chase through the summer of 1813, like Allen sailing defiantly straight through British home waters, taking and burning prizes as he went; he reached Bergen, Norway, on June 27, outrunning two British warships in an eighty-hour chase off the North Cape, returning to intercept trade passing in and out of the Irish Channel, finally running right through the British blockading squadrons and into Newport harbor on September 26, snapping up Admiral Warren's tender, the schooner *High Flyer*, on the way in; the American boarders took possession so quickly, immediately placing a guard over the captain's cabin, that the crew did not have time to destroy the squadron's signal book.

Rodgers returned with a logbook filled with sarcastic and cantankerous observations about the enemy. On May 28 he had chased, boarded, and released an American ship bound from New York to Lisbon and from her obtained a newspaper with an account of the British sack of his hometown of Havre de Grace. No other reason was offered for this attack by "the Mild, the Philanthropic, the Eloquent, the Seasoned, & the Brave Right Honourable Admiral Sir John Borlase Warren, Knight Baronite &c. &c. &c.," Rodgers said, than "because it gave Birth to a Captain of the American Navy." Halting an American ship returning from Cádiz to Boston, the *Acteon* (John H. Rogers, master), Rodgers adopted the familiar ruse of flying British colors and passing for the British frigate *Acasta*, "which gave me an opportunity, I am sorry to say, of discovering that my name sake, John Rogers, is not overburthened with patriotism." In all he had taken twelve prizes, a meager and disappointing showing, he felt, for five months at sea; he was also disappointed that he had been unable "to add any additional luster to the character of our little Navy" with any glorious victories against the Royal Navy.[39]

But Jones was full of praise and wrote back at once:

> The effects of your Cruize however is not the less felt by the enemy either in his Commercial or Military Marine, for while you have harassed and enhanced the dangers of the one, you provoked the pursuit & abstracted the attention of the other to an extent perhaps equal to the disproportion of our relative forces, and which will not cease until his astonishment shall be excited by the Account of your arrival.[40]

In fact, it was a perfect demonstration—notwithstanding Mahan's later theories about concentration of force to the contrary—of how a single marauding commerce raider at loose on the vastness of the ocean could tie up a huge portion of the enemy's navy just hunting for him. At one point, Warren had 25 ships, including 6 seventy-fours and 10 frigates, patrolling the Atlantic from the banks of Newfoundland, Cape Sable, and Georges Bank to the entrance of the Chesapeake in an attempt to block Rodgers's return to port. Warren once again found himself writing to Croker like a penitent schoolboy: "It is with extreme regret I am under the necessity of communicating for their Lordships information that Commodore Rodgers has effected his arrival in the United States Frigate *President* at Newport, I had made the best disposition in my power to intercept his return into Port and I am sure that every Captain was anxiously vigilant to fall in with him."

Warren's fleet had now grown to 129 ships, including 15 seventy-fours and 28 frigates, but still it was not enough. Even as he was preparing to obey an Admiralty order to extend the declared blockade to the northern approaches to Long Island Sound and all "Harbours, Bays, Rivers, Creeks, and Sea Coasts" south, a hurricane hit Halifax on November 12, 1813, driving 50 to 60 ships in the harbor aground, including 30 warships that required major repairs, some of which were still incomplete the following March. The seventy-fours, including Warren's flagship *San Domingo*, were especially hard hit.[41]

Warren's blockaders had sent in 225 prizes to Halifax during the year 1813 and privateers sent in another 112; at least 300 more prizes taken by Royal Navy ships were sent into Bermuda, Jamaica, and the Leeward Islands, for a total of more than 600 American merchantmen captured during the second year of the war. American exports had fallen to $28 million in 1813, down from $61 million in 1811. But American warships and privateers had still been able to get to sea, taking 435 prizes themselves during 1813. And as if to end the year with a final thumbing of their nose at the blockade, the *Congress* sailed back into Portsmouth, New Hampshire, on December 14 and the *Constitution* put out to sea from Boston on the last day of the year; neither encountered any British opposition.[42]

On December 30, 1813, Warren wearily sent another request to Croker for reinforcements in a letter that had more than a bit of the air of a defeated commander, dwelling completely on his fears and problems rather than his plans for bringing the war to the enemy. "The rapidity with which the Americans, build and fit out their Ships, is scarcely credible," he wrote in exasperation. At New York, Philadelphia, and Baltimore "every exertion" was being made to prepare vessels of war, including "a very large Class of Corvette Ships," some of which were already launched and many others nearly ready. Two ships of the line, one at Portsmouth and one at Boston, were to be finished and launched in March. The southern coast around Charleston had become a refuge for privateers. Several large clipper schooners managed to escape from the Chesapeake, "nor can any thing stop these Vessels escaping to Sea in dark Nights and Strong Winds."

Warren concluded his plea, "I take the liberty likewise to represent that as all American Men of War, Privateers and even Traders, are particularly good Sailing Vessels, such of his Majesty's Ships as are appropriated to my Command, should be of the same description."

Even Henry Hotham, the man the Admiralty had sent out to help put some order and steel into Warren's command, was ready to give up by the end of the year. Inasmuch as "your Lordship's intentions and my expectations have been disappointed," he wrote Melville in a private letter, he begged to be relieved of his duty as soon as arrangements for that purpose could be made.[43]

WITH THE end of 1813 came the final gasp of chivalry in the naval war between Britain and America. Master Commandant William Henry Allen was given a funeral with full military honors at Plymouth; his coffin was attended by eight Royal Navy post captains as pallbearers and preceded by an honor guard of two companies of Royal Marines. All of the British navy's captains in port followed the procession.[44]

An even more poignant display of mutual respect took place a month later in Portland, Maine. The morning of September 8 every business in town was shuttered as two barges, each bearing a coffin, slowly rowed to shore and a minute gun sounded alternately from the two warships standing in the harbor, one the captured British brig *Boxer,* the other the American brig *Enterprize.* Three days earlier, just north of Portland, the two ships had maneuvered to within half a pistol shot, a mere ten yards from each other, before opening fire. The outfought British ship surrendered half an hour later; again a British court-martial would admit that the enemy's "greater degree of skill in the direction of her fire" was responsible for the outcome. But both captains were mortally wounded in the first broadside, Samuel Blyth of the *Boxer* cut in two by an eighteen-pound shot, William Burrows of the *Enterprize* blasted with canister shot in the thigh, and their deaths had cast a solemn pall over the news of the American victory when the ships reached Portland the next day.

From the Union Wharf, a military escort led the procession of the two captains' coffins, Isaac Hull and other American officers following with the entire surviving crews of the two ships, British prisoners and American victors alike. At the Second Parish Meeting House the coffins lay side by side, and then the two rival captains were buried next to each other. It was, wrote C. S. Forester, "a civilized gesture in a war that threatened to become uncivilized."[45] Beyond the mutual accusations of barbarity and atrocity was a settling sense on both sides that only a war of grimly determined destruction could now bring the other to terms. By the end of 1813 the Admiralty had decided to replace Admiral Warren with a man made of sterner stuff.[46] He was Vice Admiral Sir Alexander F. I. Cochrane, who had commanded successful amphibious landings in Egypt and Martinique and who possessed a deep personal loathing of Americans, in part because his brother had been killed at Yorktown in 1781.

The loss of the *Argus* had meanwhile left Madison and Jones more determined than ever to stamp out any remaining inclinations on the part of American captains to place honor above the dispassionate calculus of destruction; there was no other way to bring the war home to the enemy. The president wrote Jones lamenting Allen's death and the loss of the *Argus* but adding:

> It proves also the great capacity of that species of vessel to make the war an evil to G.B. and particularly to the class of her

subjects who promoted it. Would it be amiss to instruct such cruisers positively, never to fight when they can avoid it, and employ themselves entirely in destroying the commerce of the Enemy.[47]

Jones's sailing instructions became even more emphatic in stressing commerce destruction and forbidding challenges: there were to be no more affairs of honor on the high seas, even when the odds were equal. "The Character of the American Navy stands upon a basis not to be shaken, and needs no sacrifices by unequal combat to sustain its reputation," he wrote in what by the end of 1813 had become a typical instruction to his captains. "You will therefore avoid all unnecessary contact with the Cruisers of the Enemy, even with an equal, unless under circumstances that may ensure your triumph without defeating the main object of your Cruise."

That object was destruction, pure and simple; American warships were to burn every British ship they took; the old game of spoils, of taking prizes and sending them into port, was incompatible with the cold strategic dictates of this increasingly modern war. "A Single Cruiser, destroying every captured Vessel, has the capacity of continuing in full vigour her destructive power, so long as her provisions and stores can be replenished," Jones stated in another order to a captain about to depart on a cruise. "Thus has a Single Cruiser, upon the destructive plan, the power perhaps, of twenty acting upon pecuniary views alone; and thus may the employment of our small force, in some degree compensate for the great inequality compared with that of the Enemy."

There was another "great object" too, Jones began emphasizing to his commanders. It was one likewise dictated by the end of the chivalrous rules with which the war had begun. American captains were now instructed to seize as many British prisoners as they could—not release or parole them, not send them home in sea cartels, which the British government in any case refused to recognize—and bring them back to America "in order to exchange against our unfortunate Countrymen who may fall into his hands."[48] It was all about evening the body count. The anonymity of numbers was beginning to speak louder than the exploits of heroes.

CHAPTER 9

"My Country I Fear Has Forgot Me"

Tattoos of early American seafarers
(Dye, "Tattoos")

AMERICAN PRIVATEERS had been contributing no small part to the growing American strategy of trying to "make the war an evil" to the British classes that Madison believed most supported it; they had also been contributing mightily to the swelling population of American captives held in British prisons. And that was the trouble in a nutshell.

From the start privateers had been enveloped in a mist of romanticism; the Republicans lauded them as "the militia of the sea" and "our cheapest & best Navy," and with the way they seemed to roll republican virtue, American entrepreneurialism, and authorized swashbuckling into one, they offered a story no newspaper editor could improve upon. Privateers were nominally subject to naval discipline and the laws of war and acted with the authority of the president—that was what distinguished them from pirates—but other than that were not under the orders of United States authorities and were free to make war on the enemy's commerce whenever and wherever they saw fit. One of the first acts of Congress upon the declaration of war was to authorize the president to issue commissions to private armed vessels empowering their captains to "subdue, seize and take any armed or unarmed British vessel, public or private," and hundreds were issued in the first months of the war. (Although the term "privateer" was often used to refer to any private armed vessel, a distinction was usually drawn between privateers in the strict sense, whose only purpose was raiding enemy shipping, and letters of marque, whose major purpose was to carry a cargo, employing their arms to fight their way through or capture any prizes they fortuitously happened upon along the way.) Any shipowner who was prepared to swear that he was an American citizen and produce two "sureties" willing to sign a bond of $5,000 as a pledge that the ship would obey the laws of war was welcome to try his fortune. From Baltimore, Salem, New York, Boston, and other ports large and small, private armed vessels set out to sea, many bearing self-consciously patriotic names or christened after American military figures of renown, past and present. The small seafaring town of Marblehead, north of Boston, supplied 120 men to the American navy but six times that number to the privateers that sailed from the port; in Baltimore some 6,000 seamen made their way onto the 122 privateers and letters of marque that set out from that city in the course of the war. Some were the usual Fell's Point rough customers, some were seamen from other ports up and down the Chesapeake, but a good many were farm boys with visions of glory and easy money or other romantics or naïfs drawn to the short stints and adventure the job offered. The rapacious recruiting agents who scoured the portside for men to make up the crews were never very particular.[1]

American privateering vessels were often beautiful to look at, rakish and distinctive: sharp-lined schooners of two hundred or three hundred tons that could be built in a month and a half, almost everything about them designed for speed over safety or comfort; they had towering masts, light planking that offered little protection against enemy fire or even the normal hazards of wind and weather, almost always relying for their main firepower on a Long Tom, an eighteen- or twenty-four-pounder mounted on a pivot amidships, and almost always relying on cramming a crew of 100 or 150 uncomfortably aboard in order to board and man the prizes they hoped to take. To windward and with enough sea room they could escape from any large warship; with their fleetness and their ability to sail two points closer to the wind than a square-rigged vessel, they could haul off in a direction no frigate or ship of the line could follow. Nipping at the flanks of a convoy, they could dash in and grab a merchant vessel under cover of dark or work in pairs, one leading an escorting frigate off on a chase while the other went in for the kill.[2]

A few of the privateers did spectacularly well marauding off Halifax and the West Indies, and even farther afield. The *Yankee* out of Bristol, Rhode Island, was the most successful of the war, taking a total of $5 million worth of enemy shipping in its five cruises, crisscrossing the Atlantic as far as Africa and earning its owners and crews $1 million from the sale of the cargoes and vessels it brought back to American ports. The *True-Blooded Yankee*, an eighteen-gun brig bought by an American in France, sailed out of Brest on March 1, 1813, and in thirty-seven days captured twenty-seven vessels, took 270 prisoners, held an island off the coast of Ireland for six days, briefly occupied a town in Scotland and burned seven vessels in the harbor, and returned to France with twelve thousand pounds of silk, eighteen bales of Turkey carpets, and two thousand swan skins, among her other booty.[3]

By the end of 1812 American privateers had brought in some 300 prizes, and a year later the total stood at 700. The trouble was that it was coming at a terrible price. Like most gambling ventures, privateering generally did not pay off at all. Of the five hundred commissions issued to private armed vessels throughout the war, more than three hundred never took a prize before returning home or being captured themselves. Privateers took an average of only 2.5 prizes apiece, a third as many as the average American navy ship. And because they most definitely operated on the "pecuniary system," they did exactly the things that vastly reduced a commerce raider's effectiveness, as William Jones had pointed out in his orders to American naval commanders: weakening their crews by manning their prizes and risking their recapture by trying to get them into friendly ports rather than burning or sinking them on the spot. Of the 2,500 prizes taken during the war by American warships and privateers, about 400 were burned, most by the U.S. navy; of the remaining 2,100, some 750 were recaptured before they could be brought into American or neutral ports as prizes.

Privateers also had little interest in taking prisoners so often simply released them. In August 1813 Congress authorized a bounty of $25 for each prisoner brought in by privateers and in March 1814 increased it to $100, but still the fact was that American privateers were rapidly shifting the prisoner balance in Britain's favor because any privateer that kept at it long enough was almost sure to wind up in enemy hands. Of forty-one privateers that sailed from Salem only fifteen remained uncaptured by the end of the war.[4]

Still, the chance of hitting the jackpot kept owners and men, or at least a certain kind of men, coming. It cost about $40,000 to purchase and fit out a typical privateer schooner and a single lucky prize—like a West Indiaman laden with coffee, sugar, or rum—could clear $100,000, even after deducting a long list of fees and court costs that went to attorneys and prize agents and auctioneers and owners of the wharves and warehouses that stored the captured ships and cargoes while awaiting adjudication. The usual arrangement was that half the spoils went to the owners and the other half was divided among the officers and crew in proportion to their rank: one share for a landsman, two shares for an able-bodied seaman, up to sixteen for the captain.

"Here was an opportunity of making a fortune," remarked George Little, a merchant sailor who entered on board the small privateer schooner *George Washington* when he found himself stranded and moneyless in Norfolk soon after the start of the war. "But then it was counterbalanced by the possibility of getting my head knocked off, or a chance of being thrown into prison for two or three years." On a typical good cruise an able seaman might stand to earn $300 in prize money for three months' work, three or four times the going wage for an ordinary seaman on a merchant ship. On an exceptionally good cruise he could literally make thousands: a single prize that the *Yankee* took, the *San Jose Indiano,* sailing from Liverpool to Rio de Janeiro filled with silks and other valuable cargo, sold for half a million dollars when she was brought into Portland, Maine, bringing the captain $15,789.69 and even the ship's two black cabin boys, the lowest men on the totem pole, $1,121.88 and $738.19.[5]

On a bad cruise, the crew—like the owners—got nothing at all, except for a small advance against their shares paid when they signed on, supplemented sometimes by what they had managed to sell their prize tickets for before the cruise. In Baltimore and other privateering ports there was a lively trade in these tickets, issued to the crew and redeemable for their share of the proceeds when the prizes were finally sold. The tickets were bought and sold like commercial paper or stock shares, or more like lottery tickets, and a good many crewmen who signed on to privateers traded away their promise of future winnings for immediate expenses that the recruiting agents and other dockside merchants, and land sharks, were all too happy to provide: lodging, and clothes, and sea chests, and gewgaws, and food and drink, and small outlays of cash.[6]

A few privateers were fitted out by experienced ex–naval officers, such as Joshua Barney, whose schooner *Rossie,* sailing from Baltimore in July 1812, was organized along tight man-of-war lines. But even though he took eighteen British ships in ninety days, Barney concluded the business was not worth it after that first cruise grossed only about $68,000 for the owners, and within a week of her return to Baltimore in October the *Rossie* was auctioned off. To try to improve the financial incentives, William Jones urged a reduction in the duties privateers had to pay on the goods they brought in; the federal duties sometimes absorbed nearly half the proceeds, while hurriedly arranged prize auctions cut into profits as well by driving down prices for vessels and cargoes such as sugar as much as 30 percent below the fair market value. In August 1813 Congress reduced duties on prizes by one-third.[7]

But the real problem lay on the risk side of the equation. As the British blockade tightened and dangers grew, the business was left more and more to men of a very different stamp from professional navy men like Joshua Barney, or even professional seafarers of the kind who had plied the legitimate trading routes before the war. George Little, warily eying his shipmates aboard the *George Washington,* concluded that "they appeared to have been scraped together from the lowest dens of wretchedness and vice . . . loafers, highbinders, butcher boys &c &c" (a highbinder meaning a paid assassin), while the captain seemed "to be fit for little else than fighting and plunder." Little was stunned when this "band of ruthless desperadoes" proceeded to plunder the personal belongings of the crew of the first prize they boarded, a merchant brig from Jamaica filled with sugar.[8]

"I had heard much of the *picked* crews of American privateers," said Benjamin Browne, similarly surveying the company he found himself among in Boston harbor on the deck of the privateer *Grumbler* (it was subsequently rechristened with the more seemly name *Frolic*). They had been recruited by laying out vast quantities of "villainous bad" whiskey, a few dollars' advance money, "and the free use of that description of rhetoric which the Irish call *blarney*," and "such a hatless, shoeless, shirt-less, graceless, unwashed, but not unwhipped set of ragamuffins, I believe never before indulged the gregariousness of their natures by congregating together." Josiah Cobb itemized the crew of the Boston privateer he joined in 1814, as a naive eighteen-year-old dreaming of adventures of the sea, as "Irish, English, French, Spanish, Portuguese, Dutch, African and American . . . and many who could hail from no quarter on the globe, but whose destination required no conjuring to ascertain." Just before sailing, a man who had signed on as gunner's mate came aboard Cobb's ship and immediately began to storm and swear, saying he had sent his baggage aboard on a boat that morning and now it was nowhere to be found. Cobb innocently offered to help the man search, and they began shifting casks and boxes, inspecting hammocks, moving vast coils of rope, but after a while he began to notice the grins of the rest of the crew, who began offering facetious suggestions—"You haven't yet searched the bottom under the ballast"; "Have you looked in the captain's breeches pockets?"—and then one deadpanned, "Had you a suit in your bag with alternate stripes of blue and drab? Because if you had, you need not despair at your loss, for yonder you can get a match," pointing toward the state prison in Charlestown, which lay in full view nearby. The man went slack-jawed and slunk away, because that was indeed where he had directly come from: he had just been released from seven years in prison and had no possessions at all, and had carried through the elaborate charade about his missing bags in an unsuccessful if imaginative bid to cover up the fact.[9]

Privateers' memoirs and logs brim with accounts of insubordination, fights among the crew, drunkenness, utterly incompetent seamanship, and men assigned stations they had no qualifications whatever to perform. Browne on joining the *Frolic* was promptly made captain's clerk, purser, *and* sergeant of marines and told to drill the other green landsmen in the use of muskets, boarding pikes, and boarding hatchets. Recruiting surgeons to serve on privateers was so difficult that the *George Washington*'s specimen seemed to have been all too typical of the type who could be enticed aboard; Little described his ship's doctor as a man "somewhat advanced in years" who had "read physic in a doctor's office, and listened to some half-dozen lectures in a medical college," and whose standard prescription for nearly every ailment was a pint of salt water.[10]

Privateers were subject to the articles of war and naval courts-martial, but discipline was often almost a parody of a man-of-war's. Even aboard the famously successful *Yankee* one of the lieutenants kept being found "dead drunk" and asleep throughout his watch. On another occasion the ship's gunner, "much intoxicated," blundered into the magazine holding a lit candle and nearly blew the entire ship to kingdom come. When the captain of the *Harpy* out of Baltimore tried to exercise his men in sail handling, having noted with concern how slow they had been in sending up the fore topgallant yard the day before, "all the crew came on deck in a mutinous spirit and absolutely refused to obey my commands," the captain recorded. A few weeks later he tried to discipline a crewman for plundering the clothes of passengers from a Portuguese brig they boarded and had the man put in irons on the quarterdeck, where he sat "swearing he did not give a damn about the vessel or anything else," and when the captain then ordered him gagged if he wouldn't keep quiet, "several of the crew cried out on the main deck they would be damned if I would gag him." Every few days the captain's log contained entries along the lines of "I reasoned the case with them . . . I found they would listen to no reason whatever."[11]

Enforcing discipline aboard hundreds of privateers was a burden William Jones had no interest in adding to the Navy Department's already overwhelming responsibilities, and when the crew of the privateer *General Armstrong* returned to Wilmington, North Carolina, in April 1813 with the captain locked below, it was clearly more than the small U.S. navy gunboat detachment in the port or the department in Washington was able to cope with. The captain demanded that sixty-one of the crew be tried not only for mutiny but the even more serious charge of piracy, since they had taken two prizes after seizing control of the ship and therefore, the captain argued, were acting without a valid privateering commission. The prisoners were confined to three gunboats in Wilmington harbor, but the situation began to spiral out of control when a local man rowing by got into an argument with the navy sentries guarding the prisoners, and in the ensuing altercation was shot and killed. In June, Jones ordered the prisoners all released, arguing that the civil courts, not the navy, had jurisdiction over piracy cases and that in any case it was an impossible burden in wartime to detach five commissioned officers to Wilmington to convene a court-martial. The captain bombarded Jones with angry remonstrances; a local jury acquitted the navy officers of murder of the local man; and the *General Armstrong*'s crew never was tried on any charges, although an almost surreal prize case arising from their captures eventually reached the United States Circuit Court, with the captain appearing as a witness against his own ship's owners while the chief witness in favor of the claimants was the leader of the ship's mutinying crew.[12]

Ill-disciplined crews and incompetent commanders on a number of occasions led to privateers' blundering directly into enemy hands. The risk of being taken was greatest when running through the blockading squadron, where the shore limited maneuver room and a privateer was likely to find himself outnumbered and surrounded by a vastly superior enemy force, but even on the open ocean American privateers sometimes threw away their considerable sailing advantages through misjudgment and atrocious seamanship. After blundering within musket shot of a British frigate in the fog on December 14, 1812, the captain of the *George Washington* ignored the advice of all his officers and insisted on running before the wind, with the result that the frigate "overhauled us without any difficulty" and the crew were all taken prisoner, and remained in British captivity until the end of the war. The crew of Josiah Cobb's privateer sailed within range of three British frigates before the sleepy lookout spotted them; the crew, then deciding that capture was unavoidable, proceeded to calmly and methodically loot their own ship, one man steadily applying himself to stuffing away most of a ham and a large wheel of cheese in the half hour before the schooner surrendered. "I goes always for the solids," he explained. The next morning the crew were taken aboard their captor, and two of the Americans immediately began fighting with each other on the deck of the British man-of-war over some simmering difference, which prompted one of the British officers to offer aloud a facetious observation: "I will bear witness to their bravery, as I have seen them fight when surrounded by their enemies on all sides."[13]

Another American privateer captain, mistaking a British seventy-four for an Indiaman, ran his ship close alongside and hailed the British ship to strike her colors. "I am not in the habit of striking my colors," the British captain called back, and at the same moment all three tiers of gunports flew open. "Well," the American captain replied, "if you won't, I will."[14]

FROM THE start, the British authorities in Canada and the West Indies were almost completely unprepared to deal with the flood of prisoners that came pouring in. As early as September 1812 there were already a thousand American prisoners being held on Melville Island in Halifax harbor; the island had a small garrison and fort consisting of a few wooden buildings, and the prisoners were crowded into the largest of them, a barnlike structure two hundred feet long and fifty feet wide. Admiral Sawyer wrote Secretary Croker that he had had to purchase a captured American ship to serve as extra prison space, but even so the situation was miserable, and explosive.

When the crew of the *Vixen* arrived on the prison hulk *Loyalist* in Port Royal harbor, Jamaica, in December 1812, it was already full of "a greater variety of living creatures" than Noah's ark, in the words of one young American who had earlier been taken prisoner from a privateer. It held not only hundreds of captured Americans but a teeming population of rats and enormous and voracious cockroaches and bedbugs that dropped down on the sleeping men at night. "Had the ark contained as much filth as this old hulk," the prisoner continued, "the dove never would have returned a second time with the testimony of her having found dry land." When five of the Americans managed to escape in a boat after bribing one of the sentries with a bottle of rum, the guard was swiftly tried by a court-martial and sentenced to a thousand lashes; the last two hundred were put on after he was dead. "Far from my friends, my country, far from thee / A wretched captive sighs for liberty," wrote the young American months later, despairing of his release.[15]

Benjamin Waterhouse, a young surgeon on a Salem privateer captured at sea in May 1813, spent his first night in the prison on Melville recoiled in nightmarish distress and shock; many of the prisoners were crawling with lice, the hammocks were slung four high, one above another, between stanchions that ran through the open space like in a cattle barn, and the whole night was filled with the moans and complaints of his fellow prisoners, some sobbing at their fate, others cursing the British, one man reciting over and over what a fool he had been to have been so headstrong and disobey his parents' wishes and go to sea. A little before dawn Waterhouse finally drifted to sleep only to be awakened almost instantly, it seemed, by the noisy grinding of locks being unbolted and the doors unbarred and the cries of "turn out—all out!" from the guards and the prodding of a bayonet when he groggily did not move fast enough. "But use makes everything easy," Waterhouse philosophically observed.[16]

Both sides were carrying on a war of nerves, the British jailers vexed and baffled by the defiance and petty retaliations the American prisoners were constantly practicing upon them. The British agent in charge of the prisoners at Halifax, a Royal Navy lieutenant named William Miller, was bombarded with complaints and demands and itemizations of rights he was violating. The jailers for their part kept up a steady stream of petty and not-so-petty harassment, forcing the prisoners to stand outside for hours on end, even in bitter cold and snowstorms, under the pretext that the barracks were being washed and that it would be injurious to their health to be allowed back in before all was "perfectly dry." When the Americans sent a delegation to Miller to complain about the putrid beef being served, he erupted in a fury, ordered the prisoners assembled, mounted the staircase on the side of the prison building, and delivered them a harangue for their "impudence":

> You are a mean set of rascals, you beg of an enemy favors
> which your own government won't grant you! You complain of
> ill treatment, when you never fared better in your lives. Had you
> been in some French prison and fed on horse-beef, you would
> have some ground of complaint; but here in His Britannic
> Majesty's royal prison, you have everything that is right and
> proper for persons taken fighting against his crown and dignity.
> There is a surgeon here for you, if you are sick, and physic to
> take if you are sick, and a hospital to go to into the bargain, and
> if you die there are boards enough for to make you coffins, and
> a hundred and fifty acres of land to bury you in; and if you are
> not satisfied with all this you may die and be damned.

Then he strutted out of the prison yard to a chorus of hisses. The prisoners then took to hurling pieces of rancid beef over the picket fence surrounding the prison yard, which finally caused the quality of the provisions to improve.[17] All the British officials who had American prisoners under their charge complained that they were ungovernable. Just days after the crew of the privateer *Frolic* arrived in Barbados, Benjamin Browne's jailer told him that their forty men were more trouble than the five hundred French prisoners he had: "A Frenchman settles down at once in a prison, into habits of quiet order, industry, mild gaiety, and respectful submission, . . . but your men have such a wild, reckless, daring, enterprising character that it would puzzle the devil to keep them in good order." When a marine sentry struck an American on a prison hulk in Hamilton harbor in Bermuda, the prisoners promptly sent a committee to the British captain "demanding satisfaction" and forcing from him an apology and an order that the guards were not to strike or abuse the prisoners. "This is all the satisfaction we recd," wrote Benjamin Palmer in his diary, "but should another American be struck Farewell Marines—These d——m Englishmen must not think they have got Frenchmen to deal with." A prison keeper in Halifax discovered another example of the Americans' "enterprising character" when a Spanish silver dollar snapped in two in his hand: it turned out that most of the dollars in circulation in the canteen had been manufactured by one of the prisoners.[18]

By the fall of 1813 there were rumors that all exchanges of prisoners had been halted. Still, Benjamin Waterhouse and his fellow prisoners in Halifax were constantly assured by their jailers that they would soon be on their way home, that cartel ships were arriving any day, and then one day Waterhouse was among a hundred Americans told to get their baggage, and soon he was being rowed out to a British warship in the harbor. Only when they were alongside the ship did they learn the truth: they were on their way not to home but to England. "Had Miller been on the boat with us," wrote Waterhouse, "we should most certainly have thrown him overboard."[19]

The ship was the *Regulus,* a thirty-year-old frigate that had been converted to a troop ship twenty years earlier. The prisoners were locked down in the dark and airless hold, two carronades loaded with canister and grape were placed on the quarterdeck pointing forward to command the hatchways, and for the entire voyage the Americans were kept on scant rations as part of an apparently deliberate policy to keep them too weak to try to take the ship. All they could think of was food, Waterhouse recalled; hunger followed them into their sleep, when they would dream of lavish meals and heavily laden tables; they had lengthy debates over whether it was better to eat the worms in the half pound of bread they received each day and whether it was more pleasurable to eat it all at once or in small portions throughout the day. The soldiers who had come to Canada in the ship had left behind an army of fleas that added to the torment of their passage.

One of the American prisoners, passing the *Regulus*'s captain with his mess's allotment of oatmeal gruel from the galley, finally burst forth with a complaint: "*Sir, Sir, but it is fit food only for hogs.*" The captain indignantly asked him what part of America he came from to be so particular about his tastes. "Near to *Bunker Hill*, Sir," the prisoner shot back, "*if you ever heard of that place.*"

On arriving in the Medway they were transferred to a prison hulk, the *Crown Prince,* one of fourteen old demasted ships of the line moored in the river. Some of the ships held as many as nine hundred prisoners at a time. "Casting a glance around," wrote an American of his arrival belowdecks on the *Irresistible,* "I found myself amidst a squalid, cadaverous throng of about six hundred, ranging from fourteen to sixty years of age; and never beheld a set of more wretched human beings. They were nearly starved and almost naked, and wholly unable to take exercise. . . . It was too dark to read, so they yielded up their minds to corroding despondency, and became sullen and morose. Their features become rigid, and to see a smile upon a face was like a sunbeam illumining a thunder-cloud."[20]

Still, the food was a significant improvement; the Americans on the *Crown Prince* drew up a constitution, a code of laws, and a court to discipline themselves; the smaller number of French prisoners already aboard, however, devoted most of their time, and all their effort, to running billiard tables and roulette wheels, that they had somehow managed to fashion, and with which they proceeded to methodically part the new arrivals from all their cash. "These Frenchmen seldom failed to win," Waterhouse noted, and were charmingly merciless in refusing to extend credit to the victims they had cleaned out: "I am sorry, very sorry indeed; it is *le fortune de guerre.* If you have lost your money you must win it back again; that is the fashion in my country—we no lend, that is not the fashion." A few of the Americans sought their revenge by proposing a wager on whether one of them could tie up a Frenchman and toss him in a sack, but the Frenchmen again demurred: "No, it is not the fashion in our country to tie gentlemen up in sacks." The Americans finally announced there would be a vote on whether to abolish gambling. The motion passed, with the French opposing.[21]

Escape might have seemed hopeless, but sixteen men got away one dark night by cutting a hole through the stern and bending the copper down, slipping into the water, and swimming ashore. The copper was then pulled back up into place, and before the next head count the following evening the prisoners also cut a small hole through the deck; after the sergeant had counted the men on one deck, sixteen men slipped through to the next deck and were counted again. But a second escape attempt gave the game away when one of the prisoners' nerves failed him and he was spotted trying to swim back. The officers searched the ship to try to discover how anyone could have gotten out and finally found the sally port, eliciting a huge roar of laughter from the Americans as they stood gaping at it.

A brasher attempt took place in broad daylight on the adjacent *Irresistible*. Four Americans, one of them an Indian of the Narragansett tribe, "a man of large stature and remarkable strength," grabbed the sentry guarding the ship's jolly boat, which was alongside with all her oars in; threw the sentry into the boat; jumped in after him; and rowed like madmen for the shore, to the uproarious cheers and shouts of encouragement of the prisoners watching from all the hulks in the river. Soon about thirty boats, with 350 British seamen and marines, were in pursuit, firing at the fleeing prisoners. On reaching shore, the fugitives abandoned their hostage and ran flat out for the fields, well ahead of the pursuing marines. But they were quickly surrounded by the local country people, who poured out of the farmhouses and brickyards and recaptured them all but the Indian, who Waterhouse, watching from the deck of the *Crown Prince*, could see "skipping over the ground like a buck." But then he too went down, spraining his ankle while leaping a fence.[22]

The attempt clearly had the British rattled, and the Americans gleefully intensified their sarcastic barrages. Some of the prisoners had taken to studying mathematics to fill the time, and now whenever one of their British jailers walked by, one of the American students would look quizzically at his slate and say aloud, as if reciting an arithmetic problem, "If it took 350 British seamen and marines to catch *four* Yankees, how many British sailors and marines would it take to catch *ten thousand* of us?" A story got around that the commander of the *Crown Prince*, a superannuated forty-five-year-old Royal Navy lieutenant named Osmore—who seemed to look upon his duties mainly for the embezzlement opportunities they presented—had poached some sheep from a field nearby for his personal use. A few days later, as Osmore was getting into the boat with his wife and family to head ashore, a raucous chorus of *"Baa! Baa! Baa!"* suddenly broke forth from all the ship's ports. Osmore retaliated by barring the boats that called daily to sell the prisoners garden vegetables; the prisoners then appealed to the commodore for a hearing, which gave them a chance to put Osmore com-

pletely on the spot by gravely begging him to explain, both to themselves and to his commanding officer, "how such an unmeaning sound
could be construed as an insult." The ban on the market boats was
lifted.[23]

A few months later all the prisoners were ordered to be put aboard
tenders for transfer to Dartmoor Prison. This was the final hardening
of the British stand on American prisoners: in January 1814 officials in
Washington learned that the British had completely "discontinued the
system of *releases on account*" of American prisoners. In May, Cockburn
reiterated his instructions that no captains were to agree to on-the-spot
exchanges; all captured Americans were to be sent directly to prisons.
"My Ideas of managing Jonathan," he wrote to Admiral Cochrane
explaining his decision, "is by never giving way to him, in spite of his
bullying and abuse."

Instructions went to Halifax from London ordering the wholesale
transfer to England of prisoners held there; a large number of ships
were due to arrive in the spring transporting fresh troops to Canada,
and on their return they were to be filled with the prisoners. At around
the same time a decision was made to concentrate all American prisoners in England into one tightly secured location. Dartmoor was a virtual
fortress, located in one of the most desolate spots of England, surrounded by miles of wild and uninhabited moorland near the south-
western coast, and usually shrouded in a bone-chilling damp and fog. It
had been built in 1806 specifically as a depot for prisoners of war, and
with the coming of peace with France in April 1814, it was going to
have plenty of room for the six thousand American sailors the British
now held in depots and prison hulks scattered around a dozen and a
half locations in England, Canada, the Caribbean, the Mediterranean,
and beyond.[24]

The night before one of the last remaining drafts of prisoners was
taken off the *Crown Prince*, there had been another spirited display of
American "impudence"; an altercation with Osmore had resulted in
thirty men having their hammocks taken away as punishment, and the
men decided that if they would not be able to sleep, Osmore would not
either. They waited quietly until ten o'clock; then all hell broke loose in
a cacophony of Indian war whoops, oaken benches battering against
bulkheads, tin and copper pans banging together. Osmore became so
enraged at one point that he threatened to order the marines to fire
down the hatches on them. Finally the men quieted down, waited

another half hour, then repeated the performance. And so it went all night.

The next morning, as the tender carried them off, a cry of *"Baa! Baa! Baa!"* came across the water, continuing without cease until the ship was out of hearing.[25]

BY THE END of 1813 the only American traders who could obtain insurance for their cargoes were letters of marque, and not just any letters of marque but only those swift, sharply built schooners of the kind that the shipwrights of Baltimore and New England had long earned a reputation for. They could carry only a fraction of their maximum load without risking their best sailing trim; insurance rates were a seemingly catastrophic 50 percent, if coverage was obtainable at all, which meant that as far as the underwriters were concerned it was no better than even money that they would successfully run through the two gauntlets of British blockaders, on the American and French coasts; but there were great profits to be made where good luck and good seamanship held. Cotton that sold for thirteen cents a pound in Charleston went for twice that in France. And although it was not their first object, there was always the chance of happening upon a convoy-dodging British merchantman that could be taken as a prize along the way.

It was a strange way to carry on trade or fight a war, but as Yankee sea captain George Coggeshall noted, by this point in the war "there were but three ways for captains of merchant ships to find employment in their ordinary vocations: namely, enter the United States Navy as sailing masters, go privateering, or command a letter-of-marque—carry a cargo and, as it were, force trade and fight their way or run, as the case might be"; and of the three, the last was the least bad on several scores. The captains and crews of letters of marque were a noticeable cut above most of the out-and-out privateers. For one thing, they paid an actual wage to their crews—thirty, forty, even fifty dollars a month—and so drew the more experienced able-bodied seamen, leaving the more desperate characters to the privateers. Like Coggeshall, their commanding officers were usually experienced merchant captains who knew how to handle a ship first and foremost, had sailed often to France and farther points before the war, and had backgrounds much like many of the American navy's officers, even if they lacked the fighting experience. Coggeshall was twenty-nine, had been at sea since he was a boy, and was the son of a sea captain.[26]

On the night of November 14, 1813, a thick nor'easter moved into Newport, and obscured behind sheets of blowing snow and propelled by the fresh gale, the schooner *David Porter* passed rapidly by the fort, out of the harbor, and soon was beyond the blockading squadron, on her way first to Charleston with a load of butter, cheese, and potatoes, then across the ocean for France with a richer cargo. Coggeshall, as captain, had put up $1,500 of his own money in the venture, a quarter of the purchase price of the schooner. The *David Porter* had the typical armament of a letter-of-marque schooner, four 6-pounders that were not much more than for show but also an 18-pounder Long Tom, that versatile weapon of intimidation, mounted amidships; she also had a far better than average crew, hired at $30 a month for an able seaman, Coggeshall having managed to find most of his thirty men and petty officers, including the gunner, boatswain, and carpenter, right out of the frigate *President*, which had just returned to Newport with many of her crew past the end of their two-year enlistments.

Nearing Charleston, Coggeshall was chased for four hours by a British brig; the wind was off the land and the brig had the weather gauge. Hoping to draw the brig off so he could tack and weather her, Coggeshall steered wide to leeward. But the brig kept her course to cut off any such attempt at getting to windward, and now Coggeshall feared he was being driven into a trap and decided to run for it as close to the wind as he could, rather than letting himself be pushed out to sea, where other enemy ships might be waiting. Hauling up to cross the Charleston bar, he passed within gunshot of the brig and fired one shot from the Long Tom, splashing water over the enemy's quarter before running in.

In Charleston he sold his New England produce for a good profit and took on 331 bales of cotton; he stood to earn $23,000 in freight and fees for delivering it to Bordeaux or any other port in France.

They made it to the port of the small, miserable village of La Teste in thirty-seven days, seeing scarcely a sail and not a single man-of-war the whole way, surviving a furious gale in the Bay of Biscay that split open the planking and nearly threw the schooner on her beam ends, the next sea threatening to capsize her. The crew frantically threw two of the guns and the water casks overboard to lighten the ship, and got her running before the wind until a smooth moment came to wear onto the other tack and relieve the strain on the damaged starboard fore shrouds that might send the mast crashing down. The schooner rode literally leaping "from one sea to another" until steadying on the other tack. The day before Wellington's army marched into La Teste on March 11, 1814, Coggeshall managed to get to sea again, holding a pistol to the head of the reluctant local pilot to persuade him to take the schooner out after he insisted the weather was too bad.[27]

At daylight on the fifteenth the crew of the *David Porter* found themselves two miles to leeward of a large frigate. Coggeshall tried the same tactic he had used with his pursuer off Charleston, trying to lure the warship to leeward so he could quickly tack and get to windward. As before, the British ship refused to be drawn, and it seemed there might be nothing for it but to ply to windward, take a full broadside at pistol shot in passing, and hope for the best. But overruling the advice of his officers, Coggeshall decided to try to run before the wind, and with more adroitness and better seamanship than the *George Washington*'s captain had displayed in executing that maneuver in the same situation, and with a crack crew that knew how to pull off such a surprise, he ordered the square sail and studding sails readied to run up at the same moment when he gave the word. And then in a flash they were running to leeward, and the frigate took five minutes before she could get a studding sail set, in which time the *David Porter* had gained a clear mile. Everything they could sacrifice went overboard; all the water except for four casks' worth was started and pumped onto the sails to keep them drawing as tight as a drum, all the sand ballast from the hold was thrown out, and by noon a good eight or ten miles separated them, and by four in the afternoon the frigate was a speck on the water.

They were short of provisions—the baker at La Teste had been unable to provide them more than two bags of bread, and in a mix-up during the chase only two water casks had been spared—but the next morning, "to our unspeakable joy," first light found them in the midst of a small merchant fleet out of England that had become separated from its escort in a gale a few days before. The first ship they captured was a brig brimming with provisions, and the schooner was soon bursting with hardtack, butter, hams, cheese, potatoes, and beer. They took three more ships before spotting, late in the afternoon, the same frigate that had chased them the day before. Coggeshall ordered the three prizes to hoist lanterns while he slipped away in the growing darkness, and "very soon after this, I heard the frigate firing at his unfortunate countrymen, while we were partaking of an excellent supper at their expense."[28]

Coggeshall turned over command of the schooner to his first lieutenant and remained in France to complete arrangements for a large purchase of wine in Bordeaux. The *David Porter* returned safely to Cape Ann later in the year, taking several more prizes on the way home and ten prisoners, which netted the owners $1,000 as a bounty from the United States government.

Later that year Coggeshall, for his return voyage, took command of "a fine Baltimore built vessel . . . a remarkably fast sailer," the letter-of-marque schooner *Leo*, lying in L'Orient harbor. For three weeks he skillfully dodged British men-of-war in the Bay of Biscay while taking several prizes, and then one afternoon there came racing across their weather quarter a prize to put all others to shame, an English packet just out of Lisbon, bound for England, almost certainly carrying a huge quantity of specie. Just as they were on a course to intercept within a pistol shot, the schooner gave a violent lurch and the foremast snapped in two places.

The only hope now was to get into Lisbon, a neutral port, before the next morning; the seas were teeming with British warships. The *Leo*'s crew worked for an hour clearing away the wreckage and rigging a jury foremast, and by four o'clock in the afternoon they were making seven knots.[29]

But with dawn and the Rock of Lisbon in sight the wind died. All day they swept and towed, and just as their hopes had risen again—four miles from land, the Lisbon pilot already aboard—Coggeshall saw coming out, on the ebb tide of the Tagus and a light land breeze, a thirty-eight-gun British frigate. In a matter of minutes they were under her guns, and prisoners of war.

The frigate was the *Granicus*, and her captain, W. F. Wise, far removed from the growing brutalities of the American war, was of the old and chivalrous school; Coggeshall was given his own stateroom and was invited almost every day to dine with the captain, who was all manners and kindness, praising the seamanship and ingenuity of American sailors and shipbuilders, and more than once urging him, "Don't be depressed by captivity, but strive to forget that you are a prisoner, and imagine that you are only a passenger." At Gibraltar the crew was immediately shipped off to England, and Coggeshall and his lieutenants were to follow in a few days, once they had given the required depositions to the admiralty court. The governor of Gibraltar had received positive orders that every American prisoner brought in was to be forwarded to Dartmoor, without exception, and the officers were not to be paroled, despite Wise's urging that they be treated civilly, all the more so since the *Leo* had voluntarily released some thirty British prisoners they had taken. "I said but little on this subject," Coggeshall said afterward, "but from that moment resolved to make my escape upon the first opportunity."[30]

It seemed an even more impossible proposition than escaping from a prison hulk in the Medway, for Gibraltar was itself a citadel, with a guarded gate leading to the mainland. The first day Captain Wise said he was prepared to let Coggeshall and his officers attend the court proceedings without a guard if they pledged their parole not to attempt to escape. Coggeshall did so, and used the chance afforded by their stroll back to conduct an hour's reconnaissance.

The next morning they were to return to the court, and Coggeshall arose, put all the money he had—about a hundred gold twenty-five-franc pieces—in his belt, and slipped a few keepsakes into his pocket.

"Well, Coggeshall, I understand you and your officers are required at the Admiralty Office at 10 o'clock," Wise greeted him, "and if you and your officers will again pledge your honor, as you did yesterday, you may go on shore without a guard."

Coggeshall gave him a careful look and replied, "Captain Wise, I am surprised that you think it possible for any one to escape from Gibraltar."

Wise, pleasantly but firmly, said, "Come, come, it won't do, you must either pledge your word and honor that neither you nor your officers will attempt to make your escape, or I shall be compelled to send a guard with you."

"You had better send a guard, sir."[31]

And so a lieutenant, with a sergeant and four marines, conducted the Americans to the office. While Coggeshall and one of his lieutenants were waiting in the courtroom for their turn to be examined, the lieutenant walked casually to the door, then urgently beckoned him over; the British lieutenant was not in sight. Coggeshall then cheerfully asked the sergeant if he would like to go up the street to the wineshop at the corner for a glass of wine with them while they waited. The sergeant thought it was an excellent idea and, leaving the rest of the marines, accompanied the two Americans up the street. The wineshop had entrances on each street; Coggeshall and the lieutenant went in one door, and while the sergeant waited there, Coggeshall slipped out the other after whispering to the lieutenant to follow and meet him two blocks over.

Coggeshall removed the eagle insignia from his cockade, and with
that gone, his blue coat, black stock, and black cockade "had, on the
whole, very much the appearance of an English naval officer." He
waited with growing apprehension at the corner he had named, but the
lieutenant did not appear. "I had now fairly committed myself, and
found I did not have a moment to spare," and so he set off with what he
hoped was an attitude of "the most perfect composure and consum-
mate impudence" toward the sentinel guarding the Land Port Gate.
Fixing the guard with a stern glare, he strode on, received a respectful
salute, and in a moment was outside the walls of Gibraltar. He went
down to the mole, where a crowd of boatmen were all too eager to row
him out to his ship; he chose one, hopped in, and as they got into the
bay the oarsmen asked, "Captain, which is your vessel?" Coggeshall
was at a loss for a moment, but seeing a Norwegian flag flying from one,
he decided that the Norwegians were probably more trustworthy than
most people and jabbed a finger toward it.[32]

He decided that his best chance was to tell the truth, and he could
scarcely finish his story before the Norwegian captain grasped his hand,
said he had been a prisoner in England and would do anything to help
him, and in two minutes flat had him fitted out in a pea jacket, fur cap,
and pipe like any Norwegian seaman. The captain then gave him dinner and said he needed to go ashore for a few hours to arrange things.

The Norwegian returned "pleased and delighted": the whole town
was in a state of pandemonium over the escape of the captain of the
American privateer. The lieutenant of the frigate had been arrested.
The next night a gang of smugglers came alongside silently in a long,
fast-rowing boat and "certainly, a more desperate, villainous-looking set
was never seen." But the Norwegian captain had arranged everything;
he did business with them all the time, selling them gin and other odds
and ends; and the smugglers said they would be all too happy to take
the "captains' brother" to Algeciras, nearby in Spain. The water was
smooth, the night dark, and the ten miles' passage was a matter of two
hours' steady rowing. A lantern was shown for a minute, then covered;
an answering signal winked from the shore; and then they were on land
crunching their way up a winding track, and at about three in the
morning they entered a small cabin, one room with a mat hanging in
the middle as a partition. This was where the chief of the smugglers
lived with his wife and two small children, and for three days the family
took Coggeshall in warmly and kindly. Venturing out cautiously to see
if there was an American consul in the town, Coggeshall was able to

find his way to an initially disbelieving diplomat, but once he had doffed his fur cap and pea jacket and "looked somewhat more like an American" he was able to tell his story, and the consul—Horatio Sprague, who had been consul in Gibraltar before the war began— immediately invited him to stay with him and offered to help him on his way. After waiting ten days in hopes of hearing news from his two lieutenants, he hired a guide and mule and, dressed as a peasant to avoid the brigands, traveled over zigzagging mountain footpaths to Cádiz, where he arrived two weeks later, just before sundown, the sun's final rays lighting the church steeples and the mountains beyond them in a burst of gold. He made his way to Lisbon on a coasting schooner, then to New York on a filthy and vermin-infested Portuguese brig, finally arriving home in May 1815 to learn that the war was over and peace had been restored. "I cannot leave this brig without warning my friends and countrymen never to take passage across the Atlantic in a Portuguese vessel of any description," he wrote.[33]

FOR THE five thousand less fortunate Americans who would be marched from Plymouth harbor during the year 1814 over sodden roads through rain and mist, Dartmoor Prison presented a paradox of leniency and misery. It was sixteen miles across the moors, and few of the men were in any condition to make the trek, deprived for so long of exercise in the prison hulks. The clay soil of the road would turn to "the consistency of mortar" in the steady rain, and many of the prisoners lacked shoes, while others lost them in the sucking ooze. "Our march might have been traced for several miles by the old boots, shoes, and stockings, which were left sticking in the mud in the hurry of the march," wrote one American sailor. A file of British soldiers on either side prodded them on their way with bayonets while officers on horseback shouted orders to keep moving.[34]

It was surreal to be on land again, but much about their imprisonment seemed to defy reality at times. The overcrowded old sixty-four that carried Benjamin Waterhouse and his companions from the Medway to Plymouth was commanded by a tyrannical captain who threatened to put any of the Americans in irons if they complained about the shortage of food and had one of his marines severely flogged for selling some of his own tobacco to a prisoner. But the lieutenant was humane, and after the captain promptly went ashore upon their arrival at Plymouth, Waterhouse was astonished at the flotilla of boats that put off from the shore filled with the hundreds of prostitutes of the town offering their accustomed trade to any arriving ship. Soon there were as many girls aboard as there were prisoners; the going rate was half a crown, scarcely fifty cents.[35]

And then a week later the prisoners were trudging from seven in the morning to half past eight in the evening across a landscape seemingly as barren as the moon's; a few of the seamen who simply were unable to take another step were thrown into the baggage carts as the ragged procession went on without a stop. Halfway there the guard was changed, a detachment from Dartmoor taking over, and the march, which had been steadily uphill, now became a steep climb, still with no halt for rest or food. One of Benjamin Browne's messmates grew so fatigued on the march that he could no longer carry his overcoat and first tried to pay one of his companions to carry it for him, then even tried to give it away but could get no takers.

The prison itself loomed "like some huge monster" through the mist. An eighteen-foot-high wall of solid granite blocks, a half mile long, surrounded the whole prison, with three guardhouses spaced around it. The arriving prisoners entered through a heavily guarded main gate, passed in and out of a courtyard that held the houses and offices of the commandant and surgeon, then through another gate in a fifteen-foot-high stone inner wall into a second courtyard and parade ground where the barracks and hospital buildings were, then finally through a gate in a twelve-foot-high iron palisade topped with sharp spikes, within which lay the actual prison buildings, seven in all.

The prison barracks were three stories high, all built of granite as well, with single huge rooms on each floor slung with hammocks in tiers three high and a foot and half apart; the walls constantly dripped with moisture and the floors were icy, the only light coming from small windows covered with iron bars and wooden shutters that gave the prisoners the choice of pitch darkness or even more dampness from the cold and constant sea wind.[36]

Most of the arriving prisoners had a similar tale to tell of their miserable first night at Dartmoor, cast onto a bare stone floor without bedding or dry clothes, their meager possessions not yet arrived in the slow-moving carts. One old man "amused himself and annoyed all others by singing a line of one and a verse of another of all the old songs he could recollect from his earliest boyhood" through the night, recalled one American sailor, but none were inclined to sleep anyway as hunger, aching limbs, and the hard floor overcame even their utter exhaustion.[37]

The next morning a clerk accompanied by a squad of soldiers arrived to record the name, age, height, physical description, and place of birth of each of the prisoners (those records would incidentally provide one of the most complete demographic portraits of American seamen of the era) and then the men were turned out into the yard "to Receive hammocks beds and Blankets that was as full of Lice as the Devil is of Wickedness," Joseph Valpey, a Salem privateersman, recorded in his diary. Guards with muskets patrolled a walk along the inner stone wall, and between the inner wall and the iron paling was the "cachot," or "Black Hole," a windowless stone hut where prisoners were confined for punishment.

The bleakness of the physical setting simply stunned many of the Americans; they could not believe, they said, that such a spot existed in England; there was not a bush or tree, and even rabbits and birds seemed to find the moor too forsaken a place to live. The local people believed it was alive with demons and ghosts at night; none set forth from the nearby town of Princetown if it meant being caught on the moor after sundown. Valpey said he saw the sun three times in the first month he was there and not at all the next two months. The yellow woolen prison jackets and trousers the men were issued made the prisoners themselves the only colorful objects in a landscape of unremitting drabness.[38]

But many of the jailers were kind and apparently felt a kinship with the Americans, at least as compared with the thousands of Frenchmen they had had charge of for the previous eight years. One day Benjamin Browne was standing with a group of Americans who were poking some fun at the imperturbable turnkey of prison number 7 when a French prisoner, who had been taken in an American privateer, decided to join in the fun and, striking a comical pose, began razzing the jailer—"Jean Bull, Jean Bull, rote beef, rote beef, pomme de terre—God tam"—whereupon the Englishman calmly raised his fist and knocked the Frenchman down, to tumultuous cheers from the Americans. The jailer explained he "could take a joke from a Yankee, because they were cousins loik," but was not going to put up with it from "a frog-eating Frenchman."[39]

The Americans were left almost completely to themselves to organize the prison, maintain discipline, and fill their time as they chose. Most of the barracks elected committees, ran their own courts to punish offenders, and carried out merciless floggings on fellow prisoners caught stealing, skimming the fat off the mess's soup for their own use ("the grand Vizier's office at Constantinople is not more dangerous than a cook's at this prison," opined Waterhouse), or letting themselves become too filthy. Every day the local farmers and tradesmen were allowed to hold a market on the parade ground from 11:00 a.m. to 2:00 p.m., and vegetables, milk, meat, butter, tea, sugar, clothes, shoes, tobacco, soap, trinkets, and books were sold to supplement the prison-issued diet of beef, bread, barley, cabbage, onions, potatoes, and herring. In January 1814 the American government began supplying a small allowance to the prisoners through the American prisoners' agent in London, initially one and a half pence a day, raised in April to two and a half pence, doled out in the form of two 1-pound notes a month to each six-man mess; and many of the men also spent their time making ship models with beef bones for the spars and hulls and twisted human hair for the rigging, weaving baskets, fashioning tinware and shoes, even building violins. Others set up shops to resell in small quantities consignments of tobacco and dry goods they purchased from the town's grocers, or peddle ersatz coffee boiled up from burnt bread, or fried codfish and potato cakes known as plumgudgeon at a penny a piece, or a stew called freco whose predominant ingredient "by an almost infinite degree" was water, at two pennies a pint. George Little earned a shilling a day washing his fellow prisoners' clothes, at sixpence per dozen.[40] Adding to their surreal circumstances, many of the two thousand Americans thrown into British prisons after being released from impressment in the Royal Navy at the start of the war started receiving the pay and prize money they had been owed. In all, probably at least $10,000 a month was coming into the pockets of the Dartmoor prisoners and promptly placed into circulation in the flourishing prison economy.[41]

At times Dartmoor seemed more "a thriving village than a notorious and unhealthy prison," as one historian put it. One American prisoner observed that "Dartmoor prison was a world in miniature, with all its jealousies, envying and strife." There were informers and the type of corrosive doomsayers that afflict every prison and army barracks: "there is a set of busy-idlers among us," Waterhouse complained, "a sort of newsmongers, fault-finders, and predictors, who are continually bothering us with unsubstantial rumors."[42] An elaborate effort to stage a mass escape by tunneling under the walls was foiled in the summer of 1814 by an informer, who received his release and a passport to the United States for his betrayal. For forty nights the prisoners had dug for hours in shifts, hiding the excavated dirt each morning by plastering it on the walls and covering it with whitewash or waiting for a heavy rain and dumping it in the water channels that ran through the yard; they had reached as far as the inner wall when one morning a thousand soldiers marched into the yard and the colonel strode right to the hidden entrance of the tunnel, thoroughly inspected the excavation, and delivered an apparently unironic tribute to the prisoners for their industry before ordering his men to fill it in. Little said his fellow prisoners vowed to kill the man if they ever caught up with him back home.[43]

There was also a gang of toughs who styled themselves "the Rough Allies" who bullied and intimidated anyone they could, knocking over rivals' market stalls, running gaming tables and pawning operations, and denouncing as "Federalists" anyone who tried to stand in their way. But there was also a lending library of several hundred books in prison number 7, purchased by a prisoner with his discharge money from the British man-of-war he had served aboard as an impressed seaman; there was a regular school in prison number 1 offering classes at sixpence a week in mathematics, navigation, French, and Spanish; there was a music society and religious services.[44]

Nothing captured the contradictions of Dartmoor more than prison number 4, which housed the thousand or so black prisoners. They had been mixed in with the rest of the prisoners until spring 1814, when the white prisoners petitioned the commandant to have the blacks separated, claiming "it was impossible to prevent these fellows from stealing."[45] That may or may not have been so, but prison number 4 soon acquired a reputation as the most well-regulated of them all. Browne observed that "many of the most respectable prisoners preferred to mess in No. 4, on account of the superior order of that prison." It was presided over by a six-foot-three black man known as "King Dick," who strode through the barracks in a bearskin cap and summarily put down any challenges to his authority with a huge cudgel he always carried at his side. King Dick held a monopoly on the gambling and beer stalls in number 4, but also staged theatrical performances, having taken over the stock of costumes and scenery left by the departing French prisoners, charging the white prisoners sixpence to see *Othello* and *Romeo and*

Juliet. A protégé of King Dick's called Simon preached feverish sermons on Sundays and succeeded in converting two white prisoners to his brand of fervent Christianity; number 4 had several schools that were popular with the white prisoners as well. "In No 4 the Black's Prison I have spent considerable of my time, for in the 3rd story or Cock loft they have reading whriting Fenceing, Boxing Dancing & many other schools which is very diverting to a young Person," Nathaniel Pierce, a privateersman from Newburyport, wrote in his journal; "indeed there is more amusement in this Prisson than in all the rest of them."[46]

There was no cure for the tedium and homesickness, though, and as the year 1814 dragged on with no release in sight, the sameness of each day after day became the prominent feature in prisoners' journals: "have done nothing this day but set down in my birth and walk about the Prisson . . . more unpleasant weather . . . wet and disagreeable weather . . . made a tour through all the prisons . . . kept My house and Received Company as it came both good and bad . . . had no imployment to Day . . . This day comes in with heavy rains and blowing weather nothing worthy of remark has transpired . . . This day comes in with more Dartmoor weather . . . Evening I past in reading—Time goes Tegeous . . ." Boredom drove two prisoners to wager a pot of porter on the outcome of a louse race, but one had to forfeit when the entrant he had been carefully keeping in the collar of his shirt vanished the day of the race.[47] Joseph Valpey filled a notebook with poems and similarly tried to make light of their verminous conditions:

> In Yellow dress from head to foot
> Just like a swarm of Bee's
> From Morn to Night you'll see a sight
> of Hunting lice and flea's.

But most of his poems were becoming maudlin laments, of fortitude gone, hopes extinguished, loves forgotten;

> My country I fear has forgot me
> And I doubt if I see you again[48]

It would have taken a paragon of administrative efficiency, psychological subtlety, and keen leadership to have successfully commanded a prison of six thousand increasingly restless American prisoners, but the commandant of Dartmoor, like all the British prison commanders, was a broken-down and over-the-hill officer given the job because the Admiralty did not know what else to do with him. The following year Captain Thomas G. Shortland would become one of the most hated men of the war when the situation at Dartmoor spiraled out of control, hundreds died of disease, and then—months after the war's end— guards opened fire on prisoners in an incident that confirmed all the worst American beliefs about British tyranny and cruelty. But Short- land was probably less evil than inept, more overwhelmed with a responsibility he did not begin to know how to discharge than deliber- ately malicious; and at the start, at least, he seemed to be making an effort at being accommodating. He told an acquaintance that he never "read or heard of such a set of Devil-daring, God-provoking fellows, as these same Yankees; I had rather have the charge of five thousand Frenchmen than five hundred of these sons of liberty; and yet, I love the dogs better than I do the damn'd frog-eaters."[49]

For most of 1814 the brunt of the prisoners' resentments fell upon the American agent for prisoners in London, Reuben Beasley, another overwhelmed man. Beasley almost never replied to the many petitions and entreaties the prisoners sent him. He visited American prisoners only twice, both times seeming to recoil in physical horror not only at the conditions the men were being held in but from the men them- selves; and his cold and aloof exterior only reinforced the growing belief among those thousands of men so far from home for so long that they had become expendable pawns in a war without end.[50]

CHAPTER 10

Fortunes of War

FOR 1814 William Jones foresaw "a bloody and devastating summer and autumn."

On December 30, 1813, a British schooner under a flag of truce had sailed into Annapolis, bearing an offer from London of direct negotiations, and throughout the spring rumors of impending peace again began to swirl. But Jones was gloomy over the reports coming back from the peace commissioners. The British absolutely refused to budge on the matter of impressment, and with Napoleon's defeat and abdication on April 11, 1814, a triumphant Britain would be even less inclined to make any offers of conciliation. The American army's land campaign had gone nowhere since its victory at the Battle of the Thames in October 1813; in March 1814 Wilkinson was relieved of his command after one final attempt to advance into Quebec ended in disaster yet again, and the prospects of any decisive American triumph against British Canada seemed to have vanished for good.

"Britain will have changed her character if under the dominating and intoxicating circumstances of her fortune she should display any thing like a rational disposition," Jones wrote Madison. "My mind is made up for the worst and my consolation is that whatever disasters we may sustain, the vindictive desperation of the enemy will unite and purify the country and I trust enable us to sustain the conflict and preserve our institutions undefiled."[1]

Jones had continued his double duty as navy and Treasury secretary but wrote a friend that the burden had become "intolerable." He called himself "as perfect a galley slave as ever laboured at the oar." Congress was also growing impatient with the extraordinary indulgence Madison seemed to be granting Gallatin in holding his place open indefinitely. In

Blue, White, Red.		
	Foretopmast head. *7*	To call in all detached ships of the convoy. If any particular ship, the bearing flag will be shewn herewith.
	Maintopmast head. *8*	To bring to and lie by.
	Mizentopmast head, or Gaff end. *9*	The Commander of the convoy sees the signal that is made to him.
any colour Under the Flag.	Foretopmast head. *10*	To make sail after lying by.
	Maintopmast head. *11*	Ships astern to make more sail.
	Mizentopmast head, or Gaff end. *12*	Alter the course to port one point. *or as 18th Compass Signal,*
Yellow, Red, Yellow.		
	Foretopmast head. *13*	To signify that an enemy is in sight.
	Maintopmast head. *14*	For the convoy to continue in the same situation if lying to, or, if sailing, to continue on the same course and under the same sail, though the ships of war act otherwise.
	Mizentopmast head, or Gaff end. *15*	For a particular ship to give immediate assistance to ships making the signal of distress.
any colour Under the Flag.	Foretopmast head. *16*	For a particular ship to take in tow a ship of the convoy, which will be pointed out by the compass Signal
	Maintopmast head. *17*	For the convoy to close nearer together.
	Mizentopmast head, or Gaff end. *18*	For the ships of the convoy to be prepared to *hoist a Union Jack over their Ensigns,* when the Commander of the convoy *hoists a White Ensign.* In order to discover if there are any strange ships in the fleet.

When this flag is hoisted at any place, signifies that the Signal hoisted at the same time, is to be put in execution un above of dark; altho the Commodore may act otherwise, and still carry the Toplights, for the purpose of deceiving a Superior Enemy and leading them from the Merchant Ships.

Signals and instructions for ships under convoy (The National Archives, U.K.)

February 1814 Madison finally nominated a permanent replacement as Treasury secretary, but no one of knowledge and ability had been willing to touch the job, and even Jones would privately admit that the man who did accept it, Senator George Washington Campbell of Tennessee, was "entirely out of place in the Treasury."[2]

Federalist congressman Samuel Taggart of Massachusetts sarcastically suggested that the new secretary's initials stood for "*Government Wants Cash!*" Jones, in one of his final tasks as acting secretary, had given Congress an estimate of expenses and revenues for the coming year, and the numbers were staggering. The cost of the war, he projected, was going to rise 50 percent over what it had been for 1813, $24.5 million for the army and $7 million for the navy. Only two-thirds of the $6 million in taxes so reluctantly approved the previous summer were likely to be collected, leaving a shortfall of $29.35 million to be raised through loans. On top of that, Madison, frustrated over the continuing failure to halt the illegal trade with the enemy and still convinced that withholding American goods could strike a lethal blow to British power, had requested and received approval from Congress for the most draconian embargo yet: no ships were allowed to leave American ports carrying any cargoes, and even fishermen had to put up large bonds before being allowed to put to sea. The loss of customs duties cut even deeper into the small stream of government income.

New England bankers, overwhelmingly Federalists, refused to subscribe to the new Treasury loans unless the administration agreed to drop impressment as an issue in the peace negotiations, and they put pressure on major banks in New York to follow suit. When the Treasury offered a $10 million loan in April, half was finally taken by a single New York financier, Jacob Barker, but he defaulted on a third of his commitment. Eventually the Treasury was offering a discount rate of 20 percent and still could not fill more than half the new loans it tried to offer. With the government floating new loans just to pay the interest on old ones, the United States was teetering on the edge of bankruptcy.[3]

So was William Jones himself. He wrote a long letter to Madison in April, laying bare his dire financial straits and begging to be permitted to return to private life so he could begin paying off his debts and redeem his personal honor. He had never sought public office; he did not regret the pecuniary sacrifice it had entailed; but "circumstances over which I have no control" now required him to leave office as soon as the next meeting of Congress was concluded, he told Madison.

I trust you will believe me when I declare that nothing but the purest attachment to the independence honor and welfare of our happy country and its inestimable institutions, for the maintenance of which we are engaged in a war *more just and inevitable* than even that of our glorious revolution, could have prevailed upon me to accept the appointment with which you have honored me.

Every motive of private interest convenience prudence and settled social habits urged me to remain in private life; but the same indignant feelings which impelled me, not to the "tented field," but to the frozen untented heights of Princeton, Pluckamen, and Morristown, when but just turned of fifteen prompted the acceptance of my present situation, with the hope of doing some good until an honorable peace should again bless our land; beyond which I never contemplated to remain in office.

Apologizing for the "egotism" of his letter, he continued:

I am poor, Sir—nay more I am embarrassed by the result of my mercantile affairs, which the untoward events of the last five years have reversed from a state of approximate independence to an inability to meet my obligations.

His voyage to India in 1808 had left him with a debt that he now had given up hopes of clearing. Due to the embargoes and America's other self-imposed trade restrictions, he had had to sell his ship for half the $47,000 it had cost him; $90,000 worth of indigo cloth he had brought back from Calcutta had sat in a warehouse at considerable expense for three years, then shipped to Archangel, then eight hundred miles by land to St. Petersburg, then finally to Vienna seeking a market. He had just now learned that a few months ago his agent had disposed of it at a considerable loss. Jones's debts totaled more than $14,000, which even his generous salary of $4,500 a year as navy secretary was not going to begin to pay off. It was time for him to go, as soon as Madison would release him from his duties.[4]

ON JUNE 3, 1814, Madison summoned his cabinet to a meeting for the seventh to decide, in effect, the future of the entire war.

Besides whatever "dominating and intoxicating" effects victory over Napoleon had brought Britain, it had also thrown open the whole continent of Europe to British trade. That had undermined whatever coercive power the American economic embargo had left, and on March 31, Madison had taken even his own party by surprise when he announced that the restrictive system that had been his article of faith for a decade and a half of public office was a dead letter, and asked Congress for immediate repeal of the three-month-old embargo. Large majorities in both houses swiftly agreed. Jones had argued several weeks earlier that repealing the embargo was the only way to restore some confidence in the government's soundness in the financial community, but Madison's reversal on so key a matter of principle was a harbinger that another one of those long-thought-out Madisonian conclusions, brewing since the news first began to arrive of the victories of Britain and her allies against Napoleon the previous fall, was coming to a head. Simply, the war was no longer winnable on the terms that Madison had launched it, and the challenge now was not to win but to find an honorable, or even a face-saving, way out.[5]

William Jones's strategic thoughts had been running on a parallel course for some time. A few weeks before the June 7 meeting he laid out for Madison a strong case for going over to the purely defensive on land, essentially conceding that the conquest of Canada was impossible. While assuring the president that he would not see "the slightest relaxation" in the navy's attention to the lakes—everything that "could or can be done has and shall be done"—Jones pointed out that offensive military operations could not seriously be contemplated, given the enemy's secure positions at Kingston and on the Niagara peninsula. The stalemate on the ground meant that the war on the Canadian frontier was now "exclusively a naval contest" for control of the lakes, and the danger was that America was being drawn into a naval war of attrition it could never win.[6] The American navy was approaching a force of 10,000 officers and men, with more than 3,000 of them on the lakes. If the buildup on Lake Ontario continued as planned, the number of men required for service on the lakes would have to more than double, to 7,000, within the next year. Even with a 25 percent pay bonus for lake duty voted in April it was proving difficult to find enough men, and then the increasingly generous bounties Congress kept voting to try to fill the chronically undermanned army had cut deeply into navy recruiting across the board. The army was now offering a bonus of

$124 plus 320 acres of land to any man who agreed to enlist for the duration of the war; the most the navy could offer was a $48 bonus, and Jones reported that the frigate *Congress*, ready for sea at Portsmouth, New Hampshire, "has been waiting a long time only for 100 men and cannot get them."[7]

But the continuing British influx of men and ships to the lakes, Ontario especially, had a more ominous strategic consequence: to "tempt us to follow his example and thus free him from trouble on the ocean and expose our Atlantic frontier to his depredations," Jones warned. The British strength at Kingston meant that they could choose the "time circumstances and force," always controlling the all-important military factor of initiative in the war on that front. "Not so on the ocean where twenty of his ships cannot check the depredations of one of our ships."[8]

On the ocean, though, the American navy's presence was down to the sloops of war that Jones had championed a year before. The *Constitution* was bottled up in Boston after barely escaping capture by the British frigates *Junon* and *Tenedos* in a mad dash into Marblehead in April, during which the ship had thrown tons of water and supplies overboard. She had subsequently slipped into Salem and then down to the navy yard at Charlestown, but there were now at least two British seventy-fours and four frigates in Boston Bay, and until the winter storms once again returned to blow them off station and provide a welcome cover of fog and snow, the *Constitution*'s chances of getting to sea were nil. At Portsmouth the *Congress* was now in ordinary, her crew dispatched to Lake Ontario; the *President* was still trapped in New York, the *United States* and the *Macedonian* in New London, the *Constellation* in Norfolk.

More frustrating, there was now the certainty that none of the new American ships being built at Philadelphia, Baltimore, or Washington—including three of the six new sloops of war, all three of the new frigates, and one of the three seventy-fours—was ever going to make it past the tight British blockade of the Chesapeake and Delaware. The seventy-fours at Portsmouth and Boston were at least further along than their stranded sister ship in Philadelphia, despite continued tinkering with their plans by Hull and Bainbridge and continual sparring by the two commodores over sharing the limited supplies of live oak stockpiled at their two yards. At Jones's orders Hull had kept sending requests to Bainbridge—"For God's sake give me all the timber you can, especially futtocks"—and received only grudging replies. Hull visited in person in March 1814, eliciting a barbed observation from Bainbridge in a letter to Rodgers: "Hull is as fat and good natured as ever."[9]

On June 18, in a ceremony meant to coincide with the second anniversary of the declaration of the war, the *Independence,* America's first ship of the line, slid eighty feet down her ways at Charlestown Navy Yard, then stuck and came to a halt. Bainbridge blamed the humid weather and the failure of the tallow that had been applied to the ways to adhere to the unseasoned wood; the next day a master joiner working to free the ship was struck and killed by a falling block. After several more days' unsuccessful struggle, Bainbridge ordered boiling tallow and oil poured on the ways; and on June 22, before a crowd of twenty thousand, the ship splashed into the harbor. The fiasco gave critics of the war a great field to exercise their wit. Federalist newspapers widely reprinted the quip attributed to a gentleman in Philadelphia when he heard the news: "It was no wonder she *stuck.* . . . The war itself *sticks;* the recruiting *sticks;* the loan *sticks;* in short everything connected with the transaction of that illfated day *sticks;* and no wonder the 74 *sticks.*"[10]

But three of the new sloops of war had gotten to sea that spring of 1814. The *Frolic,* sailing from Boston in February, was captured after a thirteen-hour chase by a British frigate and schooner in which she threw everything including her guns overboard and almost made it; but the *Peacock,* which had slipped out of New York on March 12, more than made up for her fate by taking the British brig *Epervier* in a sharp action off Cape Canaveral on April 28, at a cost of two slight casualties to the British ship's twenty-three, including nine dead. The victory netted $200,000 in specie the *Epervier* was carrying; the prize was manned and successfully brought into Savannah, the *Peacock* daringly decoying away two British frigates that tried to intercept them and then outsailing the larger enemy ships and making it safely to port two days after her prize. On May 1 the newly completed *Wasp,* built at a private shipyard in Newburyport, put out of Portsmouth on a commerce-raiding foray to the British isles; on June 4 the *Peacock,* ready for sea again, headed forth on the same orders. "Our new Sloops of war are a fair class of Vessels and sail to admiration," Jones wrote Madison, determined to use his new weapons to their utmost effect.[11]

Jones's strategic logic notwithstanding, the cabinet meeting in Washington on June 7 approved four ambitious plans to press on with the land war on the Canadian front: an expedition to Lake Huron in the far west, a landing on the north side of Lake Erie and a thrust toward York, a movement north of Kingston to secure the St. Lawrence River, and an advance toward Montreal to cut off Kingston from Quebec.

Three weeks later, Secretary of State Monroe sent the American peace commissioners a secret instruction that spoke more truly of Madison's as-yet-undeclared, but unmistakable, decision to end the war: "On mature consideration, it has been decided, . . . you may omit any stipulation on the subject of impressment, if found indispensably necessary."[12]

NEARING DUSK on the evening of July 6, 1814, a small boat came tossing through the rough surf near the town of Babylon on the south side of Long Island, and when with some difficulty it reached shore, a man in the uniform of a navy captain scrambled onto the beach. He was promptly taken prisoner by the local militia, and the story he told sounded so incredible that at first it seemed only to confirm the militia officers' suspicions that they had captured a British officer on a secret mission. Only when their prisoner produced his U.S. naval commission identifying himself as Captain David Porter did they believe he was who he claimed to be. They gave him three cheers, fired a twenty-one-gun salute from a small swivel gun, and provided him a horse and carriage to take him to New York and an oxcart to haul the boat and his six-man crew, and the news of Porter's return spread like lightning.[13]

His story was indeed incredible, and the tumultuous welcome he and the 125 other surviving men of the *Essex* received upon their arrival in New York two days later was probably more a tribute to their seemingly miraculous reappearance after nearly two years at sea than to any laurels of victory they could claim. When Porter crossed the ferry from the Brooklyn Navy Yard to Manhattan, a cheering crowd unhitched the horses from his cab as soon as he stepped in and over his protests pulled him up and down the streets of the city to roaring cheers. "The return of this distinguished naval officer," the New York *Columbian* opined, ". . . has created in the hearts of his fellow citizens a kind of melancholy joy scarcely ever equaled on any similar occasion."[14]

The melancholy came from the immediate news that Porter brought with him: the *Essex* had been taken in a murderous battle in Valparaíso harbor on March 28, 1814, leaving 60 percent of her 255 men casualties, including 89 dead. The American frigate had received some fifty broadsides during the two-and-a-half-hour fight; her carpenter reported counting two hundred 18-pound shot lodged in her hull.[15]

But their entire odyssey since leaving New York at the very start of the war had been nothing short of Homeric, and their very survival seemed, as the *Columbian*'s editorial writer put it, testimony to the "incomparable zeal" of the American sailor, even in defeat. The full story would be told by Porter in his published memoir the following year, but many of the details were in the newspapers in days, both from information Porter provided the editors and from his lengthy report to Secretary Jones, which was immediately made public.

On leaving the Galápagos the previous fall, the *Essex* and her prizes had made an easy three weeks' sail due west, and on the morning of October 25, 1813, the flotilla stood into Taiohae Bay on the Marquesas island of Nuku Hiva. The water was crystalline and smooth, and as they opened the bay a long ribbon of white beach stretched before their eyes. Behind it several neat villages clustered amid the trees in the valleys between the mountains.

The wind seemed unfavorable for reaching moorings close to shore, so Porter anchored four miles away, just inside the mouth of the harbor, and shortly afterward a boat put out from the beach and headed their way. As it neared, Porter was astonished to see it that carried three white men, one of whom had clearly gone native, as he was dressed in nothing but a loincloth and his bared body was covered in ornate tattoos in the style of the local Polynesian tribes. He turned out to be an Englishman named Wilson who had arrived on the island under mysterious circumstances several years earlier and, having acquired the language, was able to interpret for Porter. The other two were Americans from a merchant ship that had left six of her crewmen on the island to collect a cargo of valuable sandalwood while the ship proceeded to Canton, but their ship had not returned and four of the men had since died; one of the two survivors was a navy midshipman on furlough, John M. Maury, who promptly requested to enter into service under Porter.

All along the hilltops they could see clusters of men, and Porter learned that the Ha'apa'a, a neighboring tribe that occupied the mountains, had been staging raids against the villages of the valley Te I'i tribe for several weeks, destroying their houses and killing their breadfruit trees. Porter ordered four boats armed and manned and went to shore at once to make a show of both force and friendship to the Te I'i. He passed out fishhooks and old iron barrel hoops, had the marines put on a demonstration of musketry, and made a short speech promising to be "as brethren" to the people of the valley and protect them against the mountain tribe.[16]

"When I wished to assemble my officers and men to return on board," Porter recounted, "I perceived they had formed with the female part of the community, an intimacy much closer than that which brotherly relationship gave them a title to; they had soon made themselves understood without any aid of interpreters; and had wandered to the houses or perhaps the bushes, which suited their purpose as well, to ratify their treaty, the negotiating of which neither cost them much time or trouble."[17]

Word spread instantly through the ship that the girls were as lovely and accommodating as the most vivid tales they had been spinning for weeks had imagined them to be, and the crew immediately volunteered to warp the ship in to her moorings rather than stand back out to sea and wait for more favorable wind to sail in, as Porter thought advisable. When the ship was brought in, the shore was completely lined with females waving in invitation, the sailors agog at the bare breasts and slender waists exposed by the girls' white robes slung and knotted over their shoulders. Porter found it impossible to hold out against the "many applications" to go ashore, and soon it was a "perfect Bedlam," with the girls and women coming back to the ship and staying through the whole night until put back ashore the following morning, "with whatever was given them by all such as had shared their favours."[18]

Porter was disarmingly frank about the sexual mores of the islanders and the predictable reaction of his crew, at sea for over a year—at least when he wrote the first edition of his published journal.

> Far from seeming to consider it an offence against modesty, they seemed to view it only as an accommodation to strangers who had claims on their hospitality. They attached no shame to a proceeding which they not only considered as natural, but as an innocent and harmless amusement, by which no one was injured. . . . With the common sailors and their girls, all was helter skelter, and promiscuous intercourse, every girl the wife of every man in the mess, and frequently of every man in the ship; each one from time to time took such as suited his fancy.[19]

Porter suggested that some of the officers formed more serious attachments but was circumspect about his own activities, only saying, "The women were inviting in their appearance, and practiced all the bewitching language of the eyes and features, which is so universally understood; and if an allowance can be made for a departure from prudential measures, it is when a handsome and sprightly girl of sixteen, whose almost every charm exposed to view, invites to follow her."[20]

Within a few days the Americans had established a small village on a plain behind the beach, overlooking the valleys, with a cooperage to build new water casks, a rope walk to spin new rigging, and an oven made from a load of bricks found aboard one of the prizes baking fresh bread for all the men every day. The *Essex* was careened down on the beach, and the local men were employed scraping the barnacles off her bottom with half coconut shells. Work went to four o'clock each afternoon, and then a quarter of the men were allowed to stay each night ashore. David Farragut recalled that he and the other youngsters were placed under the close supervision of the ship's chaplain but were allowed to wander about during the day on the island with the native boys their age, learning to swim, throw a spear, and walk on stilts. One day four thousand men from all the nearby villages appeared, and by nightfall they had constructed houses to replace all of the Americans' tents; there were dwellings for the officers, a cooper's shop, a sail loft, a sick bay, a guardhouse.[21]

The entire population of Nuku Hiva was about forty thousand, divided among three dozen often warring tribes. Porter had sent the Ha'apa'a a message offering friendship and offering to buy their hogs and fruit, but warning he would "send a body of men to chastise them" if they did not cease their raids on the valley. That had elicited only a derisive response that the Americans were clearly afraid to fight, since all they did was make threats. Lieutenant Downes then led a detachment of forty sailors and marines from the *Essex Junior* followed by a large body of the Te I'i up the mountain. There they were met by four thousand Ha'apa'a warriors, who launched a volley of stones and spears, then a barrage of contemptuous scoffs, and then "exposed their posteriors to them." Realizing that their entire position on the island was now in the balance, Downes called on his men to charge; with three cheers they stormed the wooden fortress at the top of a hill where the enemy warriors had retreated, and rushing through another volley of spears and stones, they shot dead five of the natives at point-blank range. At that the battle was over.[22]

Almost immediately the Americans were plunged into an even larger war with the most aggressive tribe on the island, the Taipi, who were even more contemptuous of Porter's offers of peaceful trade and told him if he was so powerful he would obviously just come and take their hogs; the fact that he did not obviously proved that he was unable to. This time Porter himself led a small expedition and was ambushed in an attack that he was lucky to escape from with his life; Downes's leg was shattered by a stone, and the men beat a hasty retreat. "Perfectly sick of bush fighting," Porter again tried to get the Taipi to back down by pointing out the superiority of his force and weapons, but the Taipi sent word back that they were unimpressed by the Americans' muskets, which "frequently missed fire, rarely killed, and the wounds they occasioned were not as painful as those of a spear or stone." Only after Porter led two hundred men on a three-day expedition into the Taipi strongholds did the tribe at last sue for peace, and Porter told them because of the trouble they had caused him they would have to pay four hundred hogs as an indemnity. They agreed.[23]

By December 9, 1813, the repairs of the *Essex* were complete and a full stock of wood and water was aboard, the decks crowded with hogs and heaps of bananas and dried coconuts. Porter had ordered the crew to remain aboard the last few days preparing the ship for sea, and the men were predictably "restless, discontented, and unhappy."

One of the *Essex*'s men, while visiting the *Essex Junior* on a Sunday, boasted that they were going to refuse to weigh anchor when the order was given. "I was willing to let them ease their minds by a little grumbling," Porter recalled, ". . . but a threat of this kind was carrying matters rather too far." The next morning he mustered all the men and strode onto the deck, his cutlass in his hand, which he laid on the capstan and, as David Farragut recalled, "shaking with anger, addressed the crew."

"All of you who are in favor of weighing the anchor when I give the order, pass over to the starboard side."

To a man they all did, including the sailor Porter knew had been shooting his mouth off on the *Essex Junior*, a man named Robert White. Porter walked right up to him and demanded what he was doing on the starboard side. The man, trembling, tried to deny he had ever uttered any insubordinate words, causing Porter to reply, "You lie, you scoundrel!" and told him he had better run for his life. White leapt over the starboard gangway, was picked up by a passing canoe, and made for shore. Porter then turned back to the assembled men and told them that before he would ever let a mutiny succeed on his ship he would put a match to the magazine "and blow us all to hell." With that he gave the order to weigh, and as the fiddle struck up "The Girl I Left Behind Me," the anchor "fairly flew to the bows," Farragut recalled, and the *Essex* and the *Essex Junior* made sail and put out to sea.[24]

PORTER'S DESTINATION was Valparaíso, his intent another one of those tests of honor that had already cost the American navy far too much. Since September, Porter had known that the British squadron under the command of Captain James Hillyar was on his trail, and Porter was determined to "bring them to action if I could meet them on nearly equal terms," as he would later explain in his official report to Secretary Jones. "I had done all the injury that could be done the British commerce in the Pacific, and still hoped to signalize my cruize by something more splendid before leaving that sea." Believing that Hillyar "would seek me at Valparaiso as the most likely place to find me," that was where he accordingly would go.[25]

The *Essex* arrived there on February 3, 1814, and a few nights later Porter gave a ball for the citizens of the town aboard the ship. Early the next morning the *Essex Junior* signaled from the end of the harbor that two enemy vessels were in sight. At eight o'clock the British warships *Phoebe* and *Cherub* sailed into the harbor and began at once what would prove to be a two-month-long test of nerves as each captain tried the limits of the other's willingness to respect the neutrality of the port. The *Phoebe* made straight for the *Essex* and luffed up on her starboard bow, coming within ten or fifteen feet. The two captains knew each other from the Mediterranean: Porter had been a frequent guest of Hillyar and his family at Gibraltar.

"Captain Hillyar's compliments to Captain Porter, and hopes he is well," the English captain called from the quarterdeck.

"Very well, I thank you," Porter answered, "but I hope you will not come too near, for fear some accident might take place which would be disagreeable to you."

The *Essex* had been at quarters for some time, the deck crowded with boarders armed with cutlasses and a pair of pistols apiece, the gun crews at their stations with the smoke wafting from their slow matches, and at one gun an American—who Farragut said was still recovering from the revelries of the night before—thought he saw his opposing number on the English ship smirking at him through the gunport. "I'll stop your making faces," the American muttered, and he was just about to touch off his gun when the lieutenant caught the movement out of the corner of his eye and knocked him to the deck. "Had that gun been fired, I am convinced that the *Phoebe* would have been ours," Farragut would later write.

Above decks the conversation between the captains had quickly dropped the pretense of politeness. Hillyar innocently declared that if his ship did fall on board of Porter's it would only be by accident.

"You have no business where you are," Porter called back. "If you touch a rope-yarn of this ship, I shall board instantly."

For a few incredibly tense moments the standoff continued. Porter too clearly had his later regrets that he did not seize the opportunity then and there, especially as Hillyar's near approach was such a flagrantly hostile move that it could have offered the justification of self-defense for an attack by the *Essex*. "The temptation was great," Porter wrote, but Hillyar raised both his hands, apologized profusely, and said he had had no intention of running his jibboom across the *Essex*'s forecastle. The *Phoebe* drifted on past, anchoring a half mile away.[26]

Over the following days the officers and crews of both ships frequently saw one another ashore and even paid some friendly calls. Porter kept trying to goad Hillyar into challenging him to a one-on-one fight between the two frigates, but Hillyar replied that he was not prepared to send away the *Cherub* and abandon the advantage of superior force, and he intended to keep the *Essex* blockaded in the harbor. The Americans launched a campaign of sarcastic provocations; every night the *Essex*'s men serenaded the British ships with choruses of "Yankee Doodle" adapted with new lyrics of "nautical sarcasms," and every day a flag flew from the masthead with the motto "Free Trade and Sailors' Rights." The British tried to reply in kind. Porter observed, "The songs from the Cherub were better sung, but those of the Essex were more witty, and more to the point." The *Phoebe*'s attempt to answer "Free Trade and Sailors' Rights" with its own pithy saying similarly fell flat: "God and Country; British Sailors' Best Rights; Traitors Offend Both." A subsequent taunting challenge from the American sailors, again proposing that they send the *Cherub* away and fight it out ship to ship, was addressed to "their oppressed brother tars, on board the ship whose motto is too tedious to mention."[27]

But time was clearly on the British captain's side. Porter had received word that the sloop *Raccoon,* which had been dispatched to attack the American fur-trapping station on the Columbia River in Oregon, would soon arrive in Valparaíso and that three other British frigates were on their way to the Pacific to join the pursuit of him as well. On March 28, 1814, with a strong wind blowing from the south directly out to the sea, the larboard anchor cable on the *Essex* parted and her starboard anchor dragged free, and Porter decided to make sail at once and try to make good his escape. The *Essex* raced for the sea and was on the verge of getting to windward of the two British ships, squeezing between them and the westward edge of the harbor's mouth, when a squall struck and carried away the main topmast, plunging the men aloft into the sea, where they drowned.

The wind would not let Porter get back to the anchorage, but he sailed across the harbor's mouth and anchored within a pistol shot of the shore at the eastern edge. The *Essex* now had only Chilean neutrality to protect her; she was crippled and in a vulnerable position, and Hillyar's intentions were soon unmistakable. The *Phoebe* came up under the American ship's stern, the *Cherub* off her bow, and a little before 4:00 p.m. opened up a merciless fire, both keeping out of range of the *Essex*'s carronades. Three times during the fight the *Essex*'s men managed to get a spring attached to the anchor, a line running from the anchor cable to the capstan so that the ship could be hauled around to get her broadside to bear; each time the line was shot away by enemy fire. At one point Hillyar's first lieutenant, William Ingram, protested that it was "deliberate murder" to lay off and shoot at an enemy ship "like a target" when she was unable to return fire, but Hillyar brushed him aside and said he had his orders and was determined not to risk anything to chance.[28] It was an absolute bloodbath aboard the *Essex*. The cockpit, steerage, wardroom, and berth deck were overflowing with wounded, and nearly all of the *Essex*'s guns were out of action. One gun's crew had been manned three times; each time the entire crew was killed, fifteen men in all. At 6:20 p.m. Porter ordered the colors hauled down.

David Farragut's only injury was when a two-hundred-pound sailor ahead of him on the ladder was struck in the face by an eighteen-pound shot and fell on top of him, covering him with blood and gore and knocking him unconscious for a few moments, but leaving him no more than badly bruised. He worked through the night helping the surgeons tend to the rows upon rows of wounded and the next morning was brought aboard the *Phoebe* and ushered into the steerage. Shortly afterward he was roused from the tears of despair that had finally engulfed him when he saw a passing boy of the *Phoebe*'s crew with a pig under his arm and recognized it as his own pet pig, Murphy. Farragut demanded it back; the British sailor claimed it as a prize; "we usually respect private property," Farragut retorted. Some of the British sailors then suggested that the boys wrestle for it. Farragut agreed, quickly trounced his opponent, and emerged with the pig and the "feeling I had in some degree wiped off the disgrace of our capture." Shortly afterward Farragut was invited to join the two captains for breakfast in Hillyar's cabin, but his "heart was too full" to eat anything. When Hillyar kindly said to him, "Never mind my little fellow, it will be your turn next perhaps," Farragut quickly excused himself and left the cabin "to keep from crying in his presence."[29]

Hillyar agreed to let the survivors return to America on parole in the *Essex Junior*, and provided them a passport allowing them to pass unmolested through the blockading squadrons. On leaving, Porter thanked Hillyar for his consideration but said he would be equally frank in telling the world how Hillyar had attacked him in neutral waters. Hillyar looked stricken, grasped Porter by the hand, and said, "My dear Porter, you know not the responsibility that hung over me, with respect to your ship. Perhaps my life depended on my taking her."[30]

The *Essex Junior* set sail April 27. On July 5, approaching Sandy Hook, the ship was boarded by the British razee *Saturn*. Her captain looked at the passport, said Hillyar "had no right to make such an arrangement," and ordered the *Essex Junior* to remain under his lee for the night. Porter replied that in that case the conditions of his parole had been violated; he considered himself a prisoner of war and thus "at liberty to effect my escape if I can." The next morning he had the whale boat manned and armed and ordered the *Essex Junior* to keep between the *Saturn* and the boat as he pulled off for the shore sixty miles away, quickly disappearing into a fog bank. The *Essex Junior* was finally allowed to proceed to New York with the rest of the crew, and after a subsequent investigation both American and British authorities agreed that the Americans had been discharged from their parole as a result of the British officer's actions in detaining them.[31]

Back at Nuku Hiva, Porter had left his marine lieutenant, John M. Gamble, with the three remaining prize vessels and twenty officers and men with orders to finish preparing the ships for sea. Gamble would have an even longer and more amazing odyssey. The Americans' situation on the island began to deteriorate almost immediately. Several men deserted, joining up with Robert White, the mutinous sailor Porter had chased off the *Essex* on his departure. There were six English prisoners as well under Gamble's charge, and on May 7, Gamble was aboard the *Seringapatam* when he was suddenly grabbed and thrown to the deck, had his hands and leg tied, and was dragged into the cabin below, where a few minutes later he was joined by his two midshipmen. One of the mutineers accidentally shot Gamble in the ankle with his pistol. Later that night they put the officers into a leaky boat, and the *Seringapatam* sailed off under English colors.

Ashore things were clearly going wrong simultaneously. Possibly instigated by the Englishman-gone-native Wilson, and certainly emboldened by the Americans' sudden weakness, the once friendly Te I'i, whom Porter had praised for never having once stolen a thing from the Americans, had begun plundering the camp. When Gamble sent all his remaining hands to retrieve the items still left on shore, they were attacked by the islanders, and Midshipman William Feltus and three others were massacred. The survivors clambered into the boat and rowed for the *Sir Andrew Hammond,* where Gamble, still in excruciating pain from his bullet wound, watched in horror as canoes put off from every direction trying to cut off the fleeing boat. Hopping on one foot from gun to gun, he fired at the approaching natives with rounds of canister and grape that had already been loaded and managed to drive off the attack. Meanwhile hundreds of other Te I'i tribesmen were swarming over the American encampment, pulling down the houses. Down to a crew of eight, five of them ill or injured, Gamble ordered the *Greenwich* set on fire, then cut his cables and, with the jib and spanker sails bent, got the *Sir Andrew Hammond* under way.

Without charts and without enough men to work the ship to windward, Gamble reached the Hawaiian Islands three weeks later, took on provisions, and was heading for Valparaíso still hoping to rendezvous with Porter when he was captured by the *Cherub.* The British captain kept the Americans in tight confinement on board his ship for five months, the whole way to Rio de Janeiro. Gamble arrived home on August 28, 1815, the end of a voyage that had lasted longer than the entire war.[32]

ON ASSUMING the North American command, Admiral Cochrane had wasted no time declaring his intention to wage a more uncompromising brand of warfare than his predecessor had pursued. Cochrane had arrived in Bermuda on March 6, 1814, but Warren had brusquely rebuffed Cochrane's proposal that he take charge at once; perhaps still thinking of the prize money that was due him as long as he retained the position of commander in chief, Warren icily informed his successor that he "must decline entering into any discussion" of an early transfer and would "strictly conform to the Orders of my Lords Commissioners of the Admiralty, as to the delivering over to you the Command of His Majesty's Ships upon this Station . . . and therefore am to inform you that I shall not be prepared to place you in the Command thereof until April 1."[33]

So Cochrane bided his time but was clearly chafing to get into the fight. The day after taking charge, he issued a proclamation opening a new front in the reinvigorated campaign he was preparing to launch along the Chesapeake with the return of summer, and the expected arrival of considerable reinforcements in men and ships.

> WHEREAS it has been represented to me, that many Persons now resident in the UNITED STATES, have expressed a desire to withdraw therefrom, . . .
> *This is therefore to Give Notice,*
>   That all those who may be disposed to emigrate from the UNITED STATES will, with their Families, be received on board of His Majesty's Ships and Vessels of War, or at the Military Posts that may be established, upon or near the Coast of the UNITED STATES, when they will have their choice of either entering into His Majesty's Sea or Land Forces, or of being sent as FREE Settlers to the British Possessions in North America or the West Indies, where they will meet with all due encouragement.[34]

The notice nowhere specifically mentioned "slaves," but it did not need to: everyone knew who it was aimed at. Cochrane had a thousand copies printed up and sent them to Cockburn, who had returned to Lynnhaven Bay a few weeks earlier to begin reconnoitering and prepare a base of operations for the summer campaign. Cochrane optimistically thought he might be getting as many as fifteen thousand troops from France plus several regiments from England and Ireland. In the meantime, Cockburn established a base at Tangier Island, located almost in the middle of the Chesapeake Bay, to receive runaway slaves and begin training them for the several companies of

"Colonial Marines" he planned to organize. Cochrane also sent him £2,000 for "contingent expenses": both to buy information and to try to kidnap "Persons of Political Interest" connected to the Republican party, to be held as hostages.

While awaiting the promised reinforcements, Cockburn began looking for likely targets he could raid with the 1,500 or so men he currently had available. "You are at perfect liberty as soon as you can muster a Sufficient force, to act with the utmost Hostility against the shores of the United States," Cochrane had instructed him, pointing to American actions as justification for harsh retaliation:

> Their Government authorizes & directs a most destructive War
> to be carried on against our Commerce & we have no means of
> retaliating but on shore, where they must be made to feel in their
> Property, what our Merchants do in having their Ships destroyed
> at Sea; & taught to know that they are at the mercy of an
> invading foe. . . . Their Sea Port Towns laid in Ashes & the
> Country wasted will be some sort of a retaliation for their savage
> Conduct in Canada.[35]

Cochrane specifically suggested that he choose targets that would best facilitate the exodus of more slaves: "Let the Landings you may make be more for the protection of the desertion of the Black Population than with a view to any other advantage, the force you have is too Small to accomplish an object of magnitude—the great point to be attained is the cordial Support of the Black population with them properly armed & backed with 20,000 British Troops, Mr. Maddison will be hurled from his Throne."[36]

Hundreds of slaves flocked to Tangier through the spring and summer of 1814. Although they had had time to receive only a few weeks' training in firearms, Cockburn reported they fought extremely well in several small skirmishes. Unlike the regular troops, there was scarcely any worry of them deserting; they knew the country well; and the fear that armed black men had already induced among the Virginia and Maryland militia units had significant shock value in itself: "They expect Blacky will have no mercy on them and they know that he understands bush fighting and the *locality* of the *Woods* as well as themselves." In one well-publicized incident that sent tremors through slaveholders along the Chesapeake, an escaped slave led a British force to his former master's home, and while the troops looted the plantation, the ex-slave, armed with a pistol and sword, sat up through the night verbally tormenting his former master. At dawn the troops withdrew, taking the rest of the plantation's slaves with them.

Cockburn reported after one early raid by his black marines, "They have induced me to alter the bad opinion I had of the whole of their Race & I now really believe these we are training, will neither shew want of Zeal or Courage when employed by us in attacking *their old Masters.*" In late May 1814 the Colonial Marines had displayed notable courage during an attack on a militia battery at Pungoteague, near Tangier Island on Virginia's Eastern Shore: one of the black soldiers was shot and died instantly, but, Cockburn said, "it did not daunt or check the others in the least but on the contrary animated them to seek revenge."[37]

Cochrane's plans for revenge were on a grander scale, however. In July 1814 he wrote Lord Melville laying out options for the destruction of one of "the principal Towns of America," Boston, New York, Philadelphia, Baltimore, Washington, Annapolis, Richmond, and Norfolk among them. He issued sterner and sterner public directives to his commanders to "destroy & lay waste such Towns and Districts upon the Coast as you may find assailable." While doing so, he added, they should "take every opportunity of explaining to the people" that they would have to look to their own government for compensation, since the British actions were merely "retributory justice" for the "wanton & unjustifiable outrages on the unoffending Inhabitants" of Upper Canada. Yet Cochrane vacillated for weeks over where the brunt of the British sword should fall. He still had received no official word on how many troops would arrive or when. Croker had warily distanced himself from any responsibility for the direction of the land campaign, telling Cochrane, "Their Lordships entrust to your judgment the choice of the objects on which you may employ this Force," and advising only that he not advance too far inland as to risk having his line of retreat cut, and to give preference to "crippling the Enemy's naval Force" should such an opportunity present itself.[38]

Only in mid-July did the first even semi-official word reach Cochrane in Bermuda about the size of the army. After months of buildup in British newspapers, which had been reporting that a vast invasion force was assembling, it must have scarcely seemed believable that only a few thousand troops in the end were on the way. But the news was confirmed the last week of July when two convoys arrived in Bermuda carrying four thousand British infantry. They and a few hundred marines would be all the force available.

Cochrane still hesitated, even toying with the idea of abandoning a campaign on the Chesapeake altogether given the approach of the "sickly season." He considered instead striking New Hampshire to destroy the ship of the line under construction at Portsmouth, or perhaps Rhode Island. But Cockburn was strongly urging an attack on Washington, and a letter from him that arrived in Bermuda on July 25 aboard a schooner bearing dispatches finally persuaded the commander in chief. On August 1 Cochrane sailed for the Chesapeake with his invasion force: Washington it would be.

On August 18, 1814, a huge British flotilla entered the Patuxent River: four ships of the line, seven frigates, seven transports, and several brigs or schooners. The next day the British force of 4,500 men, led by Major General Robert Ross, a veteran of the Peninsula campaign, accompanied by Admiral Cockburn, landed at Benedict, Maryland. It was thirty-five miles from Washington on a good road, and as one of Cockburn's captains had predicted a few weeks earlier, the troops met virtually no opposition for the first twenty miles. "Jonathan is so confounded," Captain Joseph Nourse had written Cockburn, "that he does not know when or where to look for us, and I do believe it would require little force to burn Washington." He added: "I hope soon to put the first torch to it myself."

Despite weeks of warning, the defense of the capital city was in utter disarray. Another one of the many inexperienced political generals who were the bane of the United States army was in charge: Brigadier General William Winder put on an air of being knowledgeable about military matters but in fact his major qualification for office was being the nephew of the Federalist governor of Maryland, whose cooperation Madison desperately needed. Winder had spent weeks conducting a personal reconnaissance of the approaches to Washington while scarcely more than a few hundred state militia answered a summons Madison had issued on July 1 for 100,000 troops to defend the city.[39] For much of the summer the flotilla of rowed barges that Joshua Barney had organized had kept up a harassing campaign against British naval forces in the lower Patuxent, to the point that it had become a major thorn in Cockburn's side. But on August 20 Jones sent an urgent order to Barney to fall back, destroy his boats, and dispatch his 400 flotillamen for the defense of Washington. As the British troops marched toward Upper Marlboro on August 22, they heard the booms in the distance of Barney's flotilla boats blowing up. Barney's men arrived at the navy yard in southeast Washington soon afterward.[40]

Winder at last made a decision to organize a stand at Bladensburg, just northeast of Washington, with the Eastern Branch forming a natural barrier ahead of him. He placed the defenders in three lines, but the disposition was all wrong; even a Maryland militia lieutenant saw at a glance that the troops were far too scattered. On the morning of August 24, Barney received orders from Winder to deploy his flotillamen to defend the bridge in Washington across the Eastern Branch and blow it up if the British attempted to cross there; but Jones and Madison soon arrived at the scene, and as Jones noted, it was a ridiculous misallocation of force: the task of blowing up the bridge "could as well be done by half a dozen men, as by five hundred." Madison personally ordered Barney's force to head for Bladensburg and join the defense there. Barney's flotillamen, plus 120 marines from the Washington barracks, took off "in *a trot*," hauling three 12-pounder and two 18-pounder naval guns that Jones had earlier ordered mounted on carriages as part of the preparations to defend the yard.

Arriving at Bladensburg, they were placed in the third line, but the position Winder had chosen was too far back to effectively support the second line. Secretary of State Monroe, who chose that unfortunate moment to play general, having first volunteered his services as a cavalry scout and galloping about the countryside, showed up at Bladensburg just in time to make matters worse by repositioning the second line, on his own orders, so that it was incapable of supporting the first. Some seven thousand militia had arrived at last, but most had been marching without rest or food.

At 1:00 p.m. on August 24 the first British troops appeared on the other side of the river, and by 4:00 p.m. the battle was over and the British were marching on to Washington and the American forces were in headlong flight. Only Barney's men had held their line, pouring a murderous fire of grape and canister into the oncoming redcoats until the British were already completely in their rear. Barney was shot in the thigh and was pouring blood. His horse was killed. Cockburn, learning who the wounded man was, personally came up to him and spoke a few polite words and ordered a British surgeon to tend to his wounds at once.[41]

When word had arrived of the British invasion force entering the Patuxent, William Jones had ordered Rodgers and Porter from New York to head south to assist in the defense of Baltimore and Washington, but events followed far too swiftly. At the Washington Navy Yard, the chief clerk, Mordecai Booth, had spent days frantically scouring the city trying to commandeer wagons to remove the gunpowder from the yard, but there were hardly any to be found amid the mass exodus of government officers and citizens fleeing with public records and personal belongings. On the evening of the twenty-fourth Booth had been stricken by the sight of the thousands of American troops in full retreat past the yard: "Oh! *my Country*—And I blush Sir! to tell you—I saw the Commons Covered with the fugitive Soldiery of our Army—running, hobbling, Creeping & appearently panick struck." With all of the navy yard's seamen, marines, and even mechanics and laborers pressed into service in Winder's army, the yard was defenseless. Jones solemnly approved the commandant's order to set fire to the naval stores—and, with even greater pain, the newly completed sloop of war *Argus* and the nearly completed frigate *Columbia*. Shops, timber, casks of provisions, small arms, cordage, paint, tar all went up in the flames. The total loss was more than a half million dollars.[42]

Jones found his family in northwest Washington, then joined Madison across the Potomac in Virginia, where he had fled with other government officials. Cockburn, arriving on the streets of the city not long after, conspicuous astride a white horse with his sunburned face and rusty gold-laced hat, made joking inquiries of the townspeople about President Madison's whereabouts and personally supervised troops pulling down the building that housed the offices of the *National Intelligencer* newspaper, telling them to "destroy all the C's so they can't abuse my name." Cockburn then led a detachment into the White House, picked up a few souvenirs, and set the building ablaze. Other troops burned the war and navy department offices, the Treasury, and the Capitol before the British forces withdrew the way they had come and reembarked on their ships to return down the Patuxent to the Chesapeake Bay.[43]

Another squadron of British ships had meanwhile ascended the Potomac, and Jones, who had returned to Washington on August 27 with the rest of the cabinet in the wake of the British departure, was furious when he saw the abject terms of surrender the town of Alexandria had agreed to. Offering no resistance, town officials had meekly acceded to a huge demand for tribute, including all the produce and merchandise in the town. Rodgers, Porter, and Commodore Oliver Hazard Perry had now arrived in Washington, and Jones ordered them to attack the British naval force as it sailed back down the Potomac; with fire ships and artillery erected on the heights, they succeeded in delaying, though not stopping, the British force's escape.[44]

Jones was sending out a constant stream of orders to the naval detachments in the region, receiving and answering two or three express dispatches in the middle of each night. Eleanor had gone on to Baltimore, and on the way she passed through Bladensburg and was deeply affected by the scene of the battleground. On September 1 she wrote her husband of her safe arrival and her continuing fears for his safety—and for his honor, as the backlash of public opinion turned on the administration over the humiliation of the British attack.

> My Dear Husband,
>   We have separated under such distressing circumstances that I know not what evil awaits me—Now I can indulge a hope of being soon relieved from the most awful apprehensions of your safety.
>   . . . A view of the ground where the Battle was fought, and the Graves of the fallen Men, The cannon near which Com^e Barney lost his horse and where they buried it excited the most painful sensations, particularly on seeing the foot of one above the earth. Passing the hospitals in Bladensburgh we saw the wounded, Americans, and British, and preparations to bury an English soldier just expired—On the Road we met our heroes of the Navy with their crews, the Marines, Cavalry, and 800 regulars . . .
>   May the Almighty guard you
>   in the hour of danger prays
>   your Aff^te Wife
>   Eleanor Jones[45]

Admiral Cochrane wrote Melville full of high spirits over "the brilliant success" of the raid on the enemy capital, though he expressed concern that General Ross did not fully share his view that Baltimore, as "the most democratic town . . . ought to be laid in Ashes" next. Ross, he feared, was inclined to be too lenient on the Americans: "When he is better acquainted with the American Character he will possibly see as I do that like Spaniels they must be treated with great severity before you ever make them tractable."[46]

The American navy's delaying action on the Potomac bought some valuable days to prepare the defenses of Baltimore, where all signs pointed the British would indeed strike next. Here the American forces acquitted themselves far better, making amends for the debacle at Bladensburg by inflicting heavy British casualties even as they fell back behind the city's prepared defensive works in the attack that began September 12. During the initial assault an American sharpshooter killed Ross: after that the British gave no quarter to any American snipers. But the attack failed, as did the bombardment of Fort McHenry in Baltimore harbor by mortars and Congreve rockets on the night of September 13–14, an event witnessed by Francis Scott Key and immortalized in the words he began to set down the following morning in a poem titled "Defence of Fort McHenry," subsequently published under the title of its most memorable phrase: "The Star-Spangled Banner." William Jones sent Eleanor, two weeks later, a copy of the "beautiful little effusion written by Mr F. Key a respectable young lawyer of talents residing in Georgetown . . . He is a Federalist but with such Federalists I can have but a common feeling."

The British forces again withdrew to the Chesapeake, their next target a matter of intense speculation and anxiety. In the midst of everything else Jones was working "from day dawn to midnight" on a proposal for a reorganization of the Navy Department to leave to his successor and trying to wrap up his personal affairs in Washington. He had told only four congressmen of his final decision to leave office by December 1, but "people however begin 'to smell a mouse' as my home is given up," he wrote Eleanor. "May God preserve all things right at least till after the 1st of December," Jones continued. "Though all is well and my reputation high I feel as if I was standing upon gun powder with a slow match near it. Public expectation is so extravagant, opinion so capricious, and prejudice and ignorance so predominant, that millions would not tempt me to stay one year longer. . . . Though I am labouring to smooth the way for my successor I commiserate him with all my heart whoever he may be I predict his ruin if the war continues."[47]

He told her he planned to sell either his brown riding horse or their pair of grays and the carriage to begin making good on his burden of personal debt:

After all I shall return to your arms a beggar with the proceeds of our surplus furniture carriage and horses and a few dollars scraped from the late savings in all perhaps sufficient to support us 12 or 18 months in retired economy. Well never mind it, I shall return with a pure heart and peace of mind as cheerful as a lark and with sufficient common sense to keep out of the snares of public life.

He added a lament to his old dog, whose death he had just received news of. "Alas, poor Bibo! I fear he died a misanthrope for man was very unkind to him. He was a dog without guile, he loved and was faithful to his friends—would that man could say as much."[48]

ADMIRAL COCHRANE afterward tried to claim that the attack on Baltimore had been intended all along only as a "demonstration" and then blamed Ross, who was no longer around to defend himself, for having persuaded him against his better judgment to approve the failed operation.[49]

There was a lot of blame-shifting going on among the British leadership over the direction the war was taking. The new American sloops of war *Peacock* and *Wasp* had been on a rampage through the North Atlantic since setting out in the spring, leaving British merchants sputtering with outrage they directed almost entirely against their own government. On July 8, 1814, the *Wasp* arrived at the French port of L'Orient, having burned or scuttled seven prizes from the Irish coast to the mouth of the English Channel; the American ship had also destroyed the British navy brig *Reindeer* in a brief but furious action on June 28 that left the British captain's clerk the only surviving officer available to give the surrender to the American boarders that came swarming over her bloody decks nineteen minutes after the shooting began.

After refitting in L'Orient—over the indignant protests of the British government and the undisguised pleasure of the local French populace—the *Wasp* took seven more prizes while defeating another Royal Navy brig, the *Avon*, on September 1, before disappearing forever under unknown circumstances after last being seen near the Cape Verde Islands on October 9.

While the *Wasp* was refitting, the *Peacock* arrived to maraud through

British home waters in July and August, taking fourteen prizes along the coasts of Ireland and the Shetlands. The summer of 1814 also brought a number of larger and more daring American privateers into British home waters; the largest of them were ship-rigged vessels almost as well armed and well manned as sloops of war like the American navy's *Wasp* and *Peacock,* and they too set to plundering with an impunity that astonished the British merchants. The *Chasseur* of Baltimore carried sixteen long twelve-pounders and a crew of one hundred and haunted the English Channel for months, taking at least fifteen prizes while eluding the frigates and brigs sent after her. Her captain, Thomas Boyle, at one point taunted the British by sending to London on a vessel he had released as a cartel his own sarcastic version of the grandiloquent blockade declarations issued by the Royal Navy's commanders in American waters:

PROCLAMATION

Whereas it has become customary with the Admirals of Great Britain, commanding small forces on the coast of the United States, particularly with Sir John Borlase Warren and Sir Alexander Cochrane, to declare all the coast of the said United States in a state of strict and rigorous blockade, without possessing the power to justify such a declaration, or stationing an adequate force to maintain said blockade,

I do, therefore, by virtue of the power and authority in me vested (possessing sufficient force), declare all the ports, harbors, bays, creeks, rivers, inlets, outlets, islands, and sea coast of the United Kingdom of Great Britain and Ireland in a state of strict and rigorous blockade.[50]

On August 17, 1814, the directors of two major British insurance companies, London Assurance and Royal Exchange Assurance, wrote to Secretary Croker about the "numerous captures of very valuable Ships" that had been made by the American sloops of war and privateers operating in British waters and "most earnestly" requested protection to "prevent a repetition of these ruinous and unlooked-for losses to the Trade of this Country." Croker at first tried employing the usual overwhelming arrogance that was his first line of defense to any political attack, and answered that he was "commanded by their Lordships to acquaint you, that there was a force adequate to the purpose of protecting the Trade." Large meetings of merchants, shipowners, and underwriters in Liverpool, Glasgow, Bristol, and other ports involved in the coastal trade passed indignant resolutions. They pointed out that, without any precedent, even American privateers were now burning ships they captured; that insurance rates just for the passage from England to Ireland had quadrupled and quintupled and were now twice what they were even during the worst of the war with France, when the Royal Navy was surely fully occupied dealing with a much more formidable enemy than America; and that "the number, the audacity, and the success of the American Privateers with which our Channels have lately been infested, have proved injurious to the Commerce, are humbling to the pride, and discreditable to those who direct the great Naval Power of this Nation."

Croker replied this time that no fewer than three frigates and fourteen sloops of war were actually at sea patrolling the western and northern waters of the United Kingdom but that of course it was impossible to provide complete protection against "the occasional attempts of Privateers": if losses were occurring, it was the merchants' own fault for leaving the protection of the convoys. He added that it was their lordships' determination "to bring to punishment the parties who may have been guilty of such illegal acts."[51]

Croker's petulant responses were reprinted everywhere, accompanied with derisive comments. The *Naval Chronicle*'s correspondent "Albion" observed that the Admiralty was the party who should be "brought to account," for "leaving the coast of Ireland and the English Channel *blockaded by half a dozen Yankee cruisers!*" But then, he added, the entire history of the "ill fated" American war could be traced through the trail of "glaring errors of our naval administration."

The incensed merchants then appealed directly to the prince regent, noting in their petition to His Royal Highness the "coldness and neglect" with which their earlier appeals had been received by the proper departments of government.[52]

The nuisance value of a warship engaged in raiding enemy commerce was in principle many times that of a privateer; a defensive patrol or convoy escort sufficient to chase off an opportunistic privateer was one thing, a force that might have a warship-to-warship engagement on its hands another. But several of the especially intrepid American privateers began taking on the enemy's men-of-war with a show of fight that sent more shock waves through the British naval establishment in late summer and early fall of 1814, when the Royal Navy suffered two of its bloodiest defeats of the war, both at the hands of privateers. On the night of September 26, in Fayal harbor in the Azores, the privateer brig *General Armstrong* from New York—a very different vessel from the one of the same name whose crew had mutinied off North Carolina in 1813—was attacked by four heavily armed and manned boats from ships of a British squadron that had arrived that afternoon. It was a gross violation of the port's neutrality, and the British commander later tried to claim he was merely innocently going to "inquire" what ship she was. The American captain, Samuel Reid, repeatedly warned the boats off, and they were close enough to be touching the *General Armstrong* with a boat hook when the privateer opened fire, killing and wounding several of the British.

Reid then warped his ship under the protection of the fort. At about midnight the British renewed the attack, this time in twelve boats carrying hundreds of men. At one point the British seamen succeeded in boarding over the bow and starboard quarter and were beaten back with swords, pikes, pistols, and musket fire. The British even by their own account suffered more than a hundred killed and wounded; the American accounts put British losses at more than one hundred dead and more than 250 total casualties. The next day, realizing he could not hold out against the enemy determination to destroy his ship—the British captain said he would get the American privateer if he had to destroy the entire town of Fayal to do so—Reid had his men cut the masts down to stumps and blow a hole in the ship's bottom. Gathering their small arms and clothes, the crew went ashore, leaving the *General Armstrong* to her fate. When the British captain demanded that the local authorities turn over the Americans as his prisoners, the Portuguese governor demurred and the Americans vowed to fight to the last man rather than be taken, which ended the matter. A week later the whole American crew left for Amelia Island aboard a Portuguese merchant brig.[53]

On October 11, 1814, the hardest-fought naval engagement of the entire war took place off Nantucket between the privateer *Prince de Neufchatel* and five barges from the British frigate *Endymion* in an almost exact replay of the *General Armstrong*'s defiant holdout. When British boarders succeeded in gaining the forecastle of the privateer, her captain swept them overboard with a hail of canister shot and bags of musket balls fired across the deck from one of her main guns. Again the British regulars suffered a loss of a hundred or more—to the American privateer's nine killed and nineteen wounded.[54]

Neither the blockade nor the raids against American coastal cities, including even the capital, had succeeded in knocking America out of the fight. Just as in the Revolution, the British army never would commit sufficient force to occupy and hold territory, and it was most likely an impossible task in any case. Wellington himself had warned the government, when asked his opinion, that the vast and "thinly peopled" continent of America was simply ill suited to an extended military campaign that could tip the strategic balance decisively. "I do not know where you could carry on such an operation which would be so injurious to the Americans as to force them to sue for peace," he advised.[55]

The last real possibility of proving Wellington wrong evaporated in September when Governor General Prevost marched from Canada into New York with an army of ten thousand men, heading down the west side of Lake Champlain. Prevost's advance was a dramatic departure from the string of sharply fought but strategically indecisive clashes along the Canadian frontier all through the bloody summer of 1814, a bid for the decisive breakthrough on land that had eluded both sides for two years. In a two-and-a-half-hour naval battle in Plattsburgh Bay the morning of September 11, 1814, a British squadron of four ships and twelve gunboats sent to support Prevost was soundly defeated by an American force under the command of Master Commandant Thomas Macdonough. At a decisive moment in the battle, with the entire starboard battery of his flagship *Saratoga* knocked out, Macdonough warped the ship around 180 degrees using a series of anchors and cable springs he had carefully prepared ahead of time to bring the fresh battery to bear. During the battle Macdonough was twice knocked to the deck, once by a falling boom and once when the head of a decapitated midshipman smashed into his face. The British flagship *Confiance* took 105 shot holes in her hull. The casualties were horrific, with one in four men on each side killed or wounded. Prevost ordered a retreat, and Macdonough instantly became the most famous commander of the war at the time (if not so well remembered today): he was promoted by Congress to captain and showered with rewards of land and gold medals and swords and silver services from New York, Vermont, and other states. "In one month," Macdonough recounted, "from a poor lieutenant I became a rich man." He also ended the last serious threat of invasion from the north.[56]

The failure of the blockade had equally laid bare the impotence of Britain's might. Not long after taking command in April 1814, Cochrane had extended the blockade to include all of New England, and on paper the entire American coast from Maine to New Orleans was now within the British noose. But, like Warren before him, he was constantly importuning the Admiralty for more ships to make it effective. Although the West Indies stations had been removed from his command, those stations' ships had never been really available for service on the American coast anyway, and Cochrane calculated he needed more than twice as many frigates, sloops, and smaller vessels as were left him by his predecessor. In fact, the Royal Navy never deployed a force even close to what it would have taken to make the blockade complete. Cochrane concluded that ninety-eight ships were needed to maintain the blockade and that one-fourth to one-third of his force would be out of service at any given time in port refitting. With all the other demands on him to protect convoys, carry dispatches, transport troops, and support land operations, he actually never had more than twenty-five ships available for blockading. It probably would have taken the commitment of a force approaching half the entire strength of the Royal Navy to effectively seal off the American coast.[57]

The officers enforcing the blockade knew it, and it never was a completely serious endeavor for them. Lieutenant Henry Napier, aboard the frigate *Nymphe* on blockade duty in Massachusetts Bay in 1814, filled his journal with observations about the pretty girls on the coasting vessels they stopped, the many prizes they ransomed for a thousand or two thousand dollars rather than capturing or burning them, their irritation when British privateers tried to join the effort ("*Shannon*, privateer, again out. Must drive her off, as she spoils our cruising ground"), and the lobsters, clams, oysters, lambs, potatoes, green peas, newspapers, and every other comfort routinely supplied the British squadron by the local citizens they were supposedly at war with. The accommodations that blockader and blockaded alike were making after two years' fighting reinforced the sense that the war had long ceased to be about one side or the other winning; it was something to be endured and in the meanwhile made the best of. Unlike the top British commanders on the American station, who had all along overestimated the significance of

Federalist opposition to the war and who readily leapt to the conclusion that local collaboration was a sign of impending political upheaval that would knock America out of the fight, Napier thought most of the local "rascals" who eagerly filled the British squadron's orders for supplies were opportunists, not allies; they only "like the English as a spendthrift loves an old rich wife; the sooner we are gone the better."

Most of all was the boredom: endlessly plowing furrow after furrow through a field of blue-green waves, enduring nights of "hard rain, fog and anxiety," writing diary entries oddly echoing those of the prisoners of Dartmoor, as day followed day. "Oh happy Home! when shall I enjoy ye again?" wrote surgeon's mate William Begg of the frigate *Tenedos* off Boston, as he battled "the tedious hours" and "the *ennui* of a long inactive cruise."[58]

In Ghent, where the American and British peace commissioners had at last agreed to meet, the weeks wore heavily too. The negotiations began on August 8, and two full months went by with virtually no progress. John Quincy Adams, who headed the American delegation, found the notes presented by the British "arrogant, overbearing, and offensive." The British envoys were insisting on a series of "nonnegotiable" demands, including American demilitarization of the Great Lakes, cession of territory in northern Maine and the headlands of the Mississippi River, and creation of a huge reservation of land for the exclusive settlement of Britain's Indian allies, encompassing 250,000 square miles including a third of Ohio and all of Indiana, Illinois, Michigan, and Wisconsin, and necessitating the expulsion of 100,000 American settlers. But Adams also suspected the British were simply stalling; every American proposal was referred back to London.

In October, convinced that things were going nowhere, Madison took the risky step of publishing the American envoys' proposals, revealing publicly for the first time the stunning news that America had offered to drop the issue of impressment. The British opposition was emboldened enough by the news to attack the government for waging a "war of aggression and conquest."

But the American negotiators remained gloomy, convinced the British were trying to drag out the talks as long as possible in the hope of meanwhile striking a coup on the battlefield that would tilt the political calculus decisively in their favor.[59]

.   .   .

UNLIKE HER predecessor the *Independence*, the seventy-four-gun ship of the line *Washington* faultlessly glided into the water at her launching at the Portsmouth Navy Yard on October 1, 1814. But there were no guns to arm her, no men to man her, and no money to make up the lack of either. The navy had been scrambling to find guns and men for the lakes; the only foundries large enough to cast the big guns for the *Washington* were south of New York, and then they would have to be hauled overland to evade the blockade.

In Boston men were deserting from Bainbridge's command in droves, and Bainbridge was picking feuds with everyone. He wrote to Secretary Jones bitterly complaining that he could not have his marine guards flogged—under the navy's regulations, marines were subject to army discipline when ashore, and Congress had outlawed flogging in the army in May 1812—which prompted Jones to gently admonish Bainbridge, "The best examples of discipline in the universe are to be found where corporal punishment is unknown. It may brutalize, but cannot reform." Bainbridge sent a sarcastic reply to the secretary stating that in that case he presumed he would not be held responsible for the public property under his charge, as he was forbidden to punish guards found sleeping on duty.[60]

Using the pretext of his seniority in the service, Bainbridge tried to override Hull's command authority and ordered Captain Charles Morris to send him thirty of his men from Portsmouth, where they had arrived after the sloop of war *Adams* ran aground off the coast of Maine. Hull had to appeal to Jones to get the men back, and then another even more insolent note from Bainbridge arrived in Washington, informing the navy secretary, "I have received your order of the 26th ulto. and in obedience thereto, however injurious it may prove to the service, I instantly comply with it."[61]

But there was no denying the exasperating circumstances. There was no money, for new recruits or even to pay for "the most urgent contingent purposes," Jones reported to Madison on October 15. "If the salvation of a city depended upon the prompt transportation of a body of our seamen I have not a dollar." Bainbridge said that even his officers were "really suffering," with "no money, clothes, or credit and are embarrassed with debts." Following the attack on Washington, most banks south of New England suspended specie payments, and the entire financial system of the country was on the verge of collapse. Treasury notes were all the government could offer as payment, and in

Boston they were circulating at 20 percent discount; the notes of banks that had suspended specie payments were worth nothing at all outside the states where they were issued, effectively freezing the $50 million in bank credits the federal government held in the south and west.

"Something must be done and done speedily," William Jones wrote the Treasury secretary, "or we shall have an opportunity of trying the experiment of maintaining an army and navy and carrying on a vigorous war without money." But it was already too late. On November 9 the Treasury suspended interest payments on government debt, effectively declaring itself insolvent. Jones had managed to find some time to write a long proposal to the president on how the $60 million needed to keep the war going another year might be raised through a combination of new loans, a national bank that would lend the government $20 million at 6 percent interest for 12 years, more Treasury note issues, and $16 million in new internal taxes. The only trouble was that borrowing money or raising taxes did no good if it only brought in the same worthless paper the government was issuing in the first place.[62]

In New England defeatism was becoming the predominant sentiment everywhere. EVENTS OF THE USELESS WAR! ran a typical headline in the Boston *Columbian Centinel*. Bainbridge was apoplectic when a committee of Boston merchants appointed by Federalist governor Caleb Strong demanded that the *Independence* and the *Constitution* be moved outside the harbor so as not to invite a British attack on their city, and he adamantly refused to entertain their request to sink blockships at the harbor entrances. Jones solidly backed Bainbridge's decision, pointing out that there was no reason to do the Royal Navy's work for them in sealing off the harbor, thereby "relieving the enemy of the sluggish duty of blockade, to pursue a more active hostility." A large group of Irish citizens of the town, joined by Harvard undergraduates, then banded together to help erect earthworks on Noddles Island in Boston harbor that Bainbridge recommended to stiffen the more active defenses of the port.[63]

But other northeasterners flirted openly with treason. Intelligence reports from Americans in Boston and along Long Island Sound flowed into the British squadrons; Decatur's accusation about "blue lights" signaling the enemy at New London may have been ludicrous, but the willingness of more than a few disaffected northern men to spy for the enemy—even if what they provided was little more than what American newspapers reported—was real enough.[64] Many of New England's

Congregational clergy were meanwhile denouncing the war more than ever, and by 1814 were willing to suggest that America had set herself against God himself. If a war was unjust, said one minister, "it will be the duty of the Christian patriot, however contrary to the native impulse of his feelings, *to pray for the success of our declared enemies!*"65

Governor Strong went so far as to send an agent to Halifax to explore a separate peace. And beginning in October the legislatures of the New England states voted to call a convention to demand changes to the Constitution aimed at curing the ills the Federalists believed had led America into the disastrous war in the first place. The convention that met in Hartford in December 1814 approved resolutions to end the disproportionate power of the southern states through the constitutional provision that counted slaves at the rate of three-fifths of a person when apportioning representation in Congress and the Electoral College, break the hold of the "Virginia dynasty" by barring the election of a president from the same state in two successive terms, and require a two-thirds vote of Congress to declare war or restrict trade. They more than hinted that disunion would be the next step if their demands were not met. Madison, when he heard the news, was "miserably shattered and woe-begone," Washington lawyer William Wirt reported after seeing the president. Madison dismissed New England as suffering a "delusion" comparable to "the reign of witchcraft," but the outcome of the Hartford Convention seemed to have almost physically beaten him down.66

The *Federal Republican,* as vehemently anti-administration as ever, predicted in early January 1815 that there was "an explosion at hand; that the President would be called on to resign; and there must be peace by that or a future Administration." The "explosion" was expected to come from New Orleans: for weeks there had been reports of a huge British naval and military force assembling in Jamaica preparing to launch an attack there. Cochrane had included the city as a likely target back in July in a long list of options he had sent to Melville, and in mid-September approval had come back from London. Whoever controlled New Orleans would control the Mississippi River, and once again Cochrane was convinced the decisive blow was at hand.67

On December 16, 1814, after sweeping aside five American navy gunboats guarding the entrance to Lake Borgne, a British invasion force that would eventually reach 6,000 began disembarking at Isle aux Pois, about thirty miles from New Orleans. An advance column of

1,600 men reached the mainland a week later, and three small battles were fought over the ensuing week as the British force probed the defenses around the city.

Andrew Jackson, now a major general in the regular army and in command of the entire district of Louisiana, had chosen his defensive position well. The Mississippi River held his right flank, a cypress swamp his left, and an earthwork parapet protected by a four-foot-deep ditch sheltered nearly five thousand American troops. Seven artillery batteries spaced at fifty- to two-hundred-yard intervals supported the entrenched position, and before the American lines lay a broad open plain that the British would have to traverse to reach them. The British plan was to begin with a night attack to seize two guns that Jackson had unwisely placed in a weakly guarded position across the river, then turn the guns on the main American line as the major British assault began at dawn. But as the Battle of New Orleans began on January 8, 1815, the British attack fell disastrously behind schedule. It was not until daylight that the two guns were seized, and then it took an hour and a half for the main British force to begin its advance toward Jackson's breastworks. At first a heavy fog shrouded their movement, but it suddenly lifted as the British were still hundreds of yards from their enemy, and the grape and canister began cutting them to pieces. The British commander, General Edward Pakenham, was eviscerated by a blast of grape three hundred yards from the American line as he rode ahead trying to rally his men forward. In half an hour the British lost 2,000 men, including nearly 200 killed and 500 taken prisoner. Total American casualties were 70, and nearly all of those were among the men in the exposed position across the river; the Americans behind Jackson's breastworks lost 6 killed and 7 wounded. It was one of the most lopsided battles ever fought.[68]

Reports of Jackson's victory reached Washington on February 4, 1815, completely overshadowing the news of a few days earlier that Stephen Decatur had lost the frigate *President* to the British as he tried to bolt out of New York harbor during a winter storm on January 15.[69] Decatur had received command of the *President* the previous April after it became clear that the New London squadron would never escape to sea; Rodgers was shifted to Philadelphia to take charge of the new frigate under construction there (named, both to honor the American victory and annoy the British, the *Guerriere*).

It was no secret that Decatur would make the attempt. For weeks it was common knowledge that the *President* was preparing for sea and was only awaiting a good strong blow to knock the British squadron off station.[70] The blow came on the fourteenth, but the British were ready, and even though the northwest wind had driven them fifty miles to the south, they were sitting off Long Island to the east when Decatur hove into view two miles away with dawn of the next day.

It had been an ill-starred business from the start: the pilot taking them out of the harbor had miscalculated in the dark and run the *President* hard onto the bar past Sandy Hook, where the wind and sea violently beat the frigate against the bottom for an hour and a half before the rising tide finally freed her. And then Decatur stumbled right into a huge enemy force just before daylight; a blue signal rocket arced into the sky from one of the British ships; and within minutes he was running for his life from no fewer than three frigates, a brig, and the fifty-eight-gun razee *Majestic*. Decatur ordered the boats, cables, anchors, spare spars, and provisions thrown overboard, but it was clearly hopeless. The American frigate, her keel injured by the beating she had taken getting out of New York, was taking on water and was slowed by several knots. At one point in the chase Decatur proposed to his officers a desperate plan of boarding and seizing the *Endymion*, the British frigate that had succeeded in gaining the most on them, firing a howitzer down the hold of the *President* to scuttle her, then escaping in the captured British frigate, taking advantage of superior sailing qualities to run free of the rest of the enemy squadron. But the British captain of the *Endymion* never gave him a chance, staying well off his starboard quarter.

And then the two ships were running in gunshot range and for two hours exchanged fire. All four of the *President*'s lieutenants were killed, including Archibald Hamilton, the son of the former secretary of the navy, the young officer who had dramatically arrived at the naval ball in Washington bearing the *Macedonian*'s colors two years before. The *President*'s marines fired five thousand musket cartridges; Decatur himself was twice hit by splinters that left him sprawled on the deck, in severe pain from a broken rib and pouring blood from a superficial but ghastly wound to his forehead. The chase and fight went on all day, from dawn to near midnight, before Decatur bowed to the inevitable and surrendered, loudly hailing that he surrendered "to the *squadron*"—meaning not to the *Endymion* alone. The *President* was taken to Bermuda, and Decatur was swiftly released on parole to arrive back in New London on February 21.[71]

By then there was news that made any hairsplitting over the circumstances of one frigate's surrender barely worth notice. GLORIOUS NEWS read the headline of an extra edition of the *Commercial Advertiser* that hit the streets of New York early on the Sunday morning of February 12, 1815: "A Treaty of Peace was signed by the American and British commissioners at Ghent, on the 24th of December." The previous evening at eight o'clock a copy of the treaty had arrived in New York aboard the British sloop of war *Favorite*. When the news reached Hartford two days later, cannons were fired and bells rung throughout the night in rejoicing. In Albany 130,000 lights lit up the public buildings and fireworks filled the night sky. An express rider galloped to Boston in a record thirty-two hours, and schools closed, businesses shut, the legislature adjourned, and a parade of citizens with the word PEACE on their hats wound though the city. The Senate unanimously approved the treaty on February 16, and the next night at 11:00 p.m. Madison formally exchanged ratifications with the British envoy who had arrived to accept them. The following day in Washington the British and American flags flew side by side, and that night the impromptu celebration included the firing of a number of rockets, "some of them made, by one of our citizens, in imitation of the British Congreve."

In New Castle, Delaware, the Reverend John E. Latta preached a sermon on the nation's improbable deliverance from the evils of war, declaring that, in simply surviving to see the return of peace, America had defied all expectation.

> Our national character was depreciated, as to what the nations
> of the world call honor and dignity. It was supposed, that we had
> lost the spirit of national independence, and that our martial
> genius and prowess, had sunk into a fatal degeneracy. . . . Under
> all these circumstances, we, novices in war, and unhappily
> divided amongst ourselves,—our enemies veterans,—flushed
> with recent victories—retaining a grudge and denouncing a
> vengeance, who would have ventured even to surmise an early
> peace?
>   . . . The spirit of our beloved country, instead of being
> broken, is invigorated. The spirit, which contrived and executed
> the plan of our glorious independence, has been revived to
> defend it. Our citizens are inspired with a confidence, which will
> induce them to protect and defend, against all its enemies, the

only government now existing in the world, which is worthy of a free, independent people. . . . We have more astonished the world in war, than we did in peace.[72]

Only Federalist newspapers had the temerity to observe, in reading the actual terms of the treaty, that it offered nothing about free trade, sailors' rights, or any other compensations for an expensive and bloody war.[73]

CELEBRATION

OF THE RATIFICATION OF THE

Treaty of Peace

between the United States of America and the United Kingdom of Great Britain & Ireland, At Cambridge, Feb. 23, 1815.

ORDER OF PROCESSION.

The procession will be formed at University Hall, and move at 11 o'clock A. M. in the following order, to the Rev. Dr. Holmes's meetinghouse.

Military Escort.
Musick.
Marshal. | Chief Marshal. | *Marshal.*
The President of the University and the other Gentlemen, who officiate.
Government of Harvard College.
Selectmen of Cambridge.
Marshal. | Committee of Arrangements. | *Marshal.*
Strangers.
Marshal.
Resident Graduates.
Students.
Marshal.
Citizens of Cambridge.
Marshal.

ORDER OF EXERCISES.

1. **Anthem—*By Stephenson.***
 " *I was glad when they said unto me,*" &c.

2. **Prayer, by the Rev. Dr. Ware.**

3. **Reading of select portions of the Holy Scripture, by the Rev. Mr. Gannett.**

4. **Hymn, written for the occasion.**

Almighty God! to Thee we bow,
To Thee the voice of gladness raise ;
Thy mercy, that hath blessed us now,
In loud and grateful songs we praise.

Long hast Thou stretched the avenging hand,
And smote thy people in thy wrath ;
Hast frowned upon a guilty land,
While storms and darkness veiled thy path.

But light from Heaven has shone at last,
And PEACE is beaming from above,
The storm of doubt and fear has past,
And hope returns, and joy, and love.

Then praise to that Eternal Power,
Who bids our wars and tumults cease,
And hymn, in this auspicious hour,
The God of Mercy—God of Peace.

5. **Address, by the President of the University.**

6. **Poem, by Mr. Henry Ware.**

7. **Prayer, by the Rev. Dr. Holmes.**

8. **Anthem, from Handel's " Grand Dettingen Te Deum."**
 " *We praise thee, O God,*" &c.

9. **Benediction.**

Service celebrating the peace, Harvard University (Library of Congress)

CHAPTER 11

"Praise to God for the Restoration of Peace"

NEWS OF the Treaty of Ghent reached the prisoners at Dartmoor on December 29, 1814, and on every one of the prison buildings the Americans hoisted a flag with the motto "Free Trade & Sailors Rights." But the joy was brief. The winter of 1814–15 was the worst yet for the prisoners. A smallpox epidemic raged through the prison, made worse by the prison doctor's theory that the best cure was cold baths and extinguishing the fires in the barracks, and so many more succumbed to pneumonia; 270 prisoners eventually died of disease, most during that final winter.

As the weeks and then months wore on with no word about their release, the situation grew more and more volatile. Beasley, the American prisoner agent, sent a letter informing the prisoners that any who had contracted a debt and did not pay it would be detained in Britain. Then another letter arrived from Beasley stating that prisoners would be permitted to leave the country only aboard an official cartel ship, still offering no word about when the first ships would arrive.

On February 13, 1815, a prisoner who had been confined in the "black hole" for eight months was allowed out to take exercise for two hours, leapt the picket fence into the prison yard, and was quickly ushered by his fellow prisoners into number 7. The next day Shortland demanded him back; the prisoners refused; and when three hundred soldiers then marched into the yard, the prisoners declared, in Benjamin Palmer's words, that "they would never be forced in to any measure against their wills as long as there was a paving stone in the Yard to defend them." Shortland ordered the soldiers back out but sent word that he would stop the market until the man was delivered up.[1]

A new militia unit arrived to relieve one of the regiments that had been guarding the Americans, and immediately there was new trouble: a prisoner was stabbed four times by a bayonet apparently for not moving fast enough when the prisoners were ordered in at night. "Immediately prepared for Action against the morroe," Palmer wrote in his diary March 8, "fully determined to sacrifice the first Soldier that came in to the Yard." Shortland announced the next day that he would keep the soldiers out of the yard and the one who had stabbed the prisoner would received four hundred lashes as punishment.

Everyone was cracking under the strain, and control of the prison seemed to be slipping day by day. A prisoner in the hospital "became insane & stabb'd two men." Three Frenchmen "were Detected in the Act of buggery and this morning they were flog'd severely and turnd in to No 4 among the Negroes." On March 25 the prisoners "tried" and hanged Beasley in effigy. "Still no prospect of getting home How is it that our Agent is so dilatory I cant tell," Palmer wrote.[2] On April 6 he added: "The Prisoners are growing daily more and more discontented. they seem determined to make some bold attempt to escape from this dam Prison."

Two days before, tensions had risen alarmingly when a dispute over the bread ration led to a stampede of prisoners out of all the barracks; they burst open the iron gates into the market square, and an alarm bell rang as soldiers from Princetown rushed to join the guards, who were now threatening to fire on the prisoners if they did not disperse. "Fire away!" the prisoners taunted back. Again an uneasy peace was restored.[3] On the evening of the sixth the inevitable explosion occurred. Again some trivial incident was the trigger—a ball kicked into an adjoining yard by the prisoners, who then tried to retrieve it—but at around five o'clock in the afternoon the alarm bell rang, the guards turned out on the parapets, and before the prisoners could get to their barracks they began firing. Some of the prisoners later claimed that Shortland had engineered the entire episode, others that he was in the midst of the melee, raving drunk, shouting at the troops to fire, but in the chaos the truth would never be known for sure.[4] Seven Americans were killed and thirty-one wounded.

The incident finally shocked the British and American bureaucracies into action. Much of the delay in releasing the prisoners was due to the British government's insistence that each side should supply the ships to return its own prisoners, which obviously was to Britain's advantage given the imbalance in numbers. Now the British agreed to get the prisoners home as quickly as possible and work out the costs later. All Americans able to provide for themselves were released at once. Every day a contingent of freed prisoners could be seen on the road to Plymouth, marching with banners and flags inscribed "Remember the Sixth of April, 1815," "Revenge Our Murdered Countrymen!" "Dartmoor Massacre, 1815," and "Free Trade and Sailors Rights."[5]

More than one group of returning American sailors commandeered the ships taking them home when the captain tried to sail to a port far from where most of their homes were, redirecting the ships from Norfolk to New York or other ports.[6] Most arrived home without money and barely with clothes. One recalled the "deep, burning indignation" he and the two or three hundred of his fellow released prisoners felt upon arriving in Boston and, after appealing for help from the town's authorities, were given a dollar each and a certificate reading:

> This is to certify that _____, having been a prisoner-of-war, has returned to this country destitute, and is anxious to get home to his family. We therefore recommend him to those upon whom he may call for assistance while on his journey.

"Is this the reception given to men who have endured sufferings and privations unutterable," the man indignantly observed, "who have fought their country's battles, defended the fire-sides which these functionaries now enjoy in peace and security?" He scornfully tore up what he called the "begging-ticket" he had been offered and found his way home as he could, arriving there feeling "like Rip Van Winkle" awakened from his long and troubled sleep.[7]

THE FEDERALISTS were certain that they would be the political winners of the war. The country had ended up with nothing Madison had promised and everything he claimed to abhor. The war had proved the Federalists right that America needed a strong navy and a sound system of taxation to pay for it; the peace had proved them right that it was folly to think that Britain could ever be made to yield its stance on impressment and free trade. The war had cost the country $158 million and left the government with a debt of $127 million—half as much again as the "moral canker" that Jefferson had inherited and vowed to eliminate, three times what the national debt stood at just before the war. The treaty that ended the war was an almost complete return to the status quo ante; in the end, the peace commissioners had chosen to deal with every single issue of serious contention between the two countries—from the major ones of impressment and free trade to a host of secondary issues such as British access to the Mississippi River and American fishing rights in Canada—by simply omitting any mention of them from the final text. "A Treaty, which gives us peace, is represented as glorious, when it has given us nothing else," said Federalist senator Rufus King of Massachusetts.[8] Senator Christopher Gore, his fellow Massachusetts Federalist, declared, "The treaty must be deemed disgraceful to the Government who made the war and the peace, and will be so adjudged by all, after the first effusions of joy at relief have subsided."[9]

But the amnesia that sets in after all wars took hold with lightning swiftness. Simply, no one wanted to hear that a war in which men fought and died had been in vain; no one wanted to be reminded of all the blunders and incompetence and miscalculations of the generals, or all the inconsistencies and opportunism of the politicians. Almost immediately the Republicans were declaring the war not merely an American triumph but a "second war of independence." And almost immediately the Federalists found that facts were no match for the patriotic fervor that the war's end had set loose. The Hartford Convention was what Americans now remembered of the Federalist party, not their stand for a strong navy or their opposition to a futile war; the very words "Hartford Convention" became a synonym for treason in the American political lexicon for years afterward, as did "blue lights." By 1816 the Federalists had ceased to exist as a national party. "Democrat" had originated as a term of abuse for the Republicans, used by Federalists and the British because it carried the same disparaging connotation as "mob rule," but the Republicans soon adopted it themselves, and for the next four decades the Democratic party would dominate American politics. James Monroe, John Quincy Adams, Andrew Jackson, and William Henry Harrison would all ride their party's popularity, and their own service in the war, to the White House. The historian Donald Hickey tallied one future vice president, three governors, four United States senators, and twenty congressmen whose presence at Harrison's victory at the Battle of the Thames was their ticket to public office as well.[10]

Like the Federalists, many Britons were left sputtering and incredulous at American assertions of victory in the war. William James, a British admiralty court lawyer who was detained for part of the war in America and became almost unhinged over the American gloating he witnessed, quickly produced a popular account of the war that picked up where the editorials of the *Times* left off, belittling American naval triumphs and concluding that Americans were simply scoundrels who "will invent any falsehood, no matter how barefaced, to foist a valiant character on themselves."[11] In 1817 James's book *A Full and Correct Account of the Chief Naval Occurrences of the Late War between Great Britain and the United States of America* appeared, and he followed that with a huge six-volume history of the Royal Navy. The books contained a breathtaking number of inaccuracies regarding the size, force, armament, and character of the American navy but were most notable for the dripping anti-American sarcasm that filled page after page, all in the service of showing not only that the British navy had really won the war, but that in every instance when an American vessel had prevailed in battle, it was only as a result of superior force, cowardly tactics, and the employment of inhumane weapons such as bar and chain shot.

Needless to say, the only thing such attacks succeeded in persuading Americans of was that the British were not only as arrogant as ever but sore losers as well. A deep-seated Anglophobia would be one of the most enduring legacies of the war in America; among American naval officers the tradition of antipathy and suspicion of the British that stemmed directly from the War of 1812 could still be seen as late as World War II.

But British navy men on the whole took a more collected and detached view of the war's consequences, and saw the writing on the wall better and sooner than most. The war had heralded the rise of not only a new naval power but a new kind of naval warfare, more professional and less chivalric, based more on technical mastery and less on heroics. The old world, in which indignant remonstrations like James's over who had the better of points of honor still mattered, was rapidly slipping into history, like it or not. "Sic transit gloria mundi," declared the *Naval Chronicle*'s Albion in one final letter he wrote March 12, 1815, to "take my leave of the American contest" and offer a few measured observations:

An inglorious, unsuccessful, war must naturally end in such a peace as America chose to give; for assuredly we have now done our worst against this infant enemy, which has already shewn a giant's power. Soon will the rising greatness of this distant empire . . . astonish the nations who have looked on with wonder, and seen the mightiest efforts of Britain, at the era of her greatest power, so easily parried, so completely foiled.[12]

Critics of the British government in Parliament were quick to take up the theme too, attacking the Admiralty for being stuck in the past, failing to keep pace with technical advances, and honoring tradition and bureaucratic ritual over modern practicalities. Parliament reprinted a pointed and lengthy collection of documents clearly intended to embarrass the government for its handling of the war. Especially galling were the page after page of urgent requests from ships' captains to the Admiralty asking for additional firepower to match that of the American ships, and the withering replies from Secretary Croker informing them that those requests could not possibly be entertained. (One captain, unusually, was permitted to add five extra guns on his thirty-eight frigate, but when he subsequently asked for twenty additional men in order to man them, Croker replied, "As he applied himself for these Guns, the Establishment of Men cannot be altered; but he may put the Guns on Shore again if he does not think the Complement sufficient to serve them.")[13] Croker was a political survivor, though, and remained in office until 1830, continuing to savage his political and literary enemies with undiminished zeal, and leaving a small footnote to political history by being the first to use the term "conservative" as a description of his party's political ideology.

When America's first professional historians, led by Henry Adams, began examining the war three-quarters of a century after its end, they cast a perhaps inevitably jaundiced eye on all the patriotic hero worship, national chauvinism, and factional pleading that had hitherto dominated popular American accounts. Adams's brilliant, sweeping, and often extraordinarily funny account of the Jefferson and Madison administrations was hugely influential and helped solidify the settled historical judgment for most of the twentieth century that the War of 1812 was a futile miscalculation brought on by a weak and indecisive president.

But there were consequences of the war so lasting that they would become apparent only when seen across distances of time measured in a century of more. The fact was that regardless of Madison's ignominious abandonment of America's positions on impressment and free trade in the negotiations at Ghent, the British never again attempted to press an American seaman and never again attempted to hinder American neutral trade on the high seas. The American legal position that both neutral vessels and neutral goods were immune from seizure by a belligerent slowly became the accepted international norm, and was adopted by Great Britain and other major European powers in the Treaty of Paris in 1856. (Other countries were invited to join as well; the United States ironically refused, objecting to another provision of the treaty abolishing privateering, for fear that this would give large naval powers an advantage over countries such as the United States. But the United States in fact never issued a privateering commission again. The United States also was holding out for the complete abolition of the right of belligerents to capture or destroy enemy civilian property at sea, arguing that the same principles of international law that protect noncontraband civilian property on land should apply on the oceans. That position never has been adopted; international law to this day allows a combatant to capture and take as a lawful prize an enemy's merchant ships.)[14]

Though it was only clear in long hindsight, America had in fact gained a significant point even in fighting a war to such a formally inconclusive end. Henry Adams implicitly acknowledged as much in noting the cost America had succeeded in imposing on Britain. As a result of trying to maintain her traditional maritime policies, Great Britain had spent £10 million a year waging an ultimately unsuccessful war with a tiny upstart naval power one-hundredth its size. As Adams noted, that meant Britain was spending something like $50,000 a year for *each* of the impressed Americans it detained in its service. For half as much the Royal Navy could have tripled the pay of all its sailors and obtained the manpower it needed without resorting to impressment at all.[15]

While no one in Britain ever seemed to have made so explicit a calculation, there was widespread recognition that the cost of continuing the fight had indeed become intolerable by late summer and early fall of 1814, largely as a result of the adroit attacks on British seagoing commerce by the American navy and privateers. In the end, the British were as eager to end the war as the Americans were; at Ghent they soon dropped one after another of the "nonnegotiable" demands they had insisted on when the negotiations began. The British had been particularly adamant on retaining northern Maine and establishing the Indian buffer in the northwest. By November 1814 they had conceded both points, and the remaining month of negotiations was spent mainly reducing the agreement to its final wording. The British had been forced to learn a lesson that the United States would later have to relearn for itself in the seemingly one-sided fight it would find itself in a century and a half later in Vietnam: that a determined enemy facing a vastly superior military force can win simply by not losing.

For better or worse, the war's other great enduring consequence was to end the last real challenge to American sovereignty over North America by its native inhabitants. The Indian tribes who allied themselves with Britain were the war's greatest losers; the confederacy that united under Tecumseh's leadership collapsed after his death on the battlefield, and never again would the Indians be able to organize such unified or broad-scale resistance to the relentless press of American western expansion.[16]

MIRRORING THE war's untidy end, the war at sea sputtered on for months after its formal conclusion. Recognizing the time it would take for news of the peace to reach distant oceans, the treaty allowed prizes taken at sea for varying periods of time after ratification—from 12 days along the coast of North America to 120 days in the northern Pacific—to be kept by the victors. And so the American navy had the satisfaction of getting in two last blows.

On December 17, 1814, the *Constitution*, taking advantage of the momentary absence of all three British frigates that had been watching Boston harbor, quickly got to sea, for the first time in eight months. She took a number of prizes, including a British ship carrying $75,000 worth of hides and pelts and two tame jaguars, which the ship's Scottish captain asked to have back. The *Constitution*'s acting chaplain, Assheton Humphreys, remembered him pleading with Captain Charles Stewart if he "wad na restore his pet kitties," but Stewart demurred and the cats soon were at home on the *Constitution*, perfectly friendly most of the time, except that every now and then they would "capsize" the frigate's pet dog—a terrier named Guerriere—with a cuff from their paws if he got too close.[17]

In early February 1815 the *Constitution* spoke a Frenchman north of Madeira who told them of the treaty of peace having been sent for ratification to America. Then on the afternoon of the twentieth they spotted a sail east of Madeira and gave chase. Soon another man-of-war was in sight, and shortly after the two ships "appeared to be making preparations to receive us," the *Constitution*'s logbook recorded: they formed a line half a cable length from each other and hoisted the English ensign.

The two ships were the twenty-four-gun corvette *Cyane* and the sloop of war *Levant*, and together they threw a broadside slightly heavier than the *Constitution*'s 704 pounds. But most of the British ships' guns were carronades, and Stewart proceeded to engage both ships in a series of skillful maneuvers that maximized the effect of his guns while keeping out of the enemy's range. The *Constitution* came alongside the rearward of the two, the *Cyane*, and exchanged a series of broadsides. When the smoke cleared, Stewart discovered he had pulled nearly alongside the *Levant* and the *Cyane* was preparing to cross his stern and rake him. In quick succession, Stewart ordered a broadside fired into the *Levant* and the sails backed to check his ship's way and bring him back alongside the *Cyane*, and then as the *Levant* tried to cross his bow for a raking shot, he wore around the opposite direction, passing between the two ships and catching *Levant*'s stern with a raking broadside. The *Cyane* struck her colors at 6:45 p.m., less than an hour into the fight; the *Levant* was finally brought to three hours later after a long chase. "The mizzen mast for several feet was covered with brains and blood; teeth, pieces of bones, fingers and large pieces of flesh were picked up from off the deck," recorded Midshipman Pardon Whipple after going aboard the *Levant* the next morning at daylight. Aboard the *Constitution* the two British captains spent most of their time in the ensuing days blaming each other for the defeat.[18]

The *Levant* was recaptured in a long chase off the Cape Verde Islands by the very same three frigates that were to have been guarding Boston to prevent the *Constitution*'s escape, but the *Constitution* and the *Cyane* sailed free and made it to New York on May 16. Technically the recapture was illegal, as it was past the grace period allowed by the treaty, and Congress subsequently voted the *Constitution*'s crew $25,000 in compensation.

On May 18, 1815, the *Constitution* was ordered to return to her home port of Boston, and she entered the harbor on May 29 to a thundering salute. "She struck the first and last blow in the unhappy contest," editorialized the *Salem Gazette*, "and under three successive commanders has been crowned with glory." She was now back at the place of her birth and was welcomed home "as a darling child" by the citizens of Boston.[19]

The last blow of the war actually took place a few weeks later, a half a world away. Master Commandant Lewis Warrington, the aggressive-minded commander of the American sloop of war *Peacock*, refused to believe the hail from the captain of an East India cruiser he approached June 30 near Sumatra that the war was over, and ordered him to strike his colors; when the British ship refused, he fired a broadside into her. The British commander, Lieutenant Charles Boyce, was seriously injured and had his right leg amputated two weeks later. It had been five months since the ratification of the "Treaty of Peace and Amity between His Britannic Majesty and the United States of America."

IF THERE was one unambiguous victor of the war, it was the United States navy. American hostility to a standing navy vanished with scarcely a trace, and never again would there be any doubt that a permanent navy was the backbone of American security. "Experience has taught us that a certain degree of preparation for war is not only indispensable to avert disasters in the onset, but affords the best security for the continuance of peace," Madison acknowledged to Congress in his message announcing the end of the war.[20]

In August 1815, John Adams, now in his eighth decade, came aboard the line-of-battle ship *Independence* in Boston harbor, accompanied by Governor Strong. The Massachusetts governor had become notorious for his lament that America had gone to war against the country that was in so many ways the progenitor of America, indeed the very "bulwarks of our religion." Adams reviewed the six hundred assembled sailors and the magnificent ship of war and then turned to his entourage and loudly proclaimed, "Let Mr. Strong say what he will, *THESE* are the bulwarks of *OUR* religion!" Strong blushed, choked, tried to speak, failed, and the other visiting dignitaries applauded as the sailors "snickered from stem to stern."[21]

For some time Adams had been deluging the Philadelphia publisher Mathew Carey with mountains of papers from his files for a revised edition of Carey's *Naval History of the United States from the Commencement of the Revolutionary War to the Present Time.* The first edition, appearing in May 1813, had been perfectly timed to take advantage of the surge of popular enthusiasm over American victories at sea and sold out instantly. Adams hectored Carey to add a second volume in his next edition making the case for a strong permanent navy—and not incidentally vindicating the former president's long-ignored attempts to get the country to recognize "the naval resources of America as her Arm of Defense and the Instrument of her Prosperity and Glory," as Adams told him. The second edition of the *Naval History* appeared in 1814 and did just that, urging a gradual buildup of American naval power to a strength sufficient to break any blockade of the coast and recommending the establishment of a naval academy to professionalize the officer corps. It too was a huge success and immensely influential.

The stunning effectiveness of William Jones's countervailing strategy of striking at British commerce with small and fleet vessels was not lost on observers, either. With two sloops of war, an improvised supply system, and empty coffers, the American navy by the end of the summer of 1814 had succeeded in making the cost of war intolerable to the British merchant classes that had once been the most ardent advocates of vigorous prosecution of the war against America. Had the United States entered the war with the ships and money and efficient organization to fully realize Jones's commerce-raiding strategy from the start, the war might have been over in the summer of 1813, and on terms America might have had even more power to choose. With speeches noting the recent "brilliant" cruises of the navy's sloops of war, which had been "annoying, mischievous, and discreditable to the enemy," Congress in November 1814 approved with little opposition a naval expansion bill authorizing the construction of twenty vessels of eight to sixteen guns each. Though it would be 1845 before Congress would establish the Naval Academy at Annapolis, it took a major step toward professionalizing the service by quickly enacting one of William Jones's parting recommendations for reorganizing the department, establishing a board of commissioners made up of professional officers who would be responsible for overseeing naval construction and supply while relieving the secretary of some of the crushing administrative burdens that had threatened to overwhelm Jones more than once.[22]

Other measures in support of the navy sailed through Congress in the years following the war's end. In April 1816 "an act for the gradual increase of the navy" allocating $1 million a year for the next eight years for the construction of nine ships of the line and twelve heavy frigates was passed. For the first time America would possess in peacetime a fleet comparable to the European powers'.[23]

But there were many prices to be paid for the navy's emergence as a permanent establishment. A large peacetime force had all the jealousies and enmities of the young navy without the overriding sense of urgent national purpose—the "indignant feelings" that had brought William Jones out of private life and that galvanized men of energy and ability like Joshua Barney and Isaac Hull to come to the fore in a time of crisis. The following decades, which brought a return of petty rivalries and brutal discipline and prejudices large and small, were not a glorious chapter in the American navy's history. As one historian noted, the postwar navy was "torn with feuds and cliques," its leadership hidebound and conservative, falling behind in technological innovations such as steam propulsion, armored plating, rifled cannon, and explosive shells that were revolutionizing European navies in the 1820s, '30s, and '40s.[24]

It would be 1850 before public outcry over accounts of increasingly brutal discipline in the American navy led to a statutory ban on flogging, and another century before African Americans regained the ground they had held in the American navy of the War of 1812. In the midst of the war Isaac Chauncey had chastised his subordinate Oliver Hazard Perry for not wanting to recruit any blacks, who constituted probably 10 percent of the total number of American navy men and 20 percent of the privateersmen during the fight against Britain. Chauncey told him, "I have nearly 50 Blacks on board of this Ship and many of them are amongst my best men . . . I have yet to learn that the Colour of the skin, or cut and trimmings of the coat, can affect a mans qualifications or usefulness." But after the war African Americans were effectively barred from the navy except as messmen. Not until well into World War II was the wrong righted, and not until 1949 did the first African American graduate from the Naval Academy.

The four thousand slaves who had flocked to the British lines from the Chesapeake faced a miserable fate too in the war's aftermath. The Treaty of Ghent required the return of all runaway slaves still in American territory or American waters at the time of ratification, but Cockburn insisted that any blacks who had taken refuge with his forces up until that point were not going to be surrendered. Most were resettled in the Canadian Maritime Provinces, where many died from smallpox or malnutrition. In 1826 the British government agreed to pay $1.2 million in compensation to American slave owners for the loss of their property.[25]

Hull, Decatur, Porter, Bainbridge, and Macdonough became celebrities, heroes immortalized in hagiographic biographies, their portraits painted by the leading artists of the day and reproduced by the thousands on English papier-mâché snuffboxes and Staffordshire ware sold in America with a certain ironic commercialism. But, like most of the men who gave so much to the American cause, they too paid a high personal price. David Porter settled in northwest Washington on 157 acres on the highest hill in the district and tried to live the life he thought was expected of him. He imported pedigreed British bulls at $1,200 apiece, hired stable boys and dairy maids plus a gardener to tend a five-acre kitchen garden, and hauled in thousands of cartloads of manure, but nothing paid. He fought with his wife and children, the spring rains washed away the top dressing from the soil, and it took so long to erect the huge barns he thought would store his bumper crops that the crops never got planted. By 1818 he was writing navy friends trying to cadge tiny sums, even $20 at a time, to stay afloat.[26]

Bainbridge took command of the *Independence* and was appointed commander in chief of an expedition to the Mediterranean ordered in the spring of 1815 to deal once and for all with the Algerines. But the new ship was plagued by troubles: her guns were delivered late, and then she rode so low in the water that her lower row of gunports could not be opened at all. Meanwhile Decatur had been appointed to command another squadron of the expedition and got out of New York on May 20 while Bainbridge was still in Boston readying the *Independence*. Adding to the injury, Bainbridge had been kept largely in the dark by the new navy secretary, Benjamin W. Crowninshield, about the priority the Navy Department was giving Decatur behind the scenes in men and material and about the orders Crowninshield sent Decatur instructing him to depart "without delay." Bainbridge finally got under way July 2, only to learn from a passing ship at Gibraltar a month later that Decatur had already captured the dey's warships and was on his way to Algiers to dictate the peace terms. "I have been deprived of the opportunity of either Fighting or Negotiating," Bainbridge wrote his old navy friend Porter.[27]

Bainbridge returned to Boston in a seething resentment toward

Decatur. He also once again began insisting that the command of the navy yard was his by right. Hull once again had been appointed to succeed Bainbridge in that command, and Hull came downstairs to breakfast on the morning of November 20, 1815, to find a note from Bainbridge "couched in not a very pleasing style," as Hull told Rodgers, "saying that he had been ordered from this station without his consent and that he now claimed it again, that he considered his removal merely temporary, to be held for him until his return."[28]

Hull refused to budge; Secretary Crowninshield confirmed his appointment; but Bainbridge was now the senior commander afloat in Boston and did everything he could to make Hull's life miserable, constantly giving orders about details of the management of the yard and forcing Hull to appeal to the secretary to have them overruled. Bainbridge managed to get the clerk of the navy yard to secretly supply him with copies of Hull's correspondence; Susan Bainbridge began gossiping around town with disparaging stories about Ann Hull; then Bainbridge began spreading a story in navy circles that Hull had pledged to keep the place for him and had gone back on his word. He wrote sneeringly to Porter about "Hull's *just* claim," adding, "Captain Hull and myself cannot be on friendly terms." Porter was growing weary of Bainbridge's campaign and tried to suggest he desist, which prompted another typical Bainbridge plaint of wounded innocence: he was merely exercising "the honesty of self-defense," he insisted.[29]

For his part, Hull angrily wrote Secretary Crowninshield about Bainbridge, "I am not willing to allow that he has done more than I have for the good of the country, his opinion to the contrary notwithstanding." Rodgers had been asked by the secretary to provide a confidential evaluation of all the captains in the service, and his brief remarks on Bainbridge spoke volumes, especially the crossed-out word that was still perfectly legible, as it was no doubt intended to be: "An excellent officer, uniting much practice with considerable theory; he is also industrious, and if there is any objection to him, it is because he feels the importance of his own ~~consequence~~ abilities too sensibly to qualify him as well as he otherwise would for subordinate position."[30]

One day late in 1819 Decatur was walking along a street in Washington when a carriage came to a sudden stop alongside and Bainbridge leapt out, seized Decatur's hand in both of his, and said, "Decatur, I behaved like a great fool, but I hope you will forgive me; but you always contrive to reap laurels from my misfortunes."[31] Susan Decatur was instantly suspicious of Bainbridge's motives. A year earlier

James Barron had returned to the United States for the first time since the war. Barron had again appealed to be reinstated to the navy; Decatur along with almost every other senior officer opposed him. In June 1819 Barron initiated what became an increasingly heated exchange of letters between the two men that was unmistakably an attempt by Barron to generate a pretext for challenging Decatur to a duel. Decatur's official actions as an officer of his court-martial back in 1808 or now as one of three members of the new Board of Naval Commissioners could not be considered the kind of personal insult that could justify a duel. So the entire correspondence turned on an almost hairsplitting discussion of a point of honor in which Barron in effect tried to get Decatur to say that he believed Barron was unworthy of meeting on a field of honor—which would be the kind of insult that *would* allow Barron to issue a challenge. Charles Morris tried to get Decatur to agree to a short statement that would clear the air, but Decatur refused to conceal his contempt for Barron as their correspondence grew more heated. By November, Decatur's letters were running nineteen pages long and heading to their inevitable conclusion.[32]

And so Bainbridge had shown up, professing sudden friendship for a rival he had keenly disliked for years, and on March 8, 1820, Bainbridge was negotiating the arrangements for a meeting on the dueling grounds of Bladensburg as Decatur's second. Barron's second was Captain Jesse Elliott, another officer full of petty resentments who, it would later come out, had pushed Barron again and again to keep the feud with Decatur going whenever it threatened to die out. Decatur left all the details for the arrangement to the seconds, and the terms they agreed to were extraordinary in several ways. The distance was eight paces, and the parties were to take aim before the signal to fire was given, rather than standing with their arms at the side as was usual. It virtually guaranteed a fatal outcome.

On March 22, 1820, the two men met at ten o'clock in the morning. "I never was your enemy," Decatur said, a declaration that should have prompted the seconds to halt the affair then and there according to the rules of honor; but Elliott hurriedly shouted, "Gentlemen, back to your places," and gave the word to fire. Each man was struck in the hip; Barron's wound was not fatal, but the bullet he fired glanced off Decatur's hip socket and severed both arteries in the groin. Decatur died in agonizing pain twelve hours later at his house a block from the White House. He was forty-one years old.[33]

Ten thousand people came out for the funeral procession that bore

Decatur's body through Washington two days later, including President Monroe, the Supreme Court, and members of both houses of Congress. Susan Decatur was forever convinced that Bainbridge and Elliott had conspired to bring about her husband's death and was probably right, though when the correspondence between Barron and Decatur was subsequently published, public sympathy shifted somewhat toward Barron. John Quincy Adams wrote sadly that Decatur possessed "a sense of honor too disdainful of life."[34]

William Jones managed to recoup his lost personal fortune by going into business with the Philadelphia shipbuilder Joshua Humphreys in a successful venture to build steamships.[35] He died in 1831 in Bethlehem, Pennsylvania, on his way to the Pocono Mountains to escape the summer fever raging in Philadelphia, and was granted his dying request to be buried in the beautiful cemetery of the Moravian Church, whose pacifism and neutrality between Britain and America during the Revolution had made its members outcasts in a country born and periodically sustained by the disdain of life and bloodshed of war.

Notes

ABBREVIATIONS

AC *Annals of Congress*
ASP *American State Papers*
HSP Historical Society of Pennsylvania
LC Library of Congress, Manuscript Division
MeHS Maine Historical Society
MHS Massachusetts Historical Society
NDB *Naval Documents Related to the United States Wars with the Barbary Powers*
NMM National Maritime Museum, U.K.
NW1812 *The Naval War of 1812: A Documentary History*
SCL South Caroliniana Library
TNA The National Archives, U.K.
WMSC College of William and Mary, Special Collections Research Center

Prologue

1. Hickey, *Don't Give Up the Ship,* 364–66.
2. Thomas Jefferson to William Duane, August 4, 1812, Jefferson Papers, LC.
3. "Disaster on Disaster on Land," *Columbian Centinel,* February 17, 1813.
4. Osgood, *Solemn Protest,* 9.
5. Adams, *Education of Henry Adams,* 53.
6. Dye, "Early American Seafarers," 340–41.
7. Humphrey, *Press of the Young Republic,* 85.
8. William Jones to James Madison, May 10, 1814, Madison Papers, LC.
9. Adams, "Birth of a World Power."
10. Foster, *Jeffersonian America,* 5.

1. In Barbary

1. Edward Preble to William Bainbridge, March 12, 1804, *NDB,* III: 489.
2. McKee, *Edward Preble,* 47.
3. Ibid., 98–99.
4. Albert Gallatin to Thomas Jefferson, August 16, 1802, Jefferson Papers, LC.
5. Preble quoted in McKee, *Edward Preble,* 136–37.

6. Martin, *Most Fortunate Ship*, 44–46; McKee, *Edward Preble*, 123–24.

7. Preble quoted in McKee, *Edward Preble*, 137–38.

8. Morris, *Autobiography*, 18–19.

9. Edward Preble to secretary of the navy, December 10, 1803, *NDB*, III: 256–60.

10. Preble quoted in McKee, *Edward Preble*, 181–82.

11. Edward Preble to James Leander Cathcart, January 4, 1804, *NDB*, III: 311.

12. Edward Preble to secretary of the navy, December 10, 1803, *NDB*, III: 256.

13. McKee, *Edward Preble*, 227–33; Tucker, *Stephen Decatur*, 45.

14. Edward Preble to Tobias Lear, January 31, 1804, *NDB*, III: 377–78; Preble to secretary of the navy, *NDB*, III: 384–86; Preble to George Davis, *NDB*, III: 386; Tucker, *Stephen Decatur*, 46.

15. Edward Preble to Charles Stewart, January 31, 1804, *NDB*, III: 375.

16. *NDB*, III: 388.

17. Tucker, *Stephen Decatur*, 1–2, 30–32; Ray, *Horrors of Slavery*, 69–70.

18. McKee, *Edward Preble*, 193–94.

19. Edward Preble to secretary of the navy, February 19, 1804, *NDB*, III: 440–41.

20. Heermann's statement in Goldsborough, *United States' Naval Chronicle*, 257–58n.

21. Journal of Midshipman F. Cornelius deKrafft, Brig *Syren*, February 3, 1804, *NDB*, III: 388–89; Edward Preble to Charles Stewart, January 31, 1804, *NDB*, III: 375–76; Preble to Stephen Decatur, January 31, 1804, *NDB*, III: 376–77; affidavit of Midshipman Edmund P. Kennedy, *NDB*, III: 420–21.

22. Morris, *Autobiography*, 25–26; Journal of Midshipman F. Cornelius deKrafft, Brig *Syren*, February 8, 1804, *NDB*, III: 399.

23. Morris, *Autobiography*, 26–28; Midshipman Ralph Izard Jr., to Mrs. Ralph Izard Sr., February 20, 1804, *NDB*, III: 416–17; McKee, *Edward Preble*, 196–97.

24. Affidavit of Surgeon's Mate Lewis Heermann, *NDB*, III: 416–20; "Reminiscences &c by Lewis Heermann Surgeon U.S. Navy—1826," House Committee on Naval Affairs, Claim of Susan Decatur, quoted in McKee, *Edward Preble*, 197–98.

25. Stephen Decatur to Edward Preble, February 17, 1804, *NDB*, III: 414–15; Charles Stewart to Preble, February 19, 1804, *NDB*, III: 415–16; Journal of Midshipman F. Cornelius deKrafft, Brig *Syren*, February 17, 1804, *NDB*, III: 431–32.

26. Cowdery, *American Captives*, 11; Ray, *Horrors of Slavery*, 110; William Bainbridge, February 18, 1804, *NDB*, III: 432–33.

27. Cowdery, *American Captives*, 4–11.

28. Harris, *Commodore Bainbridge*, 91–92.

29. Long, *Ready to Hazard*, vii–viii.

30. Ibid., 25, 42–43.

31. Ibid., 4–5, 270–71; Harris, *Commodore Bainbridge*, 247.

32. William Bainbridge to Edward Preble, November 1, 1803, *NDB*, III: 171.

33. William Bainbridge to secretary of the navy, November 1, 1803, *NDB*, III: 171–73; Bainbridge to Edward Preble, November 6, 1803, *NDB*, III: 173; Bainbridge to Preble, November 12, 1803, *NDB*, III: 173–74. For an example of letters from Bainbridge to friends begging for reassurance that he was not being "censured" at home, see Bainbridge to William Jones, January 20, 1804, Jones Papers, HSP.

34. "Documents Referred to in Captain Bainbridge's Letter," *United States Gazette*, March 27, 1804; Ray, *Horrors of Slavery*, 75–76.

35. "Extracts of a Letter from an Officer on Board the Philadelphia Frigate Dated at Tripoli," *Salem Gazette*, April 3, 1804.

36. Long, *Ready to Hazard*, 82, 85; McKee, *Gentlemanly Profession*, 214; William Bainbridge, February 18, 1804, *NDB*, III: 432–33; Ray, *Horrors of Slavery*, 89–90, 98, 99, 104.

37. Ray, *Horrors of Slavery*, 110–11.

38. Ibid., 87, 101.

39. Ibid., 77, 84.

40. Long, *Ready to Hazard*, 57–58; Ray, *Horrors of Slavery*, 74–75.

41. Rea, *Letter to Bainbridge*, 13, 23; Smith, *Naval Scenes*, 6; Durand, *Life and Adventures*, 18.

42. McKee, *Gentlemanly Profession*, 174–77, 214–15; McKee, *Edward Preble*, 71–72.

43. London, *Victory in Tripoli*, 55, 203; McKee, *Edward Preble*, 298, 305, 336–37; Cowdery, *American Captives*, 19–20; Toll, *Six Frigates*, 248.

44. Long, *Ready to Hazard*, 98; Ray, *Horrors of Slavery*, 158–59; Cowdery, *American Captives*, 15, 16–17.

45. Long, *Ready to Hazard*, 43–44, 101; McKee, *Edward Preble*, 312–14, 335.

2. Honor's Shoals

1. Augustus Foster to Lady Elizabeth Foster, December 30, 1804, February 5, 1805, June 2, 1805, Foster, ed., *Two Duchesses*, 196–98, 203–5, 225–26.

2. Adams, *First Administration of Jefferson*, II: 363–72.

3. Perkins, *Prologue to War*, 98–99; Adams, *First Administration of Jefferson*, I: 43, 45, 52–53, 55, 129.

4. Moore quoted in Perkins, *Prologue to War*, 8.

5. Perkins, *Prologue to War*, 5, 7.

6. Foster, "Notes," 78, 102–6.

7. Adams, *First Administration of Jefferson*, I: 12–32.

8. *Historical Statistics of the United States*, 139; Adams, *First Administration of Jefferson*, I: 31–33.

9. Adams, *First Administration of Jefferson*, I: 18, 30–31; Foster, "Notes," 70–72; Perkins, *Prologue to War*, 68.

10. Albert Gallatin to Thomas Jefferson, April 16, 1807, Jefferson Papers, LC; William Bainbridge to William Jones, January 20, 1804, Jones Papers, HSP; Contract for Sale of Opium to Young Tom, Canton, September 3, 1805, Jones Papers, HSP; Balinky, "Albert Gallatin," 293–95, 304.

11. Tucker and Reuter, *Injured Honor*, 33–34; Dye, "Early American Seafarers," 339–40, 356–57; Lewis, *Social History*, 294–95.

12. Dye, "Early American Seafarers," 348–53; Bolster, "Black Seamen," 1174, 1180–87, 1194.

13. Whitbread quoted in Perkins, *Prologue to War*, 19.

14. Horsman, *Causes of War of 1812*, 33–36; Brougham quoted in Perkins, *Prologue to War*, 20; Sheffield in *NW1812*, I: 21.

15. Foster quoted in Perkins, *Prologue to War*, 28.

16. *Daily Advertiser*, February 20, 1804; June 18, 1804; August 6, 1804; August 9, 1804.

17. Hall, *Fragments of Voyages*, I: 285, 289–90.

18. Adams, *Second Administration of Jefferson*, I: 92; Crowninshield, "American Trade," 114; Baring, *Inquiry*, 95.

19. Sentence of the Vice-Admiralty Court of Nassau, New Providence, in the case of the Brig *Essex*, Joseph Orne Master, *NW1812*, I: 17–21.

20. Stephen, *War in Disguise*, 8, 12–13, 92, 155, 203.

21. Adams, *Second Administration of Jefferson*, I: 199–200; Barclay, *Correspondence*, 232–39.

22. Bainbridge quoted in Long, *Ready to Hazard*, 105.

23. Thomas Jefferson to Jacob Crowninshield, May 13, 1806, Jefferson Papers, LC.

24. Jefferson quoted in Perkins, *Prologue to War,* 121.

25. Madison, *Selected Writings,* 279.

26. Perkins, *Prologue to War,* 5; Grenville quoted in ibid., 74; Merry quoted in Adams, *Second Administration of Jefferson,* I: 202.

27. Balinky, "Albert Gallatin," 294, 296–98; 301.

28. *ASP, Naval Affairs,* I: 78–79, 104–8; Thomas Jefferson to Gouverneur Morris, May 8, 1801, Jefferson Papers, LC.

29. McKee, *Edward Preble,* 338–41; Thomas Jefferson to James Barron, May 23, 1807, James Barron Papers, WMSC; *NW1812,* I: liii, 2.

30. *AC,* 9th Cong., 1st sess. (March 5, 1806), 558–59; (March 11, 1806), 706–7.

31. *NW1812,* I: 12–15.

32. Mayhew, "Jeffersonian Gunboats," 101–2; Chapelle, *American Sailing Navy,* 208; Tucker, "Gunboats in Service," 97; *ASP, Naval Affairs,* I: 200; Paul Hamilton to Langdon Cheves, December 3, 1811, *NW1812,* I: 53–59.

33. Susan Jackson to secretary of the navy, October 31, 1808, quoted in McKee, *Gentlemanly Profession,* 156; Decatur quoted in Smith, "Means to an End," 118; *NW1812,* I: 12.

34. "By his Excellency William Shirley . . . A Proclamation," *Boston Post-Boy,* November 23, 1747; "Two Letters Sent from His Excellency Governor Shirley," *Boston Post-Boy,* December 14, 1747; Zimmerman, *Impressment,* 11.

35. Durand, *Life and Adventures,* 66, 127.

36. Lewis, *Social History,* 119, 134.

37. Durand, *Life and Adventures,* 64–65.

38. Lewis, *Social History,* 134.

39. Ibid., 86–95.

40. Ibid., 105–7, 115.

41. Zimmerman, *Impressment,* 265–67.

42. Durand, *Life and Adventures,* 49–50; Dalton, "Letters"; Perkins, *Prologue to War,* 86–88.

43. *Daily Advertiser,* May 22, August 10, August 29, October 20, 1804; *New-York Gazette,* March 22, July 24, 1805. One ship recaptured by her American crew was the *Eugenia.* Taken off Sandy Hook, she was ordered for Halifax when her American captain, pretending to be ignorant of the coast, advised the British prize master to put into New London for a pilot; once ashore, the captain rounded up thirty armed men who rowed back to the ship and overpowered the British prize crew. See *Daily Advertiser,* August 9, 1804.

44. Zimmerman, *Impressment,* 18, 26, 119; Perkins, *Prologue to War,* 92.

45. Zimmerman, *Impressment,* 109–10, 114.

46. James Madison to George Joy, May 22, 1807, Madison Papers, LC; Adams quoted in Zimmerman, *Impressment,* 176.

47. William Henry Allen to William Allen, March 30, 1807, Allen, "Letters," 206–8.

48. De Kay, *Rage for Glory,* 78–79.

49. McKee, *Edward Preble,* 310.

50. Tucker and Reuter, *Injured Honor,* 86; Toll, *Six Frigates,* 260.

51. James Barron to Franklin Wharton, September 14, 1806, and James Barron to John Rodgers, January 20, 1807, James Barron Papers, WMSC; Franklin Wharton and Thomas Tingey to Rodgers, January 31, 1807, Rodgers Family Papers, Naval Historical Foundation Collection, LC.

52. Secretary of the navy to James Barron, March 23, 1807, James Barron Papers, WMSC.

53. Heintze, "Gaetano Carusi," 75–77, 81, 85–90. Carusi never did get back to Italy. He eventually settled in America, opening music stores in Philadelphia and Baltimore and later running a concert hall in Washington; he spent his final years unsuccessfully petitioning

Congress for $4,992 he claimed as unpaid salary and compensation for a trunk containing all his valuable possessions that was thrown overboard during the *Chesapeake*'s battle.

54. Dye, *Fatal Cruise*, 48–51; Tucker and Reuter, *Injured Honor*, 70–71. All five of the *Halifax* deserters initially enlisted on the *Chesapeake*, but four quickly thought better of their action and promptly deserted from her.

55. Tucker and Reuter, *Injured Honor*, 78.

56. Dye, *Fatal Cruise*, 59.

57. Quoted in Tucker and Reuter, *Injured Honor*, 4–5.

58. "The Chesapeake and the Leopard," unidentified newspaper clipping, 1851, James Barron Papers, WMSC.

59. "Occurrences and remarks, on board the United States Frigate Chesapeak . . . Tuesday the 23 day of June year 1807," Allen, "Letters," 209–13; Tucker and Reuter, *Injured Honor*, 6–12, 151.

60. Dye, *Fatal Cruise*, 70; Tucker and Reuter, *Injured Honor*, 113–14.

61. Thomas Jefferson to Pierre S. Dupont de Nemours, July 14, 1807, Jefferson Papers, LC; Bond quoted in Tucker and Reuter, *Injured Honor*, 124.

62. Cray, "Remembering the *Chesapeake*," 445–46; Dye, *Fatal Cruise*, 68; Horsman, *Causes of War of 1812*, 103.

63. Thomas Jefferson to James Madison, August 25, 1807, Jefferson Papers, LC; Leiner, "Norfolk War Scare."

64. Canning quoted in Tucker and Reuter, *Injured Honor*, 130–31.

65. McKee, *Gentlemanly Profession*, 403–6, 498; De Kay, *Rage for Glory*, 32–34.

66. Tucker and Reuter, *Injured Honor*, 15.

67. Officers of the late U.S. Ship Chesapeake to secretary of the navy, June 23, 1807, James Barron Papers, WMSC.

68. William Henry Allen to William Allen, June 24, 1807, Allen, "Letters," 213–16; William Henry Allen to William Allen, July 17, 1807, quoted in Tucker and Reuter, *Injured Honor*, 152.

69. James Barron to Dr. Bullus, July 3, 1807, James Barron Papers, WMSC.

70. Tucker and Reuter, *Injured Honor*, 142.

71. Ibid., 163, 181.

72. Durand, *Life and Adventures*, 32–36; McKee, *Gentlemanly Profession*, 259–61.

73. Martin, *Most Fortunate Ship*, 88.

3. *"A Defence Worthy of Republicans"*

1. Joshua Humphreys to Robert Morris, January 6, 1793, letterbook, 1793–97, Joshua Humphreys Papers, HSP. Humphreys appears to have misdated this letter, which was probably written in January 1794.

2. Chapelle, *American Sailing Navy*, 5, 24–27.

3. Ibid., 57–58; Eddy, "Joshua Humphreys," 177.

4. Chapelle, *American Sailing Navy*, 13–19.

5. Lavery, *Nelson's Navy*, 228–29.

6. Otton, "*Constitution* Reborn"; Tucker, *Arming the Fleet*, 134, 139.

7. Chapelle, *American Sailing Navy*, 119–27; Fox quoted in ibid., 121.

8. Wood, *Live Oaking*, 3–4, 9–15, 40–41.

9. *ASP, Naval Affairs*, I: 11–13; Tucker, *Arming the Fleet*, 41, 124. According to Tucker, a thirty-two-pound shot requires a velocity of 1,090 feet per second to penetrate thirty inches of oak; the initial muzzle velocity of a thirty-two-pound carronade was 750 feet per second.

10. Wood, *Live Oaking*, 26–28, 55; John T. Morgan to Joshua Humphreys, October 21, 1794, letterbook, 1793–97, Joshua Humphreys Papers, HSP.

11. *ASP, Naval Affairs*, I: 8–9.

12. Dodds and Moore, *Wooden Fighting Ship*, 44; Brodine, Crawford, and Hughes, *Interpreting Old Ironsides*, 6.

13. *ASP, Naval Affairs*, I: 17–19.

14. "Principal Dimensions" Book, Joshua Humphreys Papers, HSP; William Jones to Joshua Humphreys, June 11, 1799, correspondence, ibid.; Joshua Humphreys to Thomas Truxtun, "On the Proportion of Masts and Spars," letterbook, 1793–97, ibid.

15. "To the Frigate Constitution," *Time Piece*, October 18, 1797.

16. John Barry to Joshua Humphreys, September 19, 1798, correspondence, Joshua Humphreys Papers, HSP.

17. Toll, *Six Frigates*, 95.

18. Chapelle, *American Sailing Navy*, 153–54, 161; Leiner, *Millions for Defense*, 24–27.

19. Randolph quoted in Perkins, *Prologue to War*, 163; Bentley, *Diary*, III: 414; Bainbridge quoted in Long, *Ready to Hazard*, 113.

20. Perkins, *Prologue to War*, 161–63.

21. *ASP, Foreign Relations*, III: 584.

22. Perkins, *Prologue to War*, 305–6.

23. Lowell, *Mr. Madison's War*, 11; Zimmerman, *Impressment*, 173.

24. *ASP, Naval Affairs*, I: 184–87, 193; Gallatin quoted in Adams, *Second Administration of Jefferson*, II: 428.

25. *ASP, Naval Affairs*, I: 194.

26. Bainbridge quoted in McKee, *Gentlemanly Profession*, 9.

27. John Rodgers to Isaac Hull, June 19, 1810, *NW1812*, I: 39–40.

28. Gilliam, "Letters," 54; Decatur quoted in Tucker, *Stephen Decatur*, 102.

29. *NW1812*, I: 40–50; the complete diplomatic correspondence over the *Little Belt* incident, including statements of the captains and a full transcript of the American court of inquiry, are reprinted in *ASP, Foreign Relations*, III: 476–500.

30. Clark, *Dolly Madison*, 136.

31. Wills, *James Madison*, 3–7; Smith, *First Forty Years*, 63; Gallatin quoted in Perkins, *Prologue to War*, 161.

32. Madison, *Letters and Other Writings*, IV: 491–92.

33. Stagg, *Mr. Madison's War*, 69; "Our Relations with G. Britain," *National Intelligencer*, April 16, 1811.

34. Foster, "Caviar Along Potomac," 78, 79, 89; Perkins, *Prologue to War*, 274–79, 354; Horsman, *Causes of War of 1812*, 203.

35. Stagg, *Mr. Madison's War*, 144; Stephen Decatur to Paul Hamilton, June 10, 1811, quoted in Tucker, *Stephen Decatur*, 104; David Porter to Hamilton, August 31, 1811, Madison Papers, LC; Perkins, *Prologue to War*, 291; Hamilton to James Madison, September 17, 1811, Madison Papers, LC.

36. Stagg, *Mr. Madison's War*, 59–61, 69, 74.

37. James Madison to John Quincy Adams, November 15, 1811, quoted in Horsman, *Causes of War of 1812*, 227; *ASP, Foreign Relations*, III: 405; Perkins, *Prologue to War*, 281–82.

38. Perkins, *Prologue to War*, 287–88; Taylor, "Agrarian Discontent," 498–99.

39. Jackson quoted in Horsman, *Causes of War of 1812*, 234–35.

40. Albert Gallatin, "Notes on President's message," n.d., Madison Papers, LC.

41. Paul Hamilton to Langdon Cheves, Chairman of the Naval Committee, December 3, 1811, *NW1812*, I: 53–60.

42. *AC*, 12th Cong., 1st sess. (January 18, 1812), 825–26, 840, 842; (January 21, 1812), 878.

43. Ibid. (January 18, 1812), 830–31, 833.

44. Ibid. (January 27, 1812), 999; (January 28, 1812), 1002–4; Tucker, *Stephen Decatur*, 101.

45. Long, *Ready to Hazard*, 126–29.

46. Maloney, *Captain from Connecticut*, 131.

47. Ibid., 134, 145.

48. Ibid., 46–47, 71.

49. Porter, *Constantinople*, I: 11.

50. Maloney, *Captain from Connecticut*, 140–42; Martin, *Most Fortunate Ship*, 91.

51. Maloney, *Captain from Connecticut*, 139, 143–44.

52. Ibid., 153.

53. Maloney, *Captain from Connecticut*, 156–57; Hull quoted in Smith, *Naval Scenes*, 18.

54. Morris, *Autobiography*, 47–48.

55. Maloney, *Captain from Connecticut*, 162–64.

56. Carden, *Curtail'd Memoir*, 8–13.

57. Littleton Waller Tazewell to James Monroe, February 27, 1812, reel 2, Monroe, *James Monroe Papers;* Hickey, *War of 1812*, 34–35; Forester, *Age of Fighting Sail*, 83–84.

58. Stagg, *Mr. Madison's War*, 146; Harris, *Commodore Bainbridge*, 135; Long, *Ready to Hazard*, 129–30.

59. Brant, "Timid President?"

60. Paul Hamilton to Morton A. Waring, October 17, October 19, November 30, 1810; May 11, 1812, Hamilton Papers, SCL.

61. Paul Hamilton to John Rodgers, May 21, 1812, *NW1812*, I: 118–19.

62. John Rodgers to Paul Hamilton, June 3, 1812, *NW1812*, I: 118–22; Stephen Decatur to Hamilton, June 8, 1812, ibid., I: 122–24.

63. Mahan, *Sea Power in 1812*, I: 315–18, 321–22.

64. Stephen Decatur to Paul Hamilton, June 8, 1812, *NW1812*, I: 122–24.

65. Agenda, Albert Gallatin, July 12, 1812, Madison Papers, LC.

66. Hickey, *War of 1812*, 40–44.

67. Albert Gallatin to James Madison, June 20, 1812, Madison Papers, LC.

68. Paul Hamilton to John Rodgers, June 22, 1812, *NW1812*, I: 148–49.

69. Paul Hamilton to Morton A. Waring, July 25, 1812, Hamilton Papers, SCL.

4. "The Present War, Unexpected, Unnecessary, and Ruinous"

1. Hickey, *Don't Give Up the Ship*, 42; Foster quoted in Perkins, *Prologue to War*, 416.

2. Perkins, *Prologue to War*, 316, 332–33; Horsman, *Causes of War of 1812*, 256–57; Brougham quoted in Perkins, *Prologue to War*, 340.

3. *Naval Chronicle* 28 (1812): 157–58, 246–47.

4. William Jones to Eleanor Jones, July 12, 1812, Jones Papers, HSP.

5. William Bainbridge to Paul Hamilton, July 11, 1812, *NW1812*, I: 190–91.

6. Martin, *Most Fortunate Ship*, 100–101.

7. Isaac Hull to Joseph Hull, July 5, 1812, quoted in Maloney, *Captain from Connecticut*, 170.

8. Isaac Hull to Paul Hamilton, July 2, 1812, *NW1812*, I: 160–61; Martin, *Most Fortunate Ship*, 103; Smith, *Naval Scenes*, 24.

9. Maloney, *Captain from Connecticut*, 170–71; Martin, *Most Fortunate Ship*, 104.

10. Smith, *Naval Scenes*, 25.

11. The account of the *Constitution*'s escape that follows is drawn from several eyewitness accounts: Hull's official report, Isaac Hull to Paul Hamilton, July 21, 1812, *NW1812*, I:

161–65; Morris, *Autobiography*, 56–61; Evans, "Journal," 153–56; Smith, *Naval Scenes*, 25–28. In addition, Roosevelt, *Naval War of 1812*, 47–50, and Forester, *Age of Fighting Sail*, 48–56, provide very helpful explanations of the seamanship and maneuvers employed.

12. Brown quoted in Coggeshall, *American Privateers*, 8–9, 12.

13. *NW1812*, I: 165.

14. Evans, "Journal," 158–60.

15. "Business and the Coffee House," 11–13.

16. *Columbian Centinel*, August 1, 1812.

17. Evans, "Journal," 161.

18. "Old and New Times," *Columbian Centinel*, August 1, 1812.

19. Lathrop, *Present War*, 5, 10–11, 13.

20. Hickey, *War of 1812*, 53.

21. "Address . . . to their respective constituents," *AC*, 12th Cong., 1st sess. (Appendix, 1812), 2219.

22. Ibid., 2196.

23. "Whoever Is Not for Us, Is Against Us," *Boston Gazette*, May 21, 1812.

24. Wright quoted in Hickey, *War of 1812*, 56–57; Thomas Jefferson to James Madison, June 29, 1812, Madison Papers, LC.

25. Hickey, *War of 1812*, 56–59.

26. "Effects of the War," *Federal Republican*, December 31, 1812.

27. Hickey, *War of 1812*, 60–67; "The Narrative of John Thomas," *Hagers-Town Gazette*, August 18, 1812.

28. John Adams to John Adams Smith, June 15, 1812, reel 118, MHS, *Adams Papers*.

29. Blake and Lawrence, *Nelson's Navy*, 49.

30. Lavery, *Nelson's Navy*, 241–44.

31. Ibid., 94.

32. Elias, "Naval Profession," 294, 307–9.

33. Lewis, *Social History*, 223.

34. Ibid., 206.

35. Lavery, *Nelson's Navy*, 93; Lewis, *Social History*, 222.

36. Collingwood quoted in Lewis, *Social History*, 222–24.

37. Long, *Ready to Hazard*, 133; Lewis, *Social History*, 369–71.

38. James, *Naval History*, VI: 96; Roosevelt, *Naval War of 1812*, 248; Nelson quoted in Tucker, *Arming the Fleet*, 37.

39. Adams, *First Administration of Jefferson*, I: 219–22; Jefferson quoted in Balinky, "Albert Gallatin," 302.

40. Smith quoted in McKee, *Gentlemanly Profession*, 285, 304.

41. Ibid., 282.

42. Smith quoted in ibid., 277.

43. William Jones to Joseph Anderson, July 30, 1813, *NW1812*, II: 208; Jones to James Renshaw, September 15, 1813, ibid., II: 209–10; Jones to Robert T. Spence, July 26, 1813, quoted in McKee, *Gentlemanly Profession*, 277–78.

44. Nicholas Brewer quoted in McKee, *Gentlemanly Profession*, 113.

45. Truxtun quoted in ibid., 159.

46. Valle, *Rocks and Shoals*, 43–46; Truxtun quoted in McKee, *Gentlemanly Profession*, 225–26.

47. Lewis, *Social History*, 124, 139.

48. List of Punishments, 1812–14, WAR/21, NMM.

49. Isaac Hull to Paul Hamilton, July 28, 1812, *NW1812*, I: 206–7.

50. Maloney, *Captain from Connecticut*, 180.

51. Isaac Hull to Paul Hamilton, August 2, 1812, *NW1812*, I: 207–9.

52. Isaac Hull to Joseph Hull, August 1, 1812, in Maloney, *Captain from Connecticut*, 181.

53. Evans, "Journal," 163, 165, 166.

54. Entry for August 15, 1812, Private Journal Kept on Board the U.S. Frigate Constitution, Amos A. Evans Papers, LC. This passage is not included in the published version of Evans's journal.

55. Evans, "Journal," 168–69; Isaac Hull to Paul Hamilton, August 28, 1812, *NW1812*, I: 230–33.

56. "Shipping News," *New-England Palladium*, September 1, 1812; Coggeshall, *American Privateers*, 25.

57. "Captain Dacres' Challenge," *Weekly Register* 3 (1812): 31.

58. Smith, *Naval Scenes*, 30.

59. Coggeshall, *American Privateers*, 26; William B. Orne to Phineas Sprague, April 27, 1813, George H. Stuart Papers, LC; "British Account," *Weekly Register* 3 (1812): 109; Smith, *Naval Scenes*, 34; "The Capture of the Guerriere by the Constitution," *New York Times*, January 31, 1852. The last, an anonymous account subsequently republished in several newspapers and magazines under the byline "Octogenarian" (see e.g., Orne, "Reminiscence"), appears to match other recollections definitely written by Orne, including the letter published in Coggeshall cited above.

60. "Captain Hull," *Weekly Register* 3 (1812): 159; Smith, *Naval Scenes*, 31–32; Coggeshall, *American Privateers*, 26–27; Wilson, "Commodore Hull," 106.

61. Morris, *Autobiography*, 62–63; John Contee to Franklin Wharton, August 31, 1812, *NW1812*, I: 246.

62. Smith, *Naval Scenes*, 36.

63. Maloney, *Captain from Connecticut*, 189–90.

64. Coggeshall, *American Privateers*, 27; "The Capture of the Guerriere by the Constitution," *New York Times*, January 31, 1852; "British Account," *Weekly Register* 3 (1812): 109.

65. Gilliam, "Letters," 60–61.

66. Adams, "Birth of a World Power," 519–20.

67. Maloney, *Captain from Connecticut*, 192; Gilliam, "Letters," 61; Morris, *Autobiography*, 63; "The Capture of the Guerriere by the Constitution," *New York Times*, January 31, 1852; Evans, "Journal," 376.

68. Isaac Hull to Paul Hamilton, August 28, 1812, *NW1812*, I: 237–42; James R. Dacres to Herbert Sawyer, September 7, 1812, *NW1812*, I: 243–45; Smith, *Naval Scenes*, 36; Evans, "Journal," 376.

5. Love of Fame Is a Noble Passion

1. John Rodgers to Paul Hamilton, September 1, 1812, *NW1812*, I: 262–66; Maloney, "War of 1812," 48–49; Essex Institute, *American Vessels Captured*, 96, 99, 100; Philip Broke to Sarah Louisa Broke, August 9, 1812, LBK 58/2, NMM.

2. Smith, *Naval Scenes*, 38; Maloney, *Captain from Connecticut*, 195–96.

3. "Tribute to American Gallantry," *Connecticut Herald*, September 15, 1812.

4. Gafford, "Boston Stage," 329–30; Evans, "Journal," 384–85.

5. *Columbian Naval Melody*, 15–16.

6. *American Patriotic Song-Book*, 141.

7. Gillespy, *Columbian Naval Songster*, 16.

8. "The Naval Victory," *Repertory*, September 1, 1812.

9. "Progress of the War," *Repertory*, September 1, 1812.

10. "British Account of the Capture of Detroit," *Boston Gazette*, September 3, 1812; Evans, "Journal," 379; Hickey, *War of 1812*, 82–84.

11. Evans, "Journal," 380.

12. Isaac Hull to Paul Hamilton, September 1, 1812, quoted in Maloney, *Captain from Connecticut*, 196.

13. Maloney, *Captain from Connecticut*, 192, 194, 196–97; Smith, *Naval Scenes*, 35.

14. Evans, "Journal," 382, Smith, *Naval Scenes*, 38; Maloney, *Captain from Connecticut*, 200.

15. Smith, *Naval Scenes*, 38–39; Martin, *Most Fortunate Ship*, 129; Long, *Ready to Hazard*, 143.

16. Maloney, *Captain from Connecticut*, 207–8; Wilson, "Commodore Hull," 109.

17. A List of Ships and Vessels on the West Indian and American Stations, August 7, 1812, HUL/18, NMM; The Present Disposition of His Majesty's Ships and Vessels in Sea Pay, July 1, 1812, ADM 8/100, TNA; "Naval History of the Present Year, 1812," *Naval Chronicle* 28 (1812): 159.

18. Warren, Sir John Borlase, *Dictionary of Canadian Biography Online*, www.biographi.ca; Lohnes, "British Naval Problems at Halifax," 324.

19. John Borlase Warren to the secretary of state, September 30, 1812, *ASP, Foreign Relations*, III: 595–96.

20. List of Punishments, WAR/21, NMM; Weekly Return of the Sick and Wounded, WAR/25, NMM; Disposition of Squadron, State and Condition of Ships, WAR/32, NMM.

21. Flag Officers Accounts, Sir John Borlase Warren, Account No. 1, October 31, 1813, HUL/33, NMM; Letters and Papers Relating to Prize Money, Sir John Borlase Warren, No. 2, May 24, 1815, WAR/33, NMM.

22. Lohnes, "British Naval Problems at Halifax," 319–22; Philip Broke to Sarah Louisa Broke, October 10, 1812, LBK/58, NMM.

23. Orders No. 1 (October 4, 1812), No. 2 (October 10, 1812), No. 3 (October 14, 1812), Orderbook of Adm Sir J Borlase Warren, HUL/1, NMM.

24. John Borlase Warren to John W. Croker, October 5, 1812, *NW1812*, I: 507–9.

25. Dudley, *Wooden Wall*, 69.

26. John Borlase Warren to Edward P. Brenton, November 5, 1812, Orderbook of Adm. Sir J. Borlase Warren, HUL/1, NMM.

27. James Monroe to John Borlase Warren, October 28, 1812, *ASP, Foreign Relations*, III: 598; James R. Dacres to Herbert Sawyer, *NW1812*, I: 243–45.

28. Letters relating to prisoners of war, Cartel for the Exchange of Prisoners of War, WAR/79, NMM.

29. David Porter to Paul Hamilton, August 15, 1812, *NW1812*, I: 218–19; Porter to Hamilton, August 20, 1812, *NW1812*, I: 219–20.

30. John T. Duckworth to Paul Hamilton, August 31, 1812, reprinted in "Exchange of Prisoners," *Weekly Register* 3 (1812): 89.

31. "Naval," *Weekly Register* 3 (1812): 53.

32. Evans, "Journal," 380; William M. Crane to Herbert Sawyer, August 28, 1812, *NW1812*, I: 233–34; Sawyer to Crane, August 29, 1812, *NW1812*, I: 235.

33. Anthony St. John Baker to James Monroe, September 19, 1812, *NW1812*, I: 499; John Borlase Warren to Monroe, September 30, 1812, *ASP, Foreign Relations*, III: 598.

34. David Porter to Paul Hamilton, September 3, 1812, *NW1812*, I: 443–47.

35. Farragut, *Life*, 15–16.

36. David Porter to William Bainbridge, September 8, 1812, *NW1812*, I: 468–69.

37. John Rodgers to Paul Hamilton, September 4, 1812, *NW1812*, I: 450–51; Bainbridge quoted in Maloney, "War of 1812," 49; Hamilton to Rodgers, September 9, 1812, *NW1812*, I: 471–72.

38. William Jones to William Bainbridge, October 11, 1812, *NW1812*, I: 512–15.

39. Smith, *Frigate Essex*, 266–80.

40. *NW1812*, I: 466; "Aid to Glory," 184.

41. William Bainbridge to William Jones, October 5, 1812, *NW1812*, I: 510–12.

42. Evans, "Journal," 386.

43. Carden, *Curtail'd Memoir*, 256–58.

44. Leech, *Thirty Years*, 70, 87–89, 99.

45. Ibid., 125–27.

46. Ibid., 128.

47. Testimony of Lt. David Hope, Court martial, Captain J. S. Carden and the officers and Ships Company of the Macedonian, May 27, 28, 29 & 31, 1813, ADM 1/5436, TNA.

48. The best accounts of the battle are the *Macedonian* court-martial cited above; Roosevelt, *Naval War of 1812*, 61–67; and Mahan, *Sea Power in 1812*, I: 416–22. Neither Decatur nor the officers of the *United States* left any detailed description of the action; Decatur's official report devotes no more than a single sentence to describing the actual engagement: Stephen Decatur to Paul Hamilton, October 30, 1812, *NW1812*, I: 552–53.

49. Testimony of Lt. John Bulford, Court martial, Captain J. S. Carden and the officers and Ships Company of the Macedonian, May 27, 28, 29 & 31, 1813, ADM 1/5436, TNA.

50. John S. Carden to John W. Croker, October 28, 1812, *NW1812*, I: 549–52.

51. Leech, *Thirty Years*, 147; Carden, *Curtail'd Memoir*, 264; Tucker, *Stephen Decatur*, 119.

52. Roosevelt, *Naval War of 1812*, 63; Tucker, *Arming the Fleet*, 41.

53. "Life of Captain William Henry Allen," *Port Folio* 3 (1814): 2–23.

54. Carden, *Curtail'd Memoir*, 265.

55. Tucker, *Stephen Decatur*, 121–22; Dye, *Fatal Cruise*, 93–94; Leech, *Thirty Years*, 153–59.

56. "Another Brilliant Naval Victory!" *National Intelligencer*, December 10, 1812; Latrobe quoted in Dye, *Fatal Cruise*, 93.

57. Arthur Sinclair to Paul Hamilton, October 7, 1812, *NW1812*, I: 518–19; Daniel T. Patterson to Hamilton, November 10, 1812, *NW1812*, I: 423–25; William Bainbridge to Hamilton, October 8, 1812, *NW1812*, I: 517; James Lawrence to Hamilton, October 10, 1812, *NW1812*, I: 519–20; Lawrence to Hamilton, October 22, 1812, *NW1812*, I: 522–23.

58. Paul Hamilton to Stephen Decatur, December 29, 1812, *NW1812*, I: 638–39; Hamilton to Burwell Bassett, November 21, 1812, *NW1812*, I: 577–79; Maloney, *Captain from Connecticut*, 203–4.

59. Isaac Hull to David Daggett, November 18, 1814, quoted in Maloney, *Captain from Connecticut*, 259–60.

60. Decatur quoted in Tucker, *Stephen Decatur*, 123; John Rodgers to Paul Hamilton, October 17, 1812, *NW1812*, I: 535–36; Rodgers to Hamilton, January 2, 1813, *NW1812*, II: 4–5.

61. David Porter to Paul Hamilton, October 14, 1812, *NW1812*, I: 527–28; Daniel T. Patterson to Hamilton, November 10, 1812, *NW1812*, I: 423–25; Hamilton to James Lawrence, October 17, 1812, *NW1812*, I: 522; "From the Boston Daily Advertiser," *Federal Republican*, April 2, 1813.

62. David Porter to Samuel Hambleton, February 28, 1812, quoted in Porter, *Memoir*, 100.

63. "The Secretary of the Navy," *Yankee*, October 30, 1812; Eckert, *Navy Department*, 15; Mitchill quoted in Stagg, *Mr. Madison's War*, 289.

64. James Monroe to John Borlase Warren, October 27, 1812, *ASP, Foreign Relations*, III: 596–97.

65. Mitchill quoted in Stagg, *Mr. Madison's War*, 273.

66. Paul Hamilton to James Madison, December 30, 1812, Madison Papers, LC; Madi-

son to Hamilton, December 31, 1812, Madison Papers, LC; "Mr. Hamilton," *Federal Republican,* February 26, 1813.

67. Evans, "Journal," 469–70.

68. William Jones to William Bainbridge, October 11, 1812, *NW1812,* I: 512–15.

69. Long, *Nothing Too Daring,* 77.

70. William Jones to William Bainbridge, October 11, 1812, *NW1812,* I: 512–15; Evans, "Journal," 470–73; Long, *Ready to Hazard,* 144–47; Martin, *Most Fortunate Ship,* 130–31.

71. Journal of Commodore William Bainbridge, *NW1812,* I: 639–44.

72. "A List of the Killed and Wounded of H.M.S. Java," *Naval Chronicle* 29 (1813): 348–49; Long, *Ready to Hazard,* 154–55; Roosevelt, *Naval War of 1812,* 73.

73. William Bainbridge to John Bullus, January 23, 1813, Fogg Autograph Collection, MeHS.

74. Henry D. Chads, January 4, 1813, ADM 1/21, TNA.

75. "Extract of a letter from Commodore Bainbridge, to his friend in this city," *New-York Gazette,* February 27, 1813.

6. Walls of Wood

1. "Retrospective and Miscellaneous," *Naval Chronicle* 29 (1813): 242.

2. *Times* (London), March 20, 1813.

3. Ibid., October 29, 1812; December 19, 1812; March 20, 1813.

4. "Courts Martial," *Naval Chronicle* 28 (1812): 422–24.

5. Court martial, Captain J. S. Carden and the officers and Ships Company of the Macedonian, May 27, 28, 29 & 31, 1813, ADM 1/5436, TNA.

6. *Naval Chronicle* 28 (1812): 381–82; *Naval Chronicle* 29 (1813): 117–19; "Our 'fir-built Frigates,' " *Yankee,* December 18, 1812.

7. *Naval Chronicle* 29 (1813): 288–89; "From the London Star," *Federal Republican,* March 15, 1813.

8. John S. Carden to John W. Croker, October 28, 1812, *NW1812,* I: 549–52; *Naval Chronicle* 29 (1813): 117–19; "Courts Martial," *Naval Chronicle* 28 (1812): 422–24.

9. Roosevelt, *Naval War of 1812,* 31–34, 40–41, 54–55, 63, 72; Tucker, *Arming the Fleet,* 93; Duffy, *Captain Blakeley,* 191–92.

10. Cobbett quoted in Lossing, *Pictorial Field-Book,* 140n.

11. *Naval Chronicle* 29 (1813): 472–73.

12. Ibid., 465.

13. Ibid., 402, 466–69, 473–74.

14. *Times,* October 29, 1812; Liverpool and Foster quoted in Adams, *Second Administration of Madison,* I: 15, 17, 24.

15. Croker, *Naval War with America,* 3, 12–13, 23, 38.

16. Croker, *Croker Papers,* 1–2, 18, 20–22.

17. Carden, *Curtail'd Memoir,* 281–83.

18. Gardiner, ed., *Naval War of 1812,* 160–63.

19. John W. Croker to John B. Warren, January 9, 1813, *NW1812,* II: 14–15.

20. Ibid.; John W. Croker to John B. Warren, February 10, 1813, *NW1812,* II: 16–19.

21. John W. Croker to John B. Warren, January 9, 1813, *NW1812,* II: 14–15; Dudley, *Wooden Wall,* 80–81.

22. John B. Warren to John W. Croker, December 29, 1812, *NW1812,* I: 649–51; John W. Croker to John B. Warren, February 10, 1813, *NW1812,* II: 16–19; Lords Commissioners of the Admiralty to Warren, November 27, 1812, pp. 276–78, ADM 2/1375, TNA.

23. Pack, *Cockburn,* 59–63.

24. Dudley, *Wooden Wall*, 91.

25. Vessels Captured and Detained, WAR/37, NMM; "A List of Vessels Brought into Bermuda from the Commencement of the American War," HUL/18, NMM; Essex Institute, *American Vessels Captured;* Dudley, *Wooden Wall*, 143.

26. *Narrative of Capture of Vixen*, 7.

27. Lohnes, "Naval Problems at Halifax," 322, 325.

28. Dudley, *Wooden Wall*, 11–13, 28–29.

29. Ibid., 19; John W. Croker to John B. Warren, March 20, 1813, *NW1812*, II: 75–78.

30. Dudley, *Wooden Wall*, 175–81.

31. Robert Saunders Dundas Melville to John B. Warren, March 26, 1813, *NW1812*, II: 78–79; John W. Croker to John B. Warren, March 20, 1813, *NW1812*, II: 75–78.

32. A Proclamation, John B. Warren, February 6, 1813, p. 221, ADM 1/503, TNA; Warren to John W. Croker, February 21, 1813, pp. 213–16, ibid.

33. Standing Orders on the North American Station, John B. Warren, March 6, 1813, *NW1812*, II: 59–60.

34. William Jones to Eleanor Jones, January 23, 1813, Jones Papers, HSP.

35. Robert Smith to William Jones, November 4, November 13, 1810, ibid.; Richard Rush to Jones, March 29, April 3, June 3, 1812, ibid.

36. Eckert, "William Jones," 170–71; "Copy of address presented to capt. William Jones," *City Gazette & Daily Advertiser*, May 8, 1795.

37. William Bainbridge to William Jones, March 1, 1813; George Read to Jones, January 10, 1813, Jones Papers, HSP.

38. William Jones to Eleanor Jones, March 22, 1813; Jones to James Ewell, March 10, 1813; Benjamin Homans to Jones, n.d., 1813, ibid.

39. Notes, January 1813; William Jones to Lloyd Jones, February 27, 1813, ibid.; Jones to Amos Binney, February 9, 1813, *NW1812*, II: 44; Jones to Burwell Bassett, February 2, 1813, *NW1812*, II: 24–26; Edward Cutbush to Jones, February 13, 1813, *NW1812*, II: 38–39; Eckert, *Navy Department*, 39–40.

40. William Jones to Eleanor Jones, March 8, February 10, 1813, Jones Papers, HSP.

41. William Jones to Eleanor Jones, April 10, January 23, 1813, ibid.

42. William Jones to Eleanor Jones, March 21, April 7, 1813, ibid.

43. Hull quoted in Maloney, *Captain from Connecticut*, 203; Hickey, *War of 1812*, 109–10.

44. *AC*, 12th Cong., 2nd sess. (December 15, 1812), 33; *AC*, 12th Cong., 2nd sess. (December 23, 1812), 443–50; Stagg, *Mr. Madison's War*, 291; Hickey, *War of 1812*, 118.

45. William Jones to James Madison, October 26, 1814, *NW1812*, III: 631–36.

46. Circular from William Jones to Commanders of Ships now in port refitting, February 22, 1813, *NW1812*, II: 47–49.

47. William Jones to Samuel Smith, February 22, 1813, *NW1812*, II: 45; Chapelle, *American Sailing Navy*, 256–63.

48. Charles Stewart to William Jones, February 5, 1813, *NW1812*, II: 311–13; Jones to John Cassin, February 16, 1813, *NW1812*, II: 313–15.

49. William Jones to Eleanor Jones, March 21, March 22, 1813, Jones Papers, HSP.

50. Henry, Earl Bathurst, to Thomas Sidney Beckwith, March 20, 1813, *NW1812*, II: 325–26.

7. *"You Shall Now Feel the Effects of War"*

1. *New-England Palladium*, April 16, 1813; *Statesman*, April 12, 1813.

2. William Bainbridge to William Jones, March 1, 1813, Jones Papers, HSP.

3. Ann Hull quoted in Maloney, *Captain from Connecticut*, 210.

4. John W. Croker to John B. Warren, March 20, 1813, *NW1812*, II: 75–78; Thomas Bladen Capel to Warren, May 11, 1813, *NW1812*, II: 105–6.

5. William Jones to Charles Stewart, April 8, 1813, *NW1812*, II: 346–47.

6. Garitee, *Republic's Private Navy*, 52–53; Mahon, *War of 1812*, II: 17–18.

7. William Jones to Eleanor Jones, March 22, 1813, Jones Papers, HSP; Isaac Hull to Jones, April 23, 1813, *NW1812*, II: 92; Jones to Hull, April 30, 1813, *NW1812*, II: 94–95; Maloney, *Captain from Connecticut*, 215–16; Long, *Ready to Hazard*, 175.

8. William Jones to Charles Stewart, April 8, 1813, *NW1812*, II: 346–47; Jones to Stewart, March 27, 1813, *NW1812*, II: 317.

9. Roosevelt, *Naval War of 1812*, 93–97; James, *Naval Occurrences*, 100; *NW1812*, II: 59, 68–75; *Peacock* court-martial, June 7, 1813, ADM 1/5436, TNA.

10. Craig, "Notes on Action," 75.

11. Pack, *Cockburn*, 146; Mahan, *Sea Power in 1812*, II: 162.

12. Kendall Addison to George Cockburn, March 18, 1813, p. 171, ADM 1/4359, TNA; George Cockburn to Kendall Addison, May 19, 1813, *NW1812*, II: 324.

13. Naval General Order, William Jones, July 29, 1812, *NW1812*, II: 205; John Hayes to John B. Warren, n.d. 1813, *NW1812*, II: 272–73; William Bainbridge to William Jones, December 31, 1813, *NW1812*, II: 273.

14. Hickey, *War of 1812*, 171; Wright quoted in Tilghman and Harrison, *Talbot County*, I: 53–54.

15. Hickey, *War of 1812*, 115–16, 168–71.

16. Crawford, "Licensed Trade," 166; Garitee, *Republic's Private Navy*, 50; Dudley, *Wooden Wall*, 147; Hickey, *War of 1812*, 117.

17. Hickey, "Trade Restrictions," 524.

18. *AC*, 12th Cong., 2nd sess. (February 24, 1813), 1116–17.

19. Crawford, "Licensed Trade," 166–67.

20. Long, *Ready to Hazard*, 143; *Cases Decided*, 63–68.

21. Crawford, "Licensed Trade," 168; Leiner, "*Ruse de Guerre*," 162–72, 175, 183.

22. Scott, *Prize Cases*, I: 505–6, 507, 509.

23. *AC*, 13th Cong., 1st sess. (July 29, 1813), 484–85; Dudley, *Wooden Wall*, 100.

24. Letters from Philip Broke to Sarah Louisa Broke, LBK 58/2, NMM.

25. Leiner, "Squadron Commander's Share," 74–77; Lawrence quoted in Robert Dudley Oliver to John B. Warren, June 23, 1813, *NW1812*, II: 192–93.

26. Lawrence quoted in Purcell, "Don't Give Up the Ship," 86; "Naval Battle," 375–78.

27. Tucker, *Arming the Fleet*, 48; Gilkerson, *Boarders Away*, 7, 8.

28. Roche, "Dockyard Reminiscences," 62–63.

29. An Account of the *Chesapeake–Shannon* Action, June 6, 1813, *NW1812*, II: 129–33. This was Broke's official report, but probably was not actually written by him owing to his injuries. Other sources for the account of the battle that follows are George Budd to William Jones, June 15, 1813, *NW1812*, II: 133–34; Mahan, *Sea Power in 1812*, II: 135–47; Roosevelt, *Naval War of 1812*, 100–108; Post, "Case of Captain Lawrence."

30. Gilkerson, *Boarders Away*, 11–14.

31. "Arrival of *Chesapeake*," 161.

32. Philip Broke to John B. Warren, June 6, 1813, ff. 14–15, WAR/70, NMM; Broke to Sarah Louisa Broke, August 31, September 28, 1813, LBK 58/2, NMM; Prize lists for captures by HM Ships SHANNON and STATIRA, ADM 238/13, TNA.

33. "House of Commons, Thursday, July 8," *Times* (London), July 9, 1813; Montagu, *England Victorious*, 34; "Nautical Anecdotes," *Naval Chronicle* 30 (1813): 41; "Naval History of the Present Year, 1813," ibid., 69, 161; "Impromptu," ibid., 158; Forester, *Age of Fighting Sail*, 166.

34. John W. Croker to Station Commanders in Chief, July 10, 1813, *NW1812*, II: 183–84.
35. Valle, "Navy's Battle Doctrine," 172–73.
36. William Jones to George Parker, December 8, 1813, *NW1812*, II: 294–96; Jones to John O. Creighton, December 22, 1813, *NW1812*, II: 296–97.
37. Stephen Decatur to William Jones, May 22, 1813, quoted in Dunne, "Inglorious First," 207; Jones to Decatur, May 10, 1813, quoted in Dye, *Fatal Cruise*, 118.
38. Dunne, "Inglorious First," 208–9.
39. Hardy quoted in ibid., 212.
40. Robert Dudley Oliver to John B. Warren, June 13, 1813, *NW1812*, II: 137–38; Stephen Decatur to William Jones, June 1813, *NW1812*, II: 135–36; Adams, *Second Administration of Madison*, I: 279.
41. Decatur quoted in Jordan, "Decatur at New London," 63; Adams, *Second Administration of Madison*, I: 279–80.
42. Mahan, *Sea Power in 1812*, II: 153–54; John B. Croker to Edward Griffith, July 9, 1813, pp. 140–42, ADM 2/1377, TNA.
43. Dudley, *Wooden Wall*, 94–95; Dye, *Fatal Cruise*, 139.
44. John W. Croker to John B. Warren, April 28, 1813, pp. 320–22, ADM 2/1376, TNA.
45. George Cockburn to John B. Warren, May 3, 1813, *NW1812*, II: 341–44.
46. Hickey, *Don't Give Up the Ship*, 236–38; "Events of the War," *Weekly Register* 4 (1813): 164.
47. George Cockburn to John B. Warren, May 3, 1813, *NW1812*, II: 341–44; Lossing, *Pictorial Field-Book*, 671–72; Deposition of William T. Killpatrick, *ASP, Military Affairs*, I: 365.
48. Milne quoted in Hume, "Letters Written," 290.
49. George Cockburn to John B. Warren, May 6, 1813, *NW1812*, II: 344–46.
50. "Events of the War," *Weekly Register* 4 (1813): 402.
51. Dudley, *Wooden Wall*, 96.
52. Rouse, "Low Tide at Hampton," 81–82; Mahan, *Sea Power in 1812*, II: 164–66; John Cassin to William Jones, June 23, 1813, *NW1812*, II: 359–60.
53. Napier, *Life and Opinions*, I: 217, 222, 228.
54. Report by Thomas Griffin and Robert Lively, July 4, 1813, *ASP, Military Affairs*, I: 379–81; Napier, *Life and Opinions*, I: 221.
55. Sidney Beckwith to Robert Taylor, June 29, 1813, *ASP, Military Affairs*, I: 376; John Myers to Robert Taylor, July 2, 1813, ibid., 377; Beckwith to John B. Warren, July 5, 1813, *NW1812*, II: 364–65; Hickey, *War of 1812*, 154.
56. Napier, *Life and Opinions*, I: 222; Robert Taylor to John B. Warren, June 29, 1813, *ASP, Military Affairs*, I: 375–76.
57. George Cockburn to John B. Warren, June 16, 1813, *NW1812*, II: 355–56.
58. Calderhead, "Naval Innovation," 217–18.
59. Jacob Lewis to William Jones, June 28, 1813, *NW1812*, II: 161; John B. Warren to John W. Croker, July 22, 1813, *NW1812*, II: 162–63; General orders, John B. Warren, July 19, 1813, *NW1812*, II: 164; Tucker, *Stephen Decatur*, 131.
60. James Madison to William Jones, September 6, 1813, Jones Papers, HSP; Madison to John Mason, September 23, 1813, *NW1812*, II: 248–49.
61. *ASP, Foreign Relations*, III: 633–44; John Mason to James Prince, September 28, 1813, ibid., 655; Prevost quoted in Hickey, *War of 1812*, 178.
62. Thomas Barclay to the Commissary General of Prisoners, September 17, 1813, *ASP, Foreign Relations*, III: 652; George Cockburn to John B. Warren, March 13, 1813, *NW1812*, II: 320–24; Dye, "Maritime Prisoners," 301–2; James Monroe to Commissary General of Prisoners, April 13, 1814, *ASP, Foreign Relations*, III: 632–33; Hickey, *War of 1812*, 177–78.
63. Dudley, *Wooden Wall*, 98–99; Napier, *Life and Opinions*, 218, 221–22.

64. Chandler Price to William Jones, February 12, 1813, Jones Papers, HSP; Hickey, *War of 1812*, 135–36, 139–41; Ingersoll quoted in ibid., 141.

65. Hickey, *Don't Give Up the Ship*, 149–50; Hickey, *War of 1812*, 144–45.

66. William Jones to Isaac Chauncey, January 27, 1813, *NW1812*, II: 419–20; Chauncey to Noah Brown, February 18, 1813, *NW1812*, II: 426–27; William Bainbridge to Jones, April 27, 1813, *NW1812*, II: 429–30.

67. William Jones to James Madison, October 26, 1814, *NW1812*, III: 631–36.

68. Parsons, *Battle of Lake Erie*, 12; Cox, "Eyewitness Account."

69. Hickey, *War of 1812*, 137–38.

70. Monroe quoted in Stagg, *Mr. Madison's War*, 467; William Jones to James Madison, October 26, 1814, *NW1812*, III: 631–36.

71. Parsons, *Surgeon of the Lakes*, x; Evans, "Journal," 152; Estes and Dye, "Death on the *Argus*," 184.

72. Parsons, "Surgical Account," 314.

73. Ibid., 315–16; *NW1812*, II: 561; Parsons, *Surgeon of the Lakes*, xiii.

74. Estes and Dye, "Death on the *Argus*," 186–89; Dye, *Fatal Cruise*, 137; Goddard, "Navy Surgeon's Chest"; Smith, *Frigate Essex*, 282–87; Brodine, Crawford, and Hughes, *Interpreting Old Ironsides*, 61–62; *NW1812*, II: 616; Isaac Chauncey to William Jones, December 19, 1813, *NW1812*, II: 621.

8. The Far Side of the World

1. "Events of the War," *Weekly Register* 4 (1813): 374; "Events of the War," *Weekly Register* 5 (1813): 29.

2. *NW1812*, II: 683.

3. Long, *Nothing Too Daring*, 33–34.

4. Paul Hamilton to David Porter, June 30, 1812, *NW1812*, I: 175–76; Long, *Nothing Too Daring*, 64.

5. Porter, *Journal*, I: 222; Long, *Nothing Too Daring*, 38–39.

6. Porter, *Journal*, I: 24–27. Porter omitted the "black hole of Calcutta" remark in the second, and much more widely available, edition of his book. Long, *Nothing Too Daring*, 74, quotes the original passage, and is elsewhere a useful source for other passages that appeared only in the now hard-to-find first edition.

7. Porter, *Journal*, I: 21, 2–3, 18; David Porter to secretary of the navy, July 2, 1813, *NW1812*, II: 697–99.

8. Journal of Midshipman William W. Feltus kept on board the U.S. frigate *Essex*, *NW1812*, I: 625–27; Jones, *Journals of Yankee*, 83–86; Browne, *Yankee Privateer*, 61–64; Porter, *Journal*, I: 15.

9. Porter, *Journal*, I: 48–49.

10. Ibid., I: 56–57.

11. Ibid., I: 61–63.

12. Long, *Nothing Too Daring*, 81.

13. Porter, *Journal*, I: 64–67.

14. Ibid., I: 74, 75–77; Farragut, *Life*, 20.

15. Porter, *Journal*, I: 92–93; Salas, "First Contacts," 220–22.

16. Porter, *Journal*, I: 139–40, 95, 103.

17. David Porter to the Viceroy of Peru, March 26, 1813, *NW1812*, II: 692.

18. Porter, *Journal*, I: 115; Journal of Midshipman William W. Feltus, *NW1812*, II: 694.

19. Porter, *Journal*, I: 128.

20. Ibid., I: 142, 146–49

21. Farragut, *Life,* 31.

22. Porter, *Journal,* I: 148–49; David Porter to secretary of the navy, July 2, 1813, *NW1812,* II: 696; Farragut, *Life,* 23.

23. Porter, *Journal,* I: 150.

24. Ibid., I: 151–52, 160–61, 214.

25. Farragut, *Life,* 26.

26. Porter, *Journal,* I: 174, 188, 205, 213–14.

27. Ibid., I: 195–96, 207–8, 240; Long, *Nothing Too Daring,* 100–103.

28. Farragut, *Life,* 28; Porter, *Journal,* I: 237, II: 65.

29. Porter, *Journal,* II: 3–4; Long, *Nothing Too Daring,* 110.

30. Hickey, *War of 1812,* 118–23.

31. William Jones to Eleanor Jones, July 14, 1813, Jones Papers, HSP; Eckert, "William Jones," 176.

32. William Jones to Eleanor Jones, September 17, 1813, Jones Papers, HSP.

33. Rebecca Strong to Eleanor Jones, May 12, 1813; William Jones to Eleanor Jones, September 17, 1813, ibid.

34. William Jones to Eleanor Jones, August 22, September 7, 1813, ibid.

35. *National Intelligencer,* September 6, September 7, 1813; "To the Public," *Federal Republican,* September 6, 1813; William Jones to Eleanor Jones, September 17, 1813, Jones Papers, HSP.

36. James Barron to William Jones, July 22, 1813, *NW1812,* II: 190–91.

37. William Jones to William Henry Allen, June 5, 1813, *NW1812,* II: 139–41; Dye, *Fatal Cruise,* 139–45, 264.

38. Dye, *Fatal Cruise,* 276–78; *NW1812,* II: 217–24.

39. Journal of the Frigate *President,* May 28, May 9, 1813, Rodgers Family Papers, LC; George Hutchinson to John B. Warren, September 24, 1813, WAR/70, NMM; John Rodgers to William Jones, September 27, 1813, *NW1812,* II: 250–54.

40. William Jones to John Rodgers, October 4, 1813, *NW1812,* II: 254–55.

41. John B. Warren to John W. Croker, October 16, 1813, ibid., II: 260–61; A Proclamation, John B. Warren, November 16, 1813, ibid., II: 262–63; Warren to Croker, November 13, 1813, ibid., II: 284; Dudley, *Wooden Wall,* 102.

42. Dudley, *Wooden Wall,* 100–101, 139, 143–44; List of Vessels Brought into Bermuda, HUL/18, NMM; Vessels Captured and Detained, WAR/37, NMM.

43. John B. Warren to John W. Croker, December 30, 1813, *NW1812,* II: 307–8; Hotham quoted in Dudley, *Wooden Wall,* 104.

44. Dye, *Fatal Cruise,* 287–89.

45. "Funeral Honors," *Portland Gazette,* September 13, 1813; Forester, *Age of Fighting Sail,* 192–93.

46. Forester, *Age of Fighting Sail,* 201–2; John W. Croker to Alexander Cochrane, January 25, 1814, pp. 95–97, ADM 2/1379, TNA.

47. James Madison to William Jones, October 15, 1813, Jones Papers, HSP.

48. William Jones to George Parker, December 8, 1813; Jones to John O. Creighton, December 22, 1813, *NW1812,* II: 293–97.

9. *"My Country I Fear Has Forgot Me"*

1. Hickey, *War of 1812,* 8, 96; Adams, *Second Administration of Madison,* I: 337; Coggeshall, *American Privateers,* 460; Garitee, *Republic's Private Navy,* 89–98, 133–36.

2. Coggeshall, *American Privateers*, 110–13; Adams, *Second Administration of Madison*, I: 316–23.

3. Munro, "Most Successful Privateer," 19; Coggeshall, *American Privateers*, 168–69.

4. Dudley, *Wooden Wall*, 138–39; Mahan, *Sea Power in 1812*, II: 242; Hickey, *War of 1812*, 124, 165; Chapple, "Salem and War of 1812," 55; Leavitt, "Private Armed Vessels," 57–58.

5. Garitee, *Republic's Private Navy*, 191–92, 193–94; Little, *Life on the Ocean*, 196; Maclay, *American Privateers*, 273.

6. Garitee, *Republic's Private Navy*, 128–30, 193.

7. Ibid., 152–53, 184, 186, 274.

8. Little, *Life on the Ocean*, 197–99.

9. Browne, *Yankee Privateer*, 20–21; Cobb, *Green Hand's Cruise*, 42–44.

10. Browne, *Yankee Privateer*, 21; Little, *Life on the Ocean*, 219–20.

11. Jones, *Journals of* Yankee, 113; Munro, "Most Successful Privateer," 47; Nelson, "Privateer *Harpy*."

12. Mouzon, "Unlucky *General Armstrong*"; William Jones to John Sinclair, June 7, 1813, *NW1812*, II: 68. This *General Armstrong* was a different ship from the much more famous and very successful New York privateer of the same name.

13. Little, *Life on the Ocean*, 225; Cobb, *Green Hand's Cruise*, 110–14, 122.

14. Leech, *Thirty Years*, 135–36.

15. Herbert Sawyer to John W. Croker, September 20, 1812, pp. 597–99, ADM 1/502, TNA; Sawyer to Croker, September 17, 1812, *NW1812*, I: 497–99; Giljie, ed., "Sailor Prisoner," 60, 64, 67.

16. Waterhouse, *Journal*, 17–19.

17. Ibid., 19–21.

18. Browne, *Yankee Privateer*, 82; Palmer, *Diary*, 13.

19. Waterhouse, *Journal*, 34–35.

20. "Reminiscences of Dartmoor," 23: 358.

21. Waterhouse, *Journal*, 50, 66–68, 104.

22. Ibid., 121–22, 127–28.

23. Ibid., 124–25, 130.

24. Hickey, *War of 1812*, 165; George Cockburn to Alexander F. I. Cochrane, May 10, 1814, *NW1812*, III: 63–66; Dye, "Maritime Prisoners," 305–6; Andrews, *Prisoners' Memoirs*, 76.

25. Waterhouse, *Journal*, 151–52.

26. Garitee, *Republic's Private Navy*, 116–17, 132–33; Coggeshall, "Journal."

27. Coggeshall, *American Privateers*, 178–80, 182, 183, 186–87.

28. Ibid., 186, 188–90, 192.

29. Ibid., 215, 253, 261–62.

30. Ibid., 263, 266.

31. Ibid., 268.

32. Ibid., 269–70.

33. Ibid., 271–72, 276, 291.

34. "Reminiscences of Dartmoor," 23: 360.

35. Waterhouse, *Journal*, 168–69.

36. Browne, *Yankee Privateer*, 154–57, 168–71; Valpey, *Journal*, 12; Waterhouse, *Journal*, 170–74; "Reminiscences of Dartmoor," 23: 360, 24: 520; Pierce, "Journal," 25–26.

37. "Reminiscences of Dartmoor," 23: 517.

38. Valpey, *Journal*, 12–13; Waterhouse, *Journal*, 175–76; Horsman, "Paradox of Dartmoor."

39. Andrews, *Prisoners' Memoirs*, 33; Browne, *Yankee Privateer*, 258–59.

40. Waterhouse, *Journal,* 190–91; Horsman, "Paradox of Dartmoor"; "Reminiscences of Dartmoor," 23: 519; Little, *Life on the Ocean,* 235; Browne, *Yankee Privateer,* 208–9.

41. Dye, "Maritime Prisoners," 305; Browne, *Yankee Privateer,* 210–11.

42. Horsman, "Paradox of Dartmoor"; "Reminiscences of Dartmoor," 23: 518; Waterhouse, *Journal,* 144.

43. Little, *Life on the Ocean,* 236–38.

44. Waterhouse, *Journal,* 191; Browne, *Yankee Privateer,* 197–98, 223–24, 227–28; "Reminiscences of Dartmoor," 23: 519.

45. Andrews, *Prisoners' Memoirs,* 38.

46. Browne, *Yankee Privateer,* 181–83, 193–96, 240–41; Bolster, *Black Jacks,* 102; Pierce, "Journal," 33–34.

47. Pierce, "Journal"; Valpey, *Journal;* Palmer, *Diary,* 154.

48. Valpey, *Journal,* 34, 37.

49. Waterhouse, *Journal,* 215; Andrews, *Prisoners' Memoirs,* 33.

50. Dye, "Maritime Prisoners," 300; Andrews, *Prisoners' Memoirs,* 36–37.

10. Fortunes of War

1. William Jones to William Young, n.d. 1814, Jones Papers, HSP; Adams, *Second Administration of Madison,* I: 370; Jones to James Madison, May 18, 1814, Madison Papers, LC.

2. Jones quoted in Hickey, *War of 1812,* 160.

3. Stagg, *Mr. Madison's War,* 375–79.

4. William Jones to James Madison, April 25, 1814, Madison Papers, LC; Eckert, "William Jones," 179; McKee, *Honorable Profession,* 334.

5. James Madison to Cabinet, June 3, 1814, *NW1812,* III: 497; Hickey, *War of 1812,* 174; Adams, *Second Administration of Madison,* I: 370–71.

6. William Jones to James Madison, May 25, 1814, *NW1812,* III: 495–97.

7. William Jones to Isaac Chauncey, April 18, 1814, *NW1812,* III: 402; Jones to James Madison, October 26, 1814, *NW1812,* III: 631–36; Hickey, *Don't Give Up the Ship,* 104; Jones to Madison, May 6, 1814, *NW1812,* III: 460–62.

8. William Jones to James Madison, May 25, 1814, *NW1812,* III: 495–97.

9. State and Stations of Vessels of War of the United States, William Jones to James Madison, June 6, 1814, *NW1812,* III: 785–87; Maloney, *Captain from Connecticut,* 216, 228.

10. Long, *Ready to Hazard,* 174–76; *Boston Daily Advertiser,* June 29, 1814.

11. Roosevelt, *Naval War of 1812,* 172–75, 178; William Jones to James Madison, May 10, 1814, Madison Papers, LC.

12. James Monroe to Commissioners of the United States, June 27, 1814, *ASP, Foreign Relations,* III: 704–5.

13. Farragut, *Life,* 48.

14. "The Essex," *New York Columbian,* July 8, 1814; "Capt. Porter," *New York Columbian,* July 9, 1814.

15. David Porter to William Jones, July 3, 1814, *NW1812,* III: 730–39; Carpenter's Report of Damage to the *Essex, NW1812,* III: 742.

16. Porter, *Journal,* II: 16–19.

17. This passage appears in volume II, page 22, of the 1815 edition of Porter's *Journal* but was omitted in the second edition.

18. Porter, *Journal,* II: 24–25 (1815 edition); Porter, *Journal,* II: 61.

19. Porter, *Journal,* II: 30 (1815 edition); Porter, *Journal,* II: 59.

20. Porter, *Journal,* II: 23 (1815 edition).

21. Farragut, *Life*, 27; Porter, *Journal*, II: 27, 62–63.

22. Porter, *Journal*, II: 19, 34–36.

23. Ibid., II: 87–93, 105–6.

24. Ibid., II: 137–39; Farragut, *Life*, 29–30.

25. David Porter to William Jones, July 3, 1814, *NW1812*, III: 730–39.

26. Farragut, *Life*, 32–34; Porter, *Journal*, II: 145.

27. James Hillyar to John W. Croker, February 28, 1814, *NW1812*, III: 714–15; Porter, *Journal*, II: 148; Crew of the *Essex* to Crew of the *Phoebe*, March 9, 1814, *NW1812*, III: 721.

28. David Farragut, "Some Reminiscences of Early Life," *NW1812*, III: 752.

29. Ibid., III: 754–55; Farragut, *Life*, 41, 44.

30. Porter, *Journal*, II: 175.

31. David Farragut, "Some Reminiscences of Early Life," *NW1812*, III: 757; David Porter to William Jones, July 9, 1814, *NW1812*, III: 764–65; John Mason to William Jones, August 10, 1814, *NW1812*, III: 767–77.

32. John M. Gamble to Benjamin W. Crowninshield, August 28, 1815, *NW1812*, III: 774–80; Gamble, *Memorial*, 11–16.

33. John B. Warren to Alexander F. I. Cochrane, March 23, 1814, WAR/53, NMM.

34. Proclamation of Vice Admiral Sir Alexander F. I. Cochrane, April 2, 1814, *NW1812*, III: 60.

35. Alexander F. I. Cochrane to George Cockburn, April 28, 1814, *NW1812*, III: 51–53.

36. Alexander F. I. Cochrane to George Cockburn, July 1, 1814, *NW1812*, III: 129–30.

37. George Cockburn to Alexander F. I. Cochrane, May 10, 1814, *NW1812*, III: 63–66; Cockburn to Cochrane, June 25, 1814, *NW1812*, III: 115–17; Cassell, "Slaves of Chesapeake," 149–51.

38. Alexander F. I. Cochrane to Lord Melville, July 17, 1814, *NW1812*, III: 132–35; Cochrane to Commanding Officers of the North American Station, July 18, 1814, *NW1812*, III: 140–41; John W. Croker to Cochrane, April 4, 1814, *NW1812*, III: 70–71.

39. William Jones to Richard M. Johnson, October 3, 1814, *NW1812*, III: 311–18; Nourse quoted in Mahon, *War of 1812*, 291; Hickey, *War of 1812*, 196.

40. William Jones to Joshua Barney, August 20, 1814, *NW1812*, III: 188; Codrington, *Memoir*, 315.

41. William Jones to Richard M. Johnson, October 3, 1814, *NW1812*, III: 311–18; Joshua Barney to Jones, August 29, 1814, *NW1812*, III: 207–8; Mahon, *War of 1812*, 299; Hickey, *War of 1812*, 197–98.

42. Mordecai Booth to Thomas Tingey, September 10, 1814, *NW1812*, III: 208–13; Tingey to William Jones, November 9, 1814, *NW1812*, III: 320–21.

43. Cockburn quoted in Mahon, *War of 1812*, 301; "Naval Recollections," 456.

44. William Jones to John Rodgers, August 29, 1814, *NW1812*, III: 243–44; David Porter to Jones, September 7, 1814, *NW1812*, III: 251–55.

45. Eleanor Jones to William Jones, September 1, 1814, Jones Papers, HSP.

46. Alexander F. I. Cochrane to Robert Saunders Dundas Melville, September 3, 1814, *NW1812*, III: 269–70.

47. William Jones to Eleanor Jones, September 30, 1814, Jones Papers, HSP.

48. William Jones to Eleanor Jones, November 6, 1814, ibid.

49. Alexander F. I. Cochrane to John W. Croker, September 17, 1814, *NW1812*, III: 286–88; Cochrane to Robert Saunders Dundas Melville, September 17, 1814, *NW1812*, III: 289–91.

50. Coggeshall, *American Privateers*, 361–62.

51. "II.—Further Papers Relating to the War with America," ff. 103–6, CO 42/160, TNA.

52. *Naval Chronicle* 32 (1814): 218–19; "III.—Further Papers Relating to the War with America," ff. 109–10, COC 42/160, TNA.

53. *Collection of Sundry Publications*, 3–13; U.S. Court of Claims, *General Armstrong*, 1–12.

54. "Successful Cruize—Gallant Affair," *Rhode-Island Republican*, October 19, 1814.

55. Wellington quoted in Forester, *Age of Fighting Sail*, 195.

56. Brodine, Crawford, and Hughes, *Against All Odds*, 53–72; Macdonough quoted in Hickey, *War of 1812*, 193.

57. Alexander F. I. Cochrane to John W. Croker, March 8, 1814, pp. 635–44, ADM 1/505, TNA; Dudley, *Wooden Wall*, 156.

58. Napier, *Journal*, 22, 23; entry for July 5, 1814, William Begg Journal, HSP.

59. Hickey, *War of 1812*, 287–94.

60. *AC*, 12th Cong., 1st sess. (May 16, 1812), 2300; Hickey, *Don't Give Up the Ship*, 164; Bainbridge quoted in McKee, *Honorable Profession*, 266, and Long, *Ready to Hazard*, 173.

61. Morris, *Autobiography*, 75–83; Bainbridge quoted in Maloney, *Captain from Connecticut*, 252.

62. Sketch on Financial Means, William Jones to James Madison, October 1814, Madison Papers, LC; Bainbridge quoted in Long, *Ready to Hazard*, 178; Jones to Treasury Secretary Alexander J. Dallas quoted in Hickey, *War of 1812*, 222–23, and Eckert, *Navy Department*, 67; Adams, *Second Administration of Madison*, II: 213–15, 245.

63. "Events of the Useless War," *Columbian Centinel*, August 10, 1814; Long, *Ready to Hazard*, 181–84; *Boston Daily Advertiser*, September 17, 1814.

64. Murdoch, "Reports of British Agents," 191–98; "Copy of intelligence obtained from a Gentleman lately of Boston," pp. 185–83, 193, ADM 1/508, TNA.

65. Dunham, *Oration*, 10.

66. Mason, "Federalist Agitation," 548–49; Wirt and Madison quoted in Stagg, *Mr. Madison's War*, 472–73.

67. Adams, *Second Administration of Madison*, II: 309; *Federal Republican*, December 6, 1814; *NW1812*, III: 329–30.

68. Mahon, *War of 1812*, 362, 365–68; Andrew Jackson to secretary of war, January 13, 1815, Brannan, ed., *Official Letters*, 458–59.

69. "New Orleans," *Daily National Intelligencer*, February 7, 1815; "Capture of the President," *Daily National Intelligencer*, February 1, 1815.

70. Murdoch, "Reports of British Agents," 195n43.

71. Tucker, *Stephen Decatur*, 140–49.

72. Latta, *Sermon*, 9, 15, 18.

73. "Glorious News," *Commercial Advertiser*, February 12, 1815; "Peace," *Connecticut Courant*, February 14, 1815; "Illumination," *Albany Argus*, February 24, 1815; Hickey, *War of 1812*, 298; "The Illumination, &c.," *Daily National Intelligencer*, February 20, 1815; *Connecticut Journal*, February 27, 1815.

11. "Praise to God for the Restoration of Peace"

1. Pierce, "Journal," 26, 30; Horsman, "Paradox of Dartmoor"; Palmer, *Diary*, 136, 141, 151–52.

2. Palmer, *Diary*, 159–60, 165, 171, 176; Andrews, *Prisoners' Memoirs*, 85–86.

3. Palmer, *Diary*, 179; Browne, *Yankee Privateer*, 266.

4. Waterhouse, *Journal*, 226, 231, 234; Palmer, *Diary*, 182; Adams, *Dartmoor Prison*, 16–17. The British and American authorities conducted a joint investigation of the massacre that ended up being mostly a whitewash, the American commissioner admitting that "consider-

ing it of much importance that the report . . . should go out under our joint signatures," he had "forborne to press some of the points." The American prisoners wrote their own eloquent if impassioned reply setting forth their version of events. All are reprinted in Waterhouse, *Journal*, 239–56.

5. "Reminiscences of Dartmoor," 24: 520.

6. Palmer, *Diary*, 219–20; Browne, *Yankee Privateer*, 302; Andrews, *Prisoners' Memoirs*, 120.

7. "Reminiscences of Dartmoor," 24: 522, 524.

8. King quoted in Hickey, *War of 1812*, 308.

9. Gore quoted in Adams, *Second Administration of Madison*, III: 59.

10. Hickey, *War of 1812*, 307.

11. James, *Naval History*, VI: 106.

12. *Naval Chronicle* 33 (1815): 295–96.

13. Papers Delivered from the Admiralty Relative to the War with America, p. 198, John W. Croker to R. Bickerton, May 31, 1813, CO 42/160, TNA.

14. Reid, *Consequences of Treaty of Paris*, 11–12; Petrie, *Prize Game*, 141–42.

15. Adams, *Second Administration of Madison*, I: 19–20.

16. Hickey, *War of 1812*, 303–4.

17. Humphreys, *Journal*, 19, 23–25.

18. Charles Stewart to secretary of the navy, May 15, 1815, in Brodine, Crawford, and Hughes, *Interpreting Old Ironsides*, 106–8; Whipple, *Letters*, 21; Humphreys, *Journal*, 31.

19. "The Frigate Constitution," *Salem Gazette*, May 30, 1815.

20. *AC*, 13th Cong., 3rd sess. (February 18, 1815), 255–56.

21. "A Good One!" *Yankee*, August 4, 1815.

22. *AC*, 13th Cong., 3rd sess. (November 15, 1814), 1834; (November 8, 1814), 542–48.

23. Carter, "Mathew Carey," 184–87; Bauer, "Naval Shipbuilding," 34.

24. Long, "Board of Commissioners," 66, 76.

25. Isaac Chauncey to Oliver H. Perry, July 30, 1813, *NW1812*, II: 530–31; Hickey, *Don't Give Up the Ship*, 189–90.

26. Long, *Nothing Too Daring*, 181–83.

27. Long, "Barron–Decatur Duel," 43–44.

28. Hull quoted in Maloney, *Captain from Connecticut*, 274–75.

29. Bainbridge quoted in ibid., 277, 279.

30. Hull quoted in ibid., 280; Rodgers quoted in Long, *Ready to Hazard*, 210.

31. Long, "Barron–Decatur Duel," 46–47.

32. James Barron to James Monroe, March 8, 1819, James Barron papers, WMSC; Morris, *Autobiography*, 102–3; Stephen Decatur to Barron, November 30, 1819, Barron Papers, WMSC.

33. Long, "Barron–Decatur Duel," 49.

34. Adams quoted in Tucker, *Stephen Decatur*, 182–83.

35. Eckert, "William Jones," 182.

Bibliography

MANUSCRIPTS

Earl Gregg Swem Library Special Collections Research Center, College of William and
    Mary, Williamsburg, Virginia (WMSC)
        James Barron Papers
Historical Society of Pennsylvania, Philadelphia (HSP)
        Joshua Barney Papers
        William Begg Journal
        William W. Feltus Journal
        Joshua Humphreys Papers
        William Jones Papers, Uselma Clarke Smith Collection
        Rodgers Family Papers
Manuscript Division, Library of Congress, Washington, D.C. (LC)
        Amos A. Evans papers
        Thomas Jefferson Papers, available online at http://memory.loc.gov/ammem/
        collections/jefferson_papers/
        James Madison Papers, available online at http://memory.loc.gov/ammem/
        collections/madison_papers/
        Rodgers Family Papers
        Rodgers Papers, Naval Historical Foundation Collection
        George H. Stuart Papers
Maine Historical Society, Portland (MeHS)
        Fogg Autograph Collection
The National Archives, London, U.K. (TNA)
        ADM 1, Admiralty: correspondence and papers
        ADM 2, Admiralty: out-letters
        ADM 8, Admiralty: list-books
        ADM 238, Admiralty: Prize Branch
        CO 42, Colonial Office: Canada, formerly British North America, original corre-
        spondence
        HCA 32, High Court of Admiralty: Prize Court: papers
National Maritime Museum, Greenwich, U.K. (NMM)
        AGC/23/7, James Hillyar Correspondence
        COC, Sir George Cockburn Papers
        HUL, George Redmond Hulbert Papers
        LBK/58, letters of Sir Philip Broke to his wife
        WAR, Admiral Sir John Borlase Warren Papers

South Caroliniana Library, Columbia, South Carolina (SCL)
> Paul Hamilton Papers, available online at http://www.sc.edu/library/digital/
> collections/paulhamilton.html

MEMOIRS, CONTEMPORARY VIEWS, PUBLISHED DOCUMENTS

Adams, James. *Dartmoor Prison; or, A Faithful Narrative of the Massacre of American Seamen.* Pittsburgh: S. Engles, 1816.

Allen, William Henry. "Letters of William Henry Allen, 1800–1813." Edited by Edward H. Tatum Jr. and Marion Tinling. *Huntington Library Quarterly* 1 (1937): 101–32; 1 (1938): 203–43.

The American Patriotic Song-Book: A Collection of Political, Descriptive, and Humorous Songs, of National Character, and the Production of American Poets Only. Philadelphia: W. M'Culloch, 1815.

American State Papers. Available online at http://memory.loc.gov/ammem/amlaw/lwsp.html.

Andrews, Charles. *The Prisoners' Memoirs; or, Dartmoor Prison.* New York, 1852.

Andros, Thomas. *The Grand Era of Ruin to Nations from Foreign Influence: A Discourse, Delivered Before the Congregational Society in Berkley, Nov. 26, 1812.* Boston: Samuel T. Armstrong, 1812.

Annals of Congress: Debates and Proceedings in the Congress of the United States, 1789–1824. Available online at http://memory.loc.gov/ammem/amlaw/lwac.html.

"The Arrival of the Chesapeake in Halifax in 1813 as Described by Thomas Haliburton ("Sam Slick")." *American Neptune* 57 (1997): 161–65.

Barclay, Thomas. *Selections from the Correspondence of Thomas Barclay, Formerly British Consul-General at New York.* Edited by George Lockhart Rives. New York: Harper & Brothers, 1894.

Baring, Alexander. *An Inquiry into the Causes and Consequences of the Orders in Council; and an Examination of the Conduct of Great Britain Toward the Neutral Commerce of America.* London: J. M. Richardson, 1808.

Bayard, James Asheton. "James Asheton Bayard Letters, 1802–1814." *Bulletin of the New York Public Library* 4 (1900): 228–48.

Belcher, Joshua. *An Account of the Funeral Honours Bestowed on the Remains of Capt. Lawrence and Lieut. Ludlow; with the Eulogy Pronounced at Salem, on the Occasion, by Hon. Joseph Story.* Boston, 1813.

Bentley, William. *The Diary of William Bentley, D. D., Pastor of the East Church, Salem, Massachusetts.* 4 vols. Salem, Mass.: Essex Institute, 1905–14.

Bowers, William. *Naval Adventures During Thirty-Five Years' Service.* 2 vols. London: Richard Bentley, 1833.

Brannan, John, ed. *Official Letters of the Military and Naval Officers of the United States, During the War with Great Britain in the Years 1812, 13, 14, & 15.* Washington, D.C.: Way & Gideon, 1823.

Brighton, John G. *Admiral of the Fleet, Sir Provo W. P. Wallis: A Memoir.* London: Hutchinson, 1892.

[Browne, Benjamin Frederick]. *The Yarn of a Yankee Privateer.* Edited by Nathaniel Hawthorne. New York: Funk & Wagnalls, 1926.

Carden, John Surman. *A Curtail'd Memoir of Incidents and Occurrences in the Life of John Surman Carden, Vice Admiral in the British Navy.* Edited by Christopher Thomas Atkinson. Oxford: Clarendon Press, 1912.

Cases Decided in the District and Circuit Court of the United States for the Pennsylvania District: and Also a Case Decided in the District Court of Massachusetts Relative to the Employment of British Licences on Board of Vessels of the United States. Philadelphia: R. Fisher, 1813.

Chamier, Frederick. *The Life of a Sailor.* London: Richard Bentley, 1850.

Clark, Thomas. *Naval History of the United States, from the Commencement of the Revolutionary War to the Present Time.* 2 vols. Philadelphia: M. Carey, 1814.

Cobb, Josiah [A Younker]. *A Green Hand's First Cruise.* 2 vols. Boston: Otis, Broaders, 1841.

Codrington, Edward. *Memoir of the Life of Admiral Sir Edward Codrington with Selections from His Public and Private Correspondence.* London: Longmans, Green, 1873.

Coggeshall, George. "Journal of the Letter-of-Marque Schooners 'David Porter' and 'Leo': A Yankee Skipper Who Preyed on British Shipping Relates His Wartime Experiences." *American Heritage,* October 1957, 66–85.

A Collection of Sundry Publications, and Other Documents, in Relation to the Attack Made During the Late War upon the Private Armed Brig General Armstrong. New York: J. Gray, 1833.

The Columbian Naval Melody: A Collection of Songs and Odes Composed on the Late Naval Victories and Other Occasions. Boston: Hans Lund, 1813.

Congreve, William. *The Details of the Rocket System.* London: J. Whiting, 1814.

Cowdery, Jonathan. *American Captives in Tripoli; or, Dr. Cowdery's Journal in Miniature: Kept During his Late Captivity in Tripoli.* Boston: Belcher & Armstrong, 1806.

Croker, John Wilson [Nereus]. *The Letters on the Subject of the Naval War with America, Which Appeared in the Courier, Under the Signature of Nereus.* London: B. M. Swyny, 1813.

———. *The Croker Papers: The Correspondence and Diaries of the Late Right Honourable John Wilson Croker, LL.D., F.R.S., Secretary of the Admiralty from 1809 to 1830.* Edited by Louis J. Jennings. 2 vols. New York: Scribner's Sons, 1884.

Crowninshield, Jacob. "Some Remarks on the American Trade: Jacob Crowninshield to James Madison, 1806." Edited by John H. Reinoehl. *William and Mary Quarterly* 3rd ser. 16 (1959): 83–118.

Dalton, Samuel. "Letters of Samuel Dalton of Salem, an Impressed American Seaman." *Essex Institute Historical Collections* 68 (1932): 321–29.

Decatur, Susan. *Documents Relative to the Claim of Mrs. Decatur: with Her Earnest Request that the Gentlemen of Congress Will Take the Trouble to Read Them.* Georgetown, D.C.: James C. Dunn, 1826.

Dunham, Josiah. *An oration delivered at Hanover, in the vicinity of Dartmouth college, before the several Washington benevolent societies of Hanover, Lebanon, Lime, Norwich, and Hartford, on the thirty-eighth anniversary of American independence.* Hanover, N.H.: Charles Spear, 1814.

Dunlap, William. *Yankee Chronology, or Huzza for the Constitution—a Musical Interlude.* 1812. Reprint. Tarrytown, N.Y.: William Abbatt, 1931.

Durand, James R. *The Life and Adventures of James R. Durand During a Period of Fifteen Years, from 1801 to 1816: In Which Time He Was Impressed on Board the British Fleet, and Held in Detestable Bondage for More Than Seven Years.* 1820. Reprint. Sandwich, Mass.: Chapman Billies, 1995.

Eggleston, George Cary, ed. *American War Ballads and Lyrics: A Collection of the Songs and Ballads of the Colonial Wars, the Revolution, the War of 1812–15, the War with Mexico, and the Civil War.* New York: G.P. Putnam's Sons, 1889.

The Elements and Practice of Rigging and Seamanship. London: D. Steel, 1794.

Essex Institute. *American Vessels Captured by the British During the Revolution and War of 1812: The Records of the Vice-Admiralty Court at Halifax, Nova Scotia.* Salem, Mass.: Essex Institute, 1911.

Evans, Amos A. "Journal Kept on Board the United States Frigate 'Constitution,' 1812, by Amos A. Evans, Surgeon United States Navy." *Pennsylvania Magazine of History and Biography* 19 (1895): 152–69, 374–86, 468–80.

Farragut, Loyall, and David Glasgow Farragut. *The Life of David Glasgow Farragut: First Admiral of the United States Navy, Embodying His Journal and Letters.* New York: D. Appleton, 1879.

Fay, H. A. *Collection of the Official Accounts, in Detail, of All the Battles Fought by Sea and Land, Between the Navy and Army of the United States and the Navy and Army of Great Britain, During the Years 1812, 13, 14, & 15.* New York: E. Conrad, 1817.

Firth, C. H., ed. *Naval Songs and Ballads.* London: Navy Records Society, 1908.

Foster, Augustus John. "Caviar Along the Potomac: Sir Augustus Foster's 'Notes on the United States,' 1804–1812." Edited by Margaret Bailey Tinkcom. *William and Mary Quarterly* 3rd ser. 8 (1951): 68–107.

———. *Jeffersonian America: Notes on the United States of America, Collected in the Years 1805–6–7 and 11–12.* Edited by Richard Beale Davis. Westport, Conn.: Greenwood Press, 1980.

Foster, Vere, ed. *The Two Duchesses: Family Correspondence of and Relating to Georgiana Duchess of Devonshire, Elizabeth Duchess of Devonshire.* London: Blackie & Son, 1898.

Gamble, John Marshall. *The Memorial of Lieut. Colonel J. M. Gamble, of the United States' Marine Corps, to Congress, 1828.* New York: Geo. F. Hopkins & Son, 1828.

Gilje, Paul A., ed. "A Sailor Prisoner of War During the War of 1812." *Maryland Historical Magazine* 85 (1990): 58–72.

Gillespy, Edward. *The Columbian Naval Songster; Being a Collection of Original Songs, Odes, etc. Composed in Honor of the Five Great Naval Victories, Obtained by Hull, Jones, Decatur, Bainbridge and Lawrence; Over the British Ships* Guerriere, Frolic, Macedonian, Java *and* Peacock. New York, 1813.

Gilliam, Henry. "Letters of Henry Gilliam, 1809–1817." Edited by Lilla M. Hawes. *Georgia Historical Quarterly* 38 (1954): 46–66.

Goldsborough, Charles Washington. *The United States' Naval Chronicle.* Washington, D.C.: J. Wilson, 1824.

Hall, Basil. *Fragments of Voyages and Travels.* 3 vols. Edinburgh: Robert Cadell, 1832.

Historical Statistics of the United States, Colonial Times to 1970. Washington, D.C.: GPO, 1975.

Holbrook, Samuel F. *Threescore Years: An Autobiography, Containing Incidents of Voyages and Travels, Including Six Years in a Man-of-War.* Boston: James French, 1857.

Humphreys, Assheton. *The USS* Constitution's *Finest Fight, 1815: The Journal of Acting Chaplain Assheton Humphreys, US Navy.* Edited by Tyrone G. Martin. Mount Pleasant, S.C.: Nautical & Aviation Publishing, 2000.

Inderwick, James. *Cruise of the U.S. Brig* Argus *in 1813: Journal of Surgeon James Inderwick.* Edited by Victor Hugo Paltsits. New York: New York Public Library, 1917.

Isaacs, Nicholas Peter. *Twenty Years Before the Mast; or, Life in the Forecastle.* New York: Beckwith, 1845.

James, William. *A Full and Correct Account of the Chief Naval Occurrences of the Late War Between Great Britain and the United States of America.* London: T. Egerton, 1817.

———. *The Naval History of Great Britain, from the Declaration of War by France in 1793, to the Accession of George IV.* Vol. 6. London: Richard Bentley, 1837.

Jones, Noah [A Wanderer]. *Journals of Two Cruises Aboard the American Privateer* Yankee. New York: Macmillan, 1967.

Lathrop, John. *The Present War Unexpected, Unnecessary, and Ruinous. Two Discourses Delivered in Boston: The First on the 23d of July, 1812, the Fast Appointed by the Governor of Massachusetts; the Second on the 20th of August, the Fast Appointed by the President of the United States, in Consequence of the Present War.* Boston: J. W. Burditt, 1812.

Latta, John E. *A Sermon Preached at New-Castle, (Del.) on the Thirteenth Day of April, 1815: A Day Recommended by the President of the United States, to be Observed as a Day of Public Thanksgiving and Praise to God for the Restoration of Peace.* Wilmington, Del.: Robert Porter, 1815.

Leech, Samuel. *Thirty Years from Home; or, A Voice from the Main Deck.* Boston: Tappan, Whittemore & Mason, 1843.

Lever, Darcy. *The Young Officer's Sheet Anchor; or, A Key to the Leading of Rigging and to Practical Seamanship.* 1819. Reprint, Mineola, N.Y.: Dover, 1998.

Little, George. *Life on the Ocean; or, Twenty Years at Sea: Being the Personal Adventures of the Author.* Boston: C. D. Strong, 1851.

"Log of the Chasseur: Journal of the Private Armed Brig Chasseur, Thomas Boyle Commanding." *Maryland Historical Magazine* 1 (1906): 165–80, 218–40.

Lovell, William Stanhope. *Personal Narrative of Events, from 1799 to 1815, with Anecdotes.* London: W. Allen, 1879.

Lowell, John [A Yankee Farmer]. *Peace Without Dishonour—War Without Hope: Being a Calm and Dispassionate Enquiry into the Question of the Chesapeake, and the Necessity and Expediency of War.* Boston: Greenough and Stebbins, 1807.

Lowell, John [A New England Farmer]. *Mr. Madison's War. A Dispassionate Inquiry into the Reasons Alleged by Mr. Madison for Declaring an Offensive and Ruinous War Against Great-Britain.* Boston: Russell & Cutler, 1812.

Madison, James. *Letters and Other Writings of James Madison.* 4 vols. Philadelphia: J. B. Lippincott, 1865.

Massachusetts Historical Society. *Microfilms of the Adams Papers.* Boston: Massachusetts Historical Society, 1954–1959.

Monroe, James. *James Monroe Papers, 1772–1836.* New York: New York Public Library, Manuscript Division, 1963. Microfilm.

Montagu, Montagu. *England Victorious—A Poem upon the Capture of the American Frigate* Chesapeake *by the British Frigate* Shannon, *June 1st 1813.* London, 1814.

Morris, Charles. *The Autobiography of Commodore Charles Morris, U.S. Navy.* 1880. Reprint. Annapolis, Md.: Naval Institute Press, 2002.

Napier, Henry Edward. *New England Blockaded in 1814: The Journal of Henry Edward Napier, Lieutenant in the H.M.S.* Nymphe. Edited by Walter Muir Whitehill. Salem, Mass.: Peabody Museum, 1939.

Napier, William Francis Patrick. *The Life and Opinions of General Sir Charles James Napier, G.C.B.* 4 vols. London: John Murray, 1857.

A Narrative of the Capture of the United States' Brig Vixen, *of 14 Guns, by the British Frigate* Southampton. West Chester, Pa.: Wm. Reed Lewis, 1814.

Naval Documents Related to the United States Wars with the Barbary Powers. 6 vols. Edited by Dudley W. Knox. Washington, D.C.: GPO, 1939–44.

"Naval Recollections of the Late American War." *United Service Journal,* April 1841, 455–67; May 1841, 13–23.

The Naval War of 1812: A Documentary History. 3 vols. Edited by William S. Dudley and Michael J. Crawford. Washington, D.C.: GPO, 1985–2002.

Orne, William B. [Octogenarian]. "Reminiscence of the Last War with England." *Historical Magazine* 7 (1870): 31–33.

Osgood, David. *A Solemn Protest Against the Late Declaration of War, in a Discourse, Delivered on the Next Lord's Day After the Tidings of It Were Received.* Cambridge, Mass.: Hilliard and Metcalf, 1812.

Palmer, Benjamin F. *The Diary of Benjamin F. Palmer, Privateersman.* New Haven, Conn.: Acorn Club, 1914.

Parsons, Usher. "Surgical Account of the Naval Battle on Lake Erie, on the 10th of September, 1813." *New England Journal of Medicine and Surgery* 7 (1818): 313–16.

———. *Battle of Lake Erie: A Discourse Delivered Before the Rhode Island Historical Society.* Providence: Benjamin T. Albro, 1854.

———. *Surgeon of the Lakes: The Diary of Dr. Usher Parsons, 1812–1814.* Edited by John C. Fredriksen. Erie, Pa.: Erie County Historical Society, 2000.

Pierce, Nathaniel. "Journal of Nathaniel Pierce of Newburyport, Kept at Dartmoor Prison, 1814–1815." *Essex Institute Historical Collections* 73 (1937): 24–59.

Porter, David. *Journal of a Cruise Made to the Pacific Ocean.* 2nd edition. 2 vols. New York: Wiley & Halsted, 1822.

———. *Constantinople and Its Environs.* 2 vols. New York: Harper & Brothers, 1835.

Porter, David Dixon. *Memoir of Commodore David Porter, of the United States Navy.* Albany, N.Y.: J. Munsell, 1875.

Ray, William. *Horrors of Slavery: or, the American Tars in Tripoli.* Troy, N.Y., 1808.

Rea, John. *A Letter to William Bainbridge, Esqr., Formerly Commander of the United States' Ship* George Washington: *Relative to Some Transactions, On Board Said Ship During a Voyage to Algiers, Constantinople, &c.* Philadelphia, 1802.

"Reminiscences of a Dartmoor Prisoner." *Knickerbocker* 23 (1844): 146–58, 356–60, 517–22; 24 (1844): 457–63, 519–24.

Roads, Samuel, Jr. *The Marblehead Manual.* Marblehead, Mass.: Statesman Publishing, 1883.

Scott, James. *Recollections of a Naval Life.* Vol. 3. London: Richard Bentley, 1834.

Scott, James Brown, ed. *Prize Cases Decided in the Supreme Court of the United States, 1789–1918.* Oxford: Clarendon Press, 1923.

Smith, Margaret Bayard. *First Forty Years of Washington Society.* New York: C. Scribner's Sons, 1906.

Smith, Moses. *Naval Scenes in the Last War: or, Three Years on Board the Frigate* Constitution, *and the* Adams; *Including the Capture of the Guerriere.* Boston: Gleason's, 1846.

[Stephen, James]. *War in Disguise; or, The Frauds of the Neutral Flags.* London: C. Whittingham, 1805.

A System of Naval Tactics. 1797.

U.S. Court of Claims. *Decision of the Case of the Private Armed Brig* General Armstrong, *Sam C. Reid and Others, Claimants, vs. the United States.* Washington, D.C., 1855.

Valpey, Joseph. *Journal of Joseph Valpey, Jr., of Salem, November, 1813–April, 1815, with Other Papers Relating to His Experience in Dartmoor Prison.* Detroit: Michigan Society of Colonial Wars, 1922.

Waterhouse, Benjamin. *A Journal of a Young Man of Massachusetts.* 1816. Reprint. New York: William Abbatt, 1911.

Whipple, Pardon Mawney. *Letters from Old Ironsides, 1813–1815, Written by Pardon Mawney Whipple, USN.* Edited by Norma Adams Price. Tempe, Ariz.: Beverly-Merriam Press, 1984.

NEWSPAPERS AND PERIODICALS

Albany Argus (Albany, N.Y.)
Boston Daily Advertiser (Boston)
Boston Gazette (Boston)
Boston Patriot (Boston)
Boston Post-Boy (Boston)
City Gazette & Daily Advertiser (Charleston, S.C.)
Columbian (New York)
Columbian Centinel (Boston)
Commercial Advertiser (New York)
Connecticut Courant (Hartford, Conn.)
Connecticut Herald (New Haven, Conn.)

Connecticut Journal (New Haven, Conn.)
Daily Advertiser (New York)
Essex Register (Salem, Mass.)
Federal Republican (Baltimore, Md., and Georgetown, D.C.)
Hagers-Town Gazette (Hagerstown, Md.)
National Intelligencer (Washington, D.C.)
Naval Chronicle (London)
New-England Palladium (Boston)
Newport Mercury (Newport, R.I.)
New-York Gazette (New York)
Port Folio (Philadelphia)
Portland Gazette (Portland, Maine)
Repertory (Boston)
Republican Star (Easton, Md.)
Repertory (Boston)
Rhode-Island Republican (Newport, R.I.)
Salem Gazette (Salem, Mass.)
Statesman (New York)
Time Piece (New York)
Times (London)
United States Gazette (Philadelphia)
Weekly Messenger (Boston)
Weekly Register (Baltimore)
Yankee (Boston)

BOOKS AND ARTICLES

Adams, Charles F. "Wednesday, August 19, 1812, 6:30 P.M.: The Birth of a World Power." *American Historical Review* 18 (1913): 513–21.

Adams, Henry. *History of the United States of America During the First Administration of Thomas Jefferson.* 2 vols. New York: C. Scribner's Sons, 1889.

———. *History of the United States of America During the Second Administration of Thomas Jefferson.* 2 vols. New York: C. Scribner's Sons, 1890.

———. *History of the United States of America During the First Administration of James Madison.* 2 vols. New York: C. Scribner's Sons, 1890.

———. *History of the United States of America During the Second Administration of James Madison.* 3 vols. New York: C. Scribner's Sons, 1891.

———. *The Education of Henry Adams: An Autobiography.* Boston: Massachusetts Historical Society, 1918.

"Aid to Glory." *Proceedings of the Massachusetts Historical Society* 36 (May 1902): 182–86.

Allen, Gardner W. "Naval Songs and Ballads." *Proceedings of the American Antiquarian Society* n.s. 35 (1925): 64–78.

Balinky, Alexander. "Albert Gallatin, Naval Foe." *Pennsylvania Magazine of History and Biography* 82 (1958): 293–304.

Bauer, K. Jack. "Naval Shipbuilding Programs, 1794–1860." *Military Affairs* 29 (1965): 29–40.

Berube, Claude, and John Rodgaard. *A Call to the Sea: Captain Charles Stewart of the USS Constitution.* Dulles, Va.: Potomac Books, 2006.

Blake, Nicholas, and Richard Lawrence. *The Illustrated Companion to Nelson's Navy.* Mechanicsburg, Pa.: Stackpole, 1995.

Bolster, W. Jeffrey. " 'To Feel Like a Man': Black Seamen in the Northern States, 1800–1860." *Journal of American History* 76 (1990): 1173–99.

———. *Black Jacks: African American Seamen in the Age of Sail.* Cambridge, Mass.: Harvard University Press, 1997.

Brant, Irving. "Timid President? Futile War?" *American Heritage,* October 1959.

Brodine, Charles E., Jr., Michael J. Crawford, and Christine F. Hughes. *Against All Odds: U.S. Sailors in the War of 1812.* Washington, D.C.: GPO, 2004.

———. *Interpreting Old Ironsides: An Illustrated Guide to USS "Constitution."* Washington, D.C.: GPO, 2007.

Brown, Kenneth L. "Mr. Madison's Secretary of the Navy." *United States Naval Institute Proceedings* 73 (1947): 966–75.

"Business and the Coffee House." *Bulletin of the Business Historical Society,* May 1928, 11–13.

Calderhead, William L. "U.S.F. Constellation in the War of 1812—an Accidental Fleet-in-Being." *Military Affairs* 40 (April 1976): 79–83.

———. "Naval Innovation in Crisis: War in the Chesapeake, 1813." *American Neptune* 36 (1976): 206–21.

Carter, Edward C., II. "Mathew Carey, Advocate of American Naval Power, 1785–1814." *American Neptune* 26 (1966): 177–88.

Cassell, Frank A. "Slaves of the Chesapeake Bay Area and the War of 1812." *Journal of Negro History* 57 (1972): 144–55.

Chapelle, Howard I. *The History of the American Sailing Navy: The Ships and Their Deployment.* New York: Norton, 1949.

Chapple, William Dismore. "Salem and the War of 1812." *Essex Institute Historical Collections* 59 (1923): 289–304; 60 (1924): 49–74.

Clark, Allen C. *Life and Letters of Dolly Madison.* Washington, D.C.: W. F. Roberts, 1914.

Coggeshall, George. *History of the American Privateers, and Letters-of-Marque, During Our War with England in the Years 1812, '13, and '14.* 3rd edition. New York, 1861.

Cox, Richard J. "An Eyewitness Account of the Battle of Lake Erie." *United States Naval Institute Proceedings,* February 1978: 67–74.

Craig, Hardin, Jr. "Notes on the Action Between *Hornet* and *Neptune*." *American Neptune* 11 (1951): 73–77.

Crawford, Michael J. "The Navy's Campaign Against the Licensed Trade in the War of 1812." *American Neptune* 46 (1986): 165–72.

Cray, Robert E., Jr. "Remembering the USS *Chesapeake:* The Politics of Maritime Death and Impressment." *Journal of the Early Republic* 25 (2005): 445–74.

Crosby, Alfred W. "Richard S. Smith, Baltic Paul Revere of 1812." *Pennsylvania Magazine of History and Biography* 86 (1962): 42–48.

De Kay, James Tertius. *Chronicles of the Frigate* Macedonian: *1809–1922.* New York: Norton, 1995.

———. *A Rage for Glory: The Life of Commodore Stephen Decatur.* New York: Free Press, 2004.

Dietz, Anthony G. "The Use of Cartel Vessels During the War of 1812." *American Neptune* 28 (1968): 165–94.

Dodds, James, and James Moore. *Building the Wooden Fighting Ship.* New York: Facts on File, 1984.

Dudley, Wade G. *Splintering the Wooden Wall: The British Blockade of the United States, 1812–1815.* Annapolis, Md.: Naval Institute Press, 2003.

Duffy, Stephen W. H. *Captain Blakeley and the* Wasp: *The Cruise of 1814.* Annapolis, Md.: Naval Institute Press, 2001.

Dunne, W. M. P. " 'The Inglorious First of June': Commodore Stephen Decatur on Long Island Sound, 1813." *Long Island Historical Journal* 2 (1990): 210–20.

Dye, Ira. "Seafarers of 1812—a Profile." *Prologue,* Spring 1973, 2–13.

————. "Early American Seafarers." *Proceedings of the American Philosophical Society* 120 (1976): 331–60.

————. "American Maritime Prisoners of War, 1812–15." In *Ships, Seafaring and Society: Essays in American Maritime History,* edited by Timothy J. Runyan. Detroit: Wayne State University Press, 1987.

————. "Tattoos of Early American Seafarers, 1796–1818." *Proceedings of the American Philosophical Society* 133 (1989): 520–54.

————. "Physical and Social Profiles of Early American Seafarers, 1812–1815." In *Jack Tar in History: Essays in the History of Maritime Life and Labour,* ed. by Colin Howell and Richard J. Twomey. Fredericton, New Brunswick: Acadiensis Press, 1991.

————. *The Fatal Cruise of the* Argus: *Two Captains in the War of 1812.* Annapolis, Md.: Naval Institute Press, 1994.

Eckert, Edward K. "William Jones: Mr. Madison's Secretary of the Navy." *Pennsylvania Magazine of History and Biography* 92 (1972): 167–82.

————. *The Navy Department in the War of 1812.* Gainesville: University of Florida Press, 1973.

Eddy, Richard. " '. . . Defended by an Adequate Power': Joshua Humphreys and the 74-Gun Ships of 1799." *American Neptune* 51 (1991): 173–94.

Elias, Norbert. "Studies in the Genesis of the Naval Profession." *British Journal of Sociology* 1 (1950): 291–309.

Emmons, George F. *The Navy of the United States, from the Commencement, 1775 to 1853.* Washington, D.C.: Gideon, 1853.

Estes, J. Worth, and Ira Dye. "Death on the *Argus.*" *Journal of the History of Medicine* 44 (1989): 179–85.

Forester, C. S. *The Age of Fighting Sail: The Story of the Naval War of 1812.* 1956. Reprint. Sandwich, Mass.: Chapman Billies, 1995.

Frederiksen, John C. *War of 1812 Eyewitness Accounts: An Annotated Bibliography.* Westport, Conn.: Greenwood Press, 1997.

Gafford, Lucile. "The Boston Stage and the War of 1812." *New England Quarterly* 7 (1934): 327–35.

Gardiner, Robert, ed. *The Naval War of 1812.* London: Caxton Editions, 2001.

Garitee, Jerome R. *The Republic's Private Navy: The American Privateering Business as Practiced by Baltimore During the War of 1812.* Middletown, Conn.: Wesleyan University Press, 1977.

Gilkerson, William. *Boarders Away, with Steel: Edged Weapons and Polearms of the Classic Age of Fighting Sail, 1626–1826.* Lincoln, R.I.: A. Mowbray, 1991.

Gleaves, Albert. *James Lawrence, Captain, United States Navy: Commander of the "Chesapeake."* New York: G. P. Putnam's Sons, 1904.

Goddard, Jonathan Charles. "The Navy Surgeon's Chest: Surgical Instruments of the Royal Navy During the Napoleonic War." *Journal of the Royal Society of Medicine* 97 (2004): 191–97.

Harris, Thomas. *The Life and Services of Commodore William Bainbridge, United States Navy.* Philadelphia: Carey Lea & Blanchard, 1837.

Heintze, James R. "Gaetano Carusi: From Sicily to the Halls of Congress." In *American Musical Life in Context and Practice to 1865,* edited by James R. Heintze. New York: Garland, 1994.

Henderson, James. *Frigates, Sloops & Brigs.* Reprint. Barnsley, U.K.: Pen & Sword, 2005.

Hickey, Donald R. "American Trade Restrictions During the War of 1812." *Journal of American History* 68 (1981): 517–38.

————. *The War of 1812: A Forgotten Conflict.* Urbana: University of Illinois Press, 1995.

————. *Don't Give Up the Ship! Myths of the War of 1812.* Urbana: University of Illinois Press, 2006.

Horsman, Reginald. *The Causes of the War of 1812.* New York: A. S. Barnes, 1962.

———. "The Paradox of Dartmoor Prison." *American Heritage,* February 1975.

Hoyt, William D., Jr. "Logs and Papers of Baltimore Privateers, 1812–15." *Maryland Historical Magazine* 34 (June 1939): 165–74.

Hume, Edgar Erskine. "Letters Written During the War of 1812 by the British Naval Commander in American Waters." *William and Mary Quarterly* 10 (1930): 281–301.

Humphrey, Carol Sue. *The Press of the Young Republic, 1783–1833.* Westport, Conn.: Greenwood Press, 1996.

Jordan, Douglas S. "Stephen Decatur at New London: A Study in Strategic Frustration." *United States Naval Institute Proceedings,* October 1967, 60–65.

Langley, Harold D. *Social Reform in the United States Navy, 1798–1862.* Urbana: University of Illinois Press, 1967.

Lavery, Brian. *Nelson's Navy: The Ships, Men, and Organization, 1793–1815.* Annapolis, Md.: Naval Institute Press, 1994.

Leavitt, William. "An Account of the Private Armed Vessels Belonging to Salem, Mass., During the War of 1812." *Essex Institute Historical Collections* 2 (1860): 57–64.

Leiner, Frederick C. "Saving the Big-Ship Navy." *United States Naval Institute Proceedings,* July 1977, 76–77.

———. "The Norfolk War Scare." *Naval History,* Summer 1993, 36–38.

———. *Millions for Defense: The Subscription Warships of 1798.* Annapolis, Md.: Naval Institute Press, 1999.

———. "A *Ruse de Guerre* Gone Wrong: The Sinking of the *Eleanor.*" *Maryland Historical Magazine* 101 (2006): 167–84.

———. "The Squadron Commander's Share: *Decatur v. Chew* and the Prize Money for the *Chesapeake*'s First War of 1812 Cruise." *Journal of Military History* 73 (2009): 69–82.

Lewis, Michael. *A Social History of the Navy, 1793–1815.* 1960. Reprint. Mechanicsburg, Pa.: Stackpole, 2004.

Lohnes, Barry J. "British Naval Problems at Halifax, During the War of 1812." *Mariner's Mirror* 59 (1973): 317–33.

London, Joshua E. *Victory in Tripoli: How America's War with the Barbary Pirates Established the U.S. Navy and Shaped a Nation.* Hoboken, N.J.: Wiley, 2005.

Long, David F. *Nothing Too Daring: A Biography of Commodore David Porter, 1780–1843.* Annapolis, Md.: Naval Institute Press, 1970.

———. "The Navy Under the Board of Naval Commissioners, 1815–1842." In *In Peace and War: Interpretations of American Naval History, 1775–1978,* edited by Kenneth J. Hagan. Westport, Conn.: Greenwood Press, 1978.

———. "William Bainbridge and the Barron–Decatur Duel: Mere Participant or Active Plotter?" *Pennsylvania Magazine of History and Biography* 103 (1979): 34–52.

———. *Ready to Hazard: A Biography of Commodore William Bainbridge, 1774–1833.* Hanover, N.H.: University Press of New England, 1981.

Lossing, Benson J. *The Pictorial Field-Book of the War of 1812.* New York: Harper & Brothers, 1869.

Lushington, Godfrey. *A Manual of Naval Prize Law.* London: Buttersworths, 1866.

Maclay, Edgar Stanton. *A History of American Privateers.* London: Sampson, Low, Marston, 1900.

Madison, James. *Selected Writings of James Madison.* Edited by Ralph Louis Ketcham. Indianapolis, Ind.: Hackett Publishing, 2006.

Mahan, A. T. *Sea Power in Its Relations to the War of 1812.* 2 vols. Boston: Little, Brown, 1905.

Mahon, John K. *The War of 1812.* Gainesville: University of Florida Press, 1972.

Maloney, Linda M. "The War of 1812: What Role for Sea Power?" In *In Peace and War: Interpretations of American Naval History, 1775–1978,* edited by Kenneth J. Hagan. Westport, Conn.: Greenwood Press, 1978.

————. *The Captain from Connecticut: The Life and Naval Times of Isaac Hull.* Boston: Northeastern University Press, 1986.

Martin, Tyrone G. *A Most Fortunate Ship: A Narrative History of "Old Ironsides."* Chester, Conn.: Globe Pequot Press, 1980.

————. "Isaac Hull's Victory Revisited." *American Neptune* 47 (1987): 14–21.

Mason, Matthew. " 'Nothing Is Better Calculated to Excite Divisions': Federalist Agitation Against Slave Representation During the War of 1812." *New England Quarterly* 75 (2002): 531–61.

Mayhew, Dean R. "Jeffersonian Gunboats in the War of 1812." *American Neptune* 42 (1982): 101–17.

McKee, Christopher. *Edward Preble: A Naval Biography, 1761–1807.* Annapolis, Md.: Naval Institute Press, 1972.

————. "Foreign Seamen in the United States Navy: A Census of 1808." *William and Mary Quarterly* 3rd ser. 42 (1985): 383–93.

————. *A Gentlemanly and Honorable Profession: The Creation of the U.S. Naval Officer Corps, 1794–1815.* Annapolis, Md.: Naval Institute Press, 1991.

Mouzon, Harold A. "The Unlucky *General Armstrong.*" *American Neptune* 15 (1955): 59–80.

Munro, Wilfred Harold. "The Most Successful American Privateer: An Episode of the War of 1812." *Proceedings of the American Antiquarian Society* n.s. 23 (1913): 12–62.

Murdoch, Richard K. "Intelligence Reports of British Agents in the Long Island Sound Area, 1814–1815." *American Neptune* 29 (1969): 187–98.

"The Naval Battle Between the Chesapeake and the Shannon on June 1, 1813." *Proceedings of the Massachusetts Historical Society* 21 (February 1885): 374–79.

Nell, William C. *Services of Colored Americans, in the Wars of 1776 and 1812.* Boston: Robert F. Wallcut, 1852.

Nelson, George A. "A First Cruise of the American Privateer *Harpy.*" *American Neptune* 1 (1941): 116–22.

Otton, Patrick. "USS *Constitution* Reborn." *Sea History,* Spring/Summer 1997, 40–41.

Pack, James. *The Man Who Burned the White House: Admiral Sir George Cockburn, 1772–1853.* Annapolis, Md.: Naval Institute Press, 1987.

Palmer, Michael A. *Stoddert's War: Naval Operations During the Quasi-War with France, 1798–1801.* Columbia: University of South Carolina Press, 1987.

Paullin, Charles O., and Frederic L. Paxson. *Guide to the Materials in London Archives for the History of the United States Since 1783.* Washington, D.C.: Carnegie Institution, 1914.

Perkins, Bradford. *Prologue to War: England and the United States 1805–1812.* Berkeley: University of California Press, 1968.

Petrie, Donald A. "The Ransoming of *Eliza Swan.*" *American Neptune* 53 (1993): 98–108.

————. "Forbidden Prizes." *American Neptune* 54 (1994): 165–74.

————. *The Prize Game: Lawful Looting on the High Seas in the Days of Fighting Sail.* New York: Berkley, 2001.

Post, Waldron Kintzing. "The Case of Captain Lawrence." *United States Naval Institute Proceedings* 62 (1936): 969–74.

Prudden, Theodore M. "Her Thunder Shook the Mighty Deep." *United States Naval Institute Proceedings,* January 1964, 74–83.

Purcell, Hugh D. "Don't Give Up the Ship!" *United States Naval Institute Proceedings,* May 1965, 82–94.

Reid, Whitelaw. *Some Consequences of the Last Treaty of Paris: Advances in International Law and Changes in National Policy.* London: John Lane, 1899.

Robinson, Ralph. "Retaliation for the Treatment of Prisoners in the War of 1812." *American Historical Review* 49 (1943): 65–70.

Roche, Charles. "Dockyard Reminiscences: An Account of the Action Between the 'Chesapeake' and the 'Shannon,' Gleaned from Statements Made by Eye-Witnesses." *Collections of the Nova Scotia Historical Society* 18 (1919): 59–67.

Roosevelt, Theodore. *The Naval War of 1812.* 4th edition, 1889. Reprint. New York: Modern Library, 1999.

Rouse, Parke, Jr. "Low Tide at Hampton Roads." *United States Naval Institute Proceedings,* July 1969, 79–86.

Salas, Eugenio Pereira. "First Contacts—The Glorious Cruise of the Frigate *Essex.*" Translated by A. S. Merrill. *United States Naval Institute Proceedings* 66 (1940): 218–23.

Scott, Kenneth. "The Privateer *Yankee* in the War of 1812." *American Neptune* 21 (1961): 16–22.

Smith, Dwight La Vern. *The War of 1812: An Annotated Bibliography.* New York: Garland, 1985.

Smith, Gene A. "A Means to an End: Gunboats and Thomas Jefferson's Theory of Defense." *American Neptune* 55 (1995): 111–21.

Smith, Philip Chadwick Foster. *The Frigate* Essex *Papers: Building the Salem Frigate, 1798–1799.* Salem, Mass.: Peabody Museum of Salem, 1974.

Stagg, J. C. A. *Mr. Madison's War: Politics, Diplomacy, and Warfare in the Early American Republic, 1783–1830.* Princeton, N.J.: Princeton University Press, 1983.

Taylor, George Rogers. "Agrarian Discontent in the Mississippi Valley Preceding the War of 1812." *Journal of Political Economy* 39 (1931): 471–505.

Tilghman, Oswald, and Samuel Alexander Harrison. *History of Talbot County, Maryland, 1661–1861.* Baltimore: Williams & Wilkins, 1915.

Toll, Ian W. *Six Frigates: The Epic History of the Founding of the U.S. Navy.* New York: Norton, 2006.

Tucker, Spencer C. *Arming the Fleet: U.S. Navy Ordnance in the Muzzle-Loading Era.* Annapolis, Md.: Naval Institute Press, 1989.

———. "The Jefferson Gunboats in Service, 1804–1825." *American Neptune* 55 (1995): 97–110.

———. *Handbook of 19th Century Naval Warfare.* Thrupp, U.K.: Sutton Publishing, 2000.

———. *Stephen Decatur: A Life Most Bold and Daring.* Annapolis, Md.: Naval Institute Press, 2005.

Tucker, Spencer C., and Frank T. Reuter. *Injured Honor: The* Chesapeake–Leopard *Affair, June 22, 1807.* Annapolis, Md.: Naval Institute Press, 1996.

Upton, Francis H. *The Law of Nations Affecting Commerce During War: With a Review of the Jurisdiction, Practice and Proceedings of Prize Courts.* New York: John S. Voorhies, 1863.

Valle, James E. *Rocks and Shoals: Naval Discipline in the Age of Fighting Sail.* 1980. Reprint. Annapolis, Md.: Naval Institute Press, 1996.

———. "The Navy's Battle Doctrine in the War of 1812." *American Neptune* 44 (1984): 171–78.

Wells, William R. "US Revenue Cutters Captured in the War of 1812." *American Neptune* 58 (1998): 225–41.

Wills, Garry. *James Madison.* New York: Times Books, 2002.

Wilson, James Grant. "Commodore Hull and the *Constitution.*" *New York Genealogical and Biographical Record* 11 (1880): 101–13.

Wood, Virginia Steele. *Live Oaking: Southern Timber for Tall Ships.* Boston: Northeastern University Press, 1981.

Zimmerman, James Fulton. *Impressment of American Seamen.* 1925. Reprint. Port Washington, N.Y.: Kennikat Press, 1966.

Index

Page numbers in *italics* refer to maps and diagrams.

A NOTE ABOUT THE AUTHOR

STEPHEN BUDIANSKY is a military historian and journalist whose writings have appeared in the *New York Times*, the *Washington Post*, and *The Atlantic*. His previous books include *The Bloody Shirt, Her Majesty's Spymaster, Air Power,* and *Battle of Wits.*

A NOTE ON THE TYPE

THIS BOOK WAS set in Baskerville. The face itself is a facsimile repro-
duction of types cast from the molds made for John Baskerville (1706–1775)
from his designs. Baskerville's original face was one of the forerunners of
the type style known to printers as "modern face"—a "modern" of the
period A.D. 1800.

Composed by North Market Street Graphics,
Lancaster, Pennsyvania
Printed and bound by Berryville Graphics
Designed by Virginia Tan